CHICLET'S SEASON

My Ghia's Journey Through the Oklahoma Car Show Circuit and Beyond

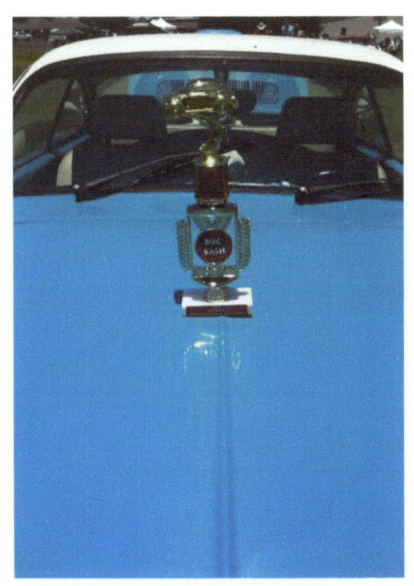

BY
TIFFY
MATEAS

Chiclet's Season

Published by Silver Wolf Publishing, Topanga, CA. To obtain copyright permission, contact the publisher at info@silverwolfpublishing.com.

Photography	Tiffany Mateas
Text	Tiffany Mateas
Concept & Design	Tiffany Mateas

Printed in the U.S.

1. Photography   2. Regional   3. Autobiography

Silver Wolf Publishing
Topanga, CA 90290

Cover photo by Margo Mateas

ISBN 978098491130-1

TABLE OF CONTENTS

ADVANCE PRAISE FOR CHICLET'S SEASON...

"Tiffany can [photographically]make something out of seemingly nothing." -
*Don Demeter Baptist Pastor, Retired MLB ball player, and member of both the Brooklyn,
New York & Oklahoma Sports Hall of Fame*

"She can frame up a shot like a pro, eliminating the need for editing programs."
Photography Professor Lyle Henry "Tuliv Ltd. Co

"These pictures are great and make everyone so happy.
I hope you make a million bucks from this project."
Dear departed car show comrad Jerry Argo

"I love Tiffany's literary voice and innovative eye."
Margo Mateas, known as The Media Relations Maven

"The pictures are all excellent. I really appreciate all of your time and efforts."
Don Garner, Canadian River Cruisers Trading Post

"Tiff's pictures turned out really well. You would never know how cold it was. They are really great."
Michael Fain Yale School of Drama

"The pictures look fantastic. It was fun! Thank you for including us in your book."
Larry Frohardt, Colorado P.T. Cruiser Club

"Thank you for taking these great pictures [including those] of the Norman Veteran's Parade
for all to see." *Lany Malysa N.C.P.A.C.E. Instructor*

"It's so wonderful when people reach out in the community and form new connections.
This is a delight." *Paseo Artist Joe Allen Gibson*

"Tiff is very good at taking pictures. The cars look great."
Dennis Damm, Wholesale Auto Norman, Oklahoma

"Tiffany is so special [to] car shows. Thank you so much for the photos that you took."
Cat Elrod, Bethany Businesswoman

DEDICATION

**DEDICATED TO LESLIE AND MONTY SMITH
IN MEMORY OF THEIR DAUGHTER, KRISTIN MARIE SMITH**

**WITH DONATIONS TO AMERICAN VETERAN CHARITIES
A CAUSE CLOSE TO HER, AND EVERYONE'S, HEART**

"LEST NOT THE VOICES OF THE FORLORN GO UNHEARD."

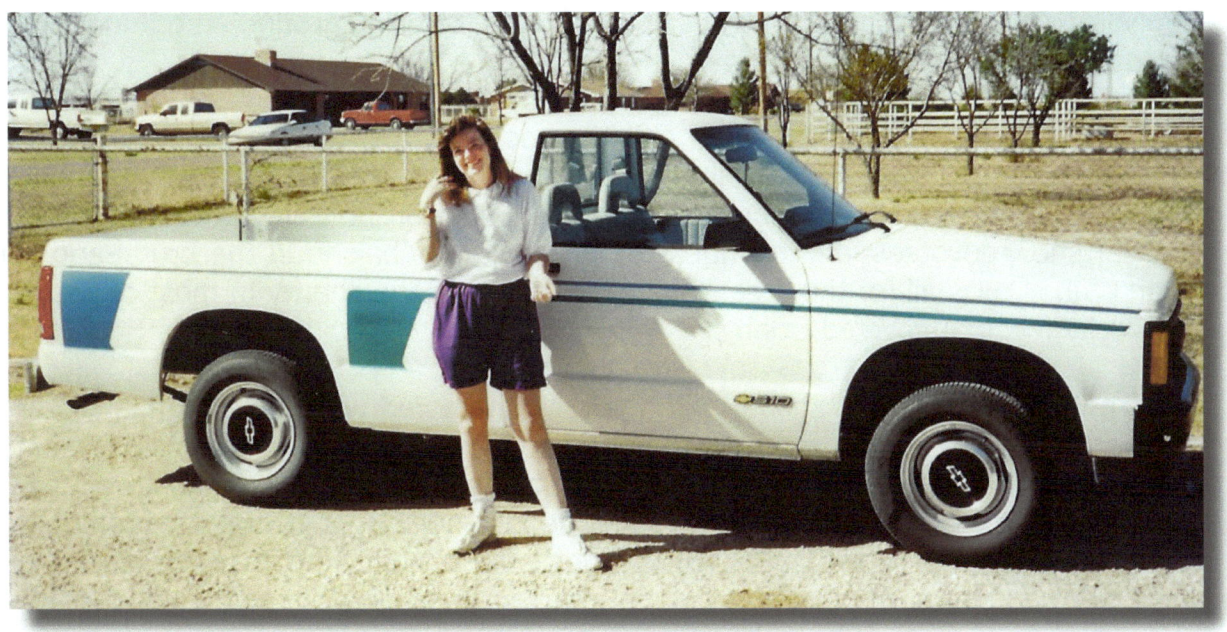

Courtesy of Kris Smith

FOREWORD

Over the course of this two-year literary process, my 1971 Volkswagen Karmann Ghia, and I have participated in at least one car show or more every month of a calendar year. "Chiclet" as I aptly address my blue and white gum-painted side kick, was quite the show girl during this run from June of 2010 to the following June and then some, accumulating an award at every competition save three. She may not be my daily driver, (an insider car show term referring to the more mundane vehicle in one's garage, whose sole purpose is one not of aesthetic or pleasurable means, but simply motors to the store and the grind stone,) sporting all the quaint little quirks a car show participant is no doubt familiar with, but she is no "Trailer Queen."

Albeit "Mission-Sorta'-Impossible," style, we have driven to every event I will mention including a two-hour St. Patty's Parade. All despite a loosely hinged door tied up before embarkation, fickle windshield wipers, and that pesky eternally-draining battery. Minor mechanical annoyances notwithstanding, this perfect annual attendance task was also quite an achievement due to the meteorological condition of the state in which I currently reside, Oklahoma. Yes, here with the four-seasoned locale during this fulfilling project the outlook ranged from the freezing winds of a blistery January day, right up to one of the state's warmest summers. Not the most welcoming environs in which to be strolling around an outdoor event every month.

2011 alone broke state records with first the coolest recorded temperature, followed by the greatest quantity of days surpassing triple-digit temperatures in mercurial Oklahoma City's entire years of tabulation. Most of those June-August local shows involved myself along with fellow car show devotees, and countless other spectators baking in the brutal arid sun for hours on end. It was all for the greater cause of camaraderie charity in most cases, and for a select lucky few that coveted trophy.

While not one to sit in the shade, and naturally enamored with the craftmanship of a well-made piece of mobile art, I attempted to hone some photography skills to wile away the tedium. Photographing so many car shows, the muse of inspiration hit and I was prompted to approach many of the afore-mentioned new found friends united by that love of automobiles. I wanted their assistance in showing off their vehicles while at the same time showcasing the interesting attractions here, in what the original native inhabitants of Oklahoma called the "Red Man's Land," and across our great country.

Please enjoy the story of my whirlwind experiences over the last smattering of car show seasons, heralded in a pictorial journey and featuring many of the stylish cast encountered along the way.

ACKNOWLEDGMENTS

I am grateful to the individuals and groups listed below for all of their contributions of love, encouragement, sponsorship, advice, assistance, prayers and kindness.

First and foremost, I am eternally grateful to God, and the powers that be who pushed together the paths of myself and soulmate Margo Mateas. I am of course ever so lucky to have the love and attention from one such shooting star as she, but I must extrapolate over the fact that honestly without her, this album would be nothing more than a shoe box of stray snap shots and memory cards. So Margsy, thank you. Thank you for your patience while I was off on what must have seemed like another wild goose chase of a photo shoot. For open arms and very often warm meals upon my harried return. Thank you for those times you tagged along, and exhibited oh so much moxy with the public when I would lean toward shyness. When the preliminary legwork phase of this creative work was complete, and I faced the daunting task of compiling, (and tracking down,) virtually acres of data, thank you for your never-quit attitude, spurring me on. Thank Heaven also for your keen editing abilities from years of traveling around the media and publishing biz. Thank you ten-fold for everything. Can't wait 'till this is hot off the press.

Tom and Mary Ballas, my devoted parents, who through the years have been steadfast in their love of all charges in their care, and who most recently have open-heartedly supported us as we painstakingly toiled over both of our individual publishing expeditions. Thank you also for instilling in your kids a sense of confidence, as well as a love of photography.

My family, including my siblings, nieces, nephews, aunts, uncles, and cousins near and far.

My friends, including those online social network pals, as well as my buds at all the attended shows. Among those I count as a friend, thank you Pam H. also for sharing your penache on all things artistic.

The generous car show family that is The "Show Your Ridez" Company.

My fellow Volkswagen fans at the OK. V.W. Cruisers Club.

The once flailing, soon-to-be thriving airline industry which afforded me the opportunity to grab some clever out-of-town photographs in a more timely manner than the national highway department allowed.

The national highways and byways, weaving hither and yon to take care of the rest of my special road trip excursions.

All of the willing model participants who graciously took time out of their busy lives to pose for me allongside their beloved autos and other modes of transportation, thereby enriching my life with their enthusiasm. Some eager photogenic heroes as you will see went above and beyond the proverbial call of duty to help achieve just the right vision.

And lastly, but certainly not least of all, I want to express my sincerest heartfelt appreciation to our United States Armed Forces, past present and still to come, who make it possible every second of every day for all here in America to breath free air. We thank you for dedicating your lives to protecting our liberties. God Bless America.

ABOUT THE AUTHOR

Some of my earliest memories include being transported within the lush black vinyl interior of my parents boat-like Mopar, their '70 Dodge Dart, dubbed the "Purple Car." Being that it was such an unusual color, it seemed more magical than any of the neighbors' motorized specimens. Thus began my love of cars. My parents even bought Matchbox cars for my young pastime activities in lieu of more infantile toys. I would spend hours running them up and down the sidewalk trying to imitate the full scale models. To this day, I possess my first mini-car, a black hot rod Paddy Wagon that I converted to a hipper, chopped-top version. It still has the dirt on it from "off-roading" in the front yard of my original Long Island, New York home. Just like the make-believe scenarios my play autos experienced, I have always loved hearing car stories.

Here are a few of my memoirs to start the ball rolling. Upon moving to Oklahoma in the mid-'70s when station wagons were all the rage, my parents welcomed more and more siblings and expanded their mobile square footage with the proud acquisition of a '77 Oldsmobile Vista Cruiser. Here we all are on one uncharacteristic Oklahoma "Snow Day" that was so cold even Dad had to stay home from his airport job. Being an adventurous band, we weren't always content for staying in with the fireplace and hot cocoa, so off we went exploring a snow-packed tunnel shoveled out by the road crews.

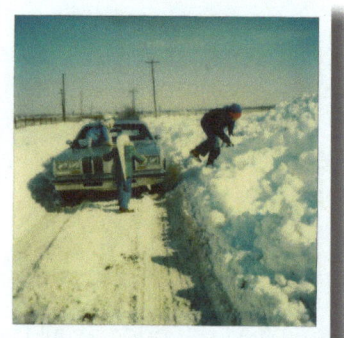 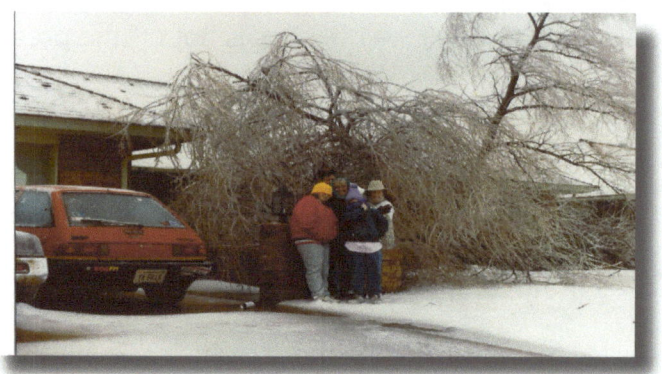

Next, Mom got her own spiffy ride for the modern family in the zippy '81 Dodge Colt. Her happiness waned not one ounce, even after the back seat spill of a crockpot fulla' steamy nacho cheese intended for a P.T.A. function she was headed to, not three hours after driving her vogue red hatchback off the showroom floor. Here, Dad grabs a shot of us huddled next to Mom's Colt on yet another icy Oklahoma day.

Over the next several years, our gang amassed a veritable wealth of automobiles. Some, like the "Purple Car," or their '89 Pontiac Grand Am, would be brought up to speed, so to speak, in order to be shared with the next coming-of-age child in the household. Some would be doled out to charitable car collection leagues. One was even stolen, but that's another story to come.

One car stands out as a trouper among the survivors until it was finally granted to an Auto Shop teacher for his students to study. That was the 1972 Datson station wagon titled over to our family from my Uncle John in Georgia. Legend has it that my letter-carrying-uncle acquired it from a co-worker who had used it in a similar delivery capacity for years. Uncle John continued to deliver his parcels daily for even more years, until he saved enough money to buy a newer car. Coincidentally, my middle sis Maureen, was due to enter engineering school and needed a mode of transport to jet about campus. The only dilemma was that she wanted to attend a school out of state. Being either daring or crazy, Dad flew to Atlanta that summer of 1993 to begin the, "lil' engine that could's," more than 18-hour crusade to Oklahoma, only stopping briefly for a tune-up check-over before heading eight more hours to New Mexico. Along the way, before the pit stop in Oklahoma, just to be on the safe side, Dad only stopped for gas, never turning off the motor. Unbelievably, it drove like a dream all the grueling hours to what would eventually become my sister's alma mater.

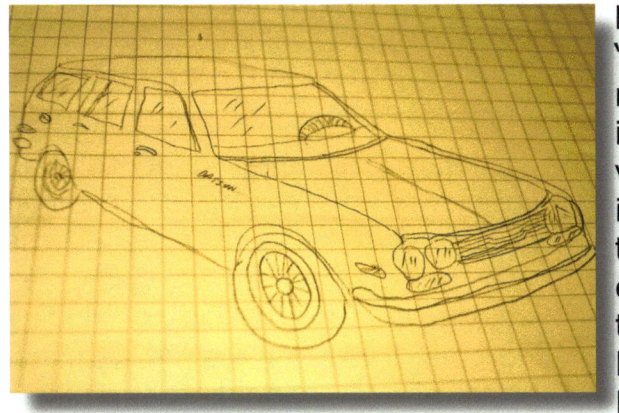
(An etching I made for my sister of her Datsun)

Maureen babied the car nicknamed the "Orange Box," and taught herself almost every minor maintenance required to keep the car running. Once it was pummeled by a campus groundskeeper's vehicle. The university paid for the car's repairs, the insurance pay out of which was actually determined to be worth more than the declared value of the entire car itself. She definitely got a chuckle out of that, and kept that car for many later years, only to be replaced by – you guessed it – another hearty Nissan, the offspring of the never-say-die Datsun.

Which car played "Houdini" as mentioned? My parent's first foreign car was an '87 Hyundai Excel. It wasn't as luxurious as the Olds, or as "coltish" as the Colt – in fact, Mom used to joke that we could probably beat it on foot down to the bus stop at the end of the street – but it was cute nonetheless, and very necessary with such a bustling household. One such hectic morning, Dad was rushing out the door to drive baby sis Megan to school early, only to find the Excel not in its typical parking spot in the driveway. Even in her sleepy state, mature-for-her age tween Megan luckily comprehended what had occurred right away. Dad first checked the street quite logically to see if he might have forgotten to park the barely one-year-old vehicle in its prime position beside the entry walk. Upon its absence, he was thrown into a disbelieving shock, causing his next action we try not to laugh at, but which can even make him smile over, after these many years... He frantically looked all around, then proceeded to, quite animatedly so, look under their patina-stained broken down Dodge Dart usually planted beside it's conspicuously painted red cousin. Come to find out, for a stretch of time the Hyundai was one of the most frequently stolen of cars. Wish someone had told us that ahead of time!

That led to my Dad getting a sports car. It wasn't, however, in the form of a mid-life-crisis high-octane million horse-powered chassis. It was an act of charity from an empathetic co-worker of Dad's named Loren, who gifted his own neglected 1978 Fiat convertible. It ran well, but needed some cosmetic attention. At first Dad had barely any time to do anything but drive it, with another school year full of extra-curricular activities to share spousal car pooling taxi duties in full swing. That next summer though, boy watch out. Dad was all over the vocation of teaching himself the art of welding and auto painting. The folks chose yet another ostentatious hue, with the color turquoise. It matched their house and celebrated the family's love of New Mexico, where three of their four children attended school.

One additional reason Dad was so intent on addressing the Fiat's more, shall we say, non-mechanical issues, was the fact that all winter long he drove his entire daily route with the damaged top down. Sure it's all fun and games with a gentle breeze shuffling the falling leaves in one's wake, until the foliage is replaced by the first and any subsequent snow flakes. Dad says he could visibly see the drivers beside him do the 'ol "double take." Can you blame them? Could you imagine the sight of a jazzy convertible in a late December snowstorm only to realize its capote wasn't attached? That messed with many a perception.

After all the years and repairs by the wayside & an economic recovery for my parents, Loren came a'calling with news that one of his children had grown to driving age. So just like the circle of life, our plucky elfin Fiat went on to help another soul. We were so grateful at the time we had with it, and fully utilized it for so many useful tasks, from teaching us all to drive the standard stick shift, to actually delivering a much-needed new dryer to our laundry room in its front seat (again probably another "believe it or not" sight for fellow motorists.) What a durable car.

The first bought-and-paid-for pink slip I had was my beloved, also purple, '94 Chevy pickup truck. It donned the license plate "Moonglo," trumpetting back to my preferred era of music, and due in part to the iridescent cast, taking on a different feel in the evening light.

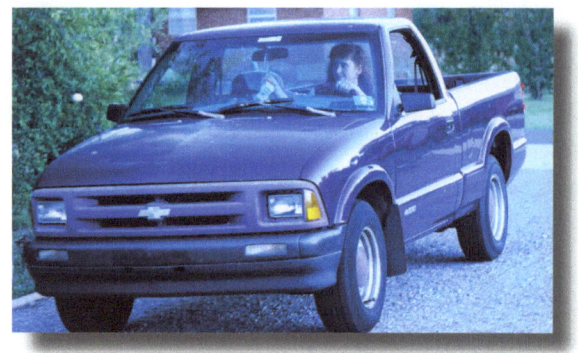

I dearly loved that S-10, keeping it through two recalls, two blown engines, not to mention repairing it after it was declared a total loss from a highway rear-end collision. Upon the third rod destroying the motor, I had already acquired my long time dream car – a '74 Karmann Ghia – and could scarcely afford the multiple repairs required on such a specialty auto, let alone raise the dough for my now equally-aging truck.

Unfortunately the road to perfection with my first Karmann Ghia, nicknamed "Ms. Smitty," wound longer than I had ever imagined with costs growing in leaps and bounds.

I found myself over my head, and having to bestow my baby to the capable hands of a colleague in my Volkswagen collector club.

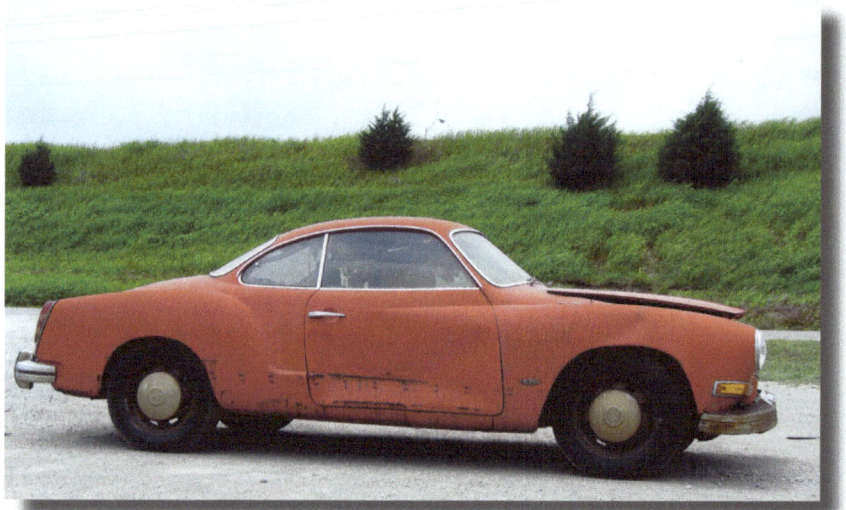

The light at the end of the tunnel came in the form of my current, quite complete Volkswagen mentioned earlier, Chiclet. It all started with a court-awarded '99 Mazda Miata. She was a 'beaut. The 10th Anniversary Edition -- signature paint job exclusive of that red letter year, spry, and still healthy enough to enable one to have the best of both worlds -- a show car one could actually use as a daily driver. But my love affair with the Ghia was stronger than reason. I had spied that model of refined German engineering, coupled with the artistic flair of Italian design, first at the formidable age of 13, and asked my folks, "What in the world is that? A Porsche?" to which one of them replied, "No, that is actually something you might be able to afford quite easily, a sportier cousin to the V.W. Beetle."

Ever since, I longed for one. It really had haunted my dreams. Those robust curves, sleek lines, classic styling. The Volkswagen Type 14 Karmann Ghia is nothing short of poetry in motion to me. So gratified am I to drive, or even just see mine. But getting back to my bargaining chip on the quest to obtain a running Ghia, my equally collectable specialty Miata. For weeks after being in possession of the Miata, we called "Sweet Pea," I subsequently tried to find a new home for it, while at the same time scouring classified ads, and internet Volkswagen sources for that sublime Ghia. I liked the continuation of the unibody construction on the coupe better than the cabrio, and definitely wanted the more traditional non-lowered pure look. Mostly given my experience however, this beggar wasn't too choosy, & required primarily a complete undamaged model. Probably at the same time, my partner in this quest, Margo, spotted "Chiclet" online while I was on a different computer checking out its details. I thought, hmm, ANOTHER turquoise car, but the ad claimed it ran like gang busters, and that white top was super evocative, almost appearing as a hard top roadster conversion to the naked eye.

Too nervous, and still not having sold the Miata for its much needed funds yet, Margo took on the task of phoning the multi-colored Karmann Ghia's peddler, Jack Chapman, on my behalf. She chewed the fat, gaining as much info as she could, when all of a sudden she had a thought, and blurted out, "Hey, would you ever consider trading that Ghia for a 10th Anniversary Mazda Miata?" She was met with silence on the line. Thinking perhaps she offended him, or threw him for a loop, she expected the worst, a hearty laugh in her face so to speak, or some other such negative response. After the pause, however, she heard the fateful words: "What did you just say?" Again worried his words conveyed indignation, she half-heartedly repeated the question. This time, Jack revealed that his girlfriend Joy had been asking him for a Miata for quite some time. Both parties nearly fell out of their chairs, and I was unbelievably estatic upon hearing the news. I still pinch myself sometimes. Thank you to Margo for that also!!!

Everything does happen for a reason, and believe it when I say, you are always in the right place at the right time. Here is a pic of us in Arkansas, where we met half way from our respective homes, sealing the deal with a handshake over Jack and Joy's new Miata.

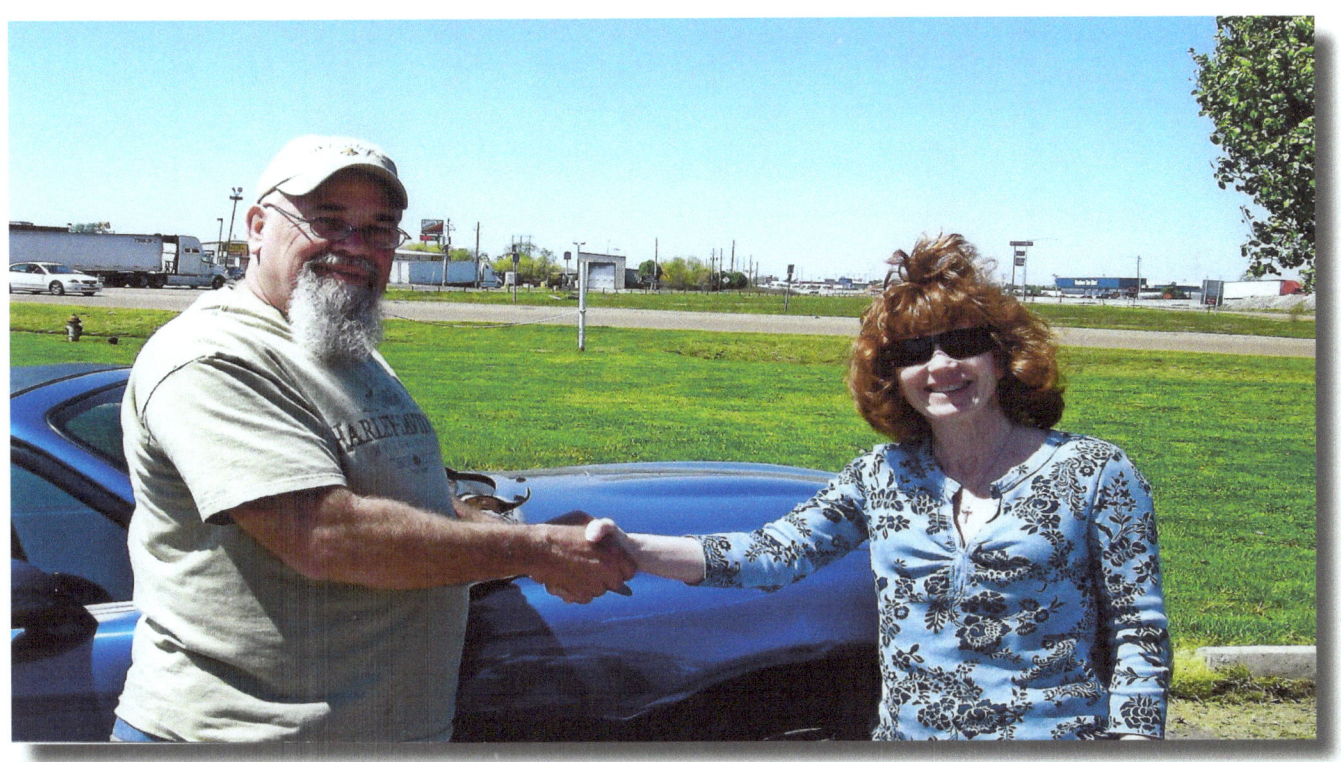

Jack and myself in West Memphis, Arkansas after exhanging our pictured turn-key dreams.

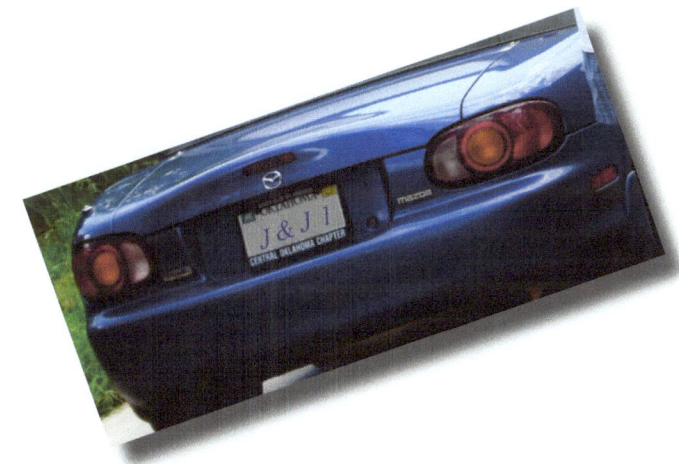

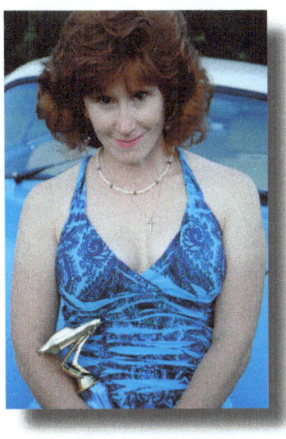

6

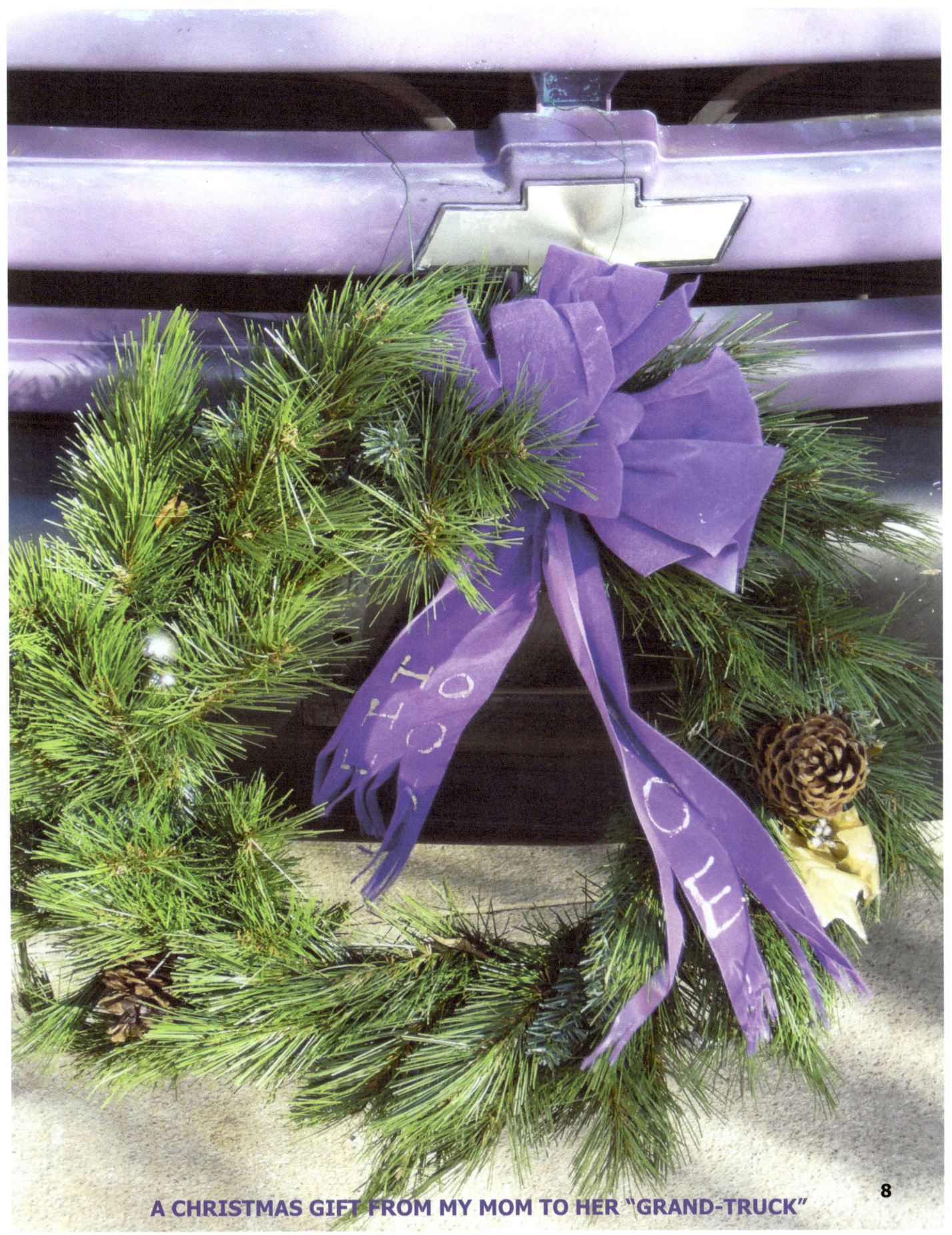

A CHRISTMAS GIFT FROM MY MOM TO HER "GRAND-TRUCK"

MARGO MATEAS

Taking a "paws," with man's best friend, is none other than my "Car Show Season Widow," Margsy. The canine pals are her faithful companions, Rose and her service dog, Max. The automotive best friend also pictured is her trusted steed, a 2002 Suzuki XL7, she calls "Victory."

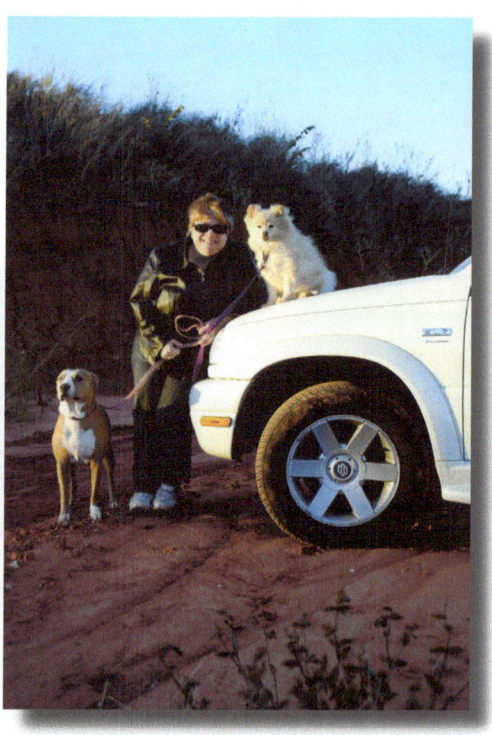

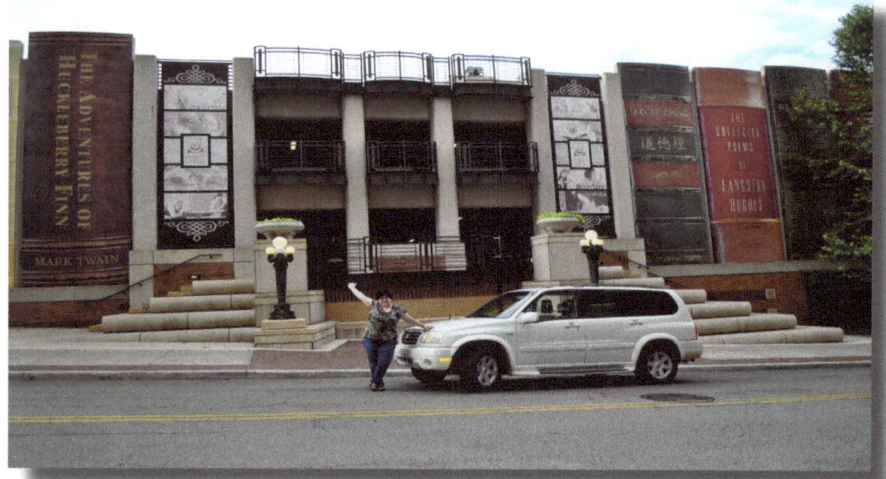

Outfitted with all the latest amenities one could ask for, "Victory" really impeccably fits her personality, and literally all the many copies of her "Career Cards" publication and deck set she has been bringing to book signings across the country. We annexed a shot of one such delivery to the cleverly-architected Kansas City Library.

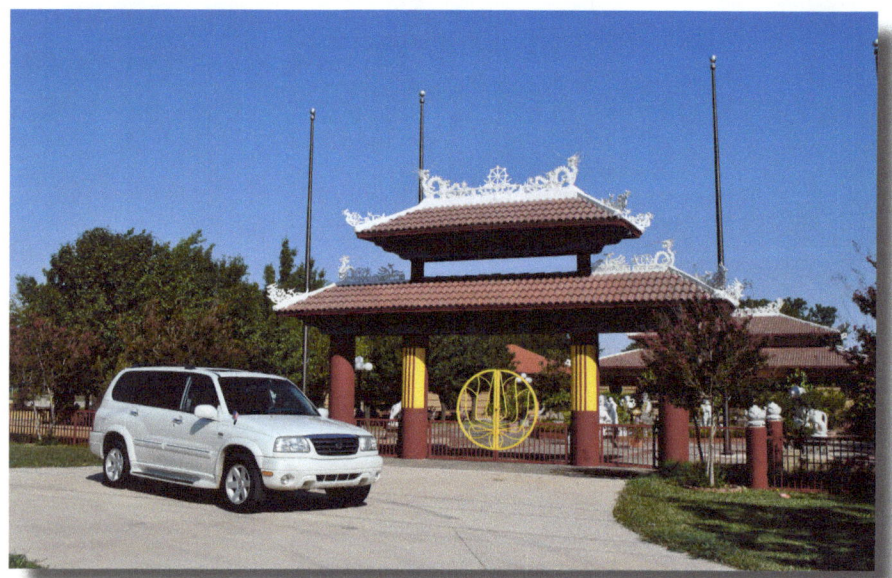

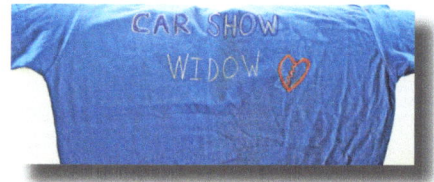

A custom-made "lady in waiting" shirt.

Like the ole' song goes... She really has been everywhere, man.

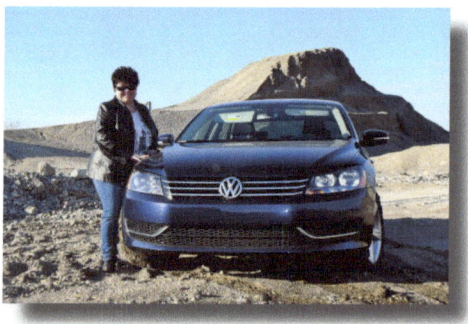

Trying to convert another to V.W.'s with a holiday rental.

My good ole' Pop Tom poses in front of idol Mickey Mantle's statue outside of the 1998 American winner for best Minor League Ball field. Both figures have a few things in common. Dad can also switch-hit and throw, but the most glaring similarity would be their loyalty.

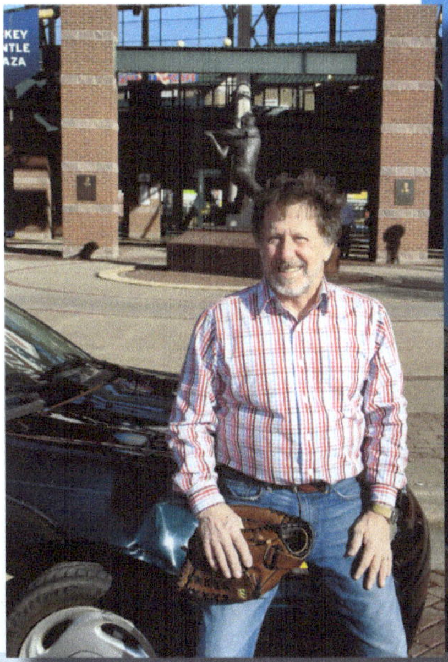

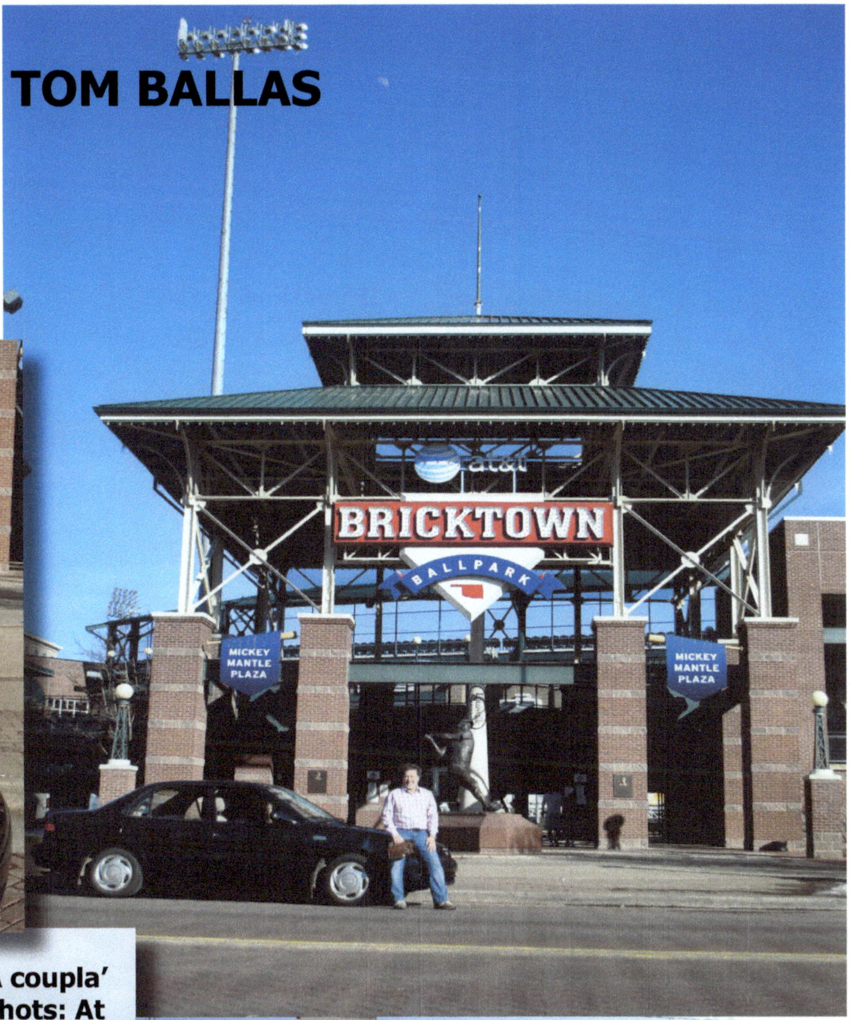

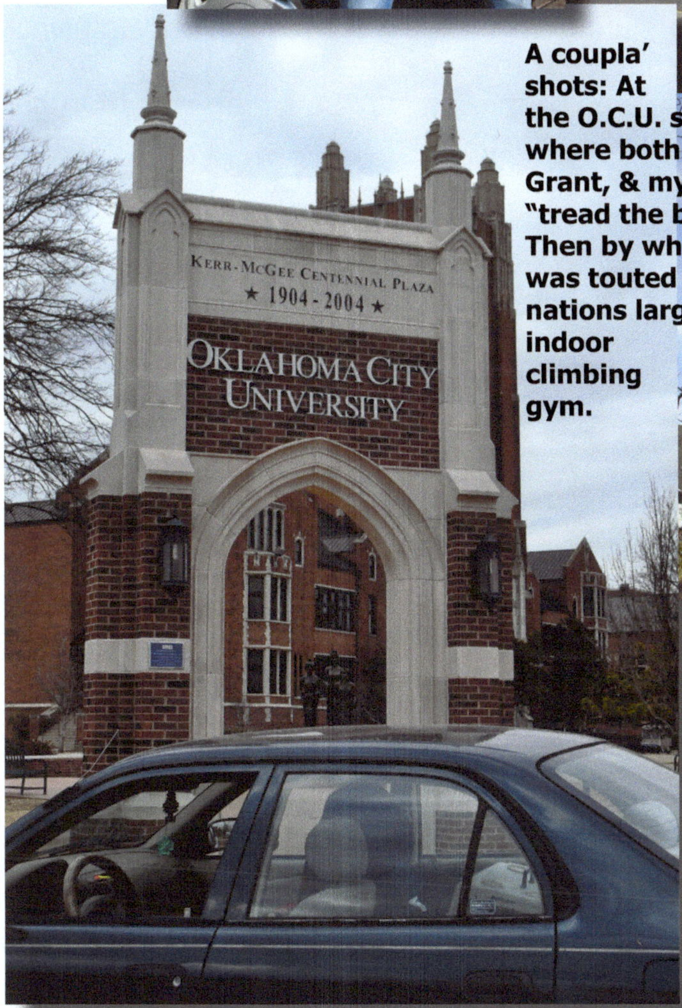

TOM BALLAS

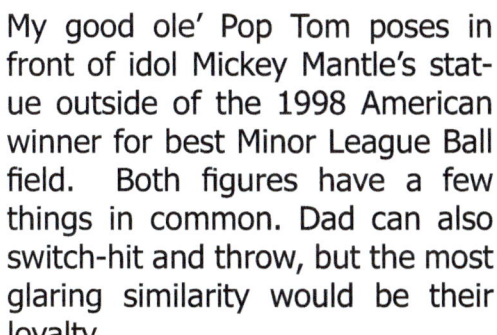

A coupla' shots: At the O.C.U. stage where both Cary Grant, & myself "tread the boards." Then by what once was touted as the nations largest indoor climbing gym.

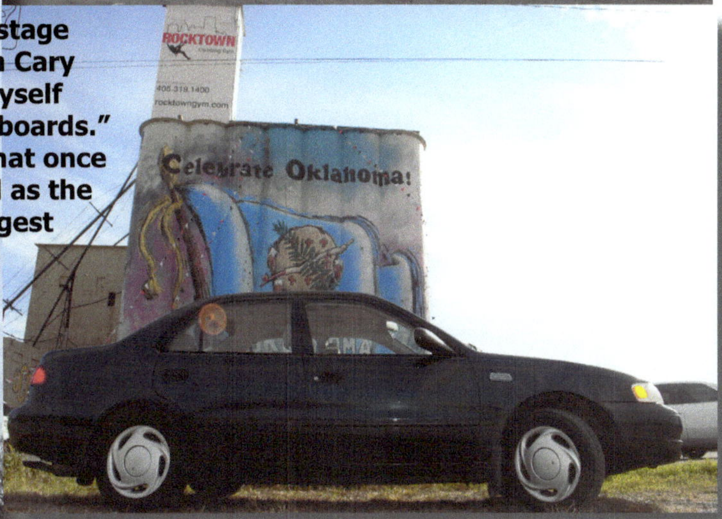

Just like Mickey's long career with none other than the Yanks, both of my folks have been steadfast exponents of their children's endeavors. From the very start of these car show trips involving intricate maintenance and storage issues, to simply helping out financially from time to time when I was holed up like a recluse feverishly composing this swan song, Dad has been there for us.

10

MARY BALLAS

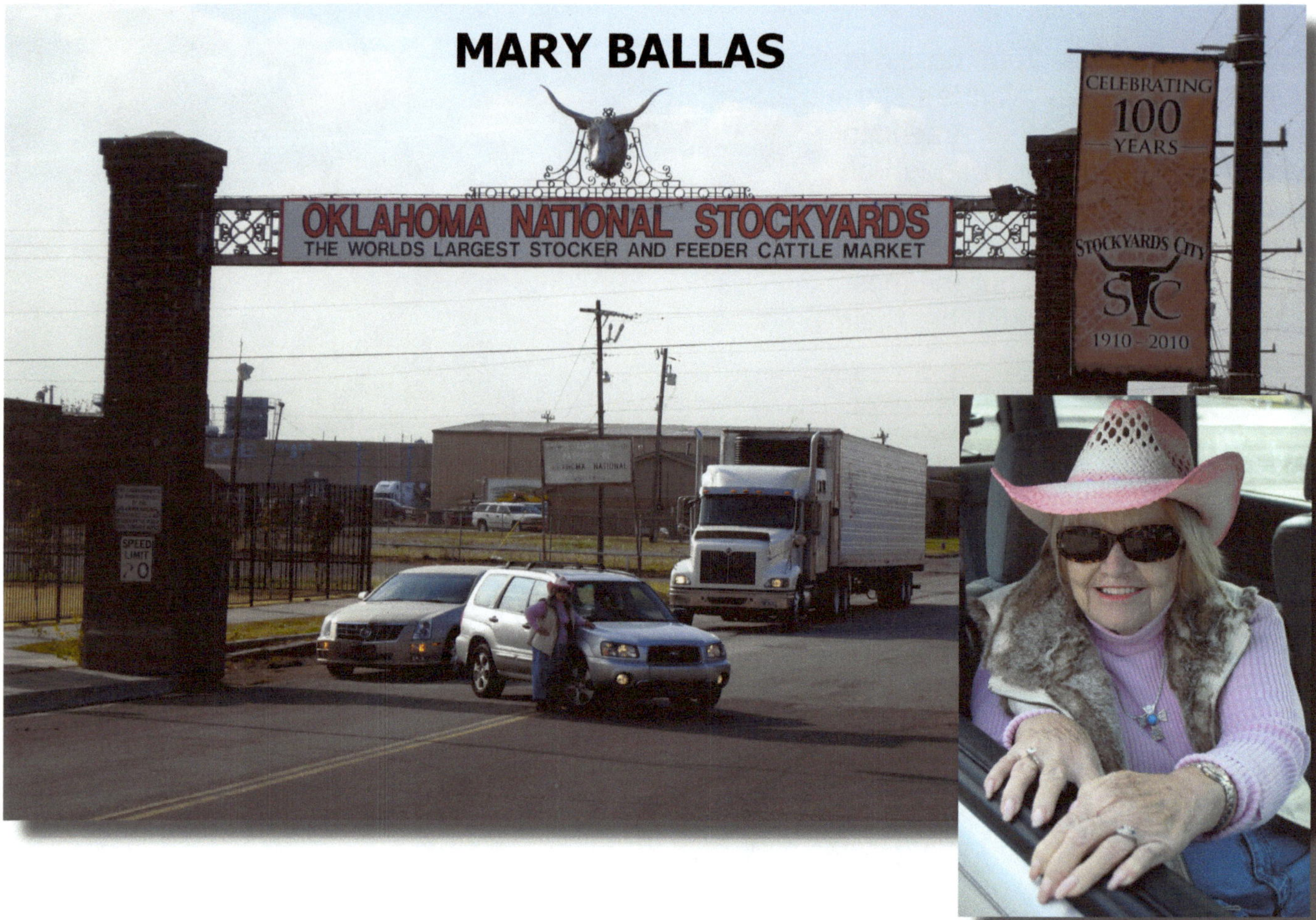

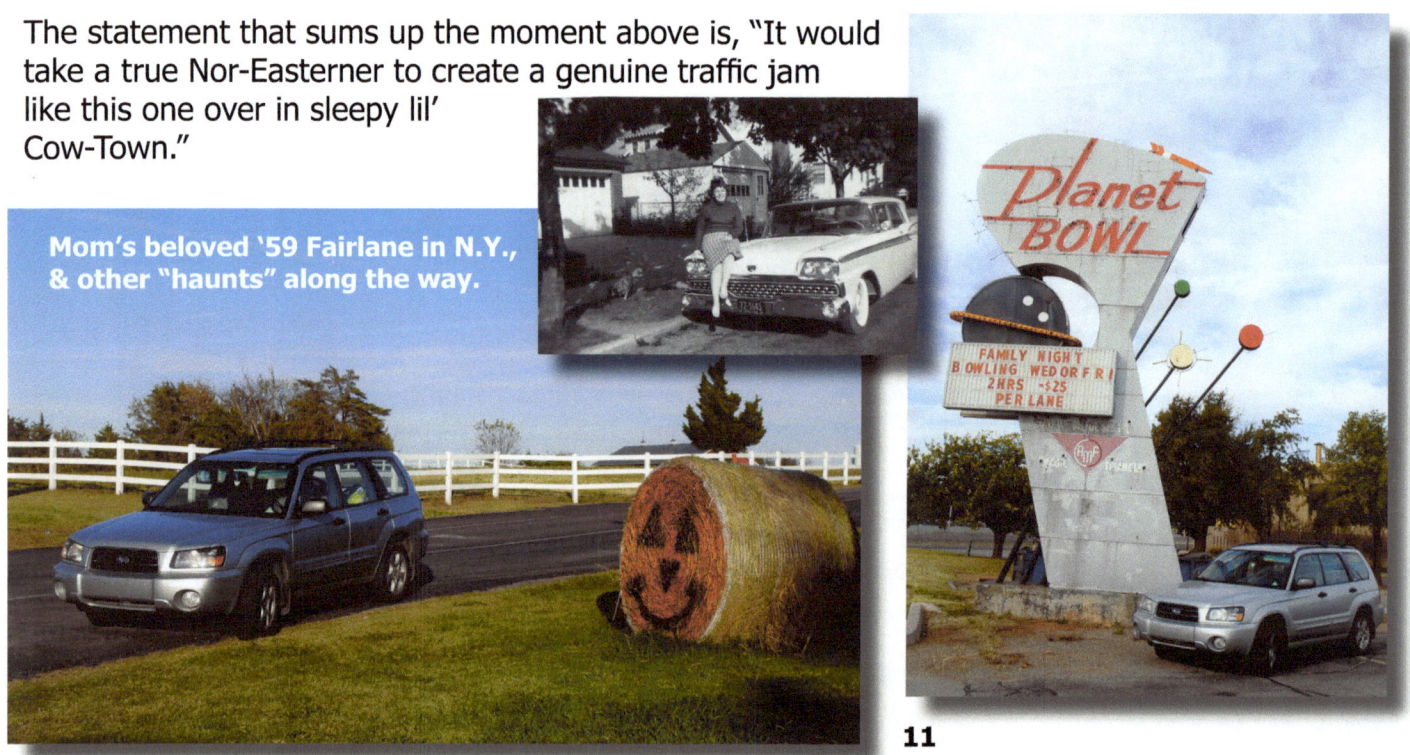

My Mom has loved cars since riding between her folks during meandering Sunday drives along what once was the potato farm-lined roads of Long Island. Her current favorite car is her '02 Suburu Forester SUV she nicknamed "Star" due to the company emblem. She may be a long way from her Brooklyn home, but she still managed to find what she's used to in her photo shoot – a touch of the country in the city. Yes it's the best of both worlds at the Stockyard's district of Oklahoma City. Thanks for always keeping things interesting, and bringing a smile everywhere you travel.

The statement that sums up the moment above is, "It would take a true Nor-Easterner to create a genuine traffic jam like this one over in sleepy lil' Cow-Town."

Mom's beloved '59 Fairlane in N.Y., & other "haunts" along the way.

11

FAMILY, FANS AND FRIENDS

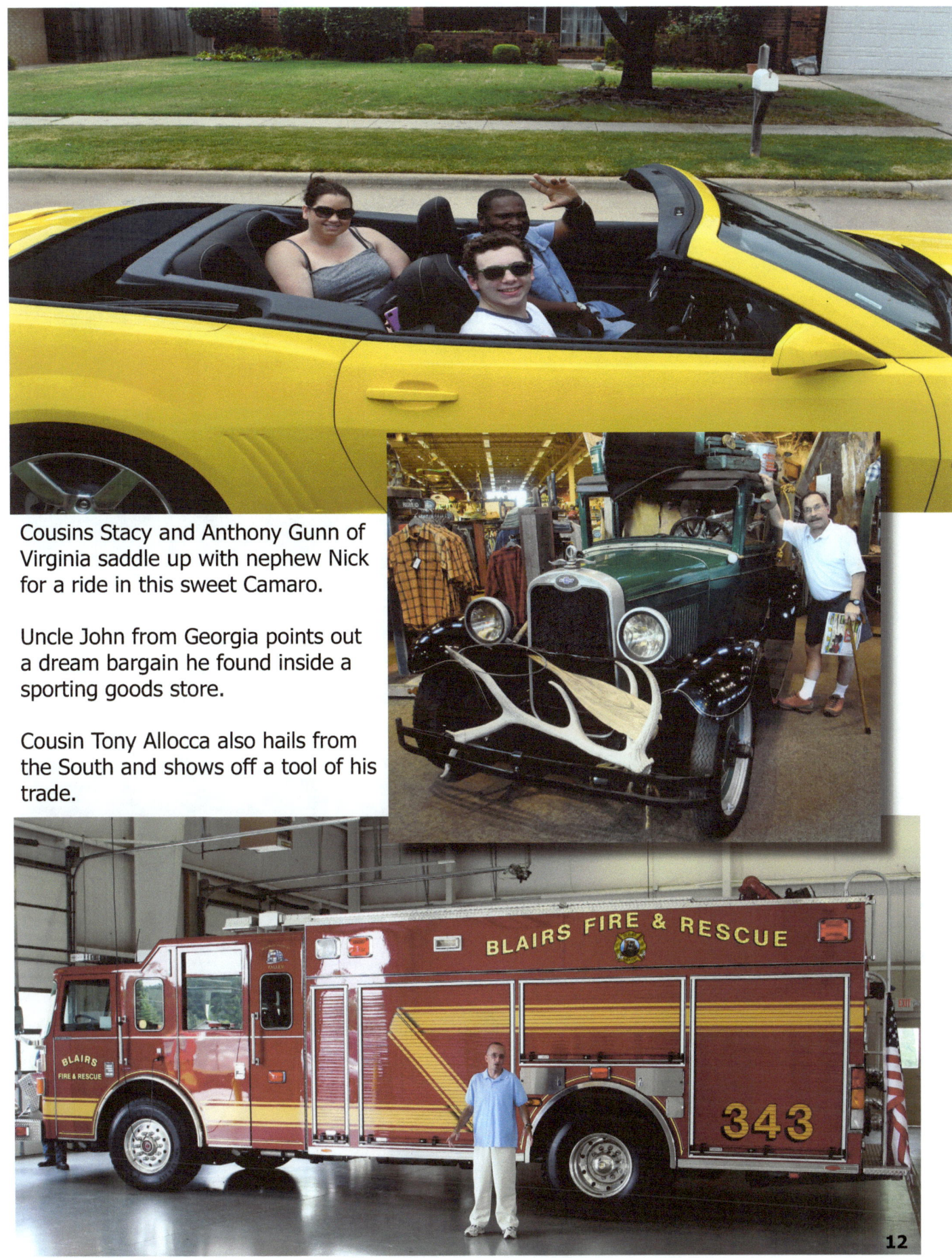

Cousins Stacy and Anthony Gunn of Virginia saddle up with nephew Nick for a ride in this sweet Camaro.

Uncle John from Georgia points out a dream bargain he found inside a sporting goods store.

Cousin Tony Allocca also hails from the South and shows off a tool of his trade.

MAUREEN & MERRILL DAVIS

Middle sister Maureen and hubby Merrill pose with their '95 Nissan midsize pickup truck outside of a bat cave near their property. This brave bantam scamp has served them well, from the blistering suns of the high desert not too far from Merrill's home town of Roswell, New Mexico, to where their computer occupations sent them, including their current Texas home near the Silicon Valley of the South. Along the way of their life's joined wayfaring, their sporty truck rarely faltered. It remains steady and strong.

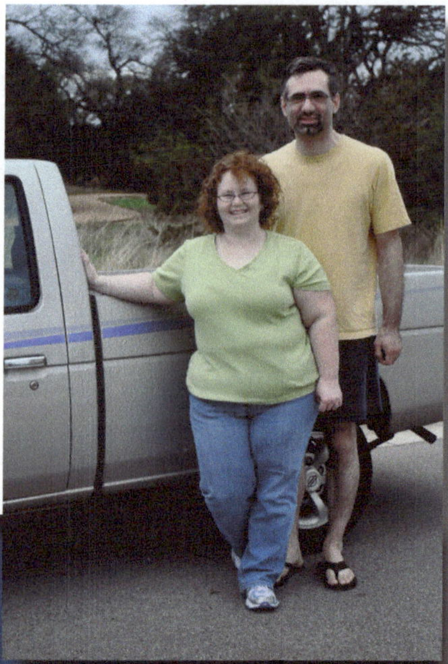

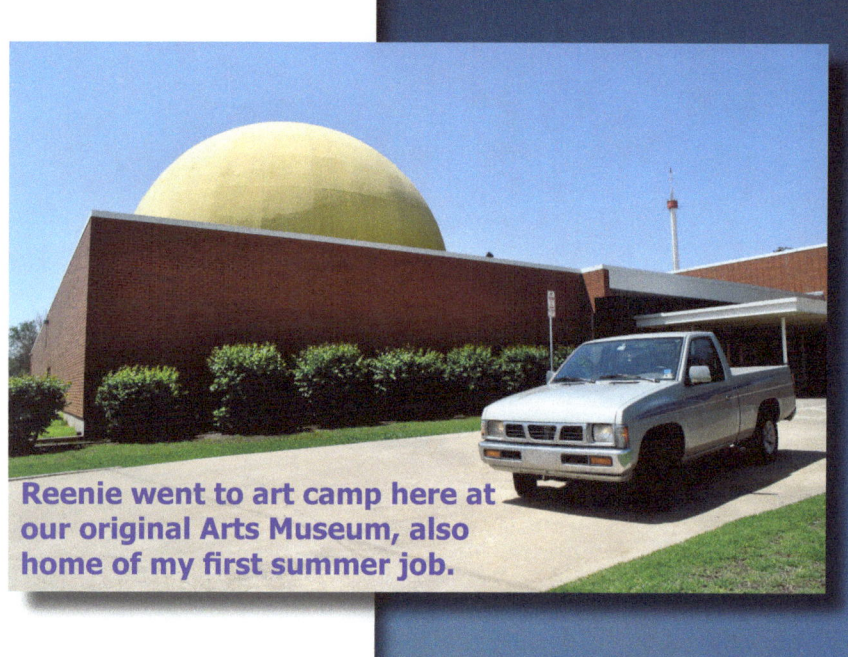

Reenie went to art camp here at our original Arts Museum, also home of my first summer job.

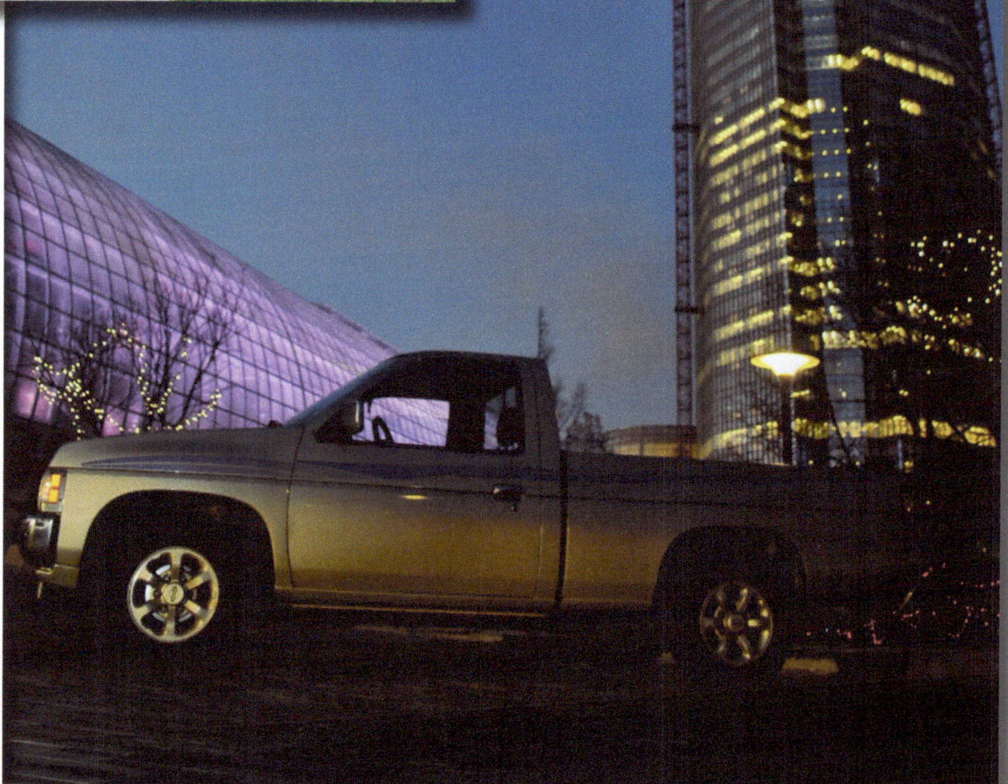

While heading to a temporary job transfer in Burlington, Vermont they encountered the town's lowest recorded temperature on the very first day they rolled in.

Their snowy silver surfer took the chilly welcome in stride, carrying them safely to and fro.

MEGAN BALLAS

Baby sis Meg shows off both her soccer savvy on the field, and her late model Honda S.U.V. Considering her involvement with soccer throughout school, and rugby in college, it was fitting for us to catch up with her near the goals.

Having recently been honored as the New Mexico Public Health Nurse of The Year, Megan's constant goal is always to stay healthy while helping others do the same. Many congratulations on your honor, and thanks for your outstanding service to the world and those around you.

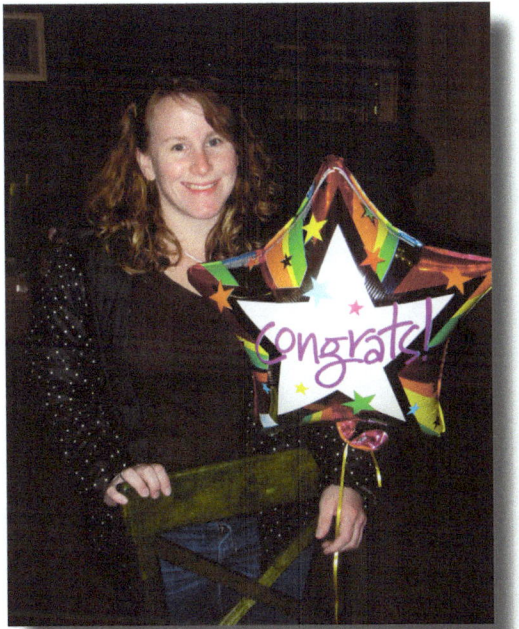

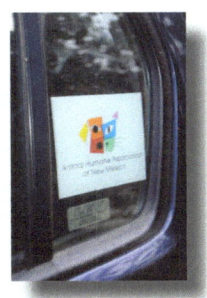

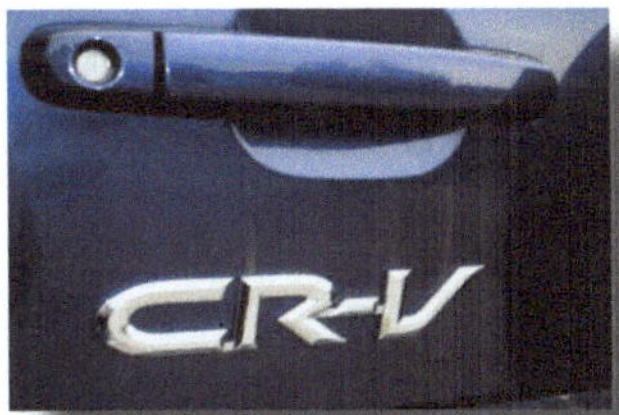

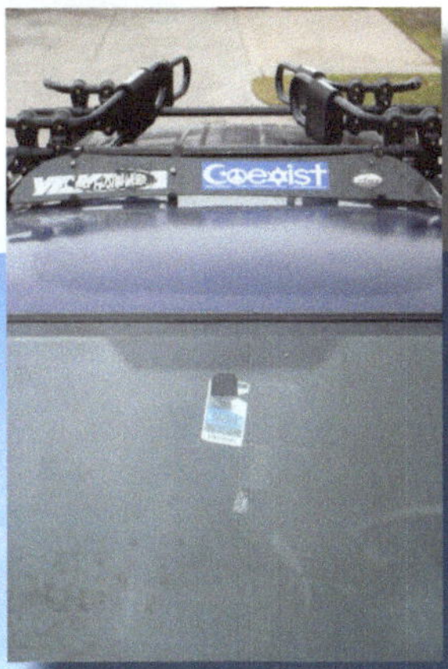

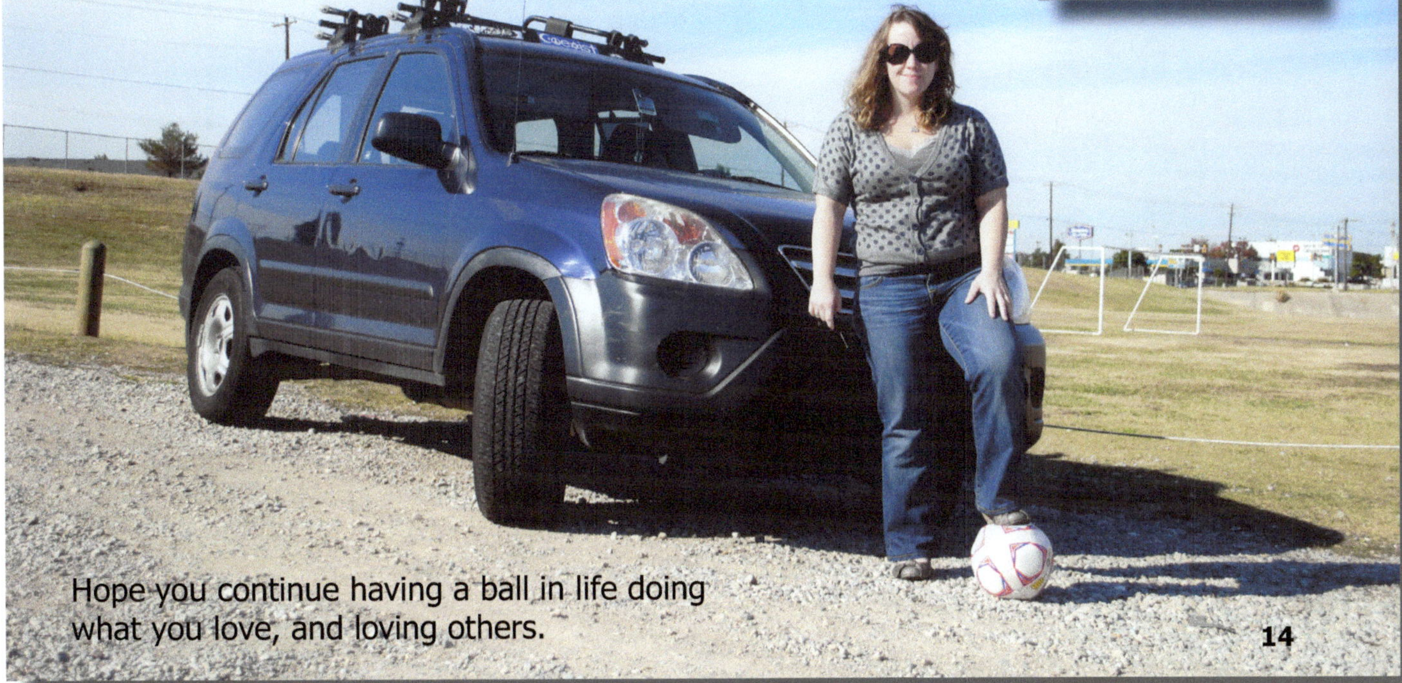

We're all so proud of you and happy to call you sister.

Hope you continue having a ball in life doing what you love, and loving others.

14

TOMMY BALLAS

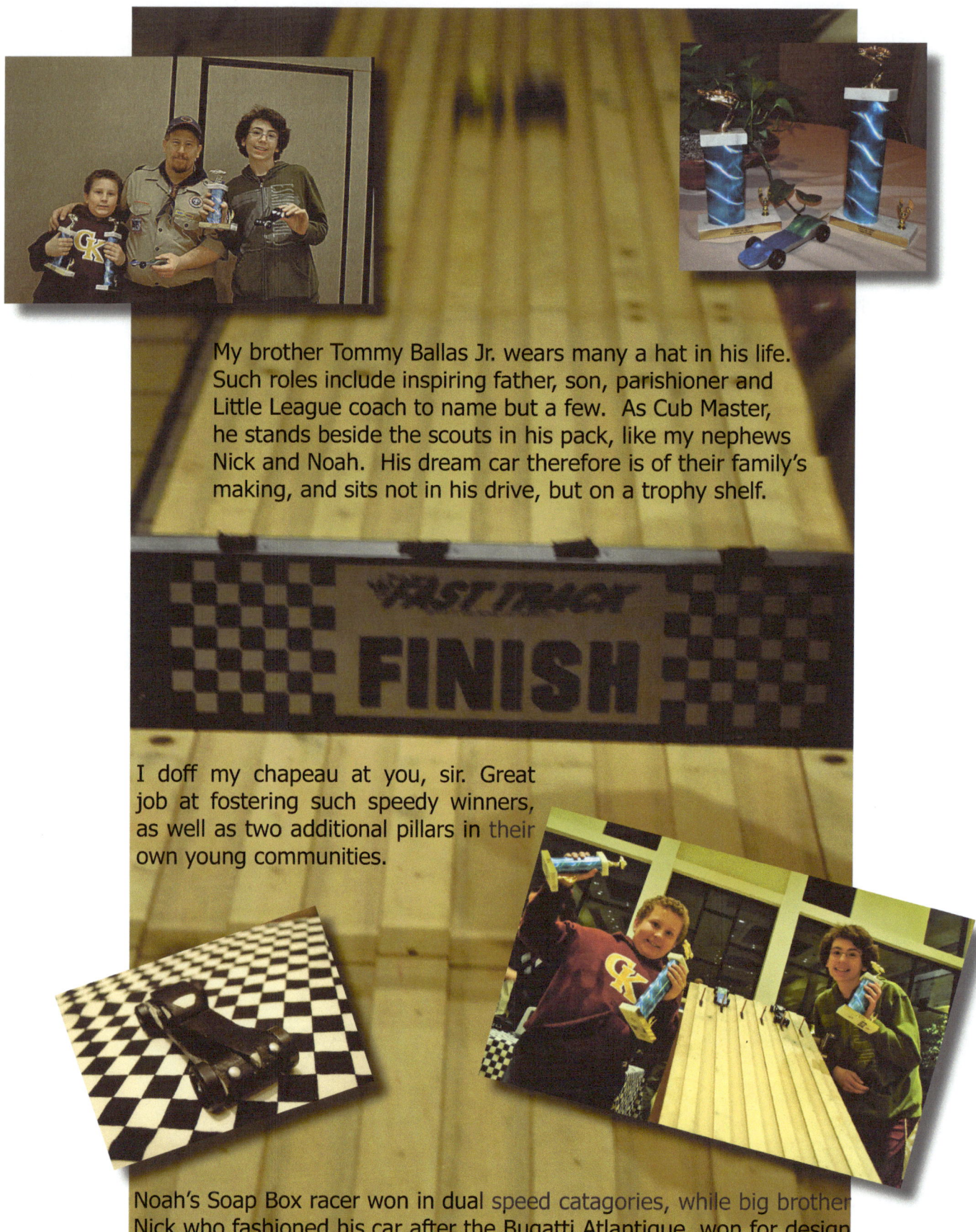

My brother Tommy Ballas Jr. wears many a hat in his life. Such roles include inspiring father, son, parishioner and Little League coach to name but a few. As Cub Master, he stands beside the scouts in his pack, like my nephews Nick and Noah. His dream car therefore is of their family's making, and sits not in his drive, but on a trophy shelf.

I doff my chapeau at you, sir. Great job at fostering such speedy winners, as well as two additional pillars in their own young communities.

Noah's Soap Box racer won in dual speed catagories, while big brother Nick who fashioned his car after the Bugatti Atlantique, won for design in his age group.

"DOUGHNUT" ADJUST YOUR SCREEN

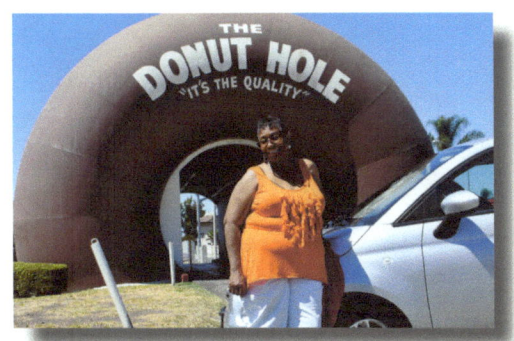

land, but also for her devoted acts of true friendship. Included would be a reminiscence where she drove all over said terrain during L.A. rush hour to deliver a pressing contract job proposal or two for out of state Margo. This instance exemplified even more her loyalty by the fact that she had a sprained arm at the time. Your inner light and kindness shines even brighter than that killer smile. Thanks for all the laughs and memories.

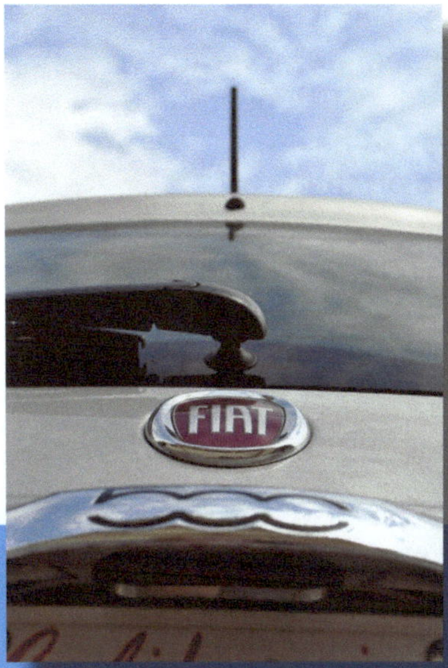

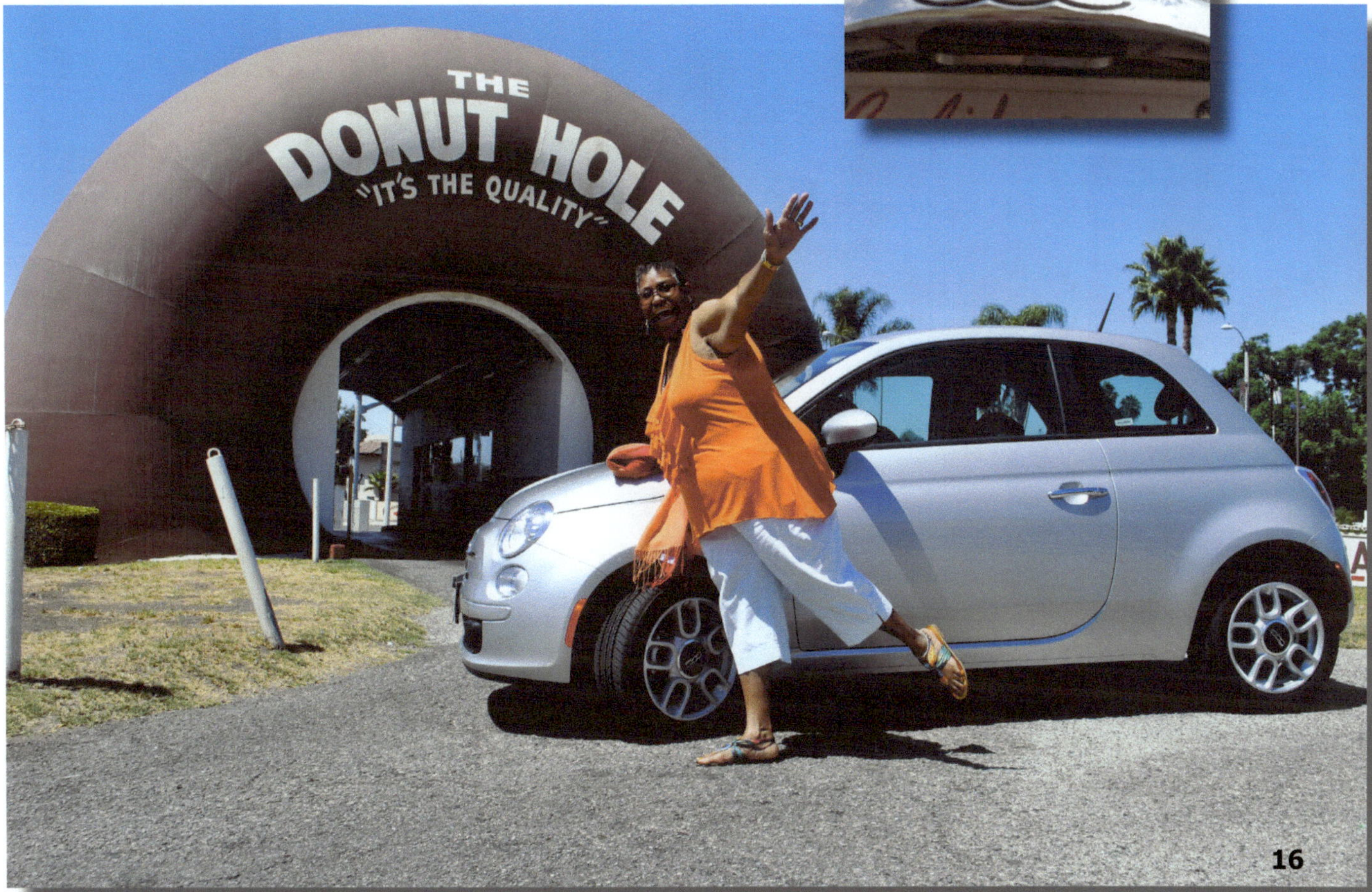

Margo's pal and "sister from another mother" Carolyn Harris prepares to "drive through" into photographic history with this peppy 2012 Fiat 500. We are with the best tour guide for our road trip around SoCal being that Carolyn has been a resident for quite some time. We found it was "Time to make the doughnuts" our snack of choice while passing through La Puente. Yes, we are so proud and fortunate to call Carolyn our ally. Not only for her extensive knowledge of the

"HUMDINGER" OF A FRIEND

A longtime neighbor, friend and Chevy lover Robert Rich easily summits a clever faux bluff, chiseled by a local car dealership, with his 2008 Hummer H3.

Our spirits were as high as the fabricated peak during this photo shoot, which really unveils the kind of vivacious, intrepid soul Rob is.

Little did we know that a short time later this pillar would succomb to an agressive form of cancer. He fought through battles that would have knocked many off their feet.

Thanks for being there for so many through the years.

We were all the better for having known you.

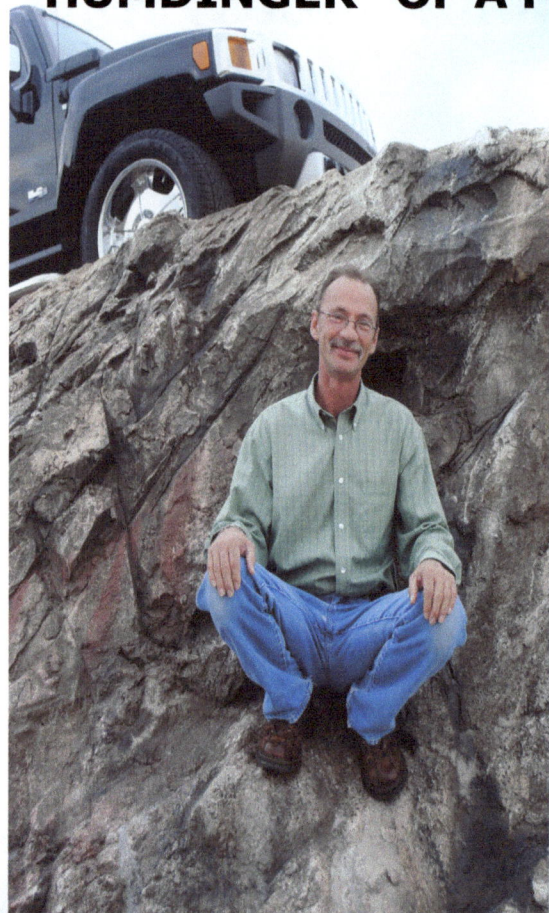

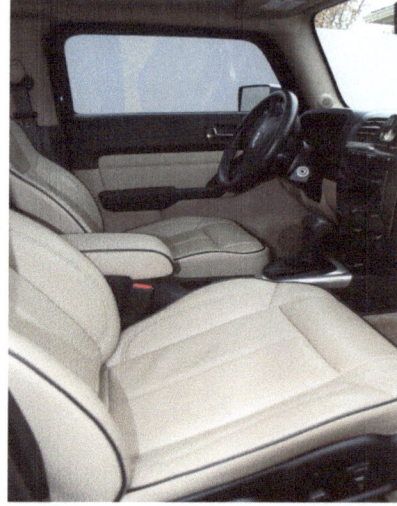

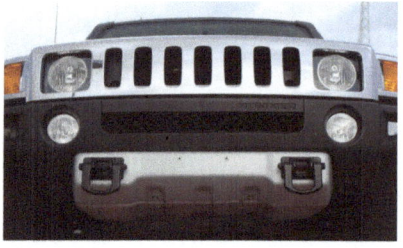

See you on the other side of the hill.

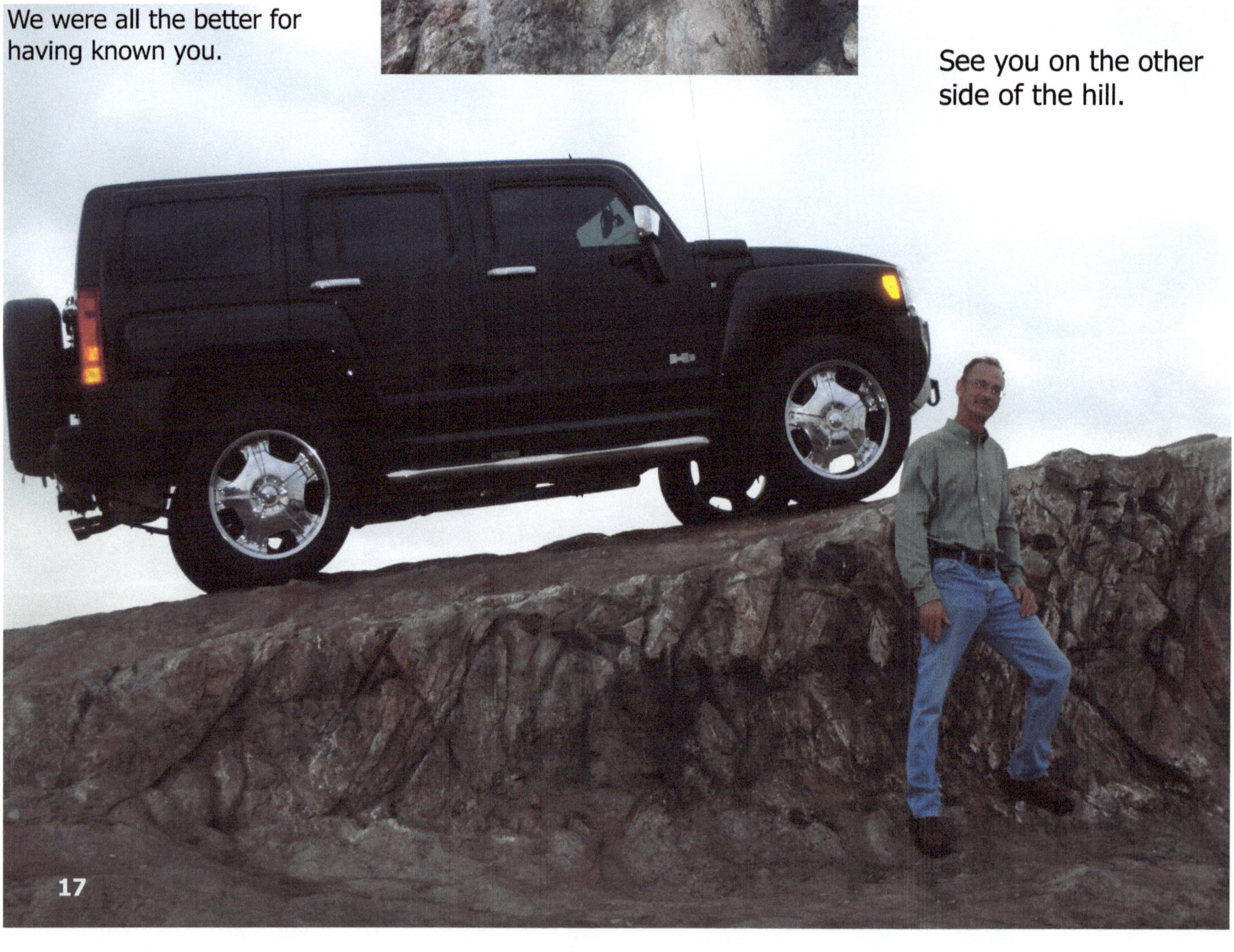

BLING BY DESIGN

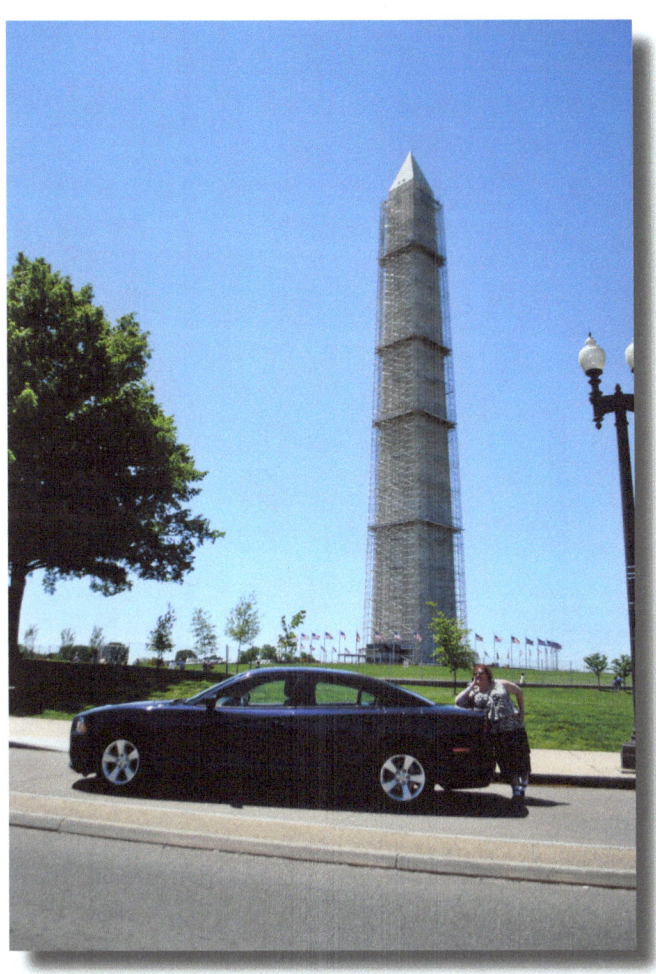

A "Nationally Treasured" confidant, and former co-worker Angela Keller, makes a D.C. land mark shimmer. Even in this earthquake repair stage of renovation, the tower shines because of Angela's styling.

She knows full well how to make an element stand out after all of her experience in jewelry composition.

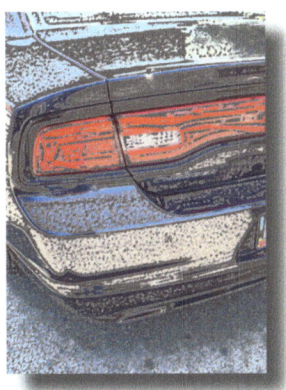

Providence smiled upon us after we landed this equally chic Dodge Charger with which to nimbly weave in and out of Washington traffic.

Here's a rendering to celebrate the joy of art for art's sake that our talented driver contributes to the world daily.

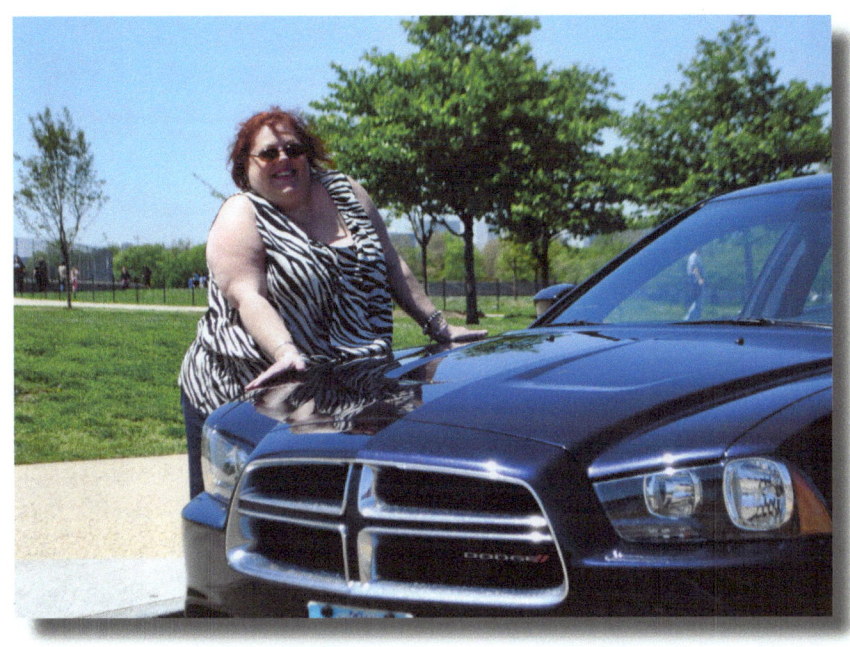

Glad we all got to tool around the Capital town in style.

NOT YOUR GRANDFATHER'S BICYCLE

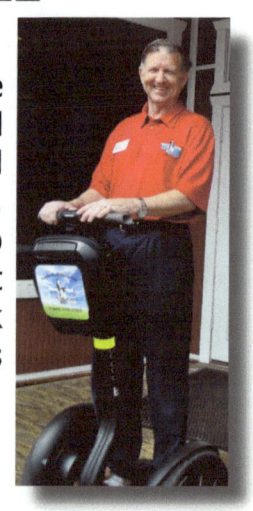

Mr. William "Skip" Knowles is an institution in the renovated historic warehouse district of Oklahoma City called Bricktown. He can be seen daily at his second (and most liberating) job, renting out a line of segway rides, of which we would love to see demoed at the local car shows. The assemblage would eat it up. In fact, he was a fan of a car show I had originally planned, being willing to give lessons near our D.J. table. This innovative two wheel mode of transport lends a revised idea on the best way to view the tourist spots. One land mark I have always felt would be a nice feature in a photography book is the city's old Well's Fargo horse Station, now a popular watering hole of a different sort.

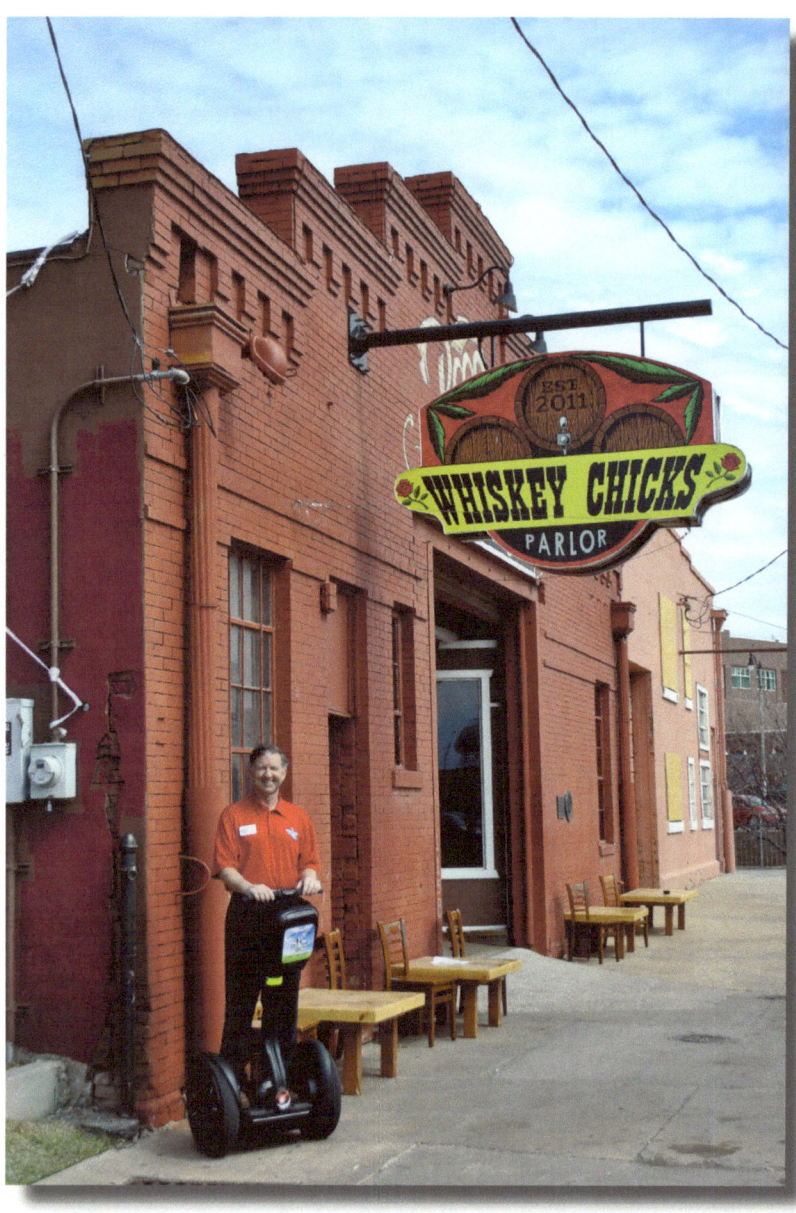

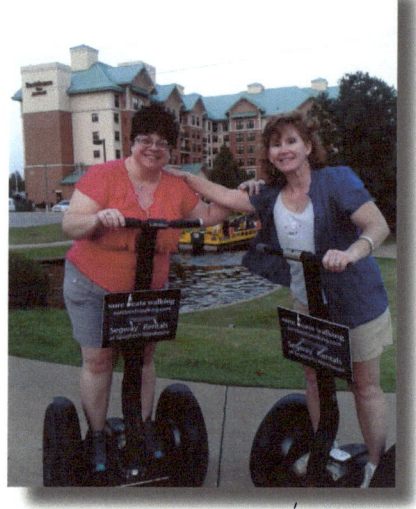

Once, we took him up on his offer of a tutorial for our anniversary. It was an exciting blast, but I am so glad we had Skip as instructor. It definitely takes a knack and as with all vehicles, demands one's full attention and the respect it deserves. Upon trying to avoid a collision with a soul that stopped short in front of me, (my darlin', if one must know,) I briefly and, probably dislexically, spaced on the breaking procedures. Suffice it to say, I found myself catapulted through the air with limbs, and even a shoe flying around me.

Realizing I was intact, and amused at the "Keys-Stone Cop-"esque spectacle I must have been, I let myself collapse back down to terra-firma in a ball of laughter. What a riot. I can-not wait to go again. And when I do, I will seek out this smiling confident face captured for all eternity by my trusty-dusty Nikon. 19

TRAVEL CHAPTER

Pardon the pun, but to "segue" into our next chapter and link them inexorably, I offer you some insight into the fresh perspectives I spied while chasing away the 'ole wanderlust we all get from time to time. Here are some pictures I caught while vacationing and assisting on various business trips over the past coupla' years... But then again I have enjoyed shooting diverse scenes and exotic automobiles since the first camera I acquired.

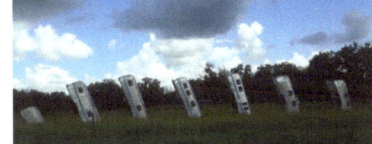

A Trailer Ranch shot from my friend Jo-Ann Prisco of lovely New Orleans, La.

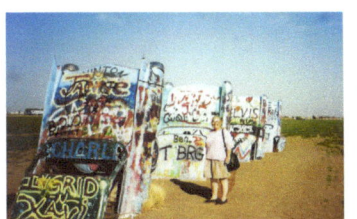

Mom at Cadillac Ranch in Amarillo, Texas.

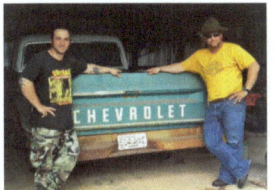

Mississippi hunting trip boys Matt & Jeff.

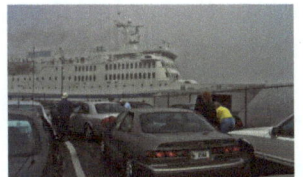

In line for a foggy Maine ferry ride. Two shots above Courtesy of the Ballas Collection.

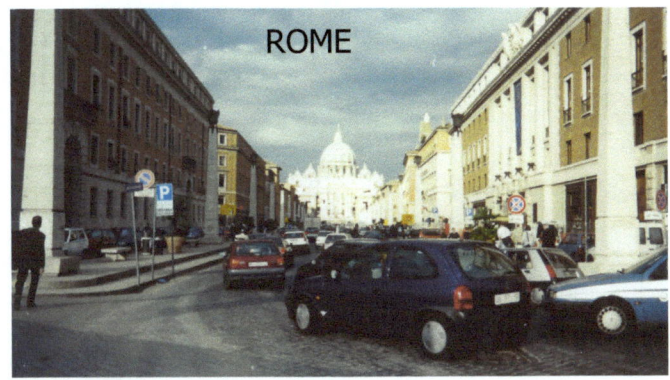

ROME

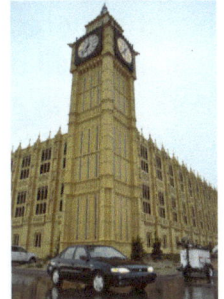

Mini "Ben" & Colliseum at the world's 2nd largest casino located in Love County, Oklahoma

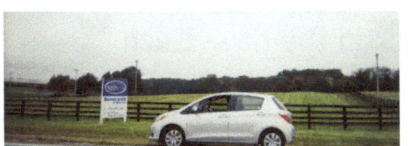

Kentucky Downs

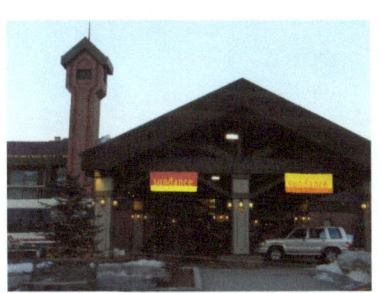

Sundance Sunset in Park City, Utah

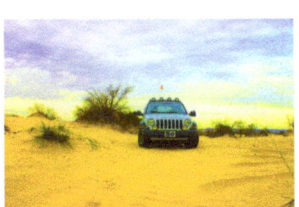

Aloha Dunes!

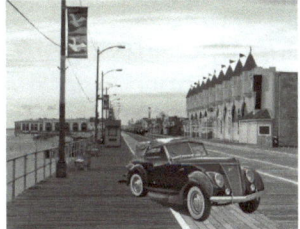

"Nostalgiatized" Darin on the Jersey shore.

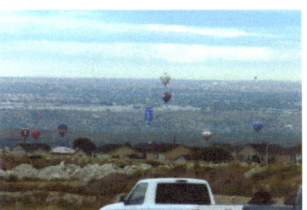

Tailgating the N.M. Balloon Fest

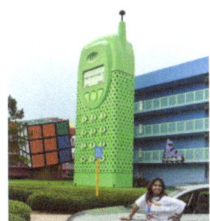

Space Coast

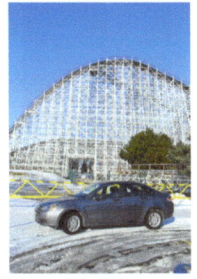

Spring dreamin' near Chi-town

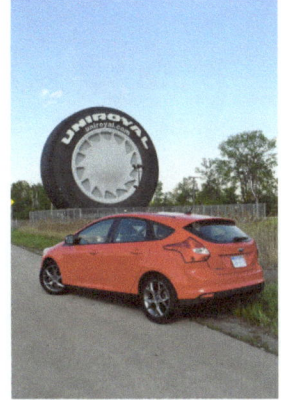

Rollin' in "MoTown"

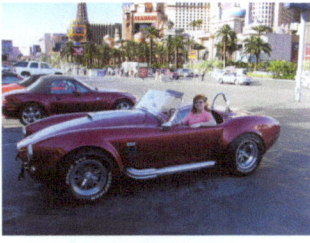

Vegas Baby!

TAGGED, BRANDY STATION STYLE

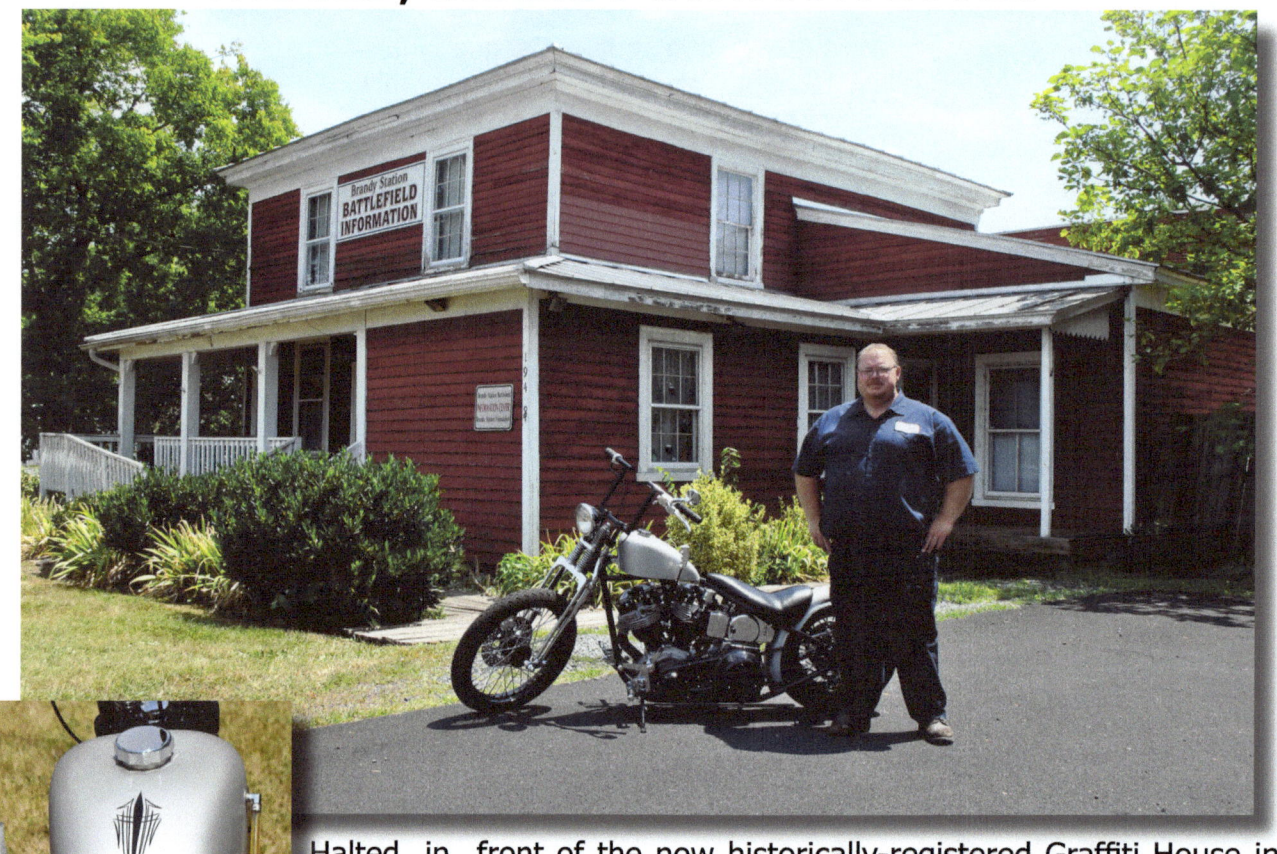

Halted in front of the now historically-registered Graffiti House in Brandy Station, Virginia, is fine artist Neil Boley and his restored '73 Harley Davidson Shovel Head, lovingly nursed back to health at his shop down the street. This significant Civil War back drop, while serving as a front-line hospital, also assisted both sides as a venting spot. As one Northerner was recuperating, the boy in blue would take kindling from the central fireplace and graffiti-ize the wall in battle-cry bragadociousness, to be followed shortly thereafter by a boy in grey to the tune of something akin to "Yankees..." well you can imagine, and really should see in person.

The graffiti still decorates the wall with even a future President signing his proverbial John Hancock back in the day. Such fragile charcoal communication had almost been all but destroyed by more than the daily elements that wreak havoc with frail antiquities of the like. It all began before its modern rediscovery when one of the previous unaware mortgagees had slated the property for demolition. Upon trying to salvage some lovely interior paneling obscuring the graffiti, the archives were spotted, and after much ado, at long last ended up in the hands of the Virginia Parks. This hallowed ground welcomes visitors to revel in the important relic it is. It's truly worth the detour

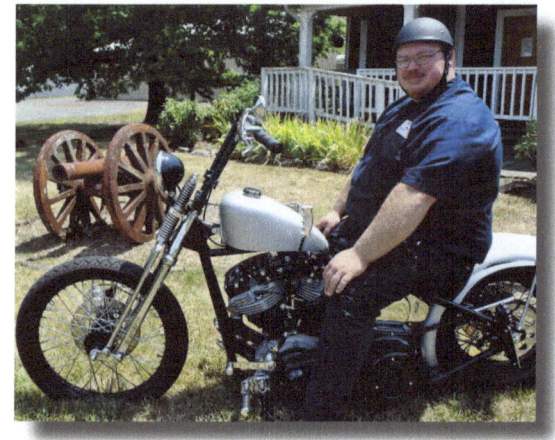

while on your list of battle spots to view. And if one cannot make a "dismount" at this site, also point of the Civil War's largest Cavalry battle, a mere hour outside of the D.C. area, please remember the house itself's much-needed preservation in your charitable considerations.

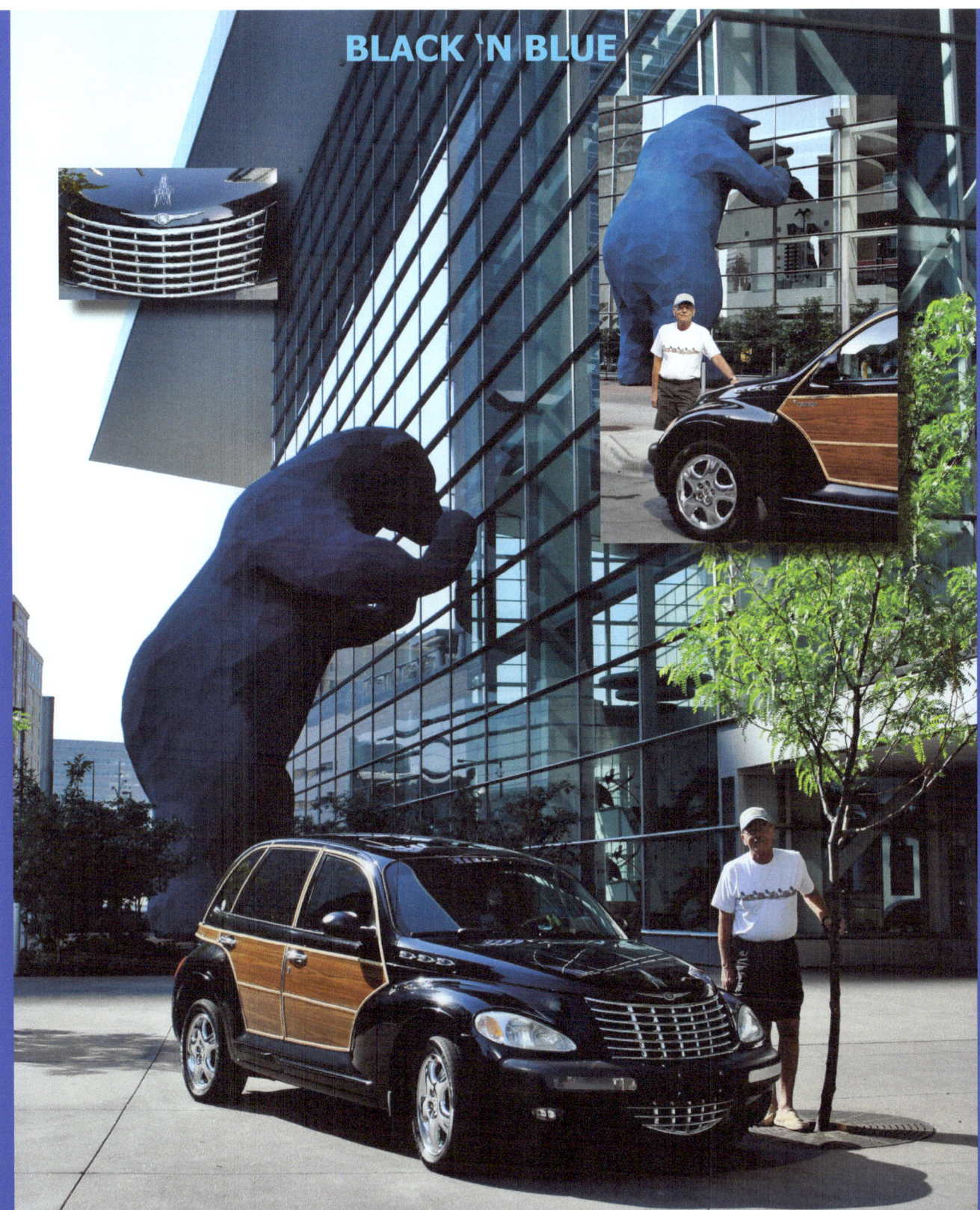

"Bearing" a grin for the camera is one of my cyber pen pals, Larry Frohardt of Colorado. I was recently in his neck of the woods attending a writer's conference. He agreed to meet me at this massive downtown Denver Convention Center mascot. It's a telling piece titled, "I See What You Mean," but is more well known as simply the Big Blue Bear. Larry & wife Jan have been longtime lovers of Denver's Metro, having been immortalized with many a sports arena and hang out in the background.
Larry with a momentary green light from Security, helped me set the perfect tone photographically, perching his paneled P.T. Cruiser at just the right vantage point.

LANE MOTOR MUSEUM

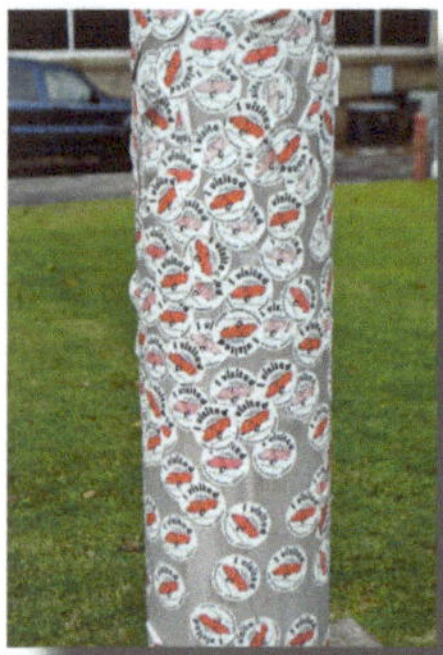

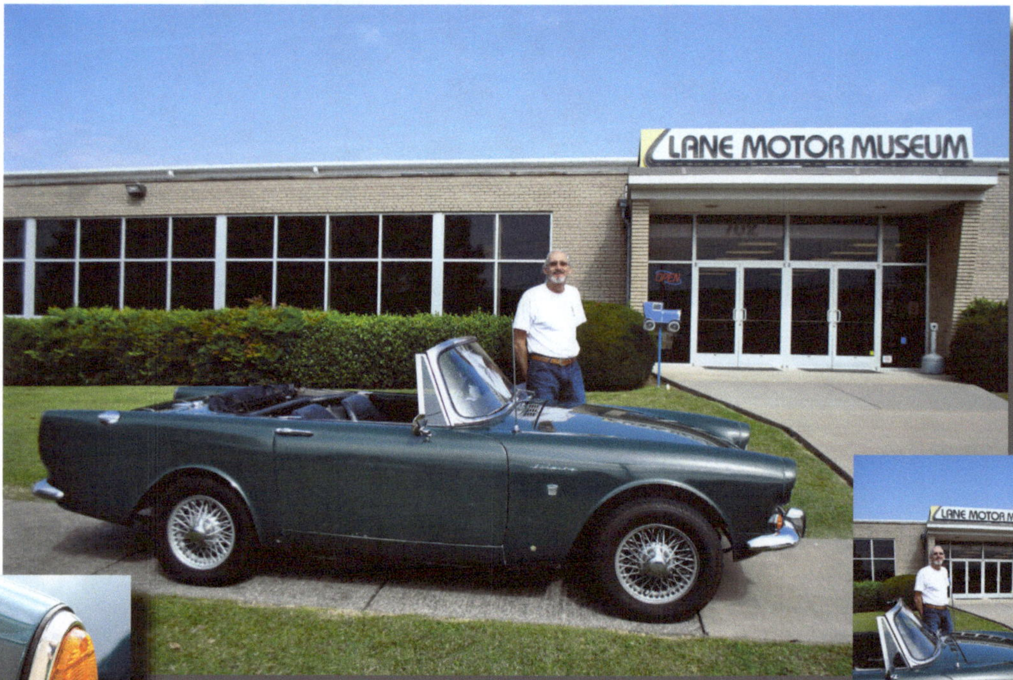

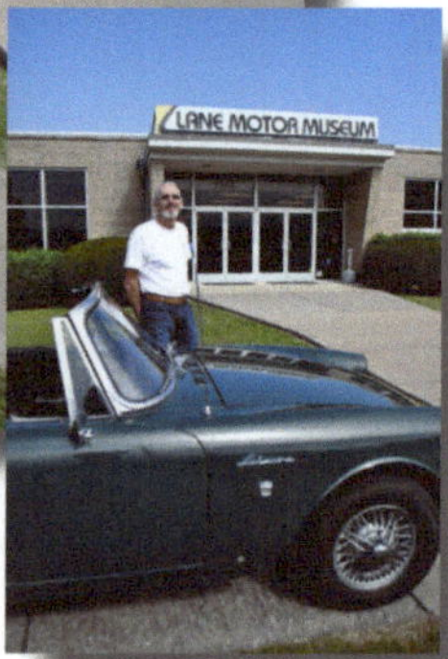

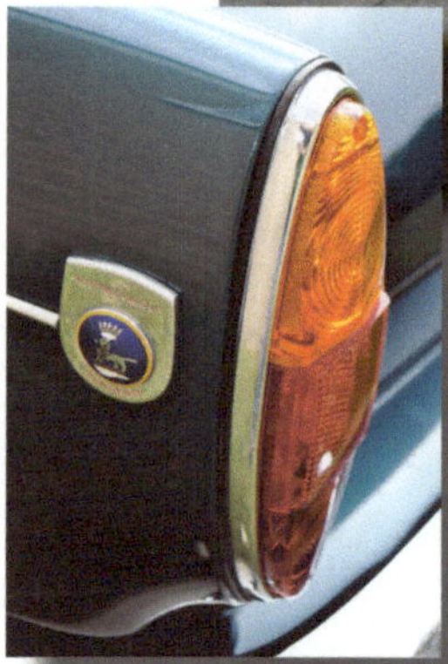

Mr. Jeff Lane surveys his automobile kingdom at his namesake's panorama, the Lane Motor Museum of Tennessee, home to the largest compilation of European cars in the U.S. On this day, a Sunbeam enthusiast clubs gather for a Round Table. The green beaut' sharing the frame with Jeff is owned by one of the museum's curators, all of whom, including my tour guide, good friend Vicki Garrison, were receptive & knowledgeable.

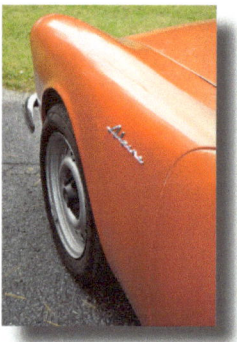

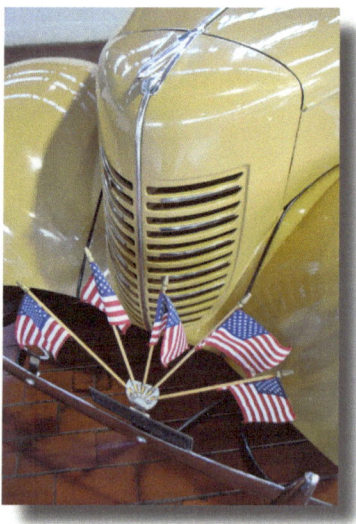

A U.S. invasion to the Europhilia with a "Star-Spangled" Bantam

Unfortunately, I was in town for this photo shoot just a day shy of their famed caravan, "The Rally for the Lane." This is a lively, biannual inner-state cruise, whereby patrons can have more than just a run-of-the mill spectator museum experience. In this case, the fans are allowed to rent particular artifacts to participate in along the cruise. So basically your everyday lay person can actually drive one of these classics the course of the route. I don't know about you, but I am saving my pennies for next year's ride during their 10th Anniversary. What an honor and utter thrill this awesome not-for-profit affords their adoring public.

LANE CONTINUED...

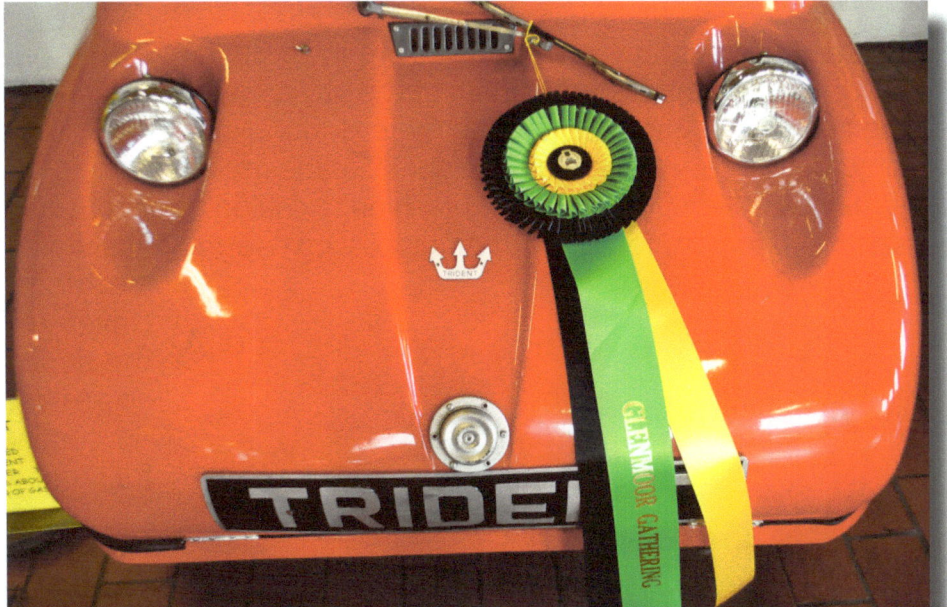

I may have had to settle with posing alongside rather than operating cars like this model of the world's smallest car, the Peel Trident from the Isle of Mann, but that truly was trip enough, as this collection is mind-blowing.

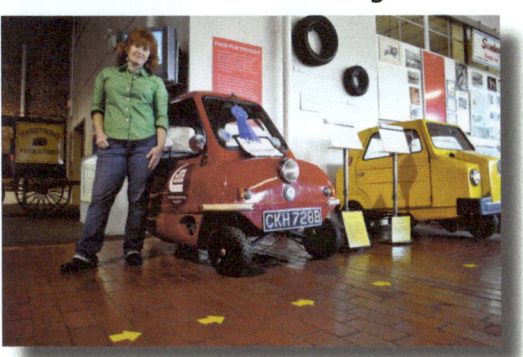

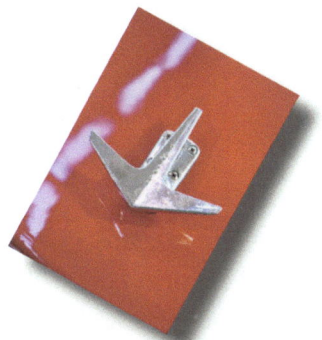

My personal favorites from the visit include this French Helico replica, and the fiercely sleek Tatra Aerouluge from Czeckoslovakia.

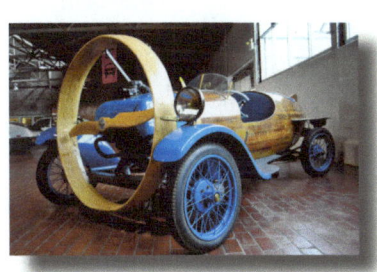

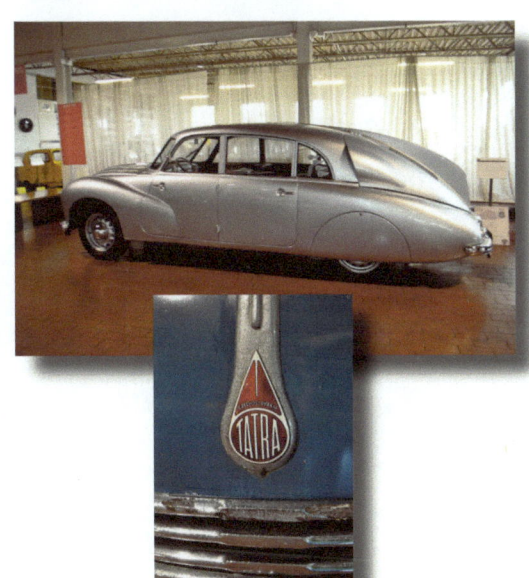

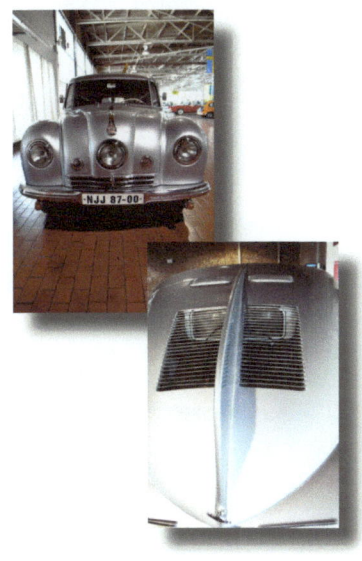

Notwithstanding the myriad of choices, I really took a liking to the opulence of the Tatra's styling.

ANNAPOLIS ANGELS

Mr. Kareem Reed, local ice cream vendor and all around great guy, won my award for nicest person in Annapolis. As I toured the finer points of the bay area's attractions, including the famous Naval Base, he dutifully manned the parking meter I found in front of his shop. He generously fed it the odd quarter here and there as I diligently made my way back to do just that. Keeping the wolves at bay as it were in such a kind fashion, I couldn't help but request his assistance further by asking him to pose for me with Annapolis' own form of hospitality found in their free electric taxi rides the GemE6. Driver Jeff will probably get the tie for nicety as he waited on my call, and braved the on coming rush hour traffic for our photo montage.

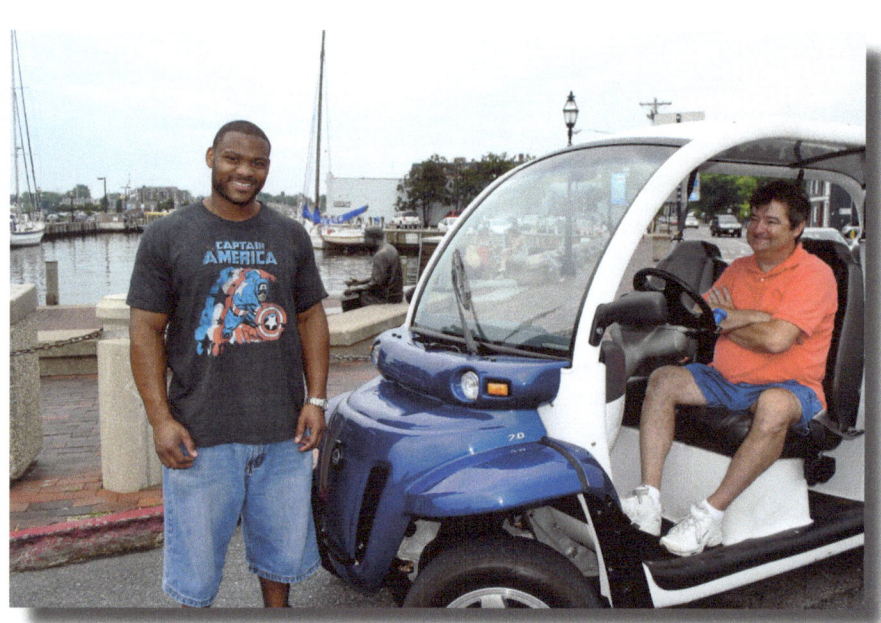

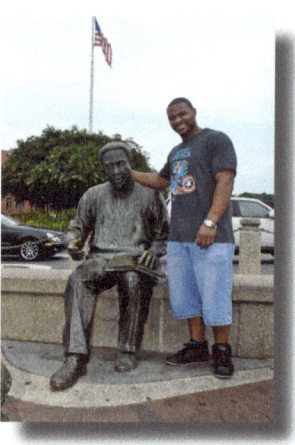

What better testimony to the poignant heart of Annapolis   than to pause beside the statue of Alex Haley tributizing Kunte Kinte at the very point where his slave ship is suspected to have made land.

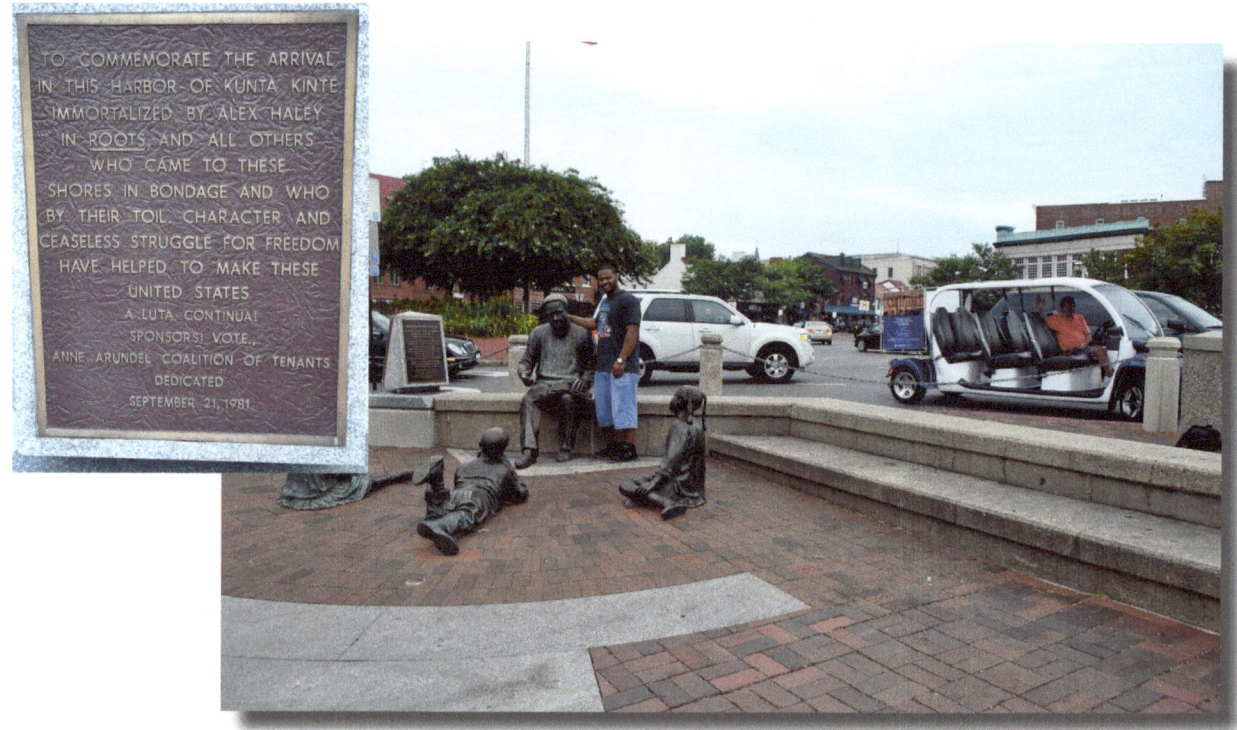

TOUGH ROAD TO HOE

Mild-mannered Bruce Davis moonlights during snowy times as the Superman of snow plow operators. His bladed side kick is a ¼ ton 2002 Chevy with a snow plow-affixed on the bow. We caught up with Bruce after another job well done in this Northern Illinois community shopping mall parking lot.

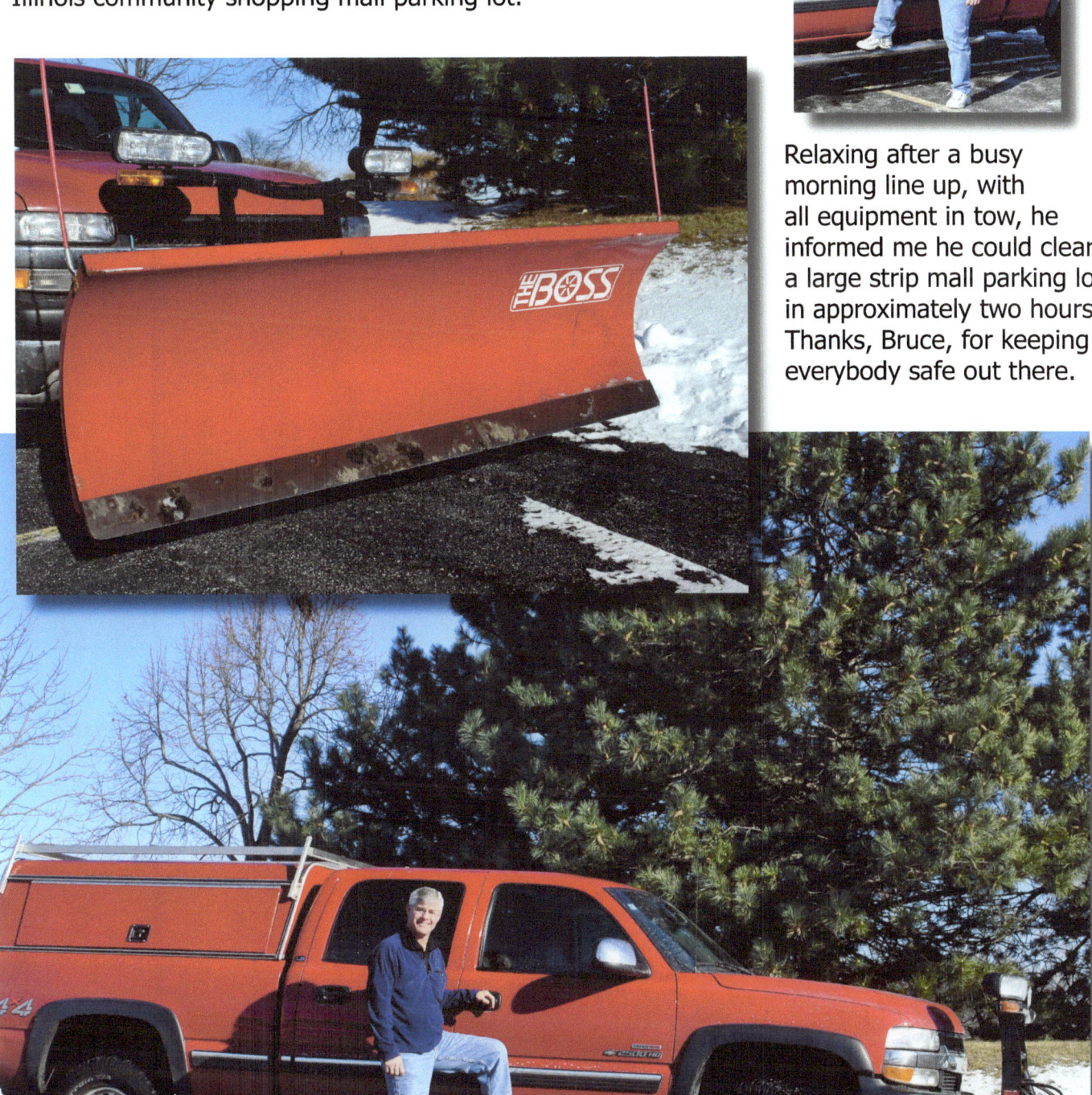

Relaxing after a busy morning line up, with all equipment in tow, he informed me he could clear a large strip mall parking lot in approximately two hours. Thanks, Bruce, for keeping everybody safe out there.

TOWEL, ANYONE?

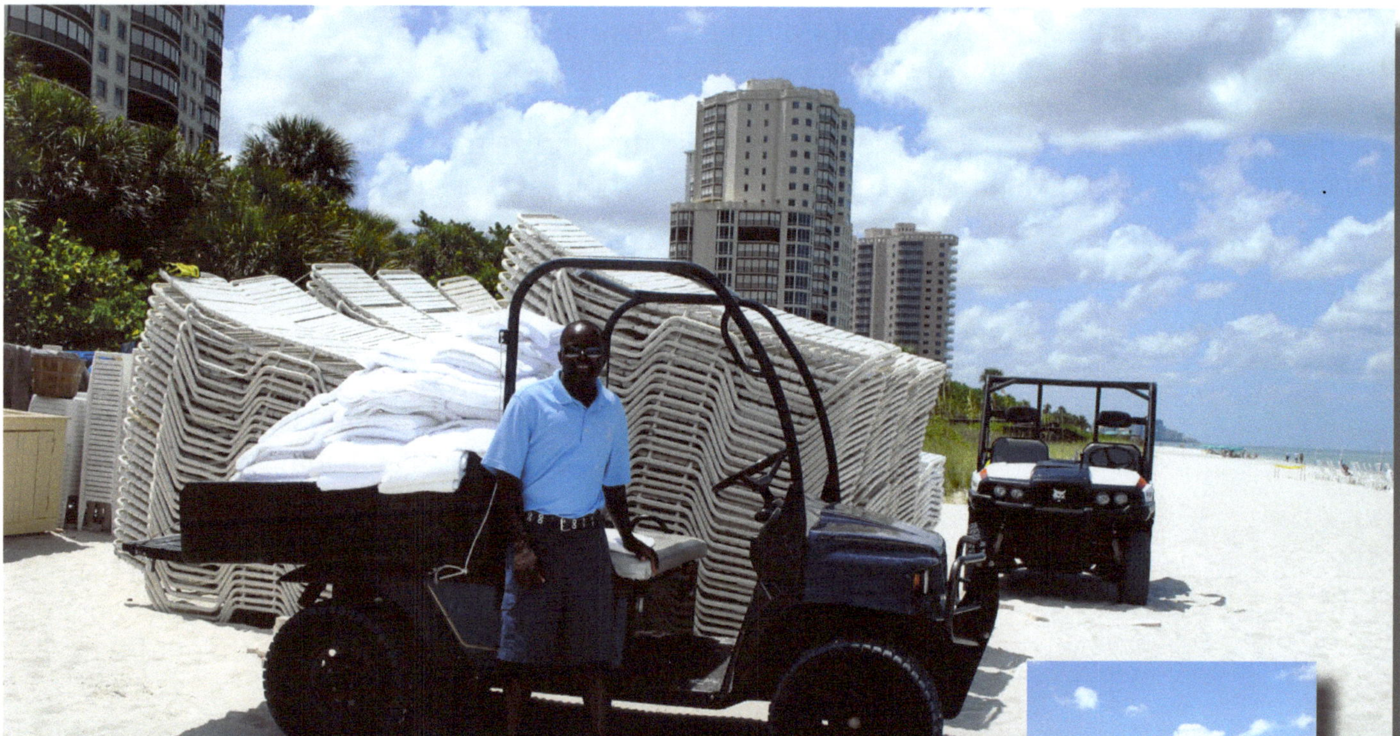

Mr. Paulny Radius is one of the hardest working beachcombers around. The only thing that probably works harder...

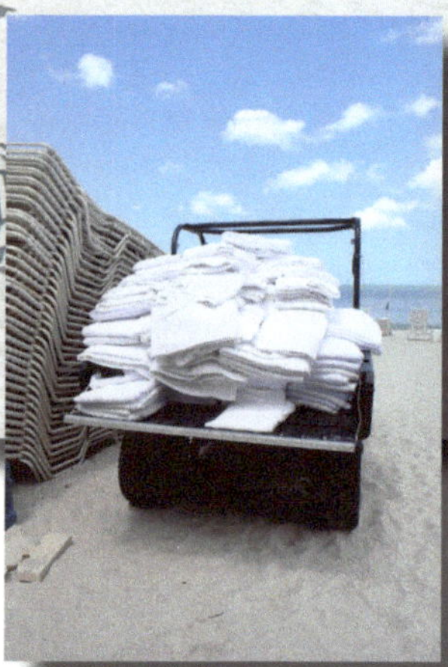

are these heavy duty four wheelers. Paulney and his colleagues utilize them in catering to the high society who oft frequent their classy, upscale seaside resort in Southern Florida.

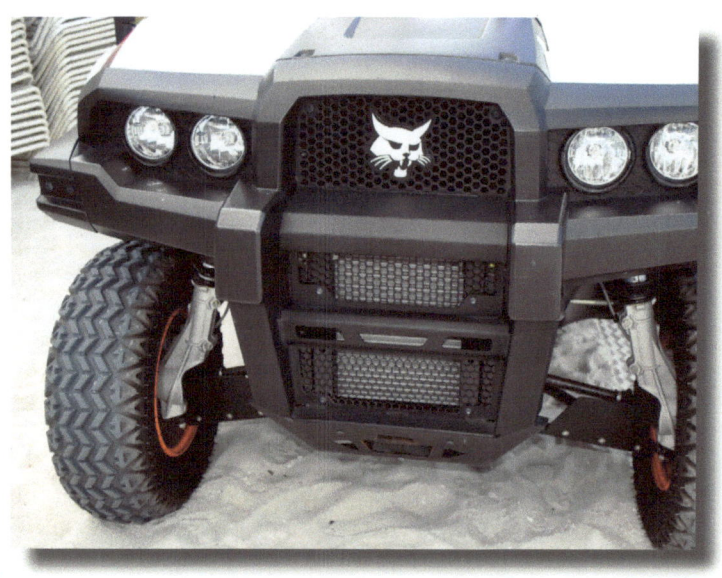

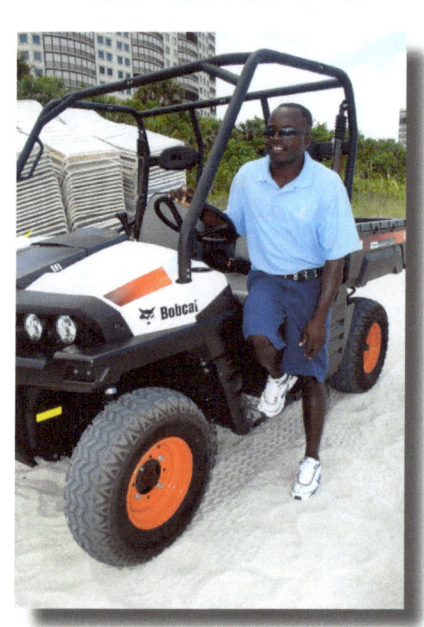

Soaking in the remaining sunlight hours of an early January evening Stephanie Vee of Sedona, Arizona poses with her compact Honda Sports sedan. The background reveals just one of the stately Red Rock vistas this area of the Southwest is famous for. Steph, along with the rest of her community, are fortunate enough to gaze upon such ever-present allure each day.

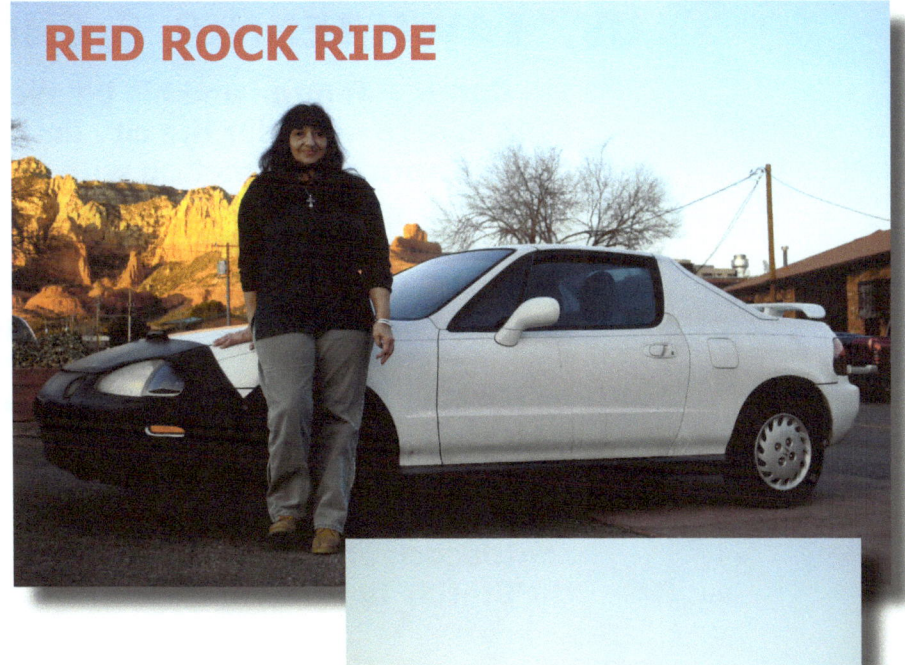

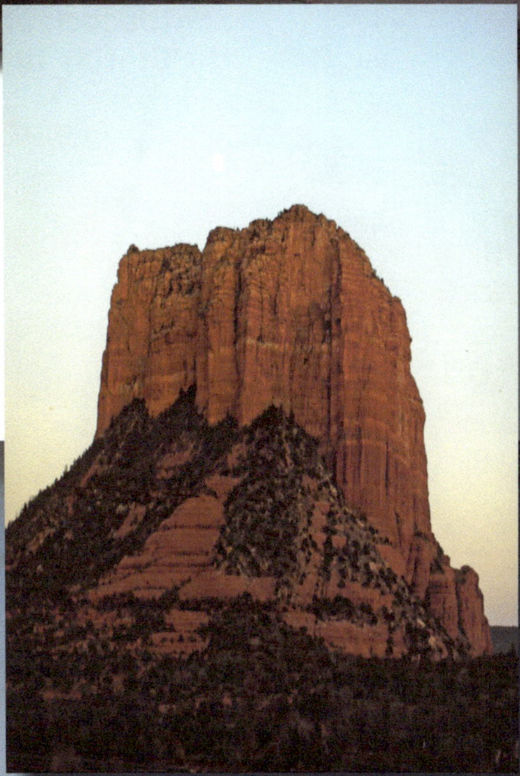

RED ROCK RIDE

It must be surreal while completing the most mundane of tasks, such as a skipping to the local grocer, or car wash, to be surrounded by the majesty that is Sedona.

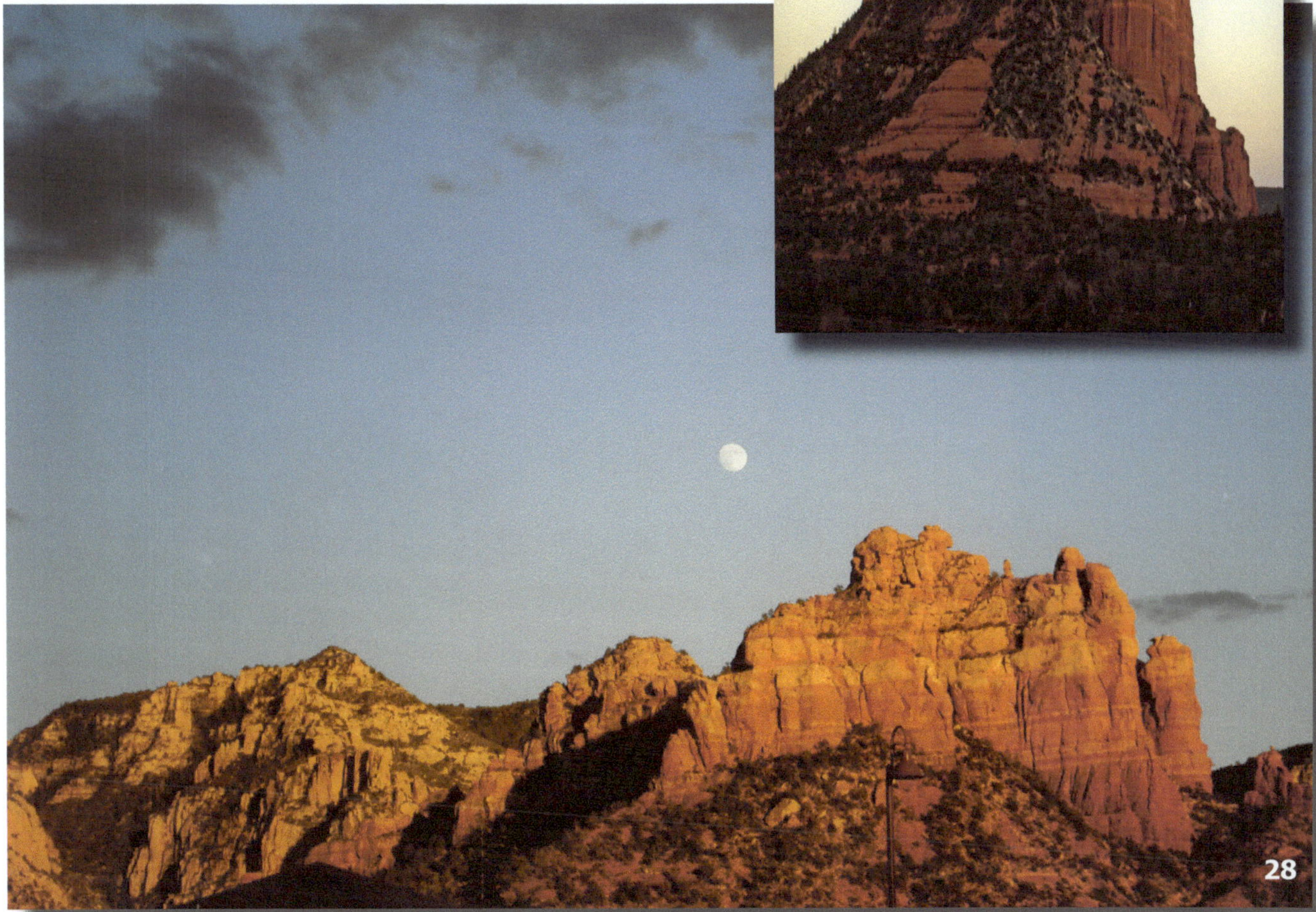

"LUV," LAWN TENNIS, & CHEVYS

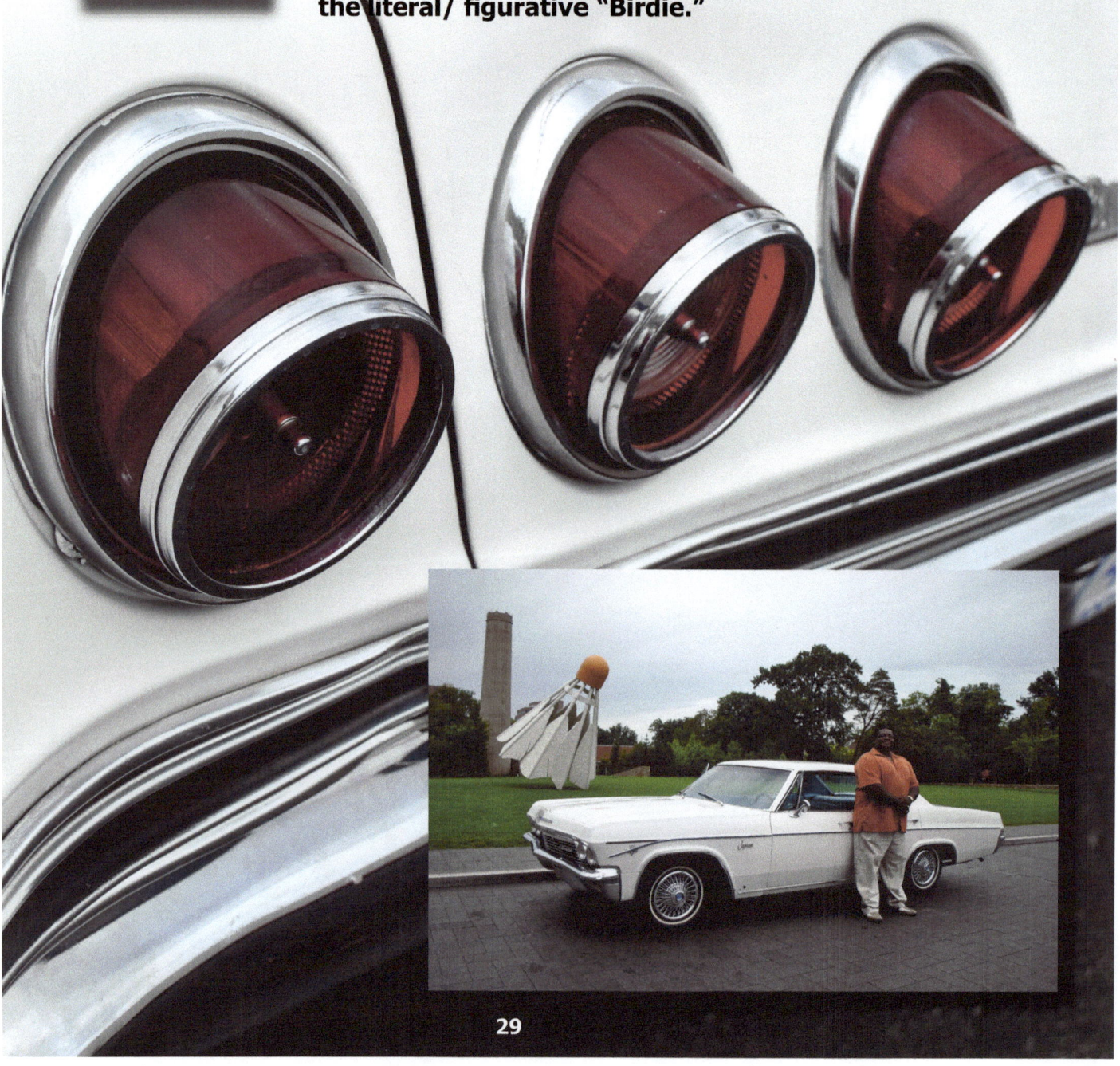

Mr. Cedric Hampton and his beloved Barbara Lynn love to meander the city limits in their '67 Chevy Caprice. We met up with them at the esteemed jewelry store, Vulcan's Forge, in the 39th Street District of Kansas City, MO, before jetting over to this KC hot spot, The Nelson Atkins Museum, for a shot or two. We hauled, as instructed by guard and posted signage. Fortunately, this Bad Boy muscle car has the capability to be nothing if not fast, so we were all back on our way to resuming that leisurely Sunday drive in no time. Even more fortunate for me and your viewing pleasure is this matching shade of corresponding hue Cedric chose to wear during our shuttlecock photo shoot. Thanks on that, and for smiling for the literal/ figurative "Birdie."

KAYAKING CANADIAN

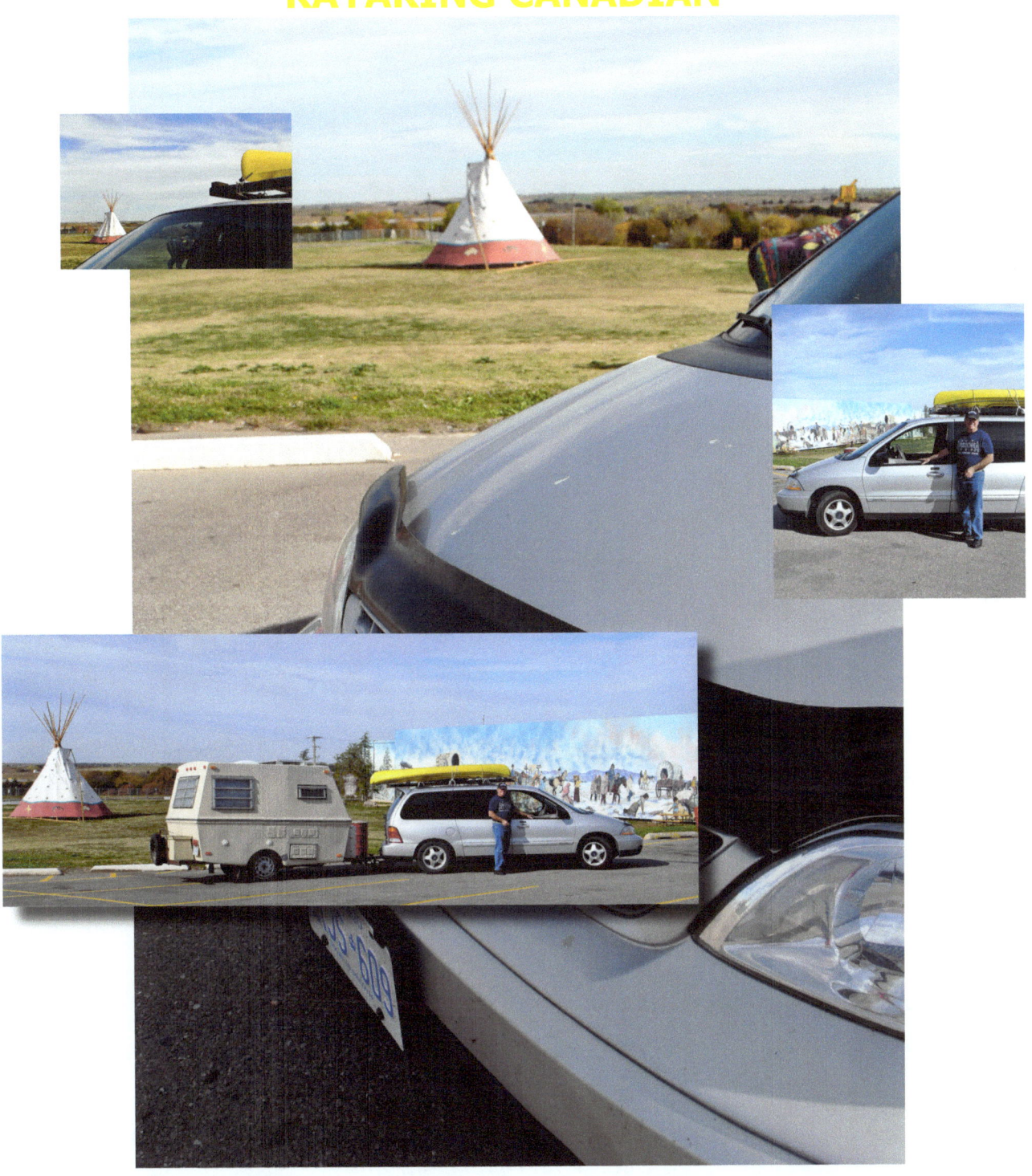

We caught up with Martin McGrath of Canada on his way south of the border toward an Arizona kayaking class he was to facilitate. As one can clearly see, Mr. McGrath is quite prepared for any contingency in his well equipped modern touring mini-van and renovated '73 camper. Marty's suburb of Kanata, was once thought to be the Mohican's name for Canada. Having been told I have Native Canadian roots somewhere back in my ancestry, we couldn't leave without "taking off" with someone from "The Great White North."

Happy Trails, and if it applies to kayakers, "Cowabunga."

"BOWLING" ON THE GREEN

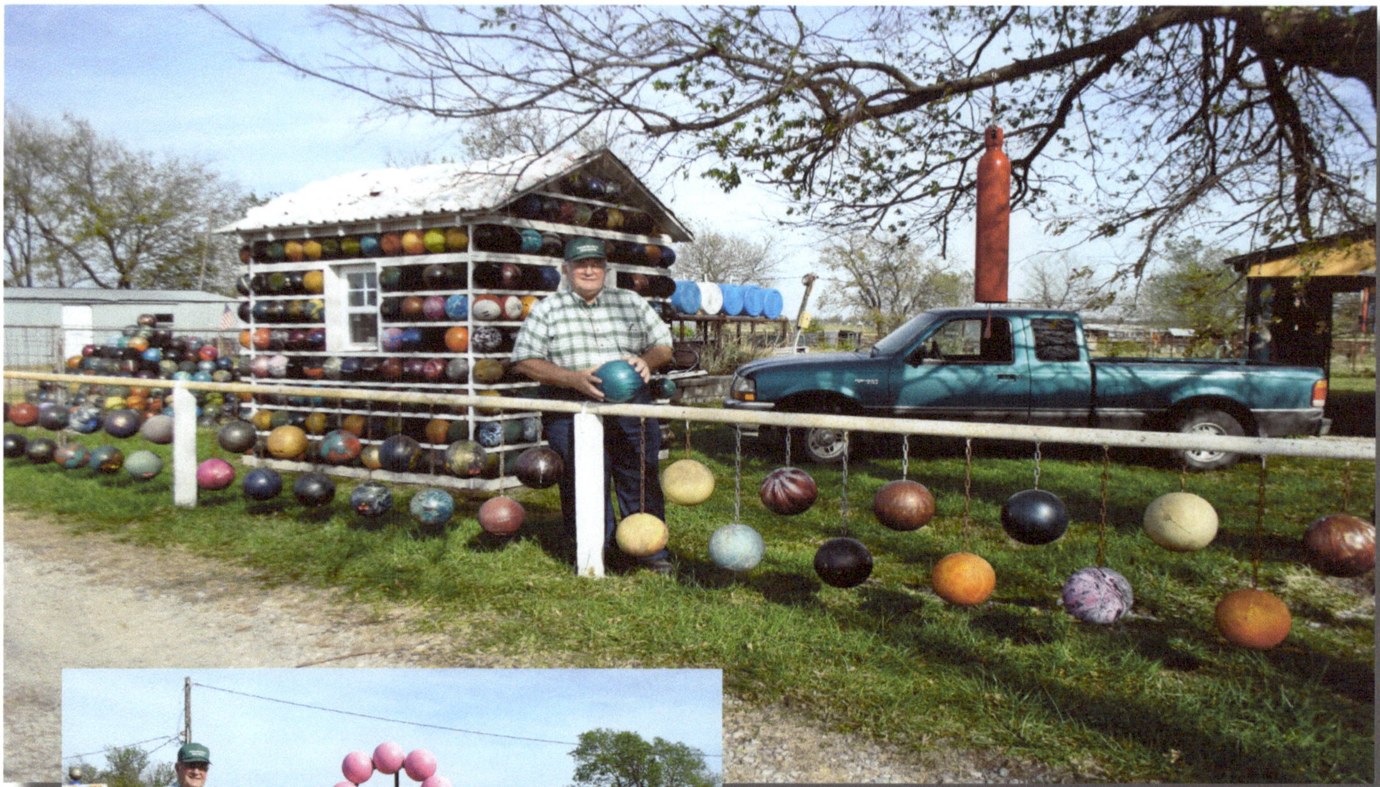

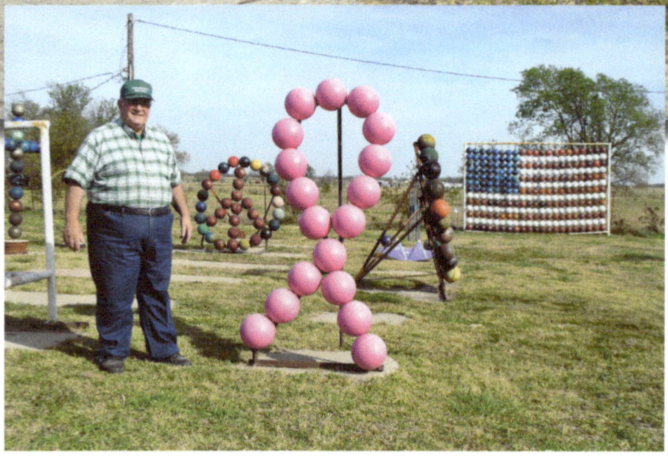

As seen in these pictures, it takes thousands of supplies (mostly donated) to compose the eclectic pop-art sculptures constructed here. Some backers swing by with their contributions and simply roll them onto Mr. Barbee's yard anonymously. One of his proudest creations represents the cancer struggles two of his daughters have undergone. Framed atop is a whimsical approach with our contributed "apple" in front of Chris' newly assembled pin-roofed visitor's shack, and the tough Ford truck, no doubt invaluable in hauling his lane necessities around. Mr.

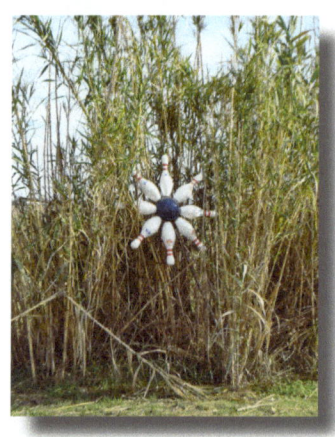

Barbee, you "strike" a chord in the place in our hearts reserved for the memorabilia of Americana.

It's not hard to observe that Mr. Chris Barbee "splits" his time between enjoying his loving extended family and expressing his creativity at home on his rambling ranch. This extensive accumulation of bowling paraphernalia began as a gazing ball project for Mr. Barbee's dearly departed wife. With that Oklahoma wind's ability to pulverize the normal glass sphere traditionally perched atop a podium, one could see how the decision to use something heavier came about. Not having had a chance to be so decorative before retirement, he has a real "ball" literally every day.

TOM STAFFORD MUSEUM

This museum may not house the most expensive car ever built, the $38 million dollar Lunar Rover, (which unfortunately had to be left behind on the moon,) but the missions it was used for would have been scant as successful without the expertise, intellect and research performed by test pilots such as the honorable Astronaut General Thomas Stafford, of the Apollo and Apollo Suyez programs. Two affable docents of the museum Julie Harms and Ashley Keel appear with us as Space

Scholarship
Just like
during the
space hand-
Cosmonaut
Leonov, thanks
continuing
generosity
educational
to these emis-
presenting the
space-related
facts amassed
structural
tribute.

students from the S.W. Oklahoma University. General Stafford's original grand act of good will waning Cold War years with his peacefully symbolic shake between himself and now long-time comrade

Aleksey
for
your
in
grants
saries
many
arti-
in your

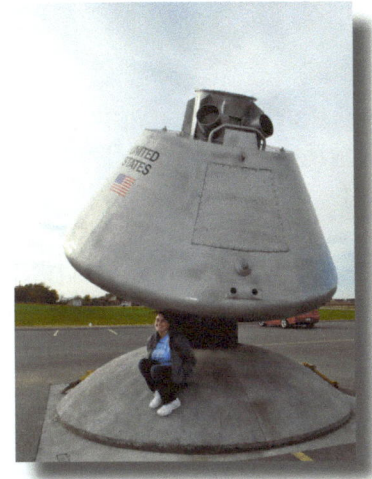

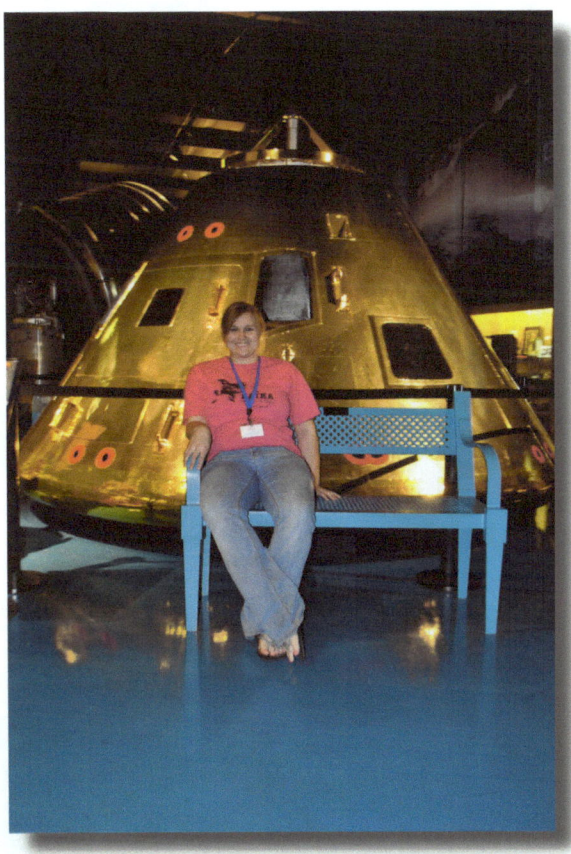

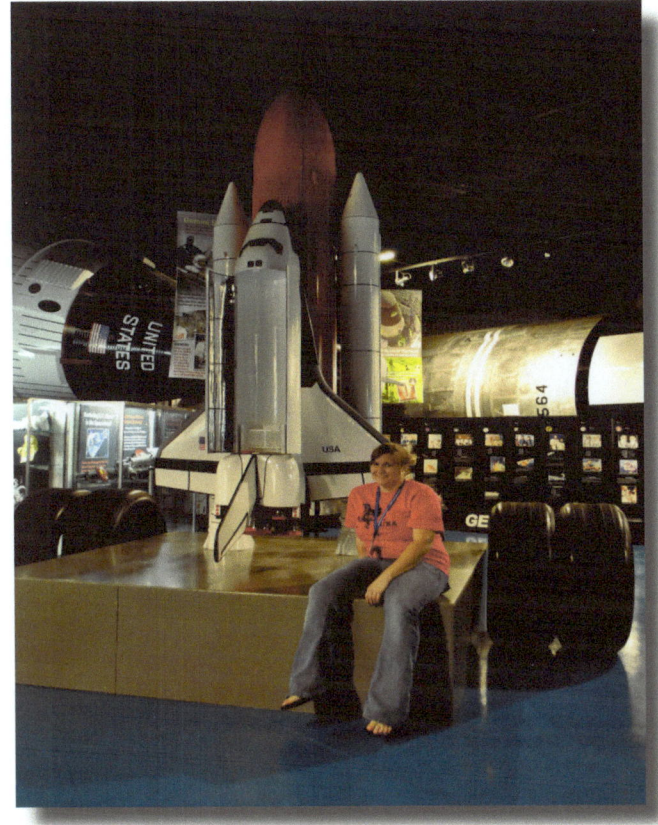

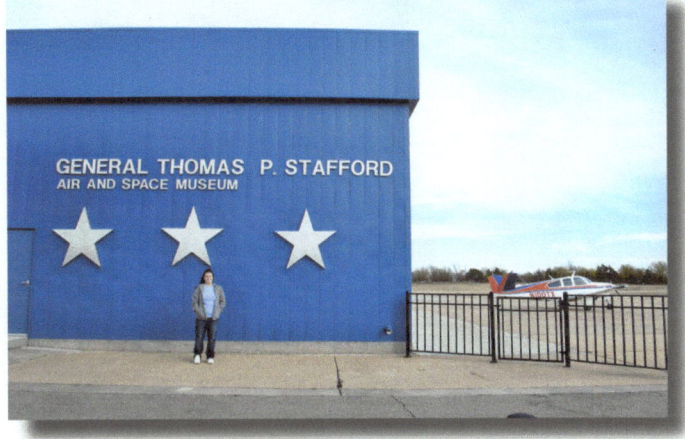

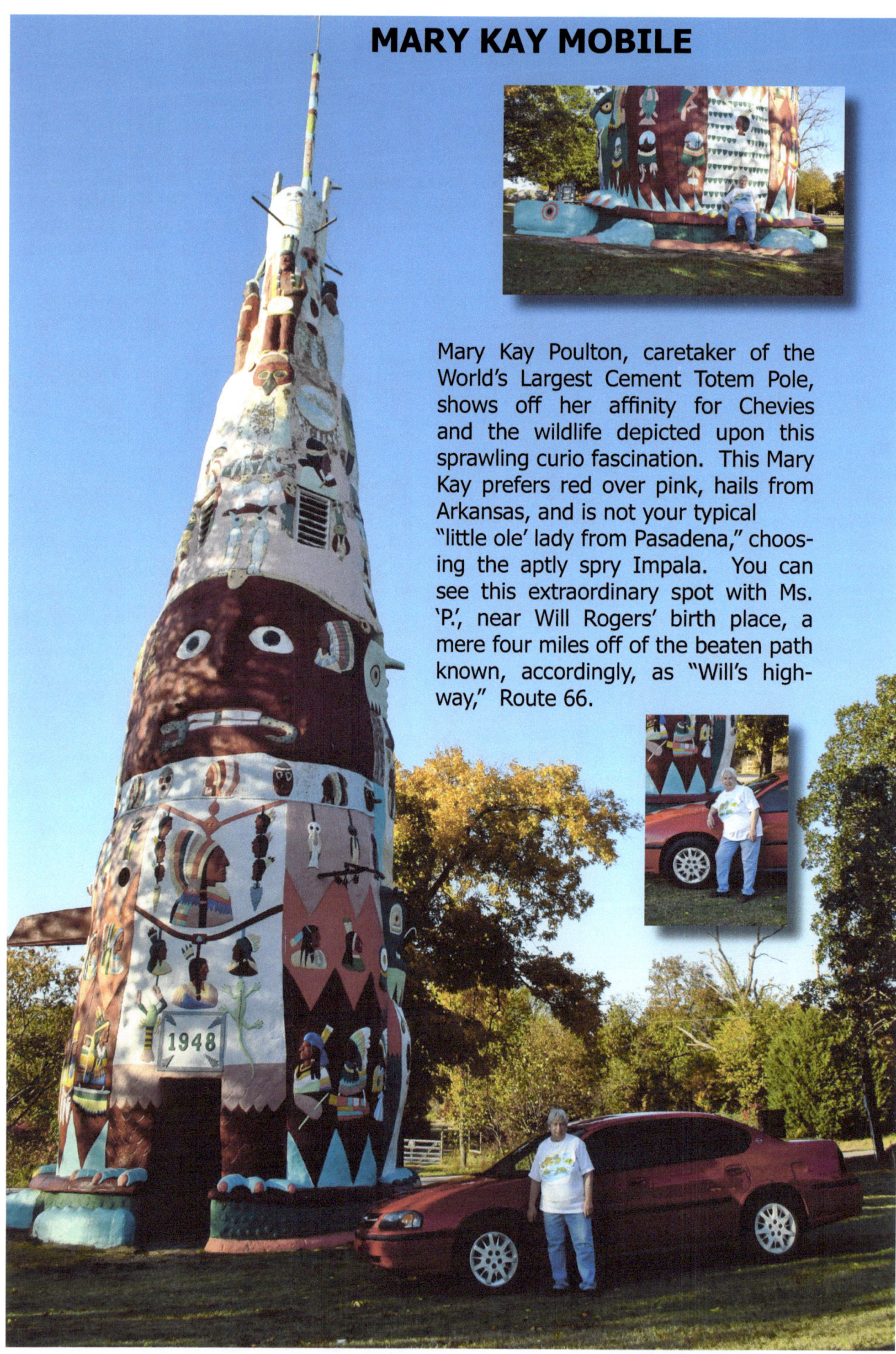

MARY KAY MOBILE

Mary Kay Poulton, caretaker of the World's Largest Cement Totem Pole, shows off her affinity for Chevies and the wildlife depicted upon this sprawling curio fascination. This Mary Kay prefers red over pink, hails from Arkansas, and is not your typical "little ole' lady from Pasadena," choosing the aptly spry Impala. You can see this extraordinary spot with Ms. 'P.', near Will Rogers' birth place, a mere four miles off of the beaten path known, accordingly, as "Will's highway," Route 66.

SEABA MOTORYCLE MUSEUM

Obliging co-owner Gerald Tims engages his kick stand by another "Mother Road" landmark, The Seaba Motorcycle Museum in Warwick, Oklahoma. This unassuming old brick filling station houses, without question, one of the superlative collections of motorcycle history in Oklahoma.

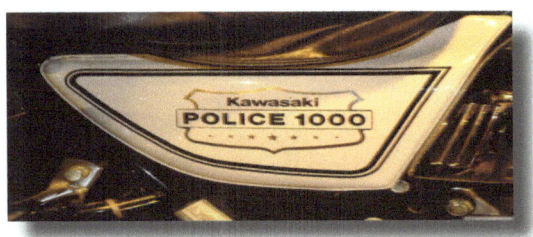

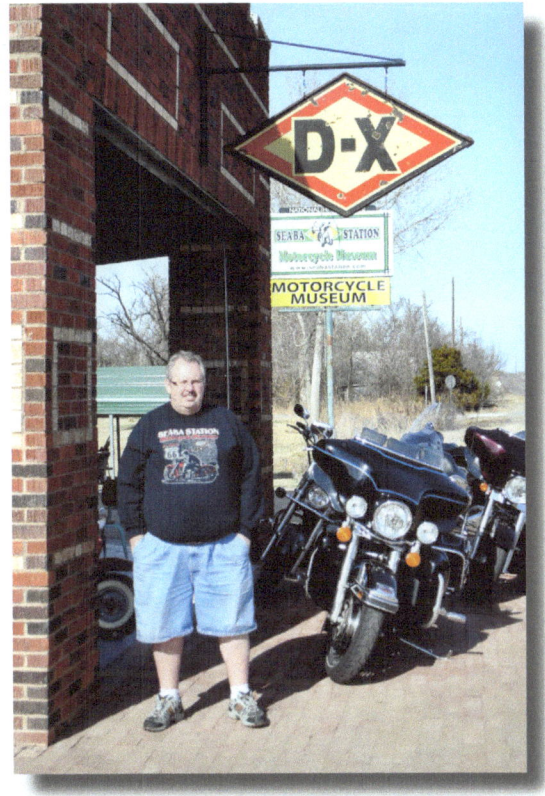

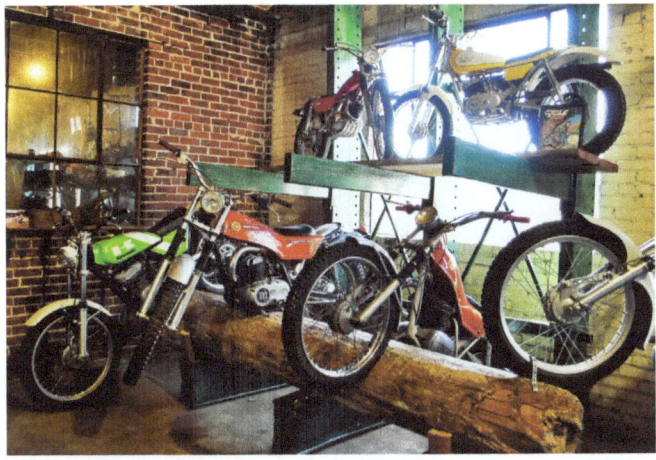

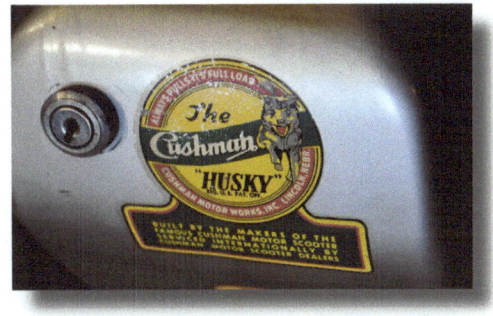

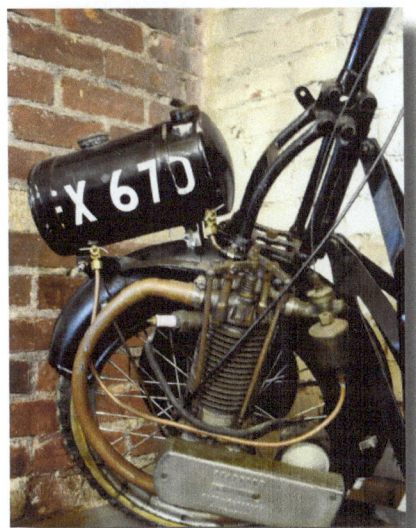

I have included a sprinkling of the exquisite aspects. An outsanding exhibit is the replica vertical board track used for racing the early 20th century, "Pope," cycle, pictured below.

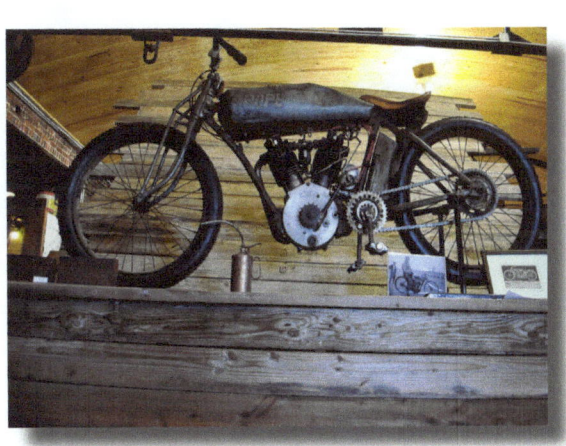

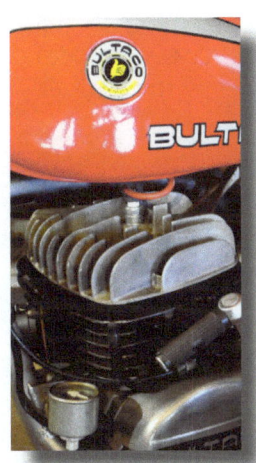

THE CAMAROS ARE COMING

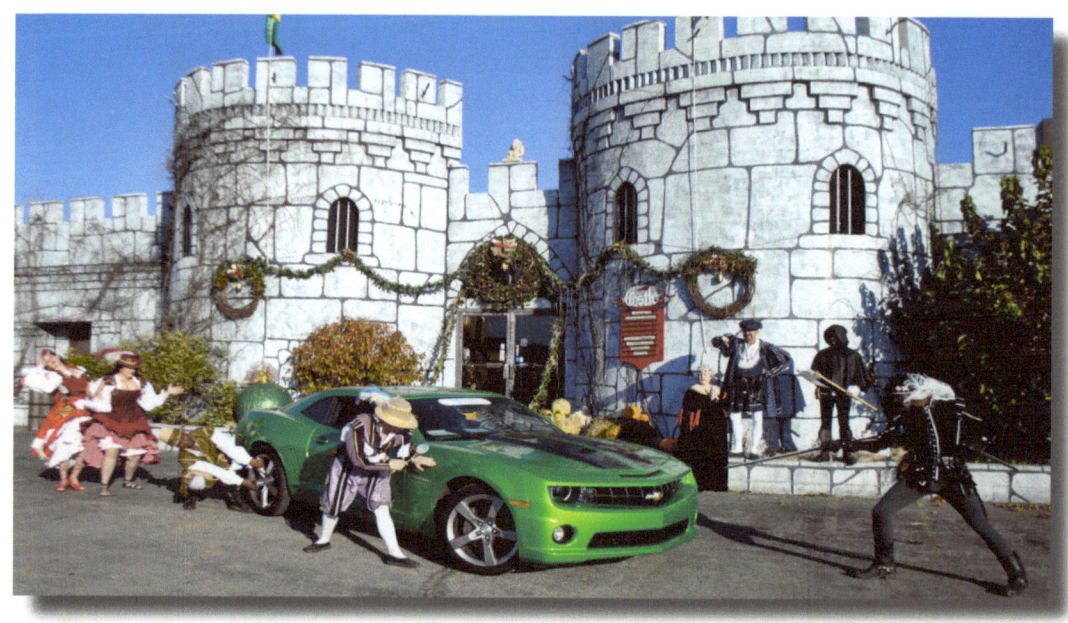

Oklahoma's own little medieval gem can be found nestled in the modest hills just west of the capital at the Castle of Muskogee. This is a delightful venue, pleased as punch, to serve up fine dining and frivoloty during the meal-time entertainment held in symbiance with various festivals and celebratory affairs occuring throughout the year. These subsequent shots were taken prior to the performance troup's curtain call for their November Boar's Head Feast.

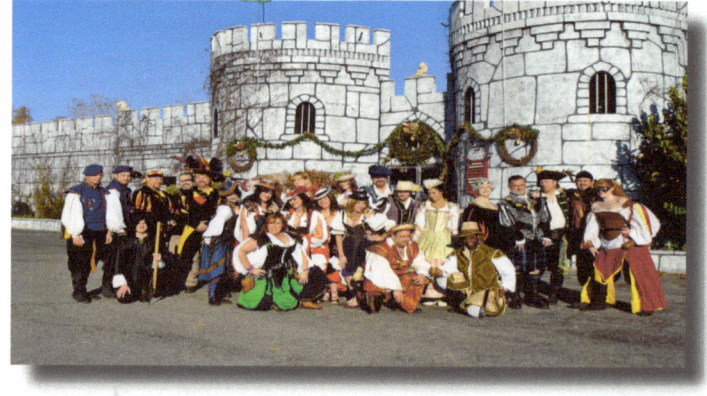

Between the Haunted Forest antics, and December's boughs of holly due to be strung, I stole a moment or two with these talented artists who were happy to ham it up during their precious prep time for one of my dream shots. Margo was crucial in her coordination skill set arranging with the local Chevy dealer to send over not just any car, but this raucus "Belle of The Ball", a 2011 Camaro to serve as our focal point.

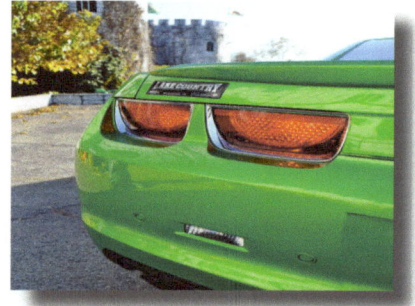

With the scene set, we gaze, as do all of the villagers, upon a fearful sight. Who, or what is this anachronistic glowing green stranger that has rolled into town? Its very presence baffles yet magnifies, meeting with mixed reactions. The women and children were instructed to run for cover, and they did, save for a few curious wenches on the verge of fainting.

CAMAROS SEQUEL PAGE

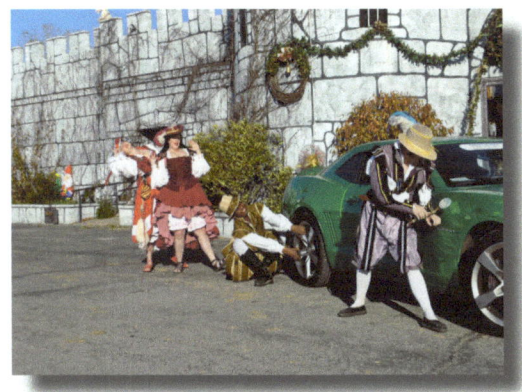

An intrigued man of science leans in with his magnifying spectacle for a closer examination, whilst one of the hamlet's knaving beggars attempts to acquire a chink of the beast's armour to sell on the black market.

At the bequest of the sequestered King, a brave knight, with weapon drawn, subdues the tresspasser, while the Sheriff's sympathetic spouse pleads for mercy on the presumably innocent lost traveler.

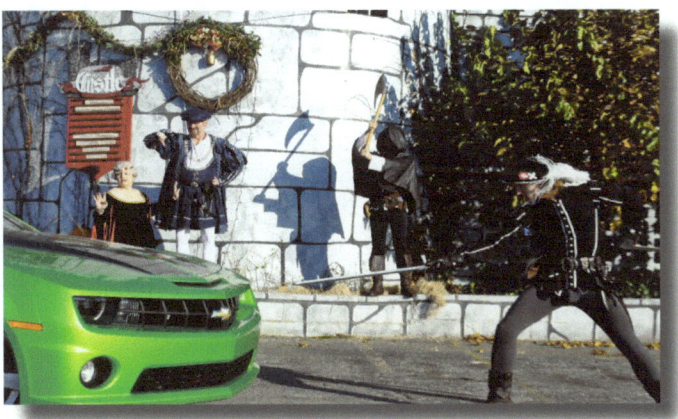

The Sheriff, in the interest of safety, obviously perceives the situation otherwise, and calls in the executioner to relieve everyone of this troublesome burden, thereby restoring peaceful activity among his hysterical public, the King's royal subjects.

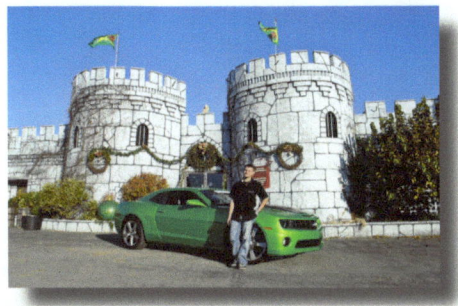

Thanks again to the players for their cooperative attitude and generosity of craft. Thanks also to the very adept chauffeur from Muskogee's Chevy proprietors, who deposited this bewitching green machine at our disposal for an afternoon. Every soul, young and old, was envious as he drove off into the sunset, in an oddly ever so cinema-esque happy ending to our fanciful slice of time-travel merriment. Glad he was able to rescue the creature from the grim reaper's clutches.

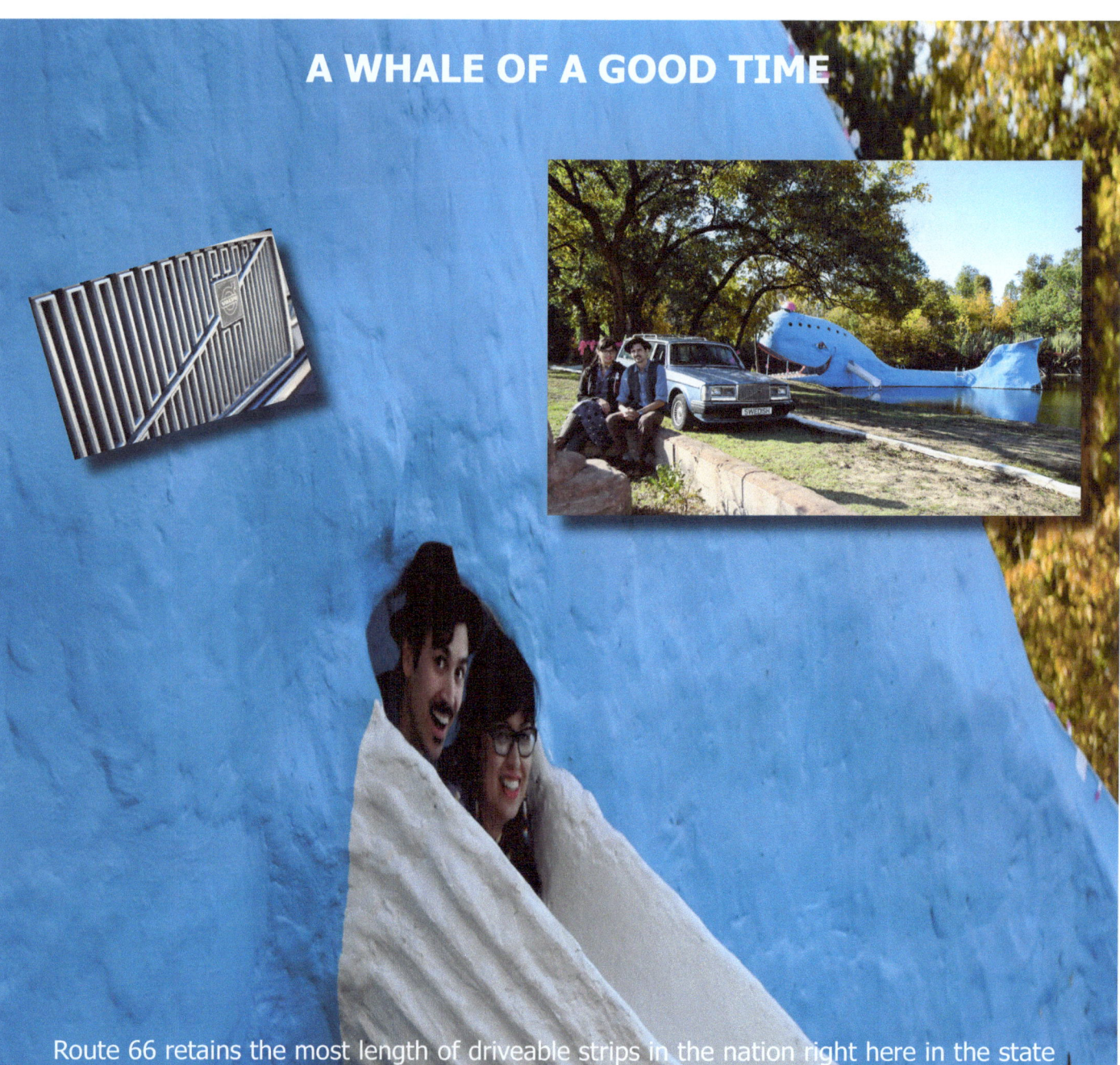

Route 66 retains the most length of driveable strips in the nation right here in the state of Oklahoma. One of the iconic highway's most famous inhabitants, The Blue Whale near Tulsa, has seen millions of visitors drive past its port hole's portal including our two love birds Apolonia Pina and Ian Pico. It originally served as a gift form another lovebird to his wife, with the actual kitschy cement whale opening up to become a slide atop an elaborate swimming hole.

I thoroughly delighted in this autumn photo shoot. Apolonia's Volvo just had to be blue to match. The foliage was awe-inspiring. Speaking of prevalent tones, the whale and the adjacent metropolis of Catoosa were decked out in pink, to advocate Breast cancer awareness. These kids were smiling amenable models, even taking it upon themselves to mug for the camera through the whale's chute near its peeper. The current owner, whose Dad was the afore-mentioned architect of the pool, had a blast watching all of our antics. Their enthusiasm was contagious, as I found myself smiling also.

CELEBRITIES AND HEROES

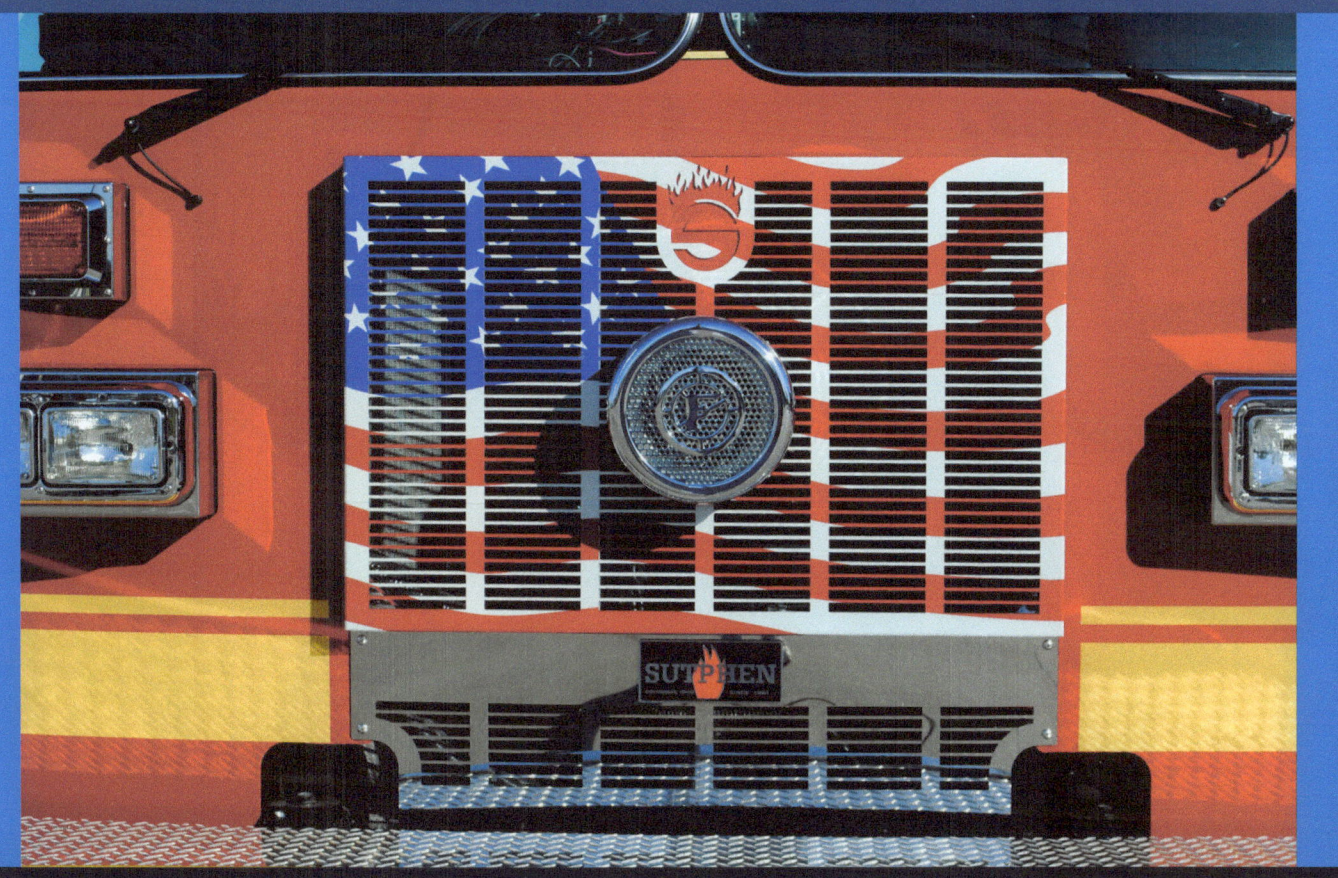

I now pose the question: Who wouldn't want to spot a celebrity or hero at their local car show, or anywhere for that matter? I know I savor such brief brushes with stardom. Feast your eyes on these lingering photographic moments I got to spend while rubbing famous elbows and honoring heroism...

JOHN FERGUSON a.k.a. COUNT GREGORE

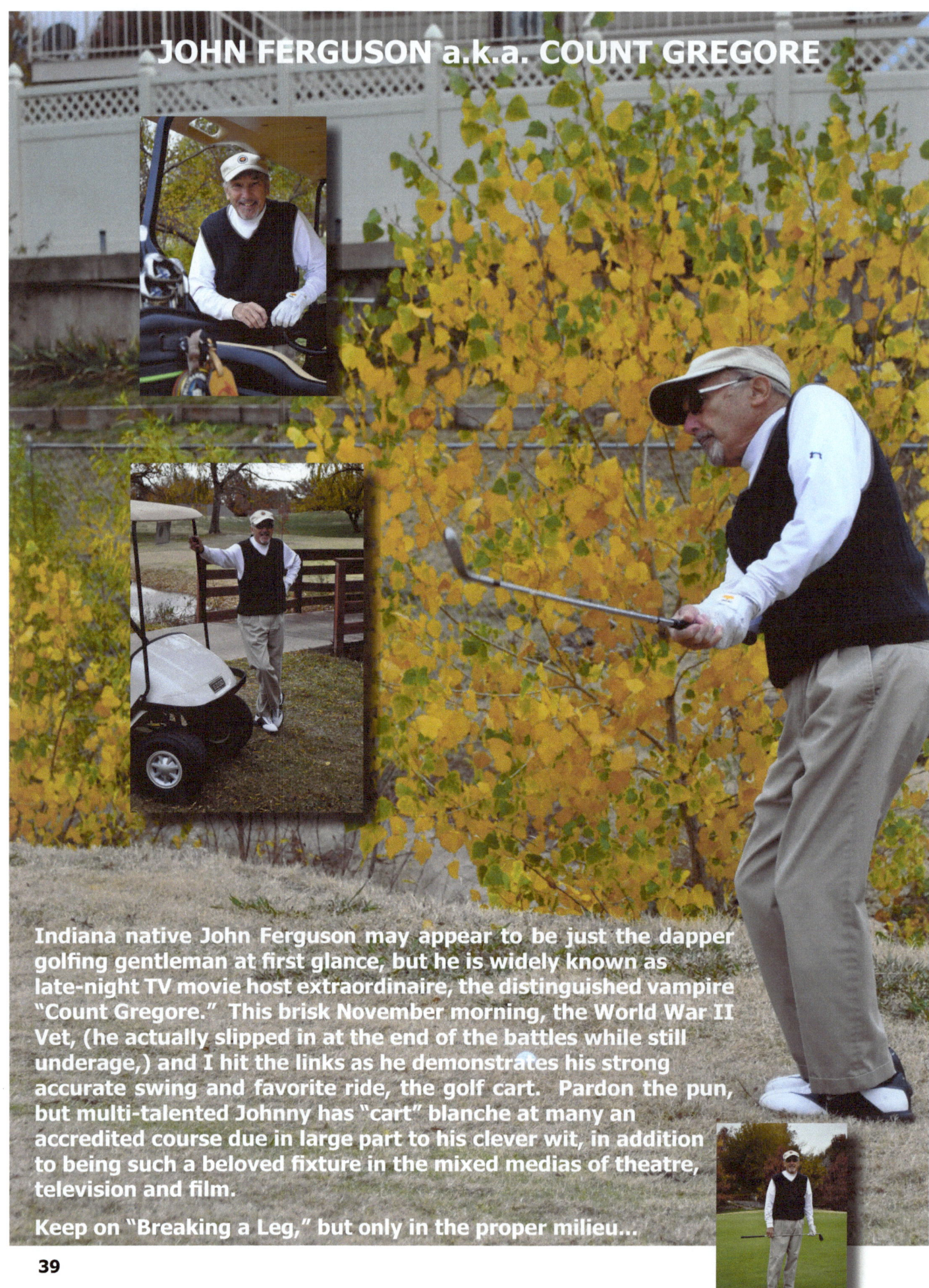

Indiana native John Ferguson may appear to be just the dapper golfing gentleman at first glance, but he is widely known as late-night TV movie host extraordinaire, the distinguished vampire "Count Gregore." This brisk November morning, the World War II Vet, (he actually slipped in at the end of the battles while still underage,) and I hit the links as he demonstrates his strong accurate swing and favorite ride, the golf cart. Pardon the pun, but multi-talented Johnny has "cart" blanche at many an accredited course due in large part to his clever wit, in addition to being such a beloved fixture in the mixed medias of theatre, television and film.

Keep on "Breaking a Leg," but only in the proper milieu...

RISING STAR JOSH CUNDIFF

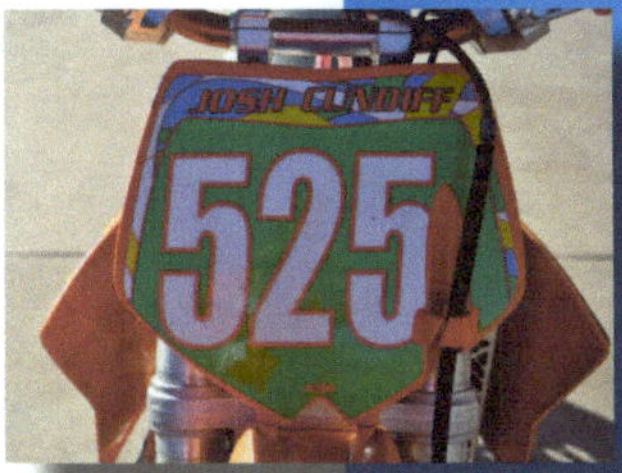

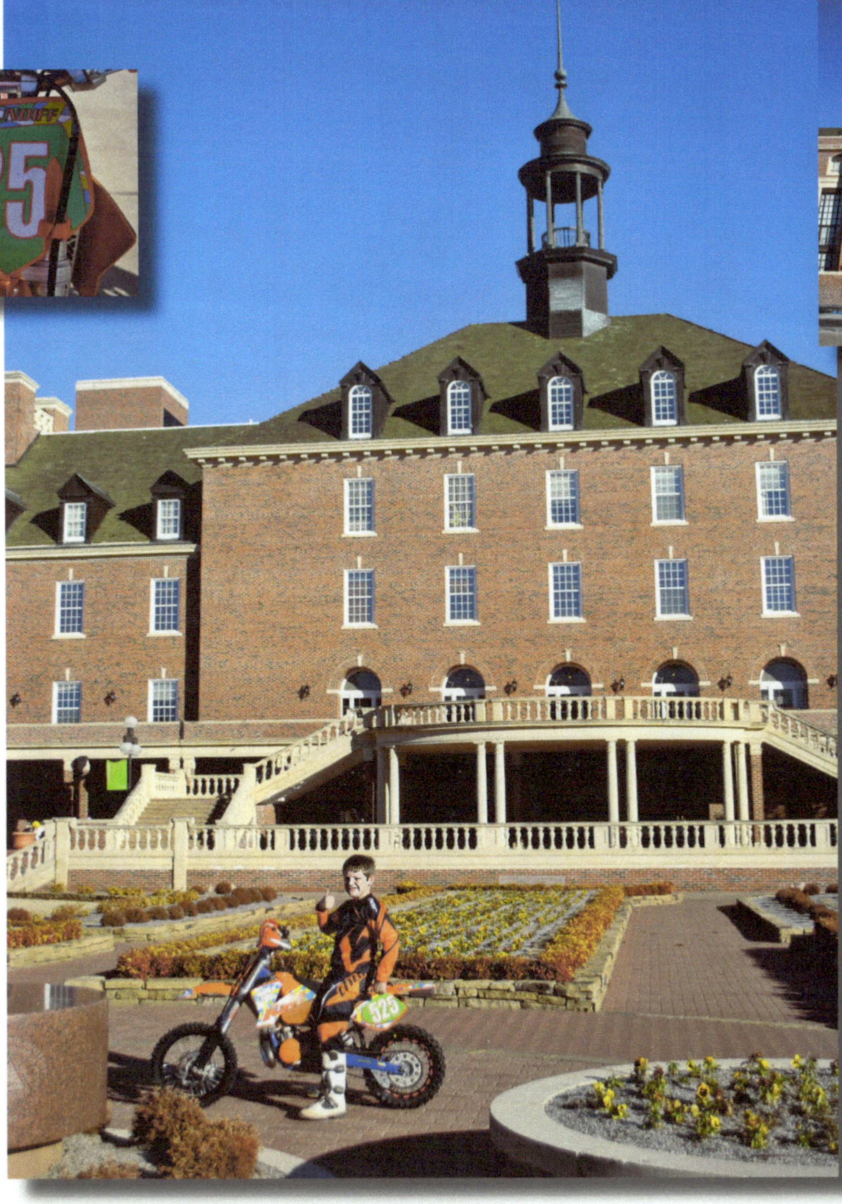

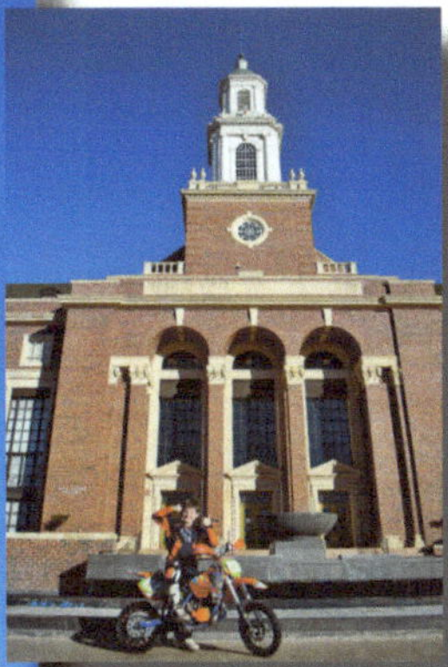

There's a saying in Stillwater, Oklahoma, that one's veins run orange in support of the Oklahoma State University. Well, little Josh Cundiff and family took it one step further waving the school colors in other areas of their lives also. Here our award-winning BMX biker parks his high end, German engineered KTM racer at various bright spots on the famed campus including the statuesque library and the nation's largest student union building. I see this astute, jovial young man going places, including Oklahoma's home of excellence in higher education, and beyond.
God speed, bright star.

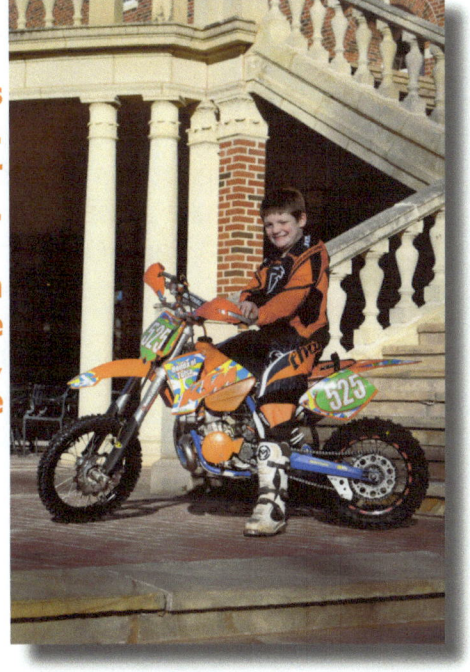

OFFICER CHUCK WHEELER

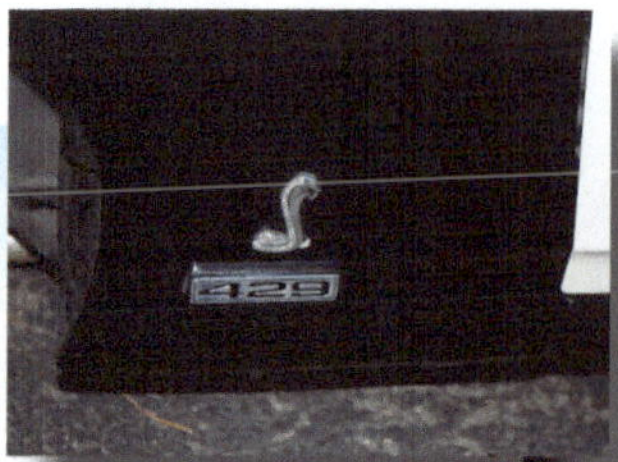

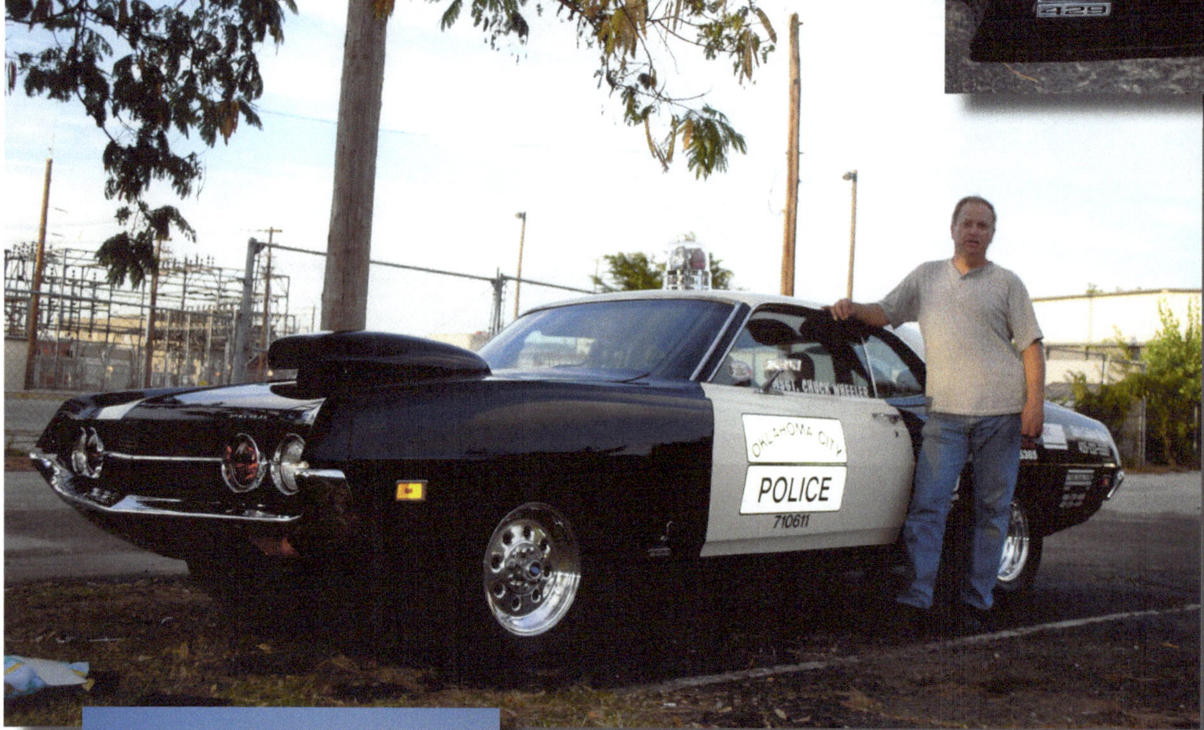

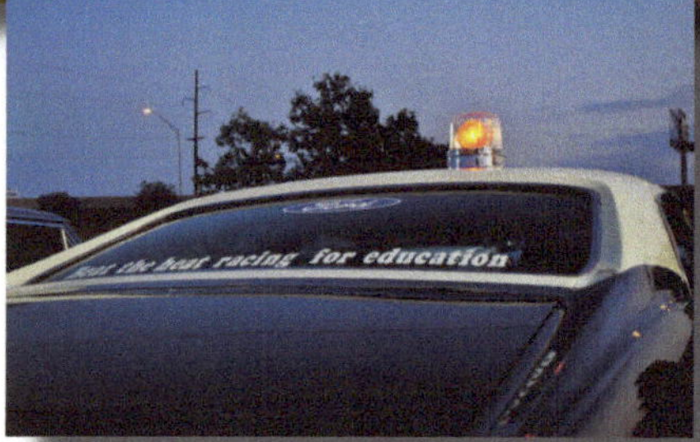

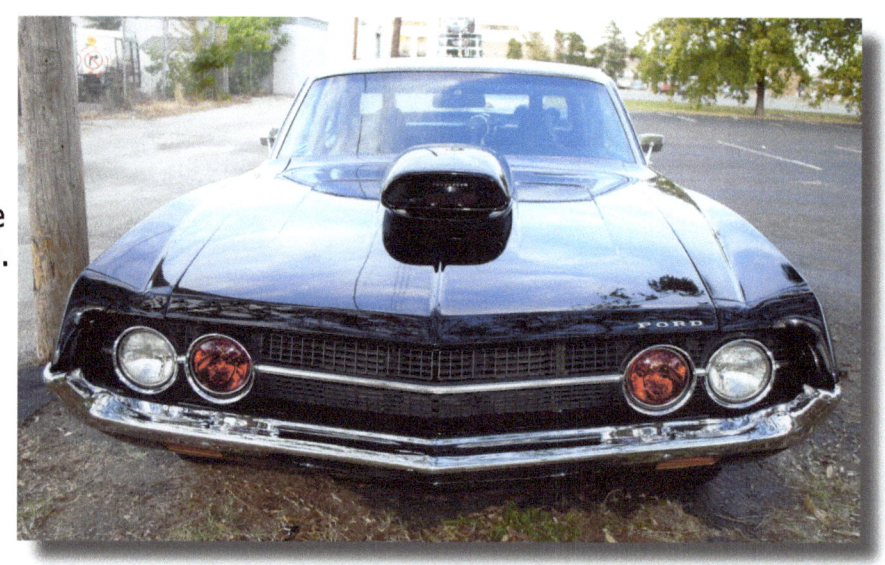

Master Sergeant Chuck Wheeler uses his actual squad car, a 'suped-up 1971 Ford 429, in the organization called "Beat The Heat- Racing for Education."

It pairs up high school students with police officers for safe, regulated competitions, often on their designated quarter-mile track in Nicoma Park, Oklahoma.

SCOUT NORQUIS L. DAWSON

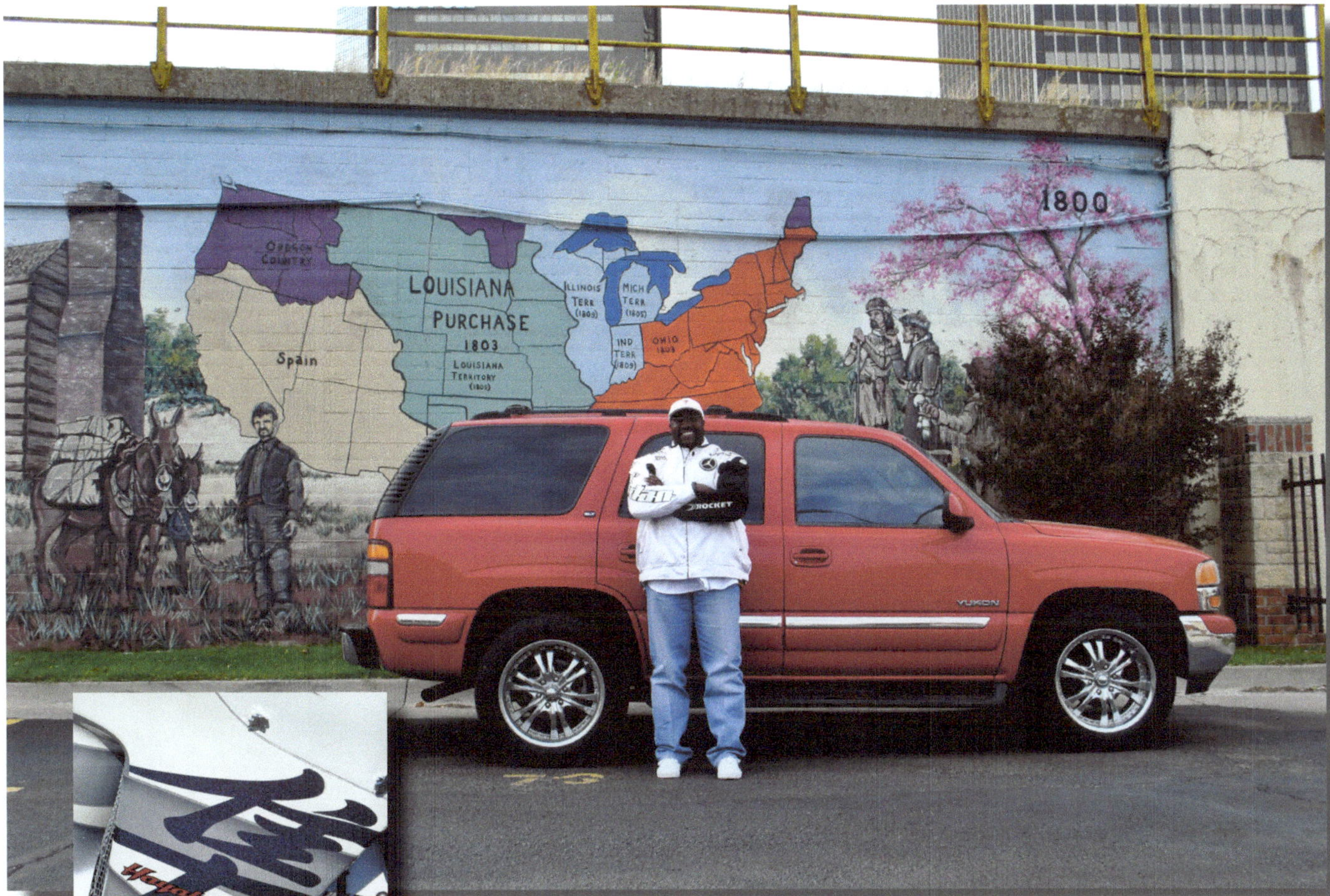

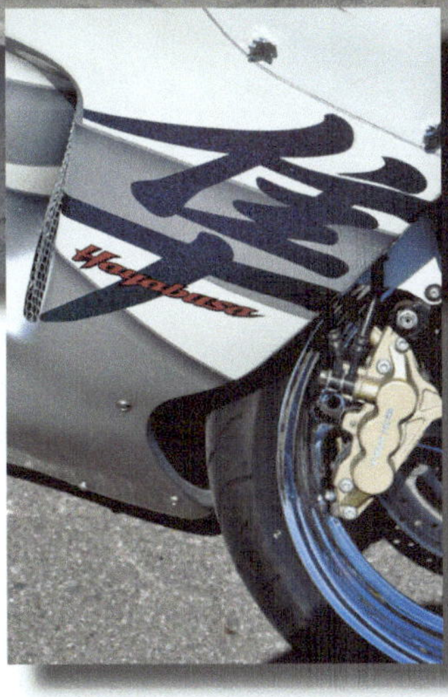

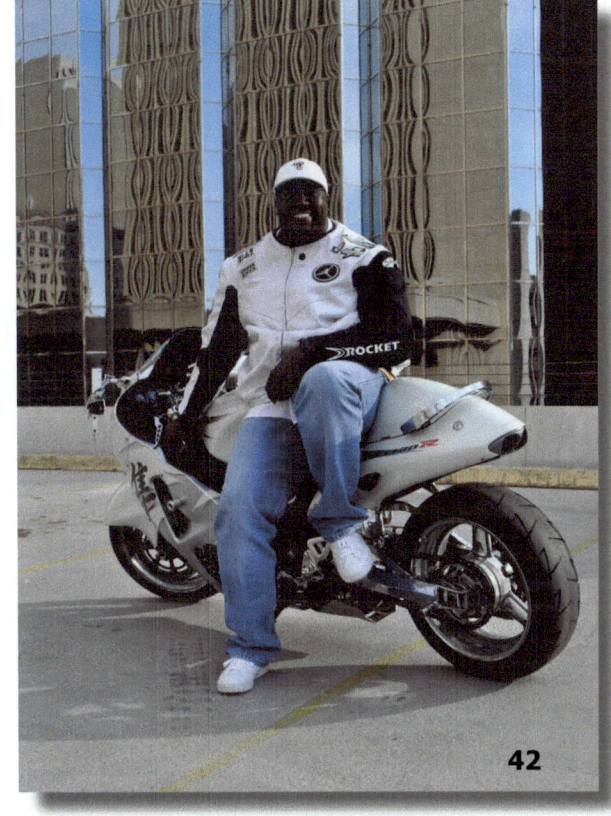

Norquis Dawson is famous for making other people famous by discovering their potential skills in his role as a scout for both the major Oklahoma school football programs. Alongside his winning attitude, complete with well rounded smile, I wish his talents were not so behind the scenes, as he is a photogenic fellow for sure. He revels in every opportunity snagged to ride his customized Suzuki when not dutifully driving to seek out new talent. Keep up the good work, Mr. Dawson. Fans may not cheer your efforts toward the end zone, but they appreciate your keen eye everywhere someone in American soccer touches down.

GEOIST JOE ALLEN GIBSON

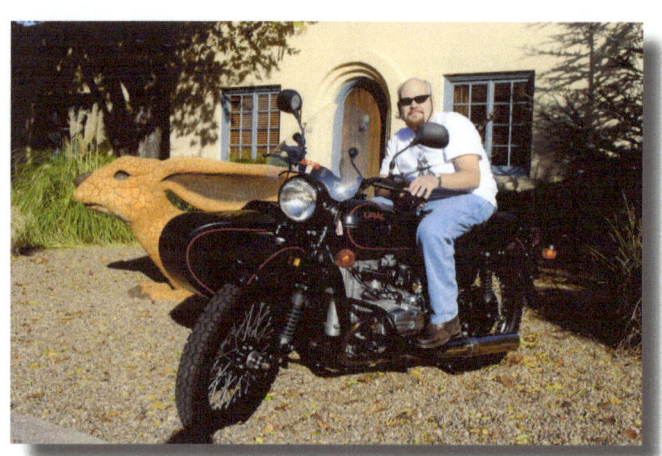

Former geologist Mr. Joe Allen Gibson is a famed local artist known for having the media in which he works coined as the descriptive phrase "Geoism."

His art combines the geology of his youth spent largely around the oil fields prevalent in his home of Okla. with elements of three-D and abstractism. How apropos then, to find him posing with his 2010 Russian manufactured Ural motorcy- 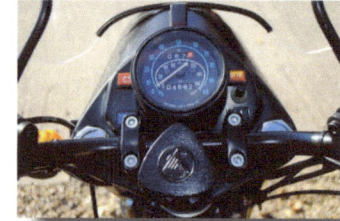 cle in front of a favorite sculp- ture in Oklaho- ma City's artistic Paseo district. The montage truly encom- passes all of the elements just specified...an oil-run all busi- ness machine, the Ural, with a whimsical 3 D bunny. It cer- tainly does make for a psychedelically groovy photo opp.

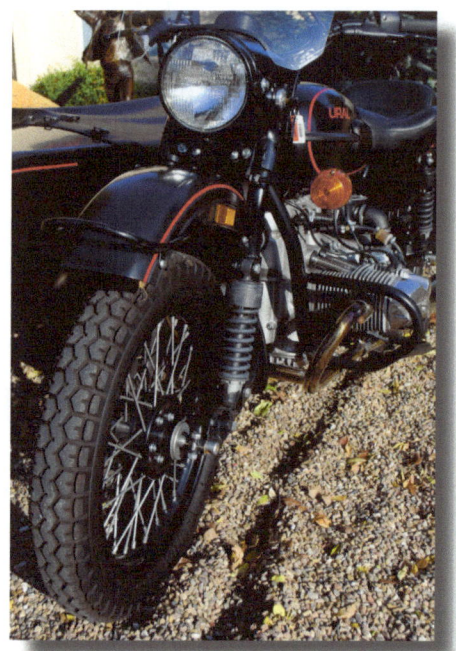

Thanks Joe for divulging this rabbit hole. Here's hoping for the best of success in all of your future endeav- ors. I incorporate your website to encourage others to check out an overview of your unique offerings.

www.geoism-art.com

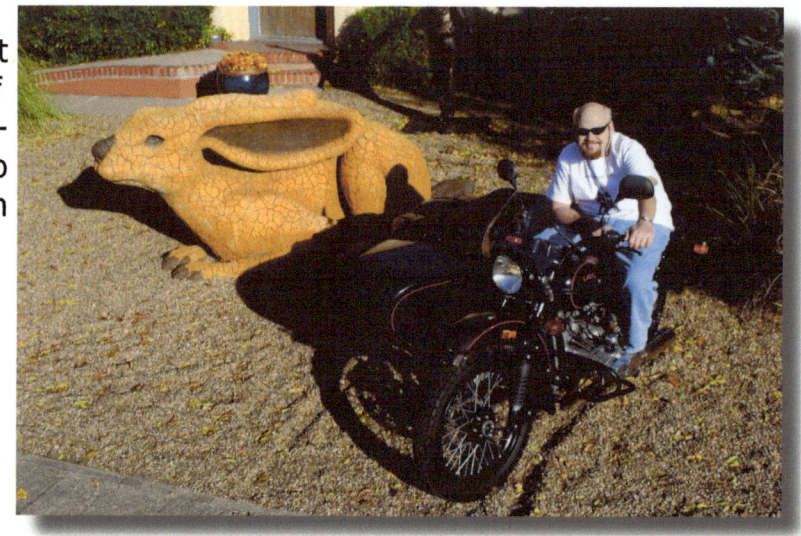

BOXING LEGEND STEPHANIE DOBBS

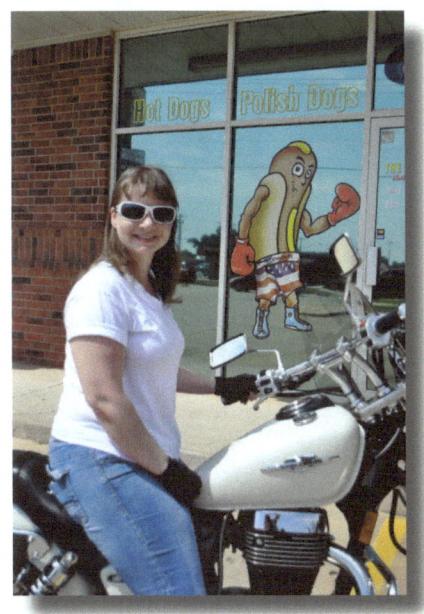

Stephanie, "All Action," Dobbs, boxing's real superstar, holds tight to her Suzuki Boulevard in front of the delicious coney dog business she started upon hanging up her gloves.

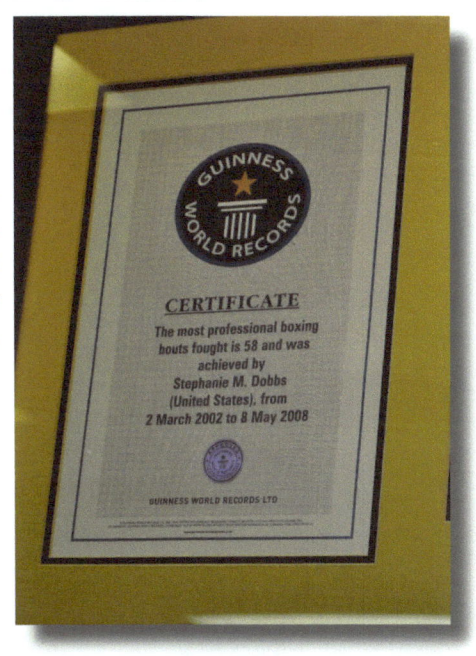

Another keepsake she holds dear to her heart is her Guinness Book record for any boxer (male or female) who has competed in the most amount of bouts. An energetic powerhouse, she chose not to remain in the corner, but keeps coming out swinging in all aspects of life. Thanks for sharing that knock-out personality, and for taking a time out to show off in this book.

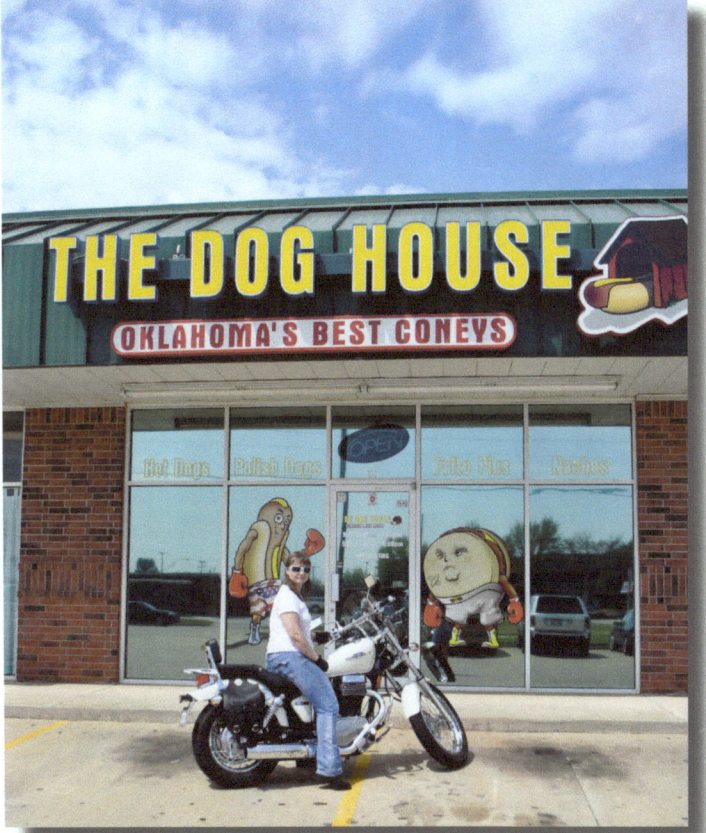

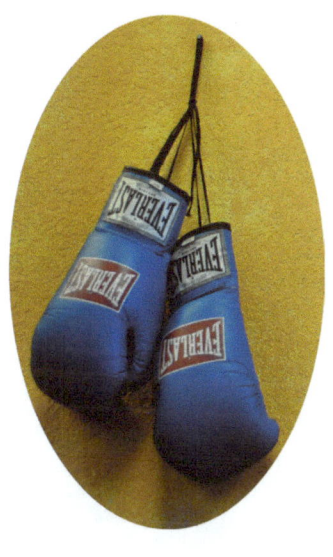

COACH LES ELWOOD AND FAMILY

Les Elwood, patriarch of the Elwood Family of Oklahoma City, proudly stands with some members of said family including wife Janet, son Shawn, as well as his other pride and joy a 1948 Fire Truck once in active use for the town of Canton, Oklahoma. The Elwoods are a staple, afoot at almost all of the shows I have attended locally.

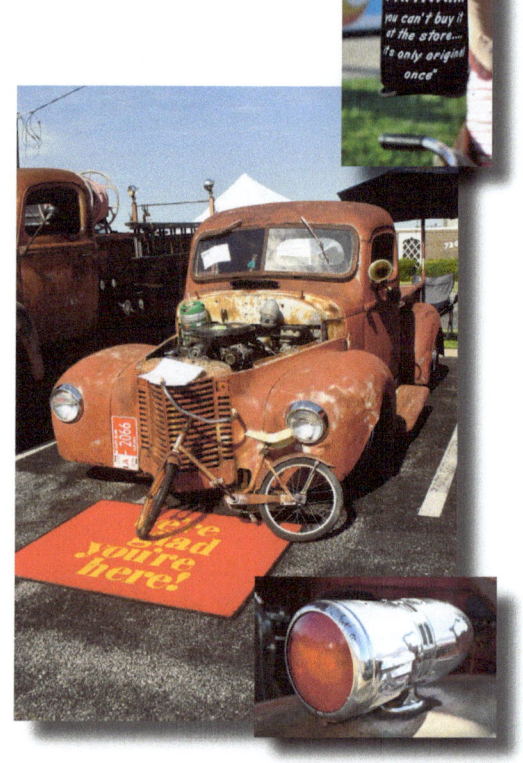

They belong to an elite group at these functions known as the Rat Rod category. The division has a stringent set of rules to be adhered to, including a lack of aesthetic formalities such as shiny paint jobs, preferring to strictly stick to the mottled shade called Patina.

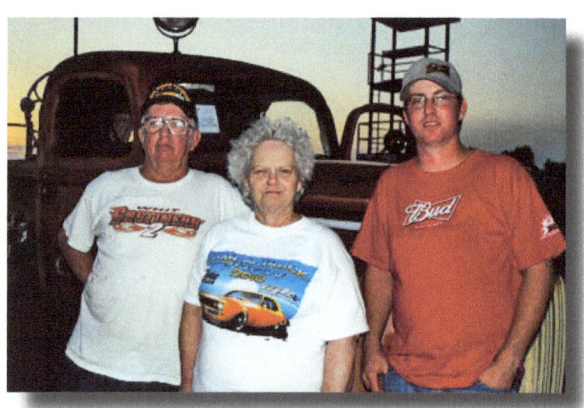

Mr. Elwood is a hero indeed, but not for the reason you might think... Les or "Coach" as I have always referred to him, was quite the gentle leader to a bunch of rumble-tumble girls including myself, who were fortunate enough to be under his softball tutelage in our formative years.

Still in possession of our medals, and my South Side "Bears" cap, I will never forget the memories we all made. I love how you just laughed off one of my debut base running attempts. I remember my shaky knees in the batting box, as I made actual contact with a pitch. Off I hustled toward first base. Then is when the fun began, either through bravery, or a sheer manic aim to please, I ignored the base coaches, and kept running right from the moment my miniscule in-field plinker hit the ground. I imagine the gal on second must have been a smidge surprised to see me rounding first without being waved in. I know for sure the runner on third was terrified, seeing two teammates headed her way as she also took off for home, amid the confused chaos, and frantic attempts by the opposing team to futilely fumble a ball our way.

Coach is still great with the wide-eyed kids who crowd his rusty ole' ride at the shows, hoppin' out of the cab, and enabling them to climb around and investigate his mobile art, which by the way, IS a daily driver.

In fact, when the children of customers seeking consultation at his family's mechanic shop, spy the multitude of trophies scattered around, he offers them one to take home.

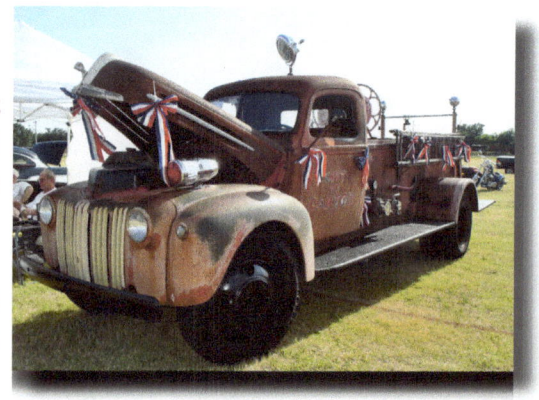

DON DEMETER, H.O.F. ROOKIE

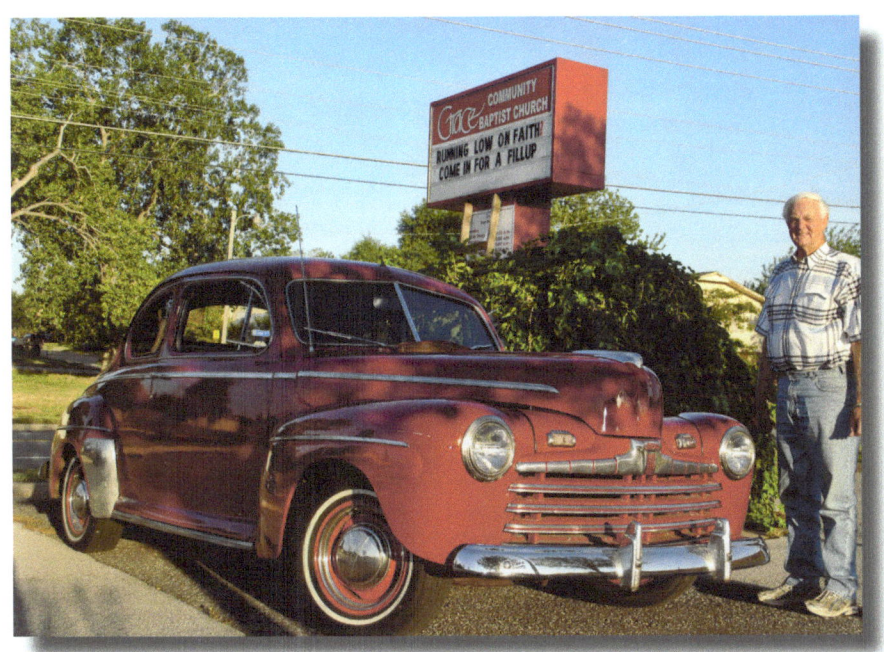

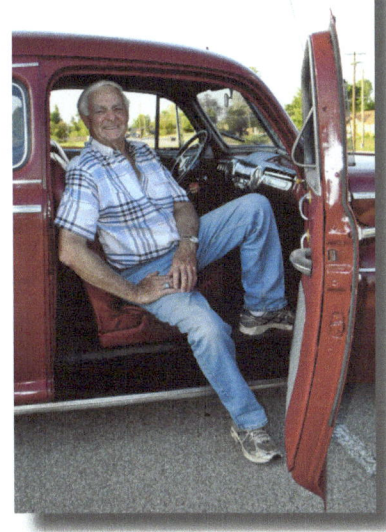

The boys in Brooklyn may only be playing AAA baseball now that the beloved "Bums," as the original Dodgers were affectionately dubbed, have moved out West like so many before them. Alas, the lure of those fabulous summers will live on forever, as long as gentlemen like Oklahoma Sports Hall of Famer Don Demeter share their living story and warm smile. Prior to following his major league team to L.A., Mr. Demeter gained a short-lived 0&1 status upon his first two at-bats in Brooklyn, putting his average at 500, and also earning a hall of Fame nod in Brooklyn.

Now, Don bats a thousand as he oversees his congregation at church in Moore, Oklahoma. He "Graced" us with an afternoon out of his busy schedule to pose in front of his other source of beatitude, a 1947 Ford Sedan. In the process, I couldn't help but notice the flash from this National League West Coast Division Championship ring. Thanks for stepping up to the plate for your parishioners and community including this blissful ball fan.

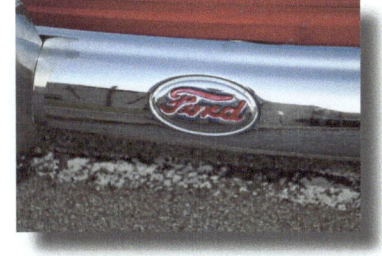

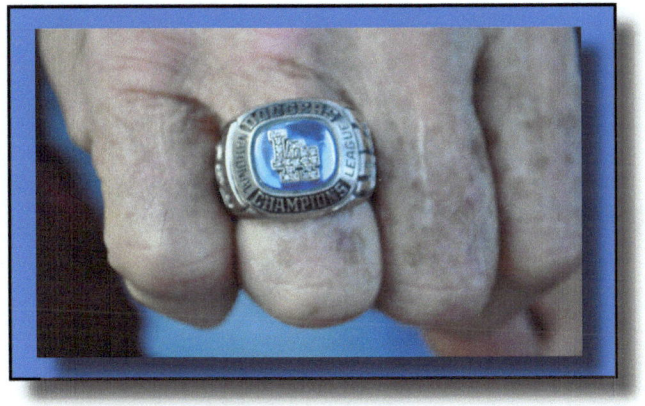

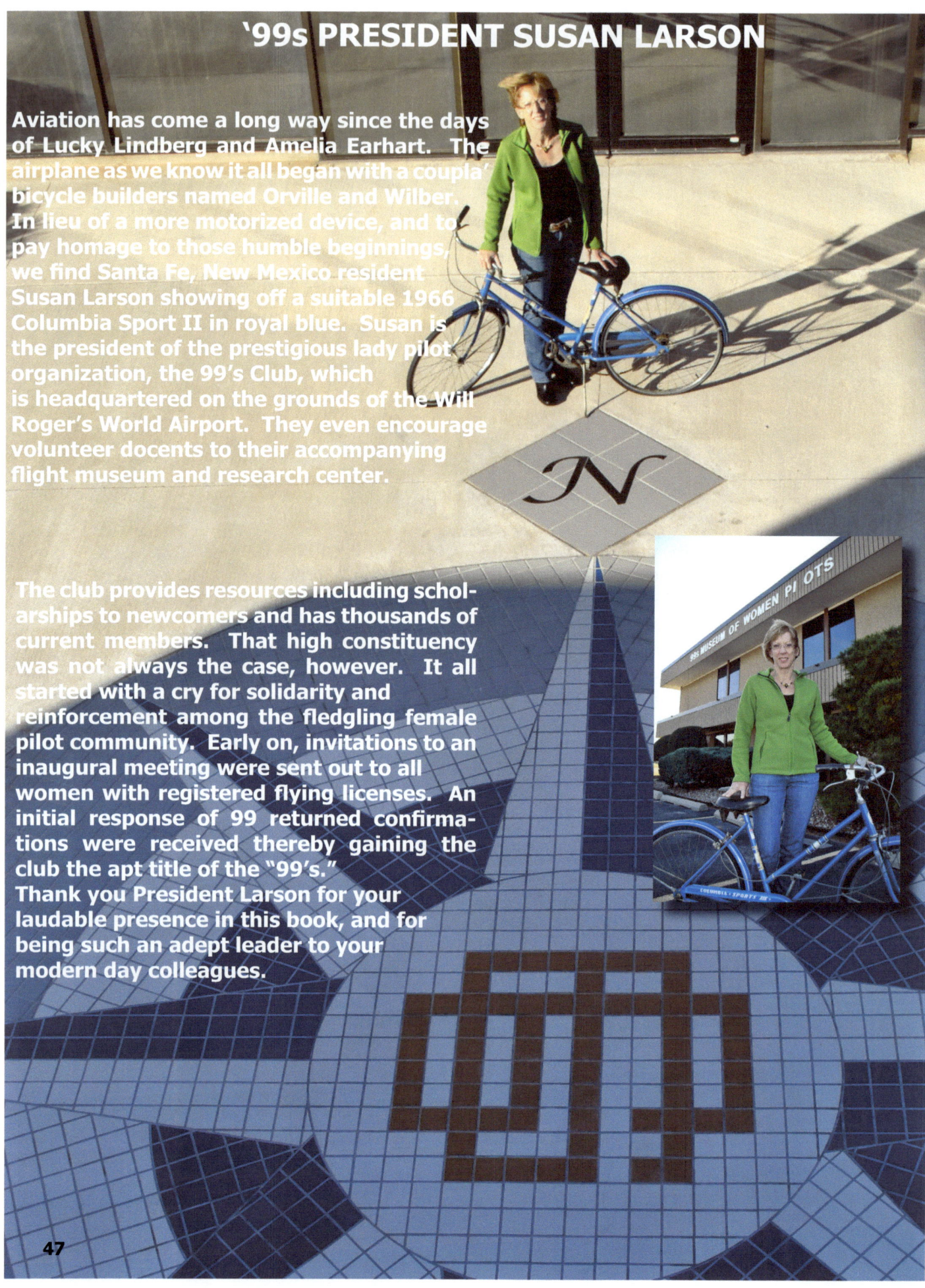

'99s PRESIDENT SUSAN LARSON

Aviation has come a long way since the days of Lucky Lindberg and Amelia Earhart. The airplane as we know it all began with a coupla' bicycle builders named Orville and Wilber. In lieu of a more motorized device, and to pay homage to those humble beginnings, we find Santa Fe, New Mexico resident Susan Larson showing off a suitable 1966 Columbia Sport II in royal blue. Susan is the president of the prestigious lady pilot organization, the 99's Club, which is headquartered on the grounds of the Will Roger's World Airport. They even encourage volunteer docents to their accompanying flight museum and research center.

The club provides resources including scholarships to newcomers and has thousands of current members. That high constituency was not always the case, however. It all started with a cry for solidarity and reinforcement among the fledgling female pilot community. Early on, invitations to an inaugural meeting were sent out to all women with registered flying licenses. An initial response of 99 returned confirmations were received thereby gaining the club the apt title of the "99's."
Thank you President Larson for your laudable presence in this book, and for being such an adept leader to your modern day colleagues.

CAPTAIN PRESTON F. WILLOUGHBY

Retired officer Preston F. Willoughby marches us around his favorite museum's also retired defense machine stockpile. After serving our country for 43 years, Preston chooses not to merely partake of the wide array of pasttimes available to someone of his stature, but rather takes a different path. He is now in service to his community as the current Vice President and General Chairman of the 45th Infantry Division Association based in Oklahoma City.

Thank you, Captain, for all that you do as proponent of this museum and its consequential, all-important artifacts. Foremost, a salute of thanks goes out to all that you have done for our country through these many years.

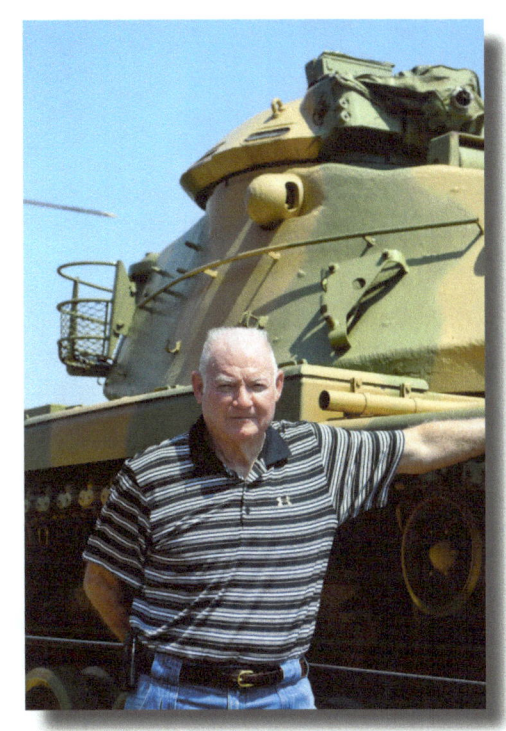

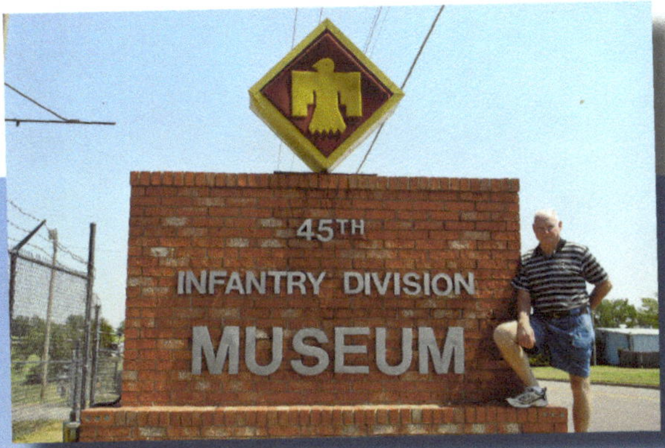

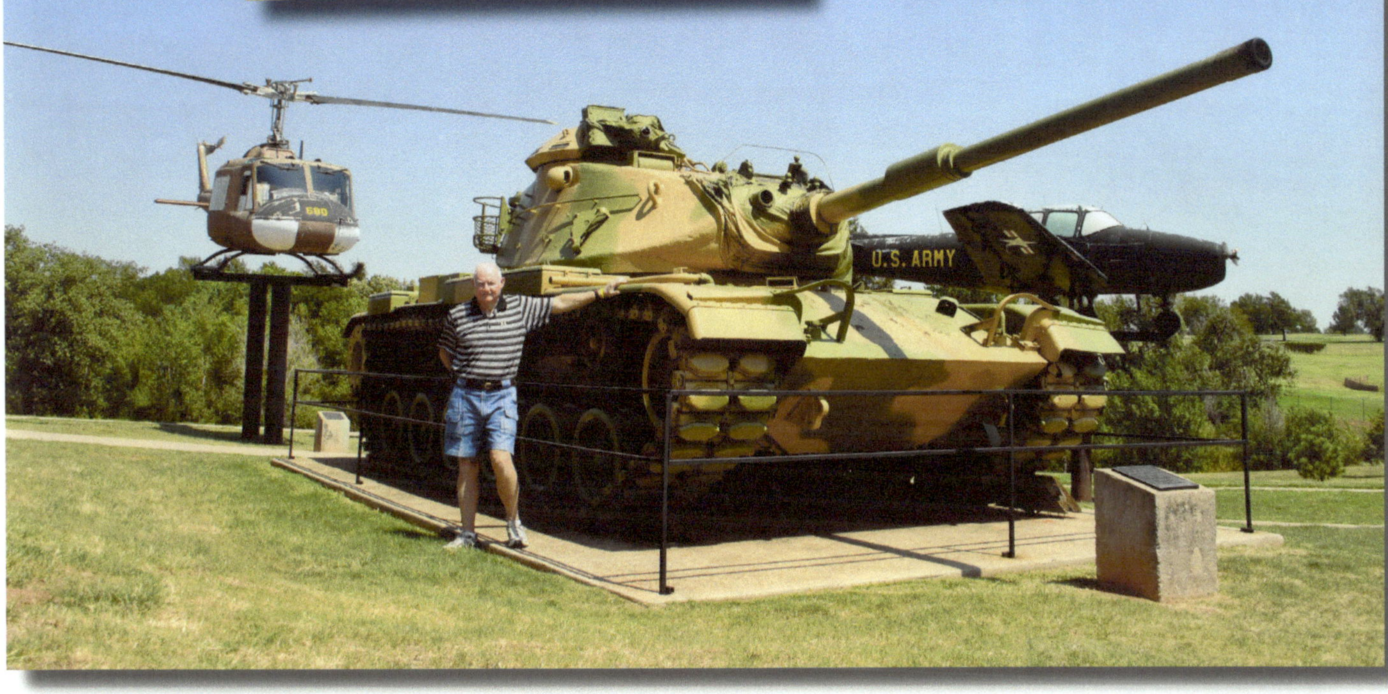

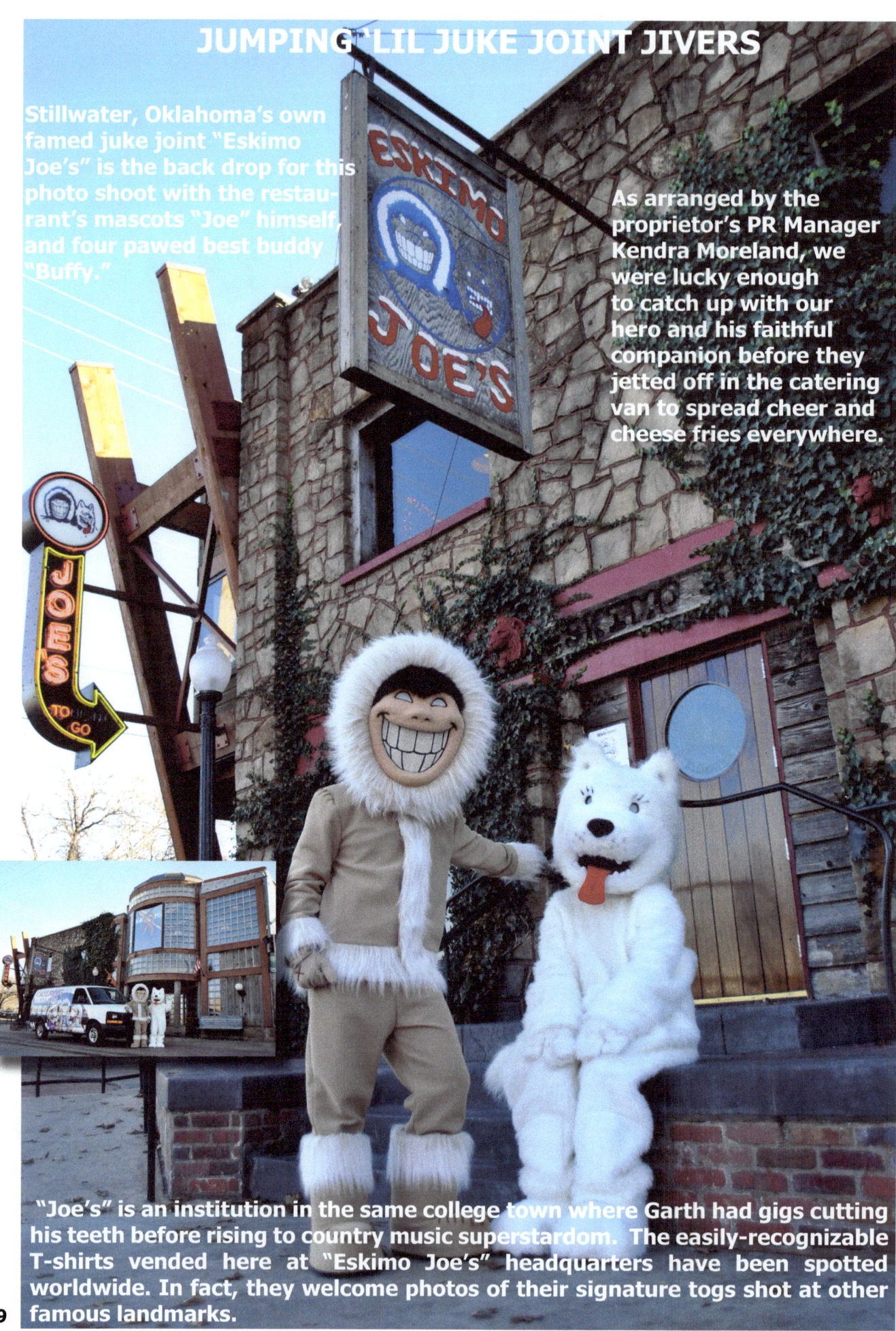

JUMPING 'LIL JUKE JOINT JIVERS

Stillwater, Oklahoma's own famed juke joint "Eskimo Joe's" is the back drop for this photo shoot with the restaurant's mascots "Joe" himself, and four pawed best buddy "Buffy."

As arranged by the proprietor's PR Manager Kendra Moreland, we were lucky enough to catch up with our hero and his faithful companion before they jetted off in the catering van to spread cheer and cheese fries everywhere.

"Joe's" is an institution in the same college town where Garth had gigs cutting his teeth before rising to country music superstardom. The easily-recognizable T-shirts vended here at "Eskimo Joe's" headquarters have been spotted worldwide. In fact, they welcome photos of their signature togs shot at other famous landmarks.

49

HANDLEBAR MOUSTACHE WORLD CHAMPION

Nocturnal view

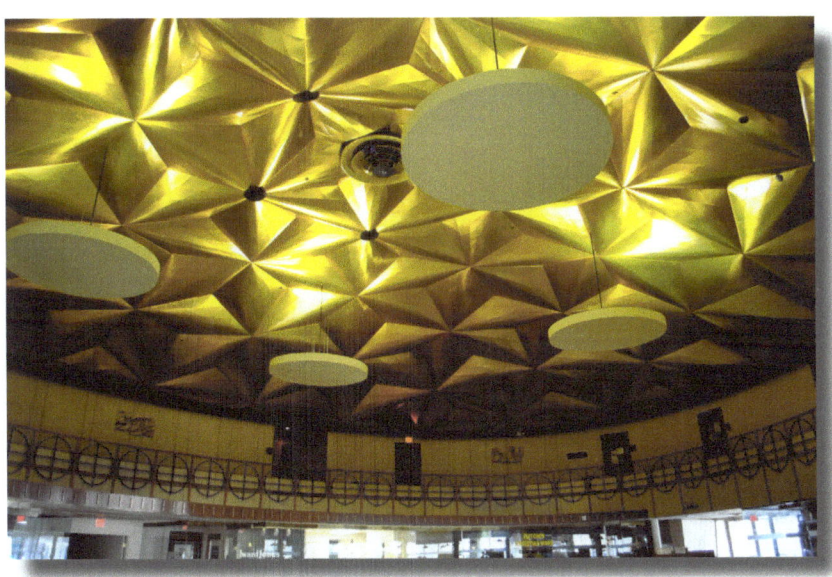

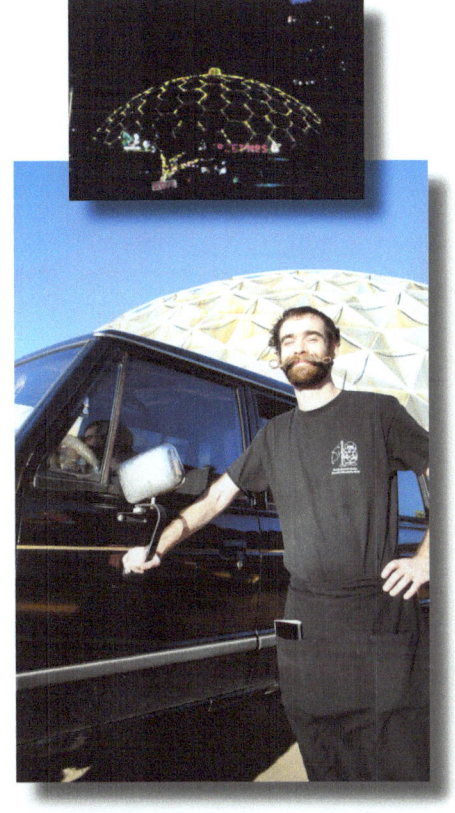

The Honorable Devon Holcombe winner of the World Beard and Moustache Championship held in Anchorage, Alaska, displays not only his well-trained facial hair, but also a well-traveled Mitsubishi s.u.v. while parked in front of this historically-protected structure, "The Gold Dome." When not turning his attention toward the next competition in line for himself, he focuses on his grateful customers at the stimulating restaurant "The Prohibition Room" inside of this adored geometric shape. Best of luck to you and your famous handlebars at the upcoming whiskered events. Keep charming the judges with those twinkling eyes.

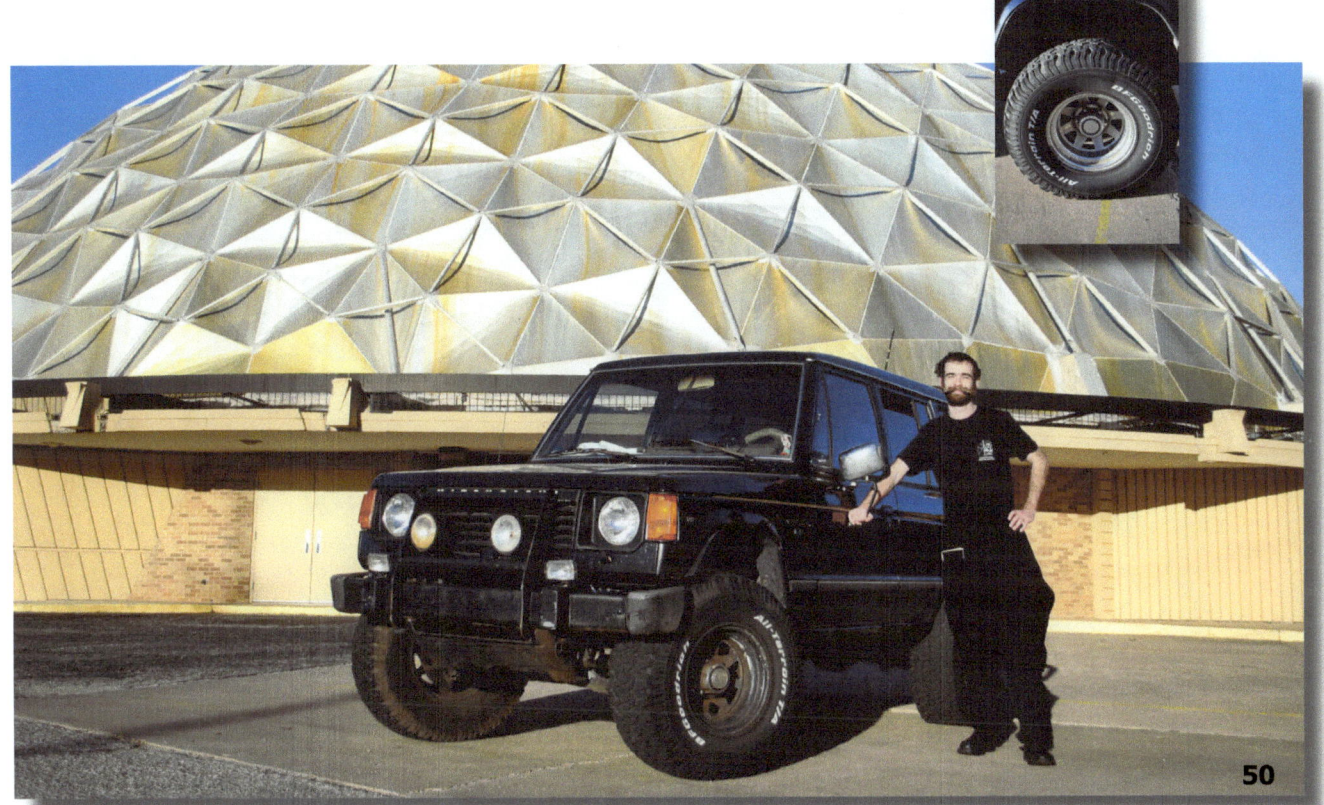

FRONT MAN OF SECOND CITY CHUCK BONA

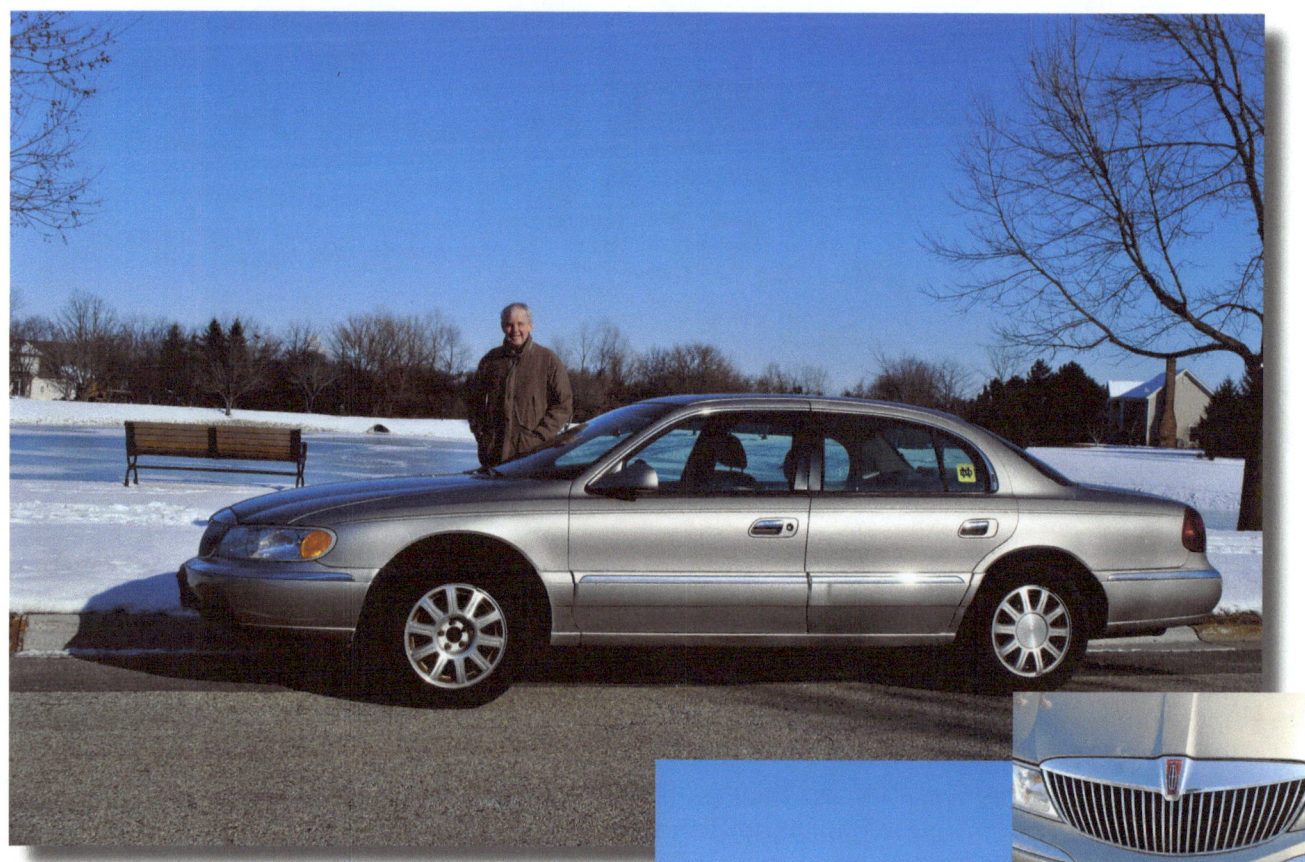

Chuck Bona, of Northern Illinois, "Zambonis'" with his sophisticated Lincoln near one of the many frozen over ponds the Midwest is known for. As we drank in the wintry pageant surrounded by shivering flora & flauna, he nonchalantly imparted to me a time he spent in Chicago's 2nd City Comedy Troupe. He regaled with stories of antics from the likes of John Belushi and company. Skating on thinner ice than we conversed near, I craved to hear more about his early career.

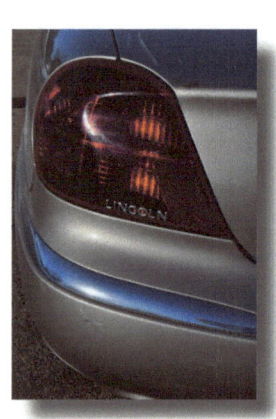

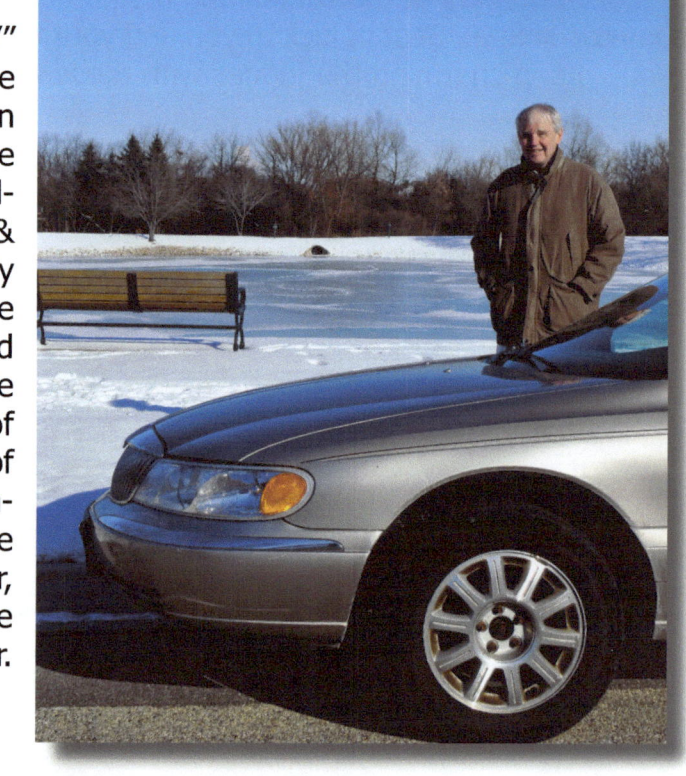

Hope to see Chuck's comical talents again soon. From one actor to another when convey good luck... "Break a Leg" pal.

SANTA & MRS. CLAUS

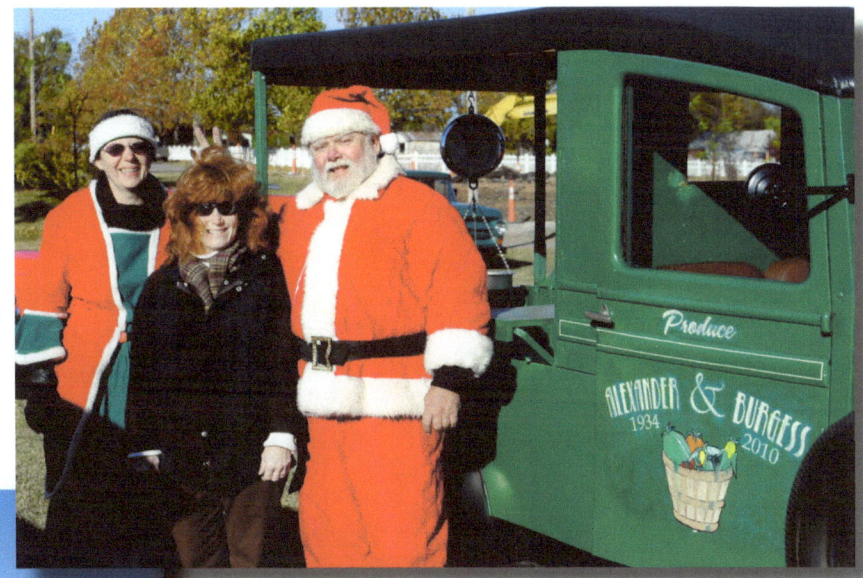

Lane and Carolyn Bullock of Midwest City, Oklahoma, also known as Mr. and Mrs. Claus in our motorcycling circles, have hopped not upon their sleigh this time, but on a 1998 Honda Valkyrie.

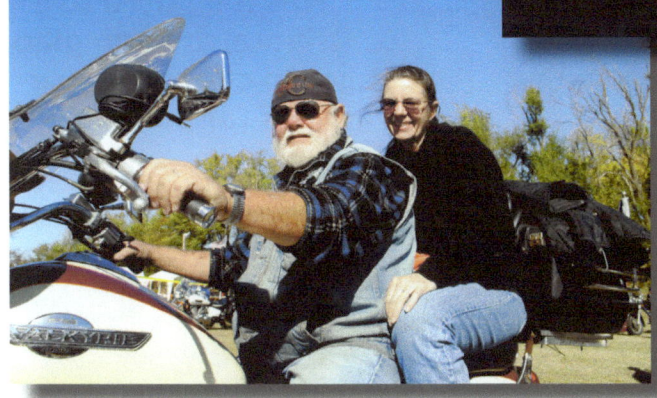

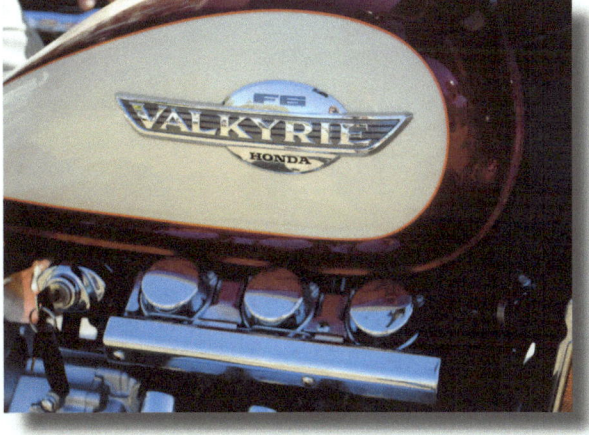

Yes, Rudolph took a break in preparation for the big day while these two season-minded citizens helped raise funds and mirth for a local toy run and holiday bike and car show.

They also spread joy to my all grown-up heart when my sleepy eyes peered out at them in their jolly attire, as evidenced by this semi-candid shot a passerby captured of us.

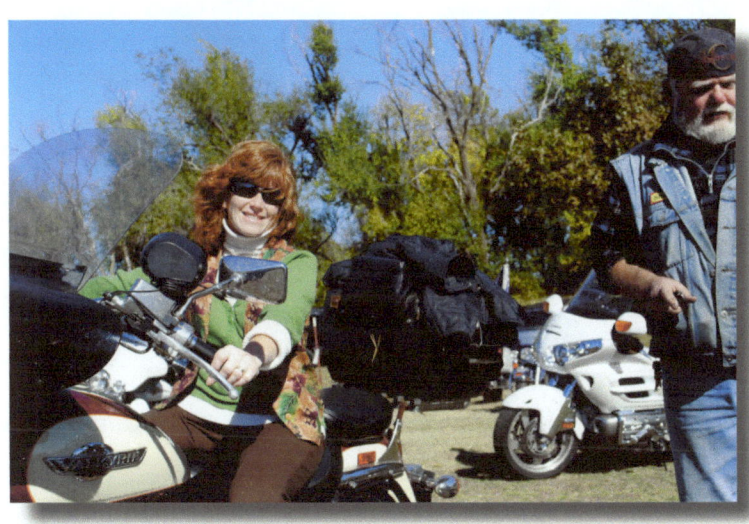

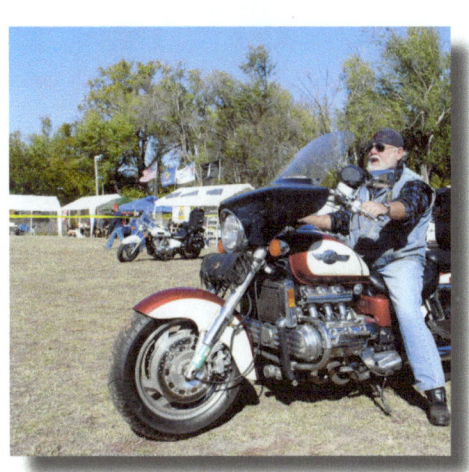

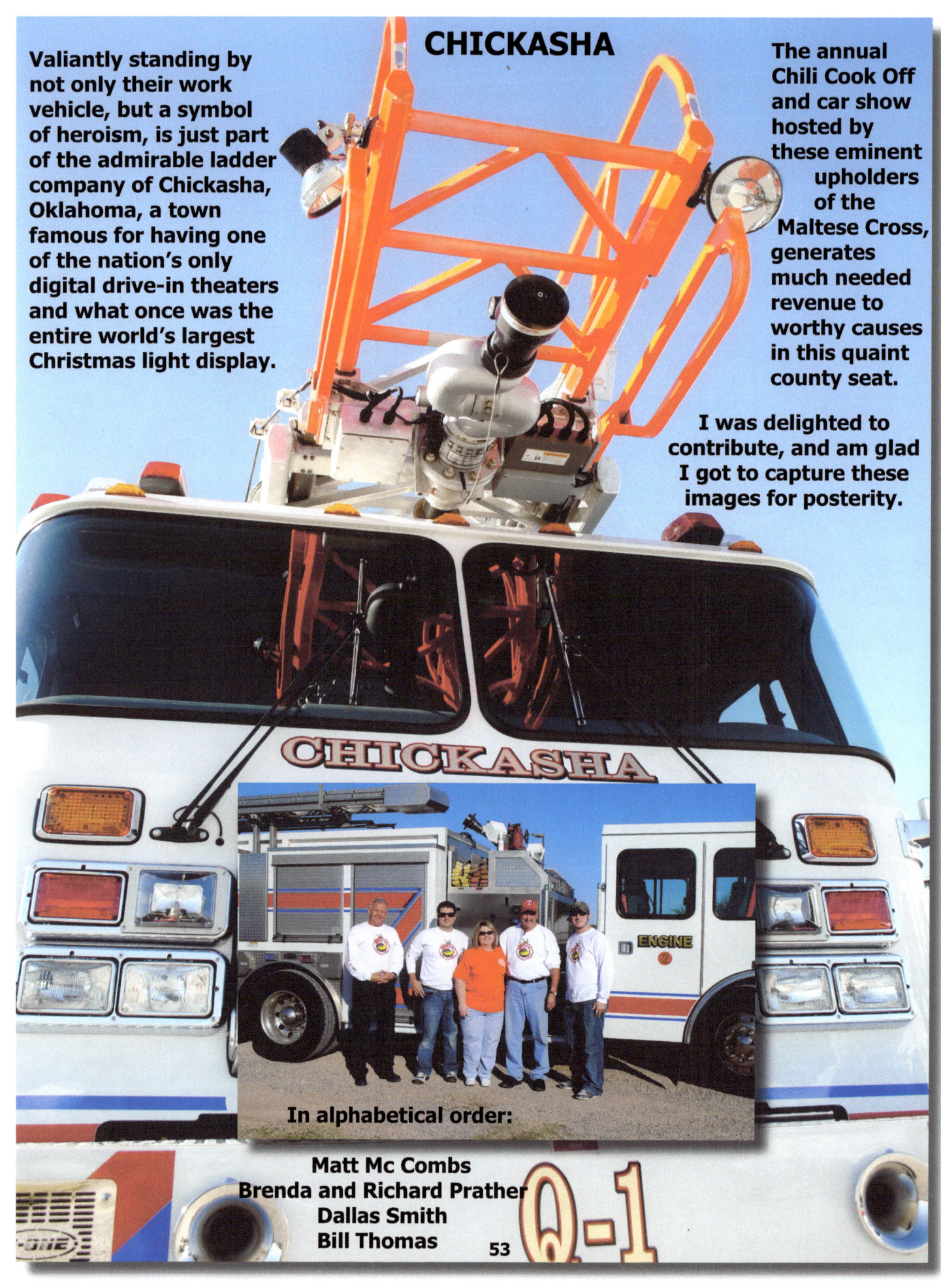

CHICKASHA

Valiantly standing by not only their work vehicle, but a symbol of heroism, is just part of the admirable ladder company of Chickasha, Oklahoma, a town famous for having one of the nation's only digital drive-in theaters and what once was the entire world's largest Christmas light display.

The annual Chili Cook Off and car show hosted by these eminent upholders of the Maltese Cross, generates much needed revenue to worthy causes in this quaint county seat.

I was delighted to contribute, and am glad I got to capture these images for posterity.

In alphabetical order:

Matt Mc Combs
Brenda and Richard Prather
Dallas Smith
Bill Thomas

53

PRAGUE CITY MANAGER JIM GRAFF

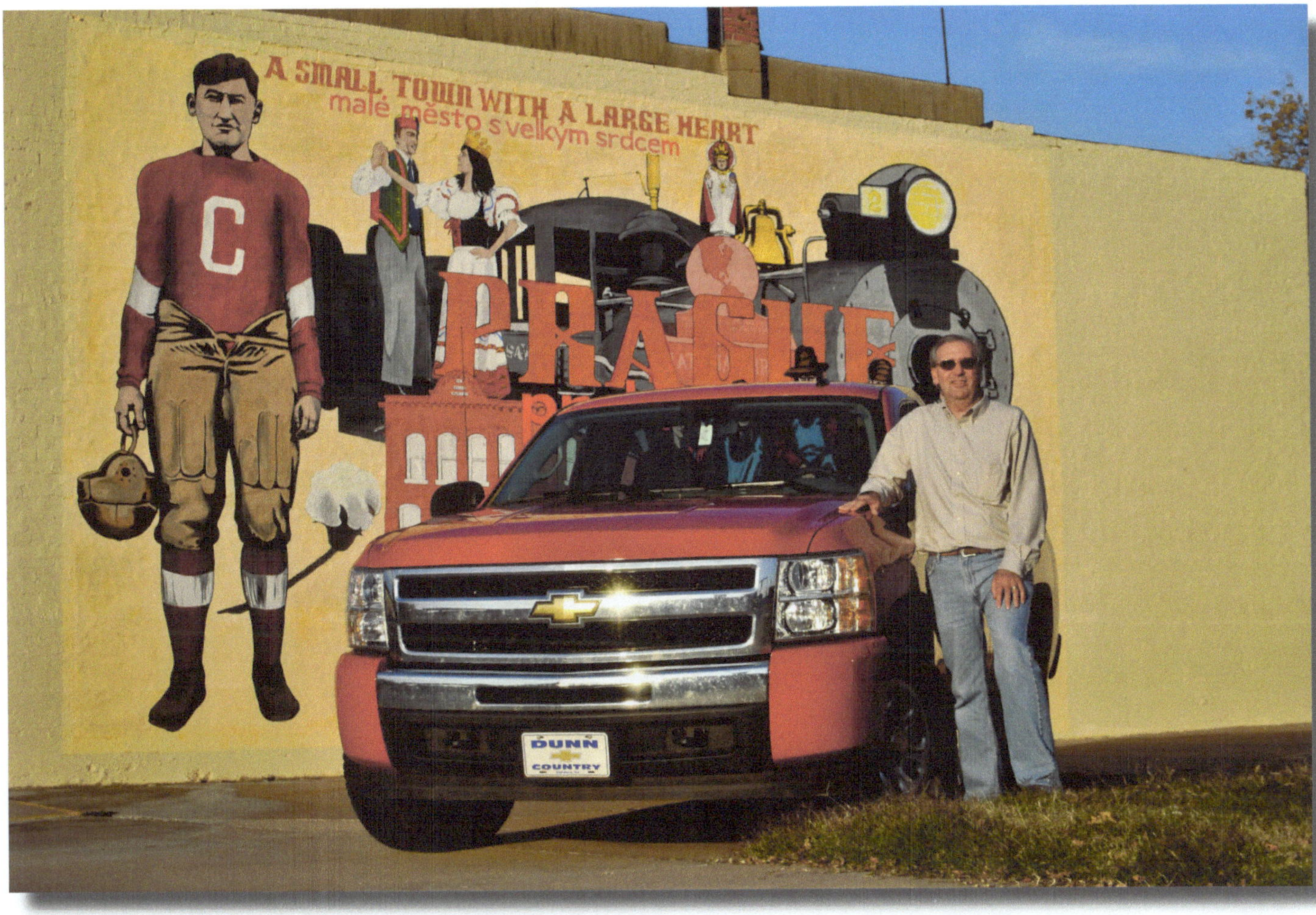

Prague, Oklahoma, sister city to the fair hamlet of the same name in Czechoslovakia, is pretty famous in its own right. Recently in November of 2011, this area claimed fame by being the epicenter of the state's most powerful earthquake. Registering at 5.6 on the Richter scale, it succeeded in shaking up this sleepy township in every way. Shortly following the aftershock's rumble on to the next fault line, we had the pleasure of meeting the honorable Mr. Jim Graff, Prague's City Manager, who agreed to pose with his treasured full size Chevy.

According to some of the locals we interviewed, the seismic event really was quite a terrifying ordeal, as are any major shakers to first-timers, and fledglings not accustomed to such displays of the ground's power. Just experiencing it from the comfortable two-hour distance away in the Capitol, I can personally attest that the quake was disturbing and felt like its duration was interminable. I know if the starting point had been in my proverbial back yard, I would want the calming presence of Mr. Graff presiding at my municipality's offices to bring about order and tranquility again. In these shots he shows off the birth place of arguably the 20th Century's greatest athlete, Jim Thorpe, and the "thorp's," graceful and pious Infant of Prague Shrine.

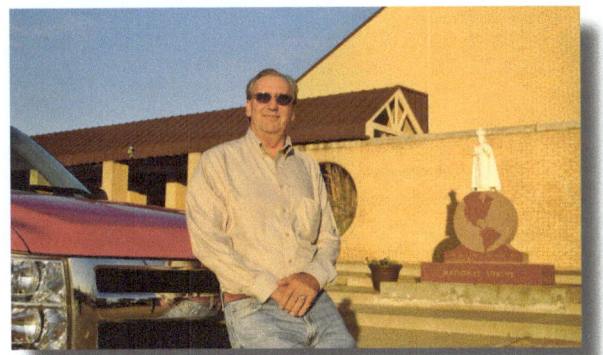

NORMAN MAYOR CINDY ROSENTHAL

To kick off the Grand Ball, or parade as it were, is Cindy Rosenthal, the honorable mayor of college town Norman, Oklahoma. She solemnly served as Grand Marshal for the first Veteran's Day parade the 'burg has hosted since the Vietnam Conflict. It was a reverent occasion, drawing classic car and cycle aficionados such as Lani Malysa, also featured in our motocycle chapter. She was only too willing to volunteer her chauffeur services to the cause aboard this 1971 Chevy. On deck are a handful of other highlights from the morale-boosting procession, including one of the author herself with a more satyrical soldier.

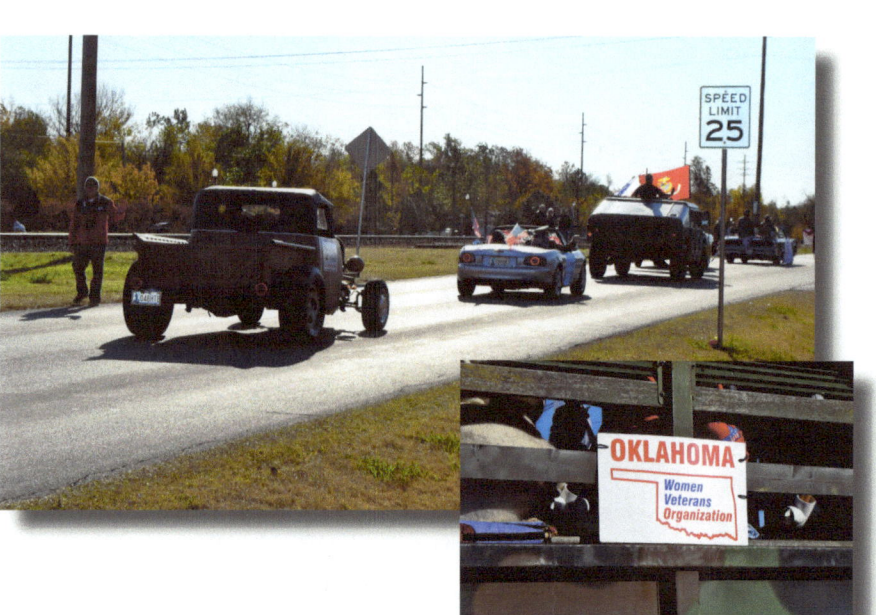

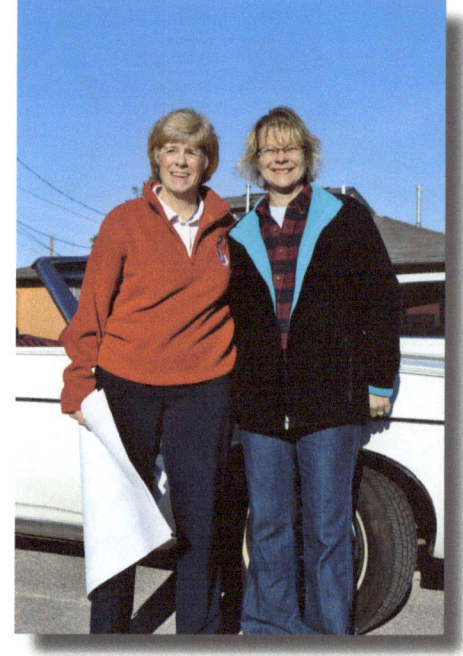

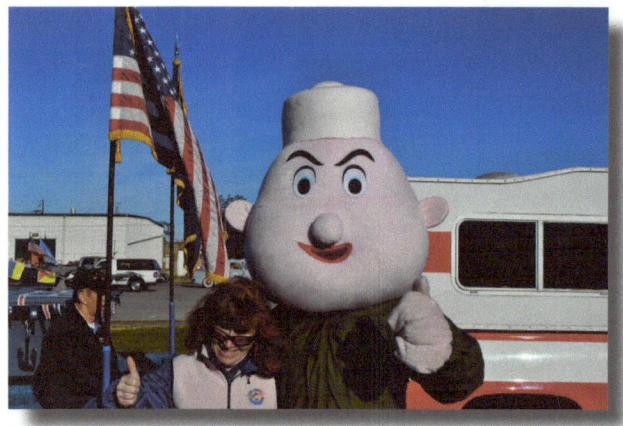

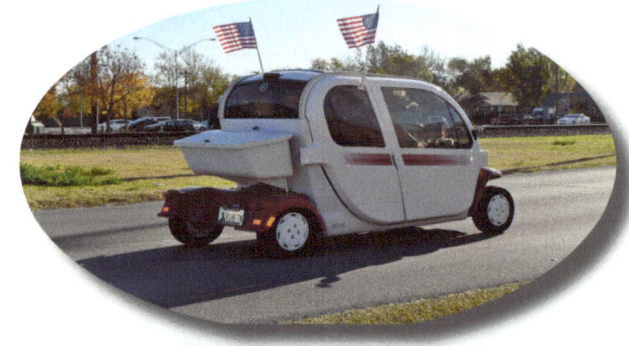

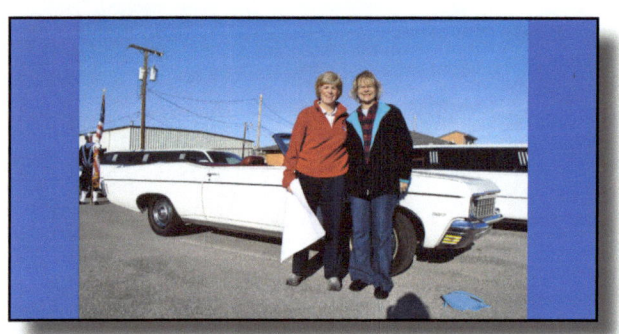

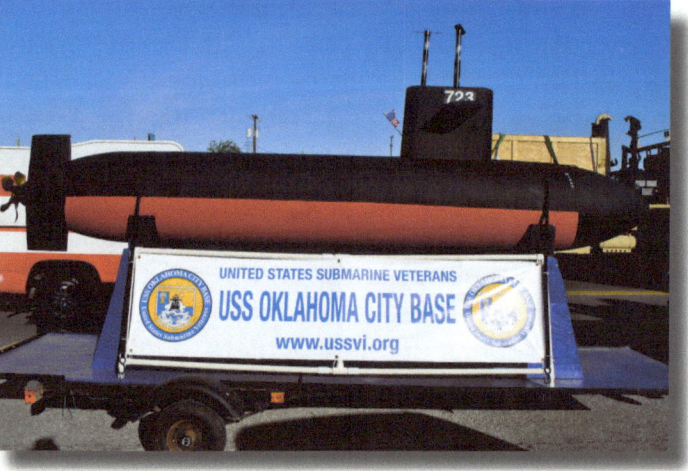

THE HOT DOG TO GO A.W.O.L. OVER

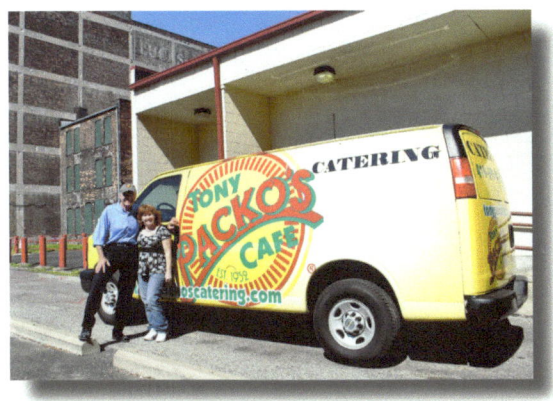

In business for over 80 years, the Packo Family of Toledo, Ohio has a knack for creatively merging the recipes of the "Old Country" with the desires of their modern-day public. One such invention would be their world reknowned "Hungarian Hot Dog."

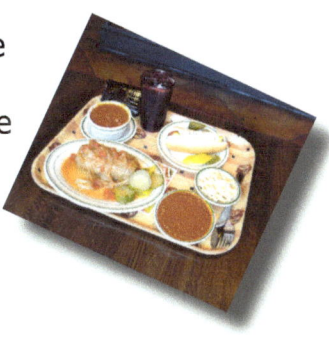

Even Toledo native Jamie Farr incorporated his affinity for this hometown favorite into his character, "Klinger's," vernacular, mentioning the historic Birmingham neighborhood staple during several episodes of the hit sitcom M*A*S*H.

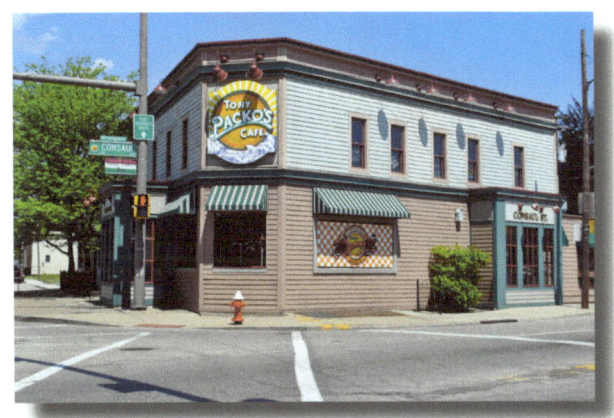

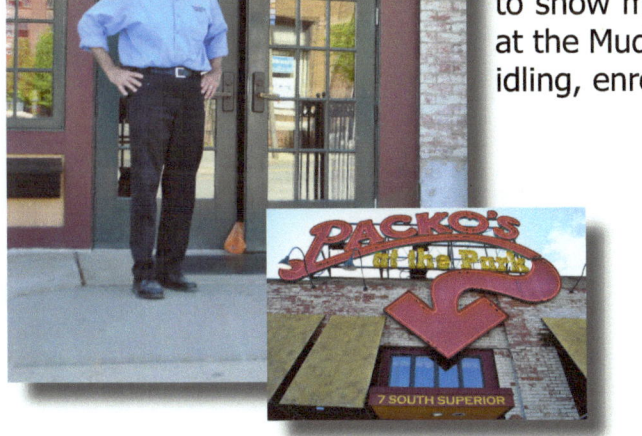

Now with numerous central Ohio locations, Mr. Tony Packo Jr. carries on the culinary tradition of his descendants before him . He ever so genially took time out of his engaging day to show me around and quickly adjourn for my eager lens, at the Mud Hen stadium shop. Their catering truck is always idling, enroute to the next hungry crowd.

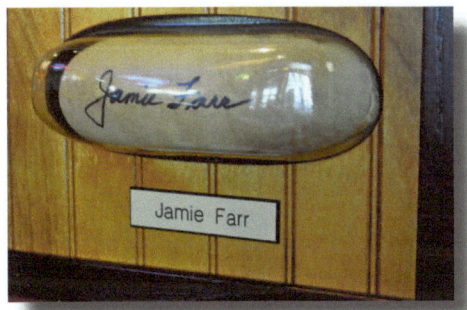

Whenever a celebrity is near "Glass City" situated on the life-sustaining Maumee River, they are invited to sign a commemorative hot dog bun at Packos... I will be back when I am of that caliber... That's a promise I am striving to accomplish. In the meantime I'll be content with simply "relishing" a home made cabbage roll, and those mouth-watering hot pickles.

Within this chapter are some shots, to name a few, from many of the car shows throughout that golden time span between the composing of the first page of this book, and the moment I took my last shot. I, along with my felicitious Karmann Ghia, attended at least one show in every month.

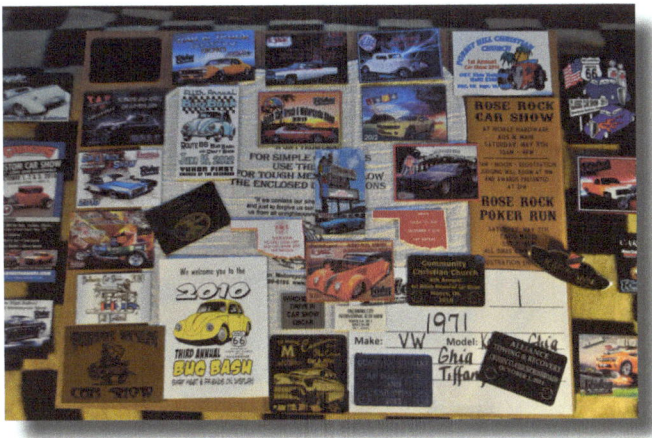

February: includes the big Votech school in the lil' town of Drumright, Oklahoma. This fund raiser is beneficial in creating job-ready individuals, giving a helpful boost to the dynamic community.

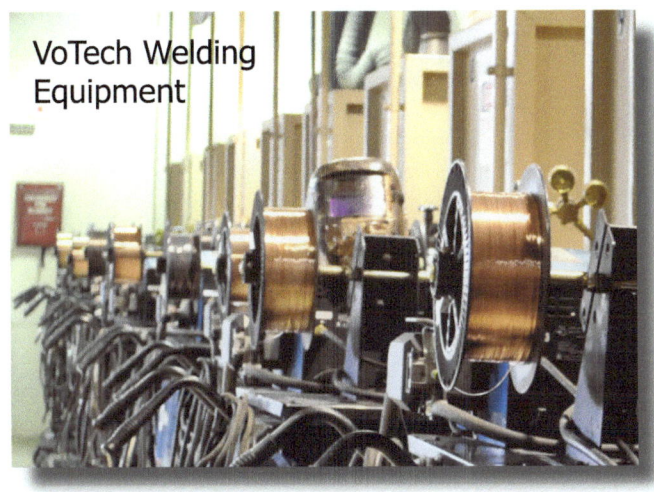

VoTech Welding Equipment

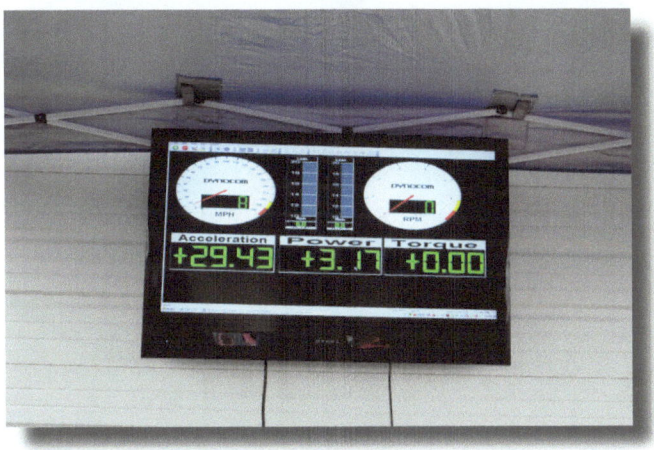

THE SHOWS...

January: A nationally renowned coffee house hosted a Coffee and Cars event. My prize was getting to meet a fella mentioned in the upcoming Import category, who owns multiple Lamborghini's.

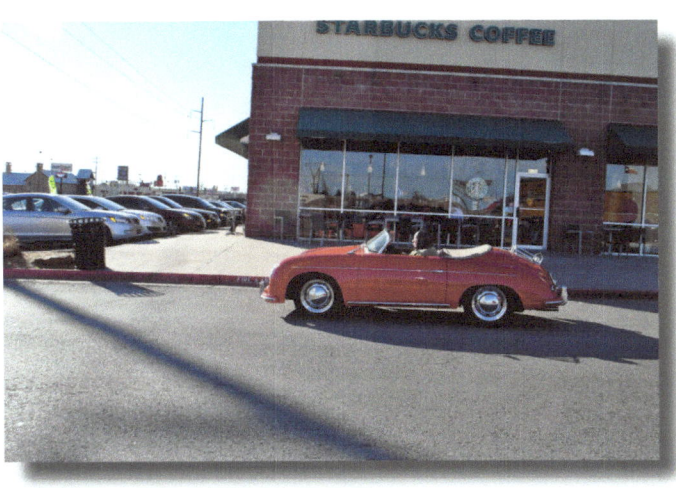

March: was a particularly busy month in 2011 for me, as I participated in my first parade on St. Patrick's Day.

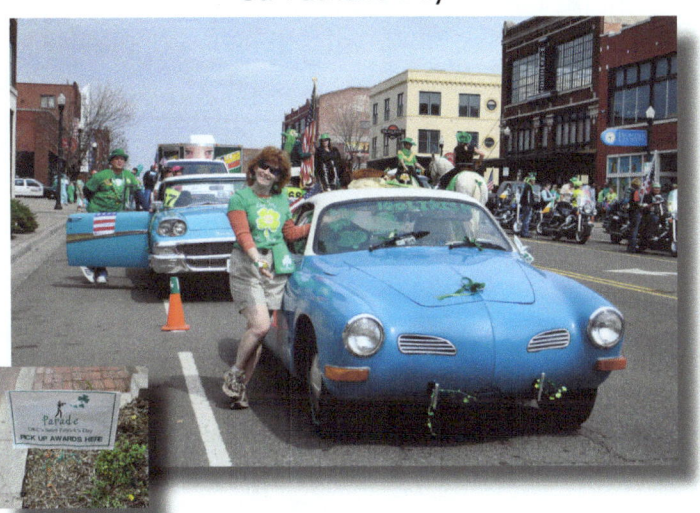

Rounding out the "Ides" month, I entered into a concours which also had a "Dyno-Pull" option. This apparatus is a nifty invention designed to see how powerful a vehicle's motor is, by connecting sensors between an automobile and a computer. The operators then rev the engine to full capacity while recording the data. I contemplated putting my trusty rusty VW up on the lift for this free demonstration associated with the show. That second passed, quickly replaced by the fear that I would be bringing my cherished auto home in pieces after the impending explosion invariably sent blazing shrapnel raining down. 58

THE SHOWS, CONTINUED...

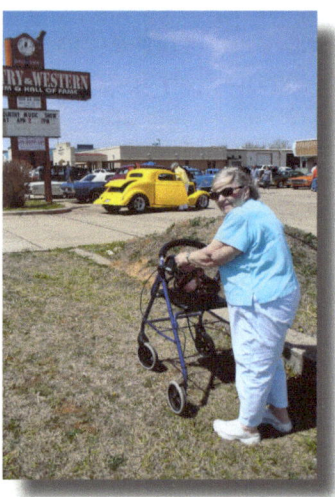

April: many shows in Oklahoma are available, including this early spring event for the Lion's Club of the Air Force-oriented Midwest City. Here my Mom is enroute to the location they hold said show, The Country Western Hall of Fame Museum. **May:** also offered Fraternal functions. The Shriners put on the best party with a Piston Throw, and Hydraulic competion. I like their picturesque sphinx also.

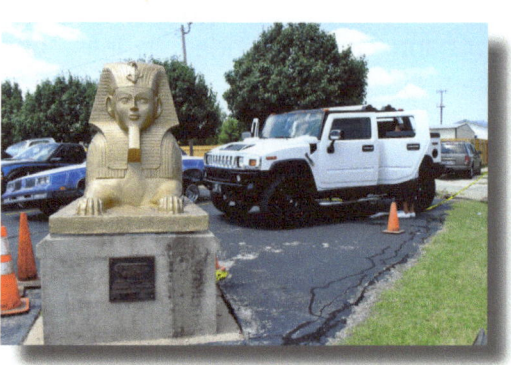

June: in Oklahoma to me means it's time for the flowers, and "flower powerers" to bloom at the Annual Oklahoma VW Car Show. This was my first show ever attended, shortly before this book's junket began. We took home 2nd place in the entire Karmann Ghia category. Not too shabby for a first try. Way to go "Chiclet."

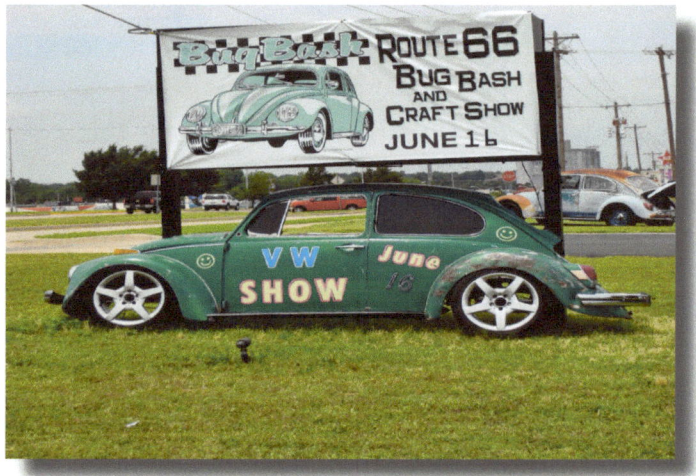

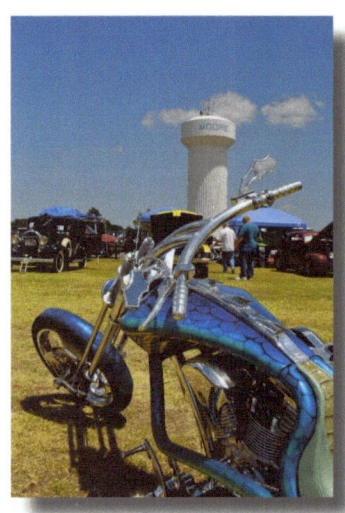

July: the month of Independence Day, holds in store more than watermelon & fireworks for car lovers. It includes one truly first-rate Art Fest near my childhood home's adjoining township of Moore, Oklahoma. Coinciding with the festival is yet another charitable car show, put on by the company "Show Your Ridez," with proceeds going to the local Rainbow Girls scout-like organization.

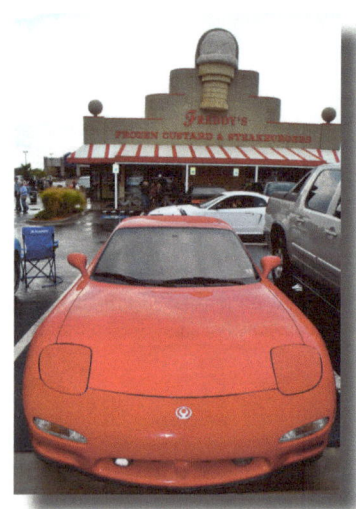

August: is a convivial car show month for the Oklahoma City area, as the Freddie's Custard and Steak burger establishment puts on their birthday series of shows at many metro locations. Each shindig includes inflatable jump houses & face painting for the kiddos, not to mention a hot dog eating contest. Freddie himself was a WWII Vet in the Philipines conflicts. Thank you for serving our country and having such a booming business.

THE SHOWS... SEPTEMBER

September... Oh don't get me started about this month. The first days of Fall in Oklahoma are no stranger to the car show sect. In fact with the kids and grandkids back in school, or departed for home from summer vacation, the amount of show participation seems to increase.

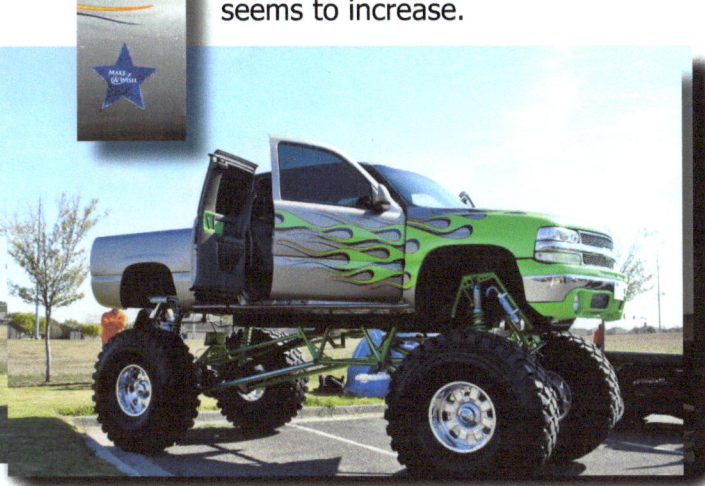

The afore-mentioned, "Show Your Ridez," really puts on a show-of-shows with what is typically their season finale. This would be none other than their highest attended happening, the Make A Wish foundation fundraiser. The altruistic car show company donates all of their earnings made from that show to the not-for-profit. Some of their patients, who serve in a judging position, receive rides in this Monster Truck. Many onsite donations are elicited, with even the 50/50 drawing winners usually giving their drawn prize back to the cause. God bless all involved.

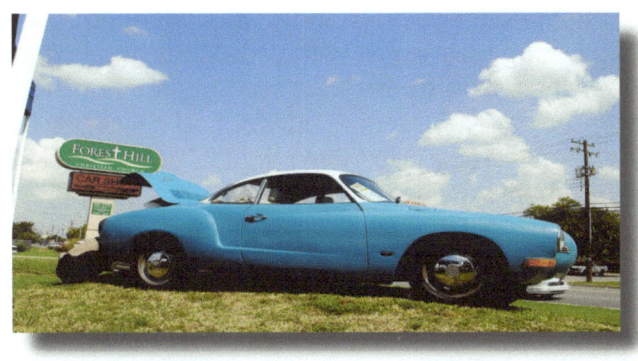

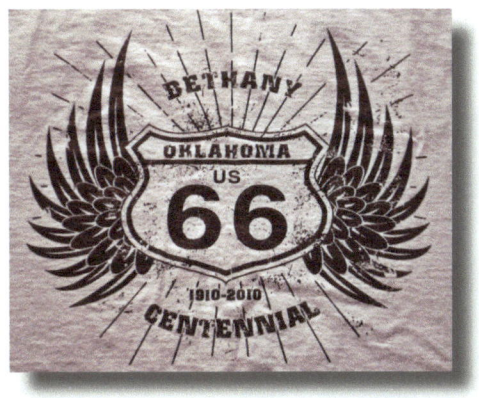

September: also saw Bethany, Oklahoma's Centennial celebration and car show, thrown by Cathy Elrod, who will be featured in our Host chapter. It attracted so many visitors it will now be an annual undertaking with the reins going to Cat, and the Elrod family, operators of the Main street staple Norma Jean's Antiques.

Another big September show is presented by The Forest Hill Christian Church, run by another gentleman soon to be mentioned in our Host chapter, youth pastor Darin Troutman and family. They, as done by so many church organizations, also choose to donate this event to charity. They give back to the participants as well providing a free lunch in the admission price. It's a delish lunch, and an even better show. It brings benefactors out in droves. How could it not, with all of that, as well as helicopter rides?

THE SHOWS... OCTOBER - NOVEMBER

Aww, October. Barring an extended "Indian Summer," this tenth month of the year brings the long-awaited cooler weather to our "Red Man's Land," which can also cause a spike in show activity.

As mentioned, although a relieving few degrees more algid, October also brings on the heat, with chili cook off/car show combos, not to mention the raised pulse from spookily frightful trick or trunk type shows. Hosts like Rustic Iron boast a Halloween block party complete with carnival motif, & costume clad drivers, who festoon their shined up hoods with bowls of candy for the tykes.

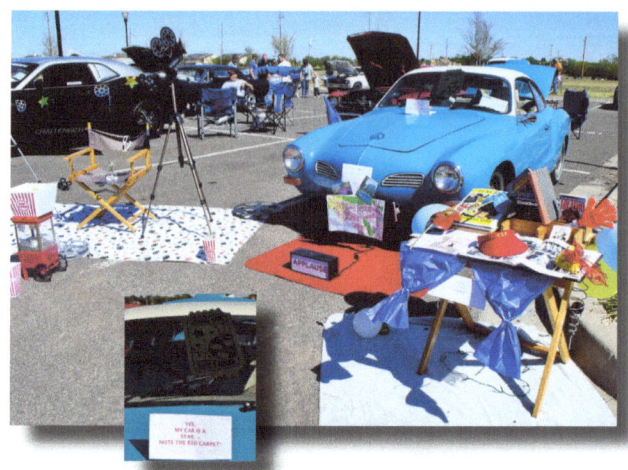

One of my favorite shows supports the Drama Department at a fledgling new school called Southmoore. The theatrical leader Kay Baugus used to be my graduating class' Thespian coach. I therefore created some displays surrounding my car chronicling how her guidance from a tender impressionable age encouraged myself, as well as all of her students. I summarily was influenced to further pursue an acting career onward with one of the most prestigious programs at The College of Santa Fe. What was meant as a tribute to the I am sure often thankless efforts of the teaching profession, and one of its shining stars, Mrs. 'B,' garnered me a Best of Show award with the show host's favorite pick trophy. I am grateful for all of life's rewards.

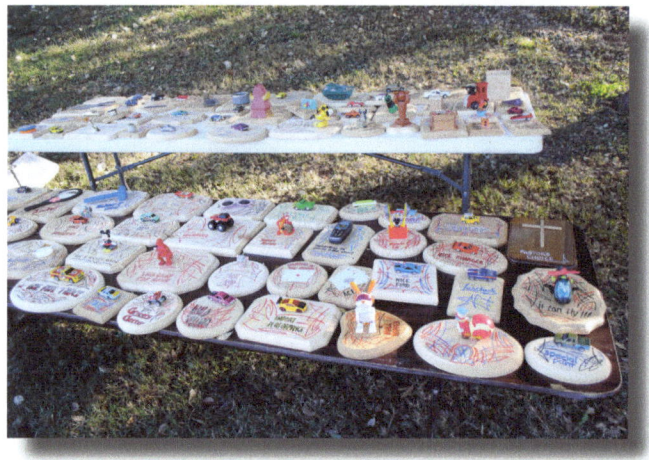

November: saw me driving a bit further out of town to the sleepy hamlet of Harrah, Oklahoma for the lakeside "Rods n' Custom's" toy drive. This commendable cycle/car show affair benefitted the neighboring rural areas with provisions and holiday necessities, akin to the Toys For Tots mission. The entry fee called for a new unwrapped children's toy or non-perishable food item, in lieu of a monetary requirement. Donations were also highly appreciated. Each entrant received a custom, homemade trophy. Mine, being that I own a Volkswagen, consisted of a hot wheel type Beetle affixed to a plaque, and was decorated by a local student proficient in graffiti art. In years past the prize was constructed of car parts, such as speedometers etc. mounted on pedestals. Glad such jovialness is affixed to alleviating poverty and hunger issues.

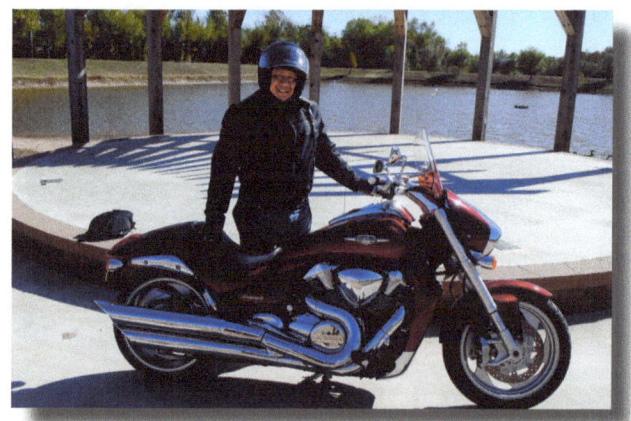

Charles Davis Rides in for the riparian event

DECEMBER

December I took a non-heated almost 40-year old rumbling suspension for a bump-filled ride two hours north to the state's second-largest metropolitan area of Tulsa-Town. I was eager to support the first car-included show sponsored by the normally cycle exclusive A.B.A.T.E., or A Brotherhood Aim Toward Education organization. I felt compelled to pack up the old extra seat cushion and parka to make the all-important chilly trek. And hey, how cold could it be once I got there, as it was to be an indoor spectacle? In the spirit of the holidays, I planned for weeks how my December-themed display would appear. Gathering boxes of candy canes to distribute, as well as all the turquoise Christmas decorations I could find, from battery operated lights to shiny eye-catching metallic blue wreaths, I headed for the hills. Upon arrival at the fairgrounds where the bike poker run and car show was to be held, I discovered only one other die-hard automobile lover, besides myself, had shown up, hence making that the smallest car show that I have ever

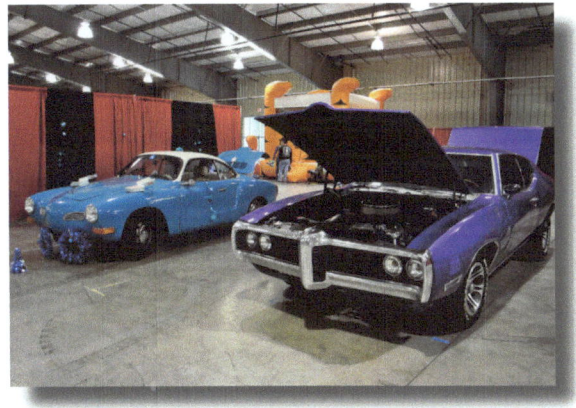

been a part of. It was also the only show I ever had the opportunity to commune with animals such as the ones pictured, from a local wildlife sanctuary's exhibit.

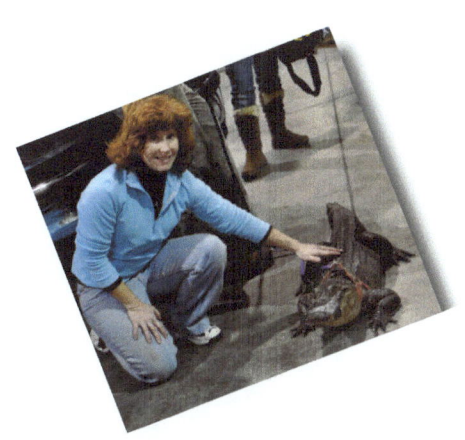

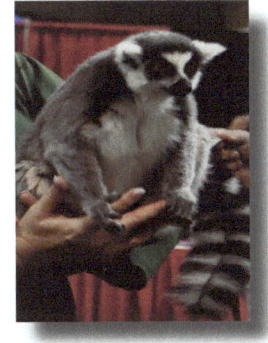

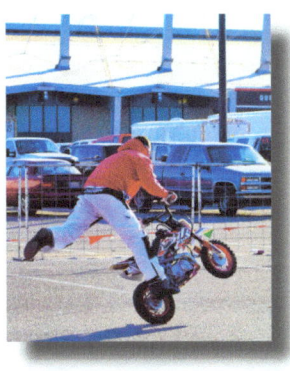

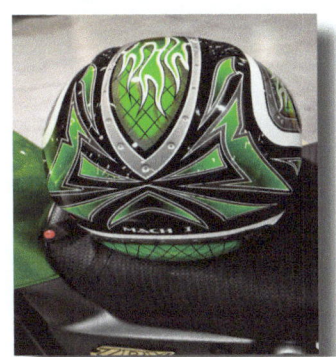

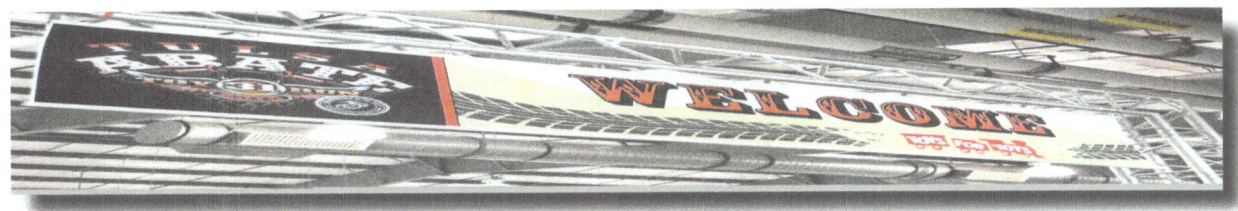

HOSTS
Well if it weren't for these well-meaning industrious hosts, we wouldn't even have a show to go to. So I present the ringleaders who usually present our trophies to us...the Hosts.

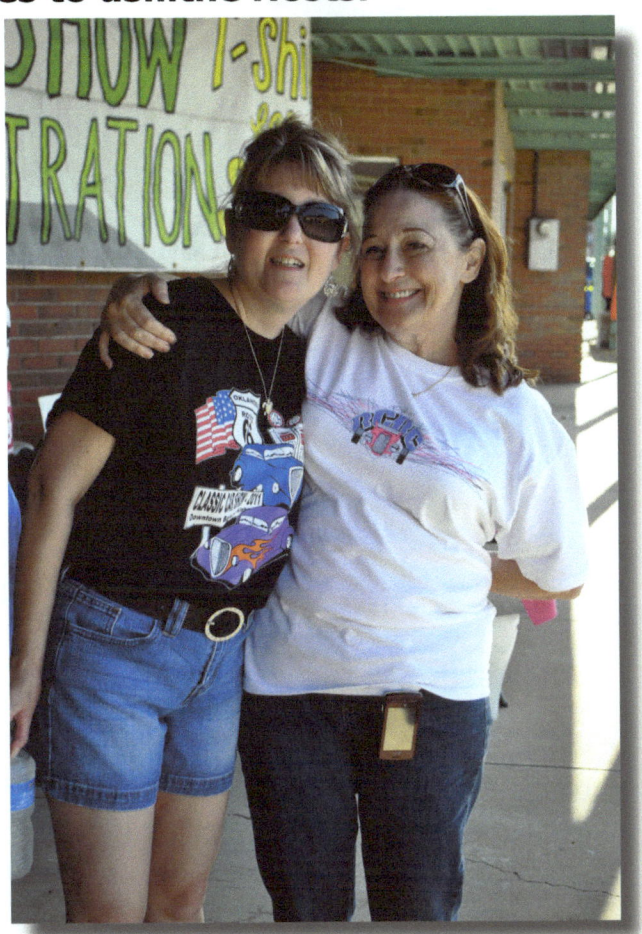

Cathy "Cat" Elrod, host of the Bethany Oklahoma Centennial and continuing Route 66 Car shows, and Mom, THE Norma Jean.

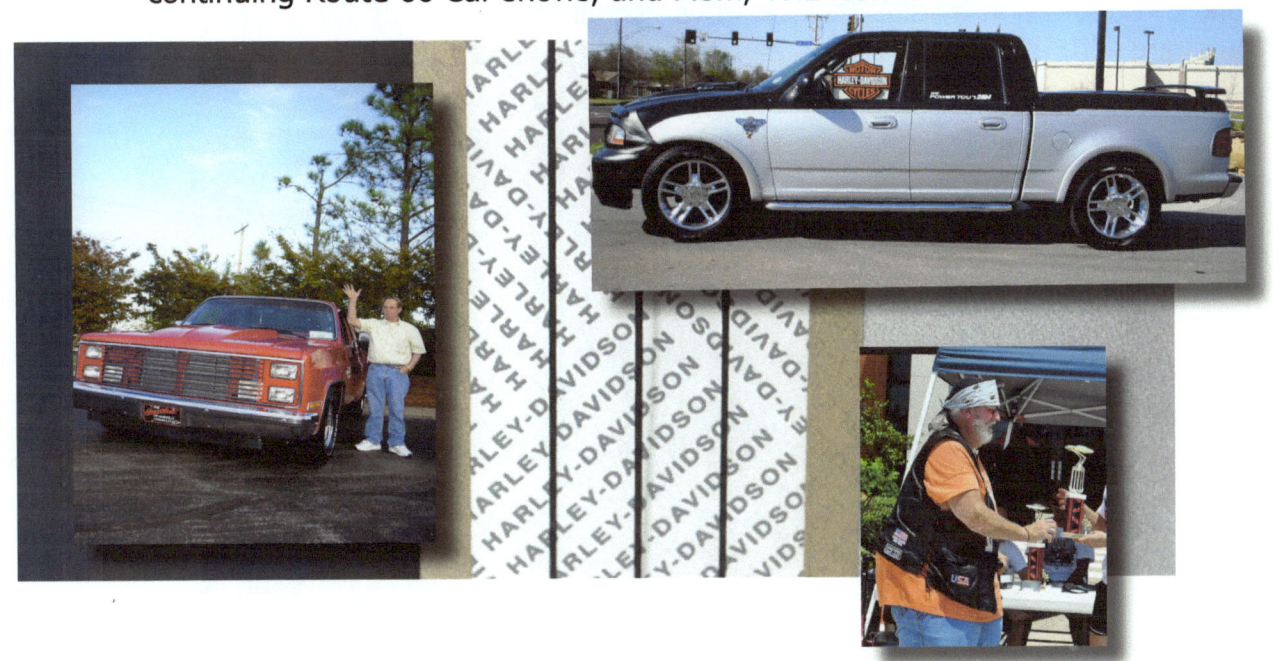

The Rustic Iron in the Heartland car show host team Veteran J.C. Chandler, & Sonny Rickett. with their dueling '85 Chevy and 100th Anniversary H.D. Edition Ford pickup trucks.

SHOW YOUR RIDEZ

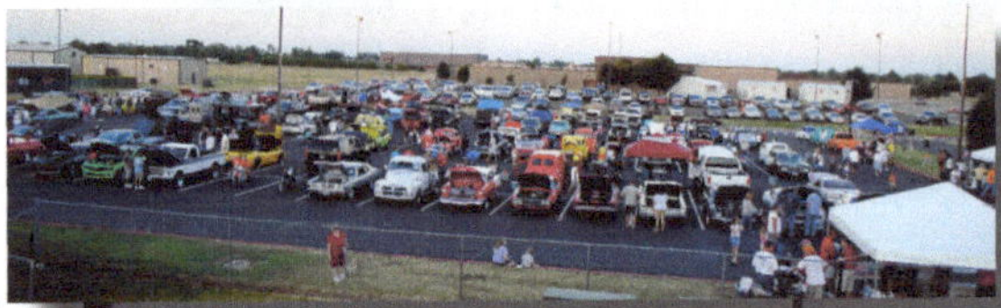

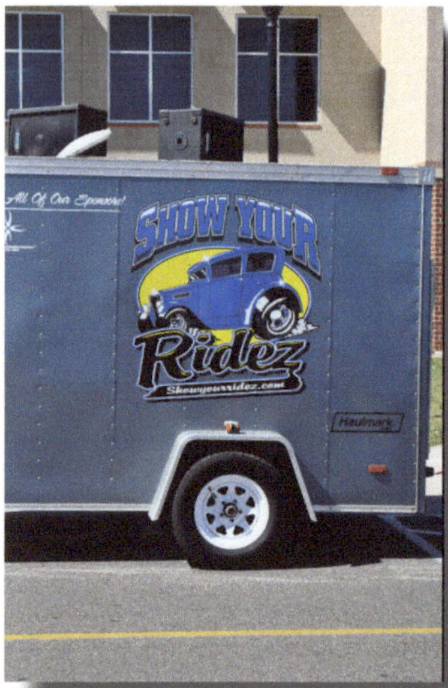

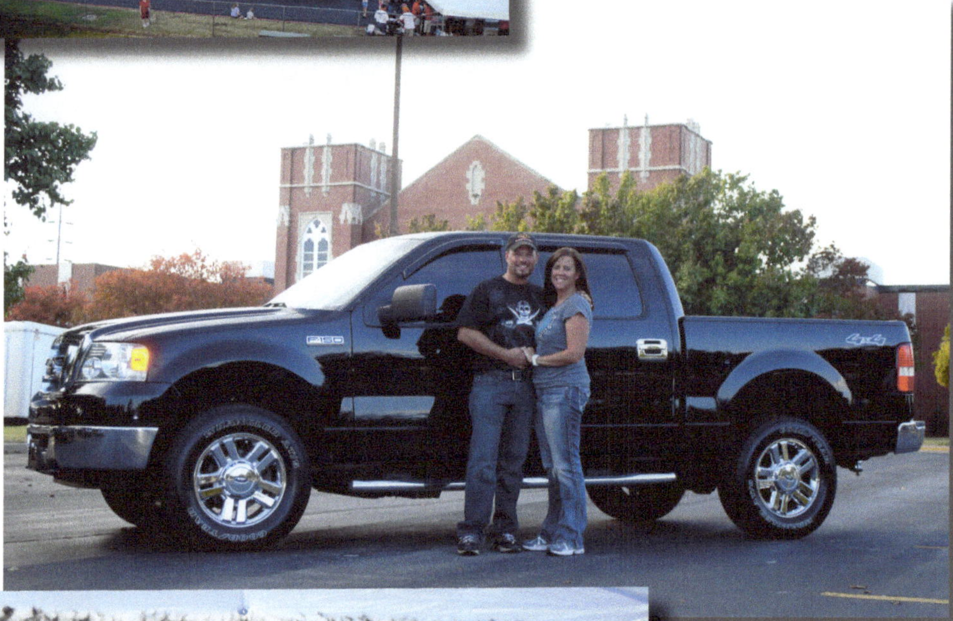

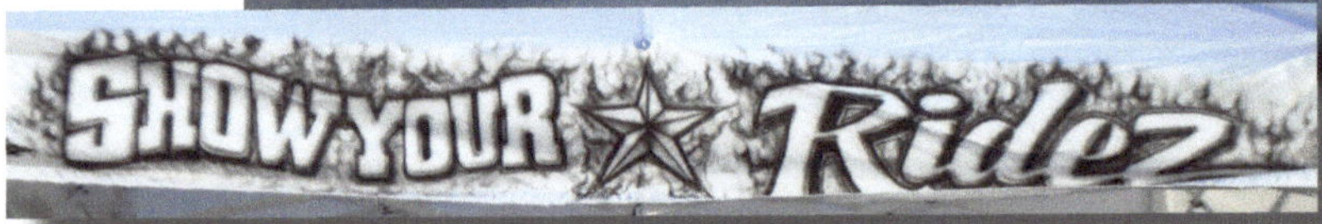

The Show Your Ridez car show company is run by helpmates Leanne and Jeff Weigel with a hand from their children, and other family members such as Leanne's sister Jeniffer, and their mom Cheryl (below,) all of whom have second jobs. That would include Jeff, who actually works at our local Air Force Base, most early Saturday mornings before heading home to help load the trailer full of necessities for the day's show. They usually do not get home until well after midnight following an evening event, making for, suffice it to say, a long day full of hard work and dedication by all. Thanks, guys, for all the charitable generosity, and colorful gifts, you share with the world. You make it look so easy, and I tried to never miss your events.

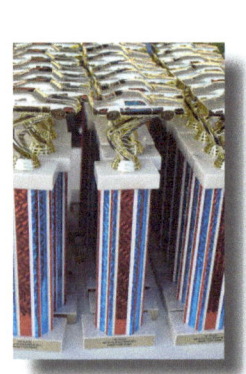
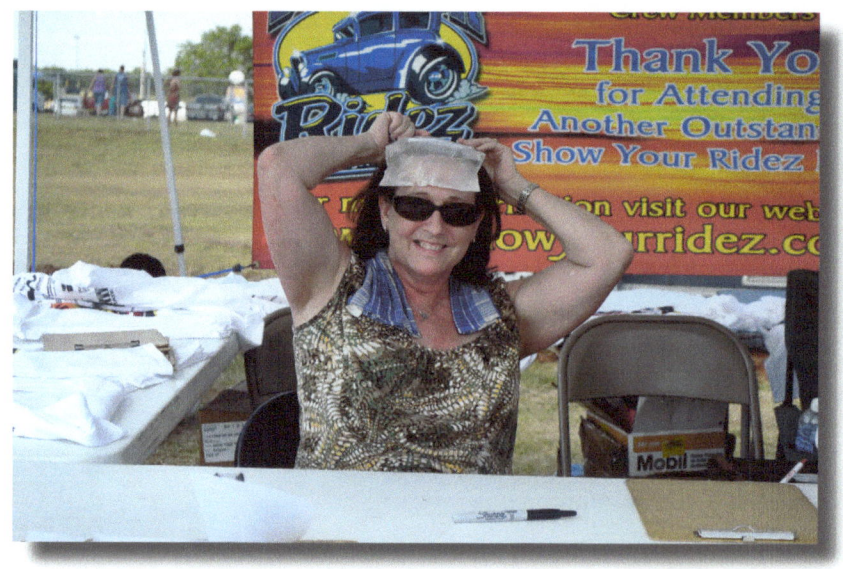
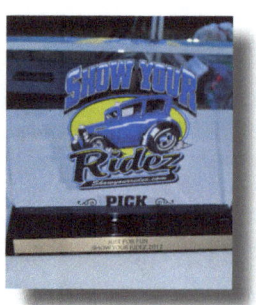

Keep on keepin' cool...

THE TROUTMAN FAMILY

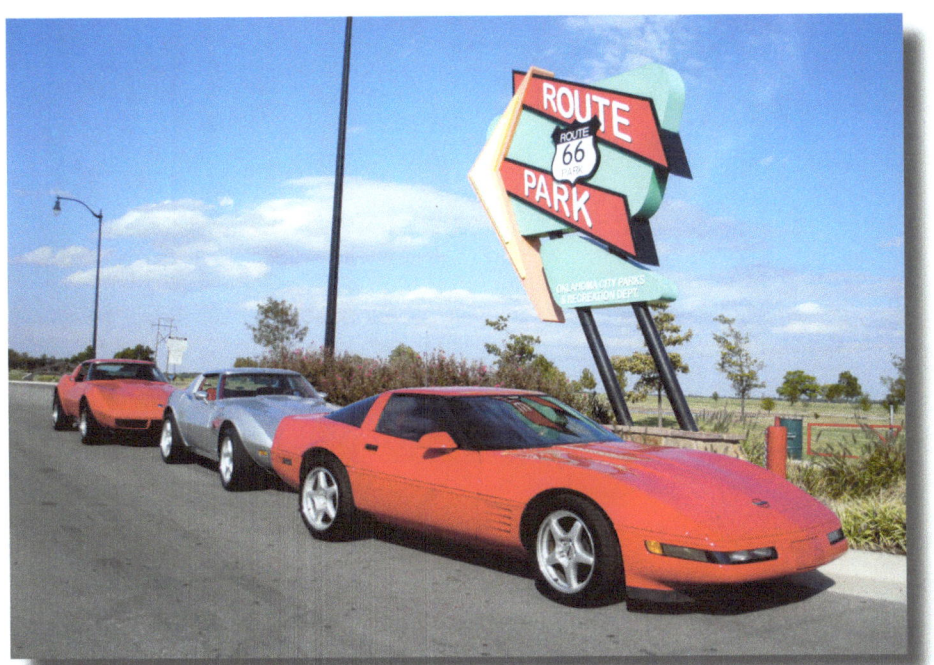

Darin, Kim, and Blake are definitely a Chevy family, as demonstrated by their three Vets and Camaro. Darin is the Youth Pastor at OKC.'s Forest Hills Christian Church. A number of his young children parishioners recently became pen pals with some of Haiti's church children.

Upon learning that the Hatian kids do not get to rejoice in such simple pleasures as playground equipment, one of the items we Americans take for granted, the Oklahoma counter parts started to diligently seek out generosity around them to afford their less fortunate newfound friends at least this creature comfort. In addition to the other funds raised, the church also held their annual car show for this purpose.

They donated enough for those swing sets, and then some.

Here we found a winsome spot or two along America's Main Street, Rt. 66, to divert with this loving, upright bunch. I even got to drive my first Corvette during this photo shoot. I eschew traditional narrative by just stating, it rocked!

Thanks for not only giving to those around you, but for remembering a land just a bit further south, in not so well-off a position as our own.

BETH WHITE

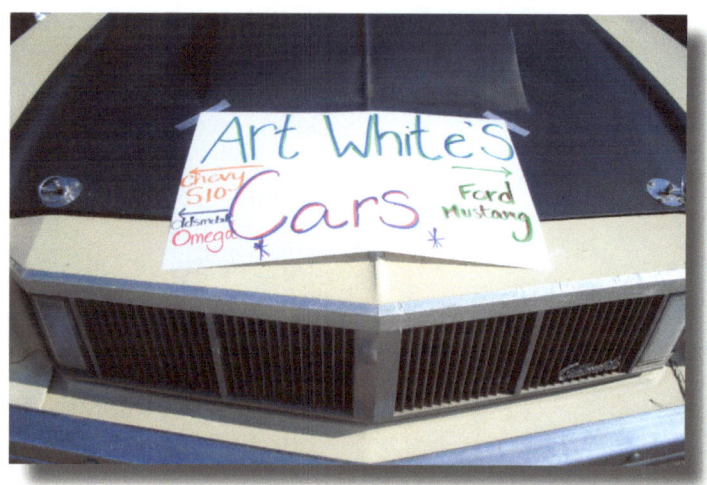

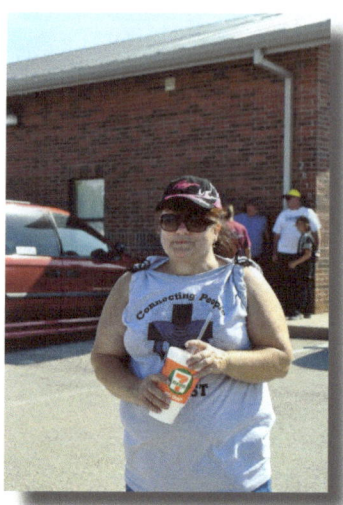

Beth White abides with a trifling of the cars she inherited from her dear departed husband Arthur, including her '05 Mustang and 1976 Omega. They shared many interests through the years, including their love of cars. Each year to honor that companionated kinship, Beth, in conjunction with her place of worship, hosts the Art White Memorial Car Show. It draws hordes from across the Midwest, and has a lot to offer for one of the less advertised shows, including a delicious home-cooked lunch, and often an Elvis impersonator. One constant is that these two autos are always center stage and prominently featured. Thanks for such a devoted retrospective.

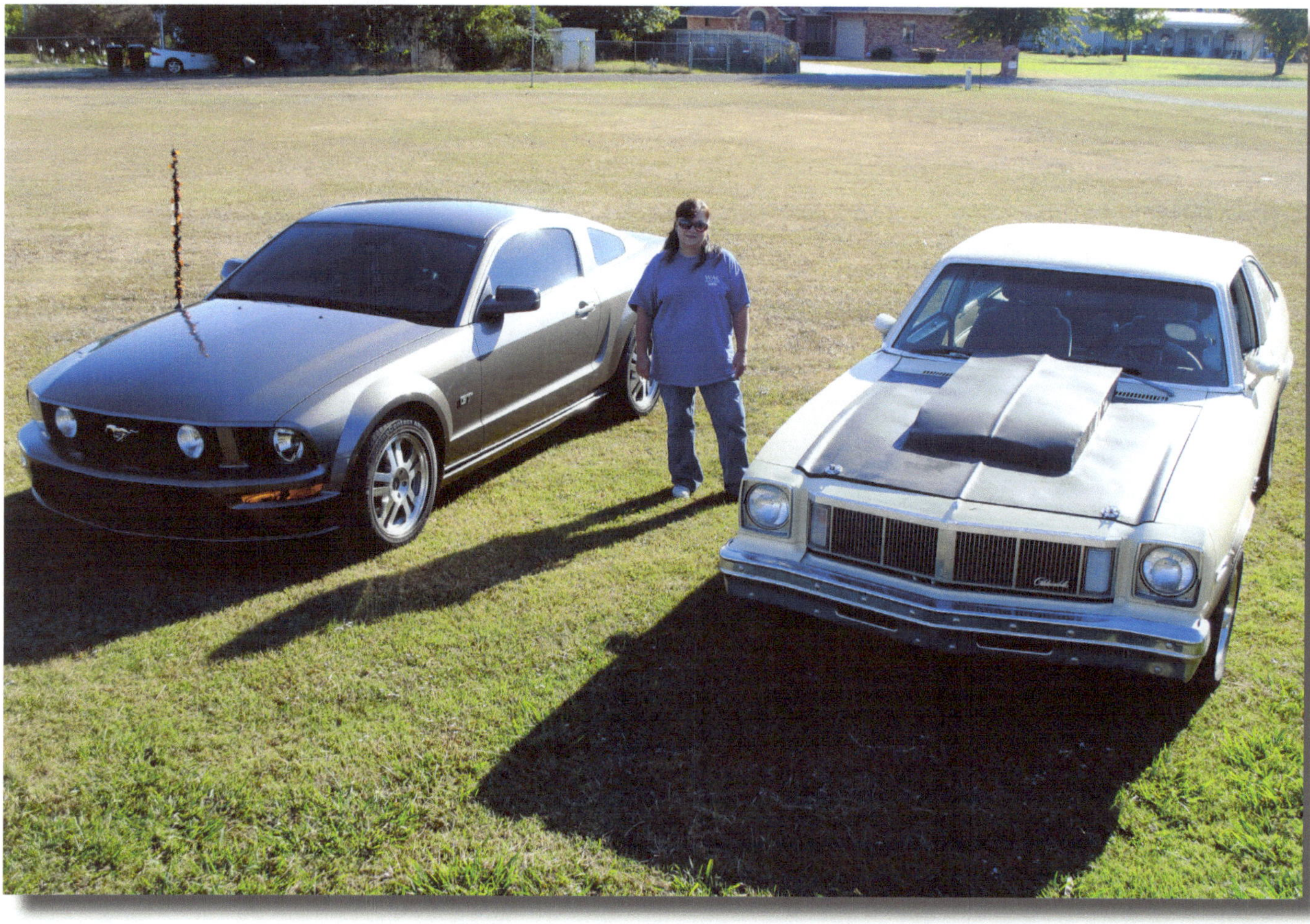

HEARTLAND CHRISTIAN HOTRODS AND CUSTOMS

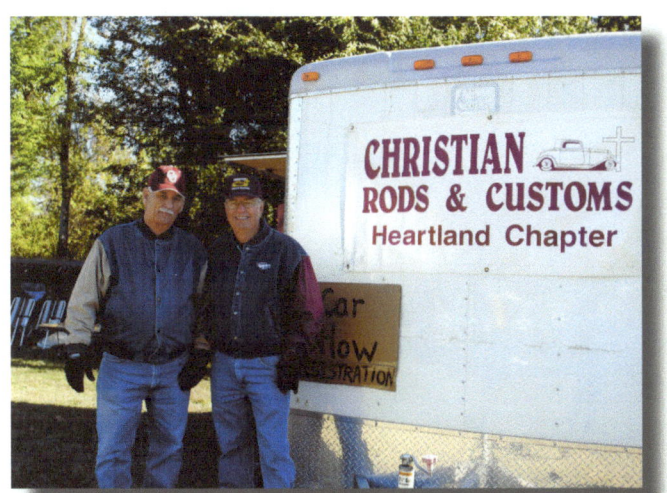

Charles Clifton and Floyd Dalton are illustrious leaders of their car show organization, and club, joining forces to meet and greet several times throughout the year. Each year, in early November, to kick off the holiday months, and round out the car show season in Central Oklahoma, they have the distinction of hosting the charitable show I discussed in the "Shows" chapter. It's comparable to a Toys For Tots type event, which helps many families who may have been struggling with hunger and poverty.

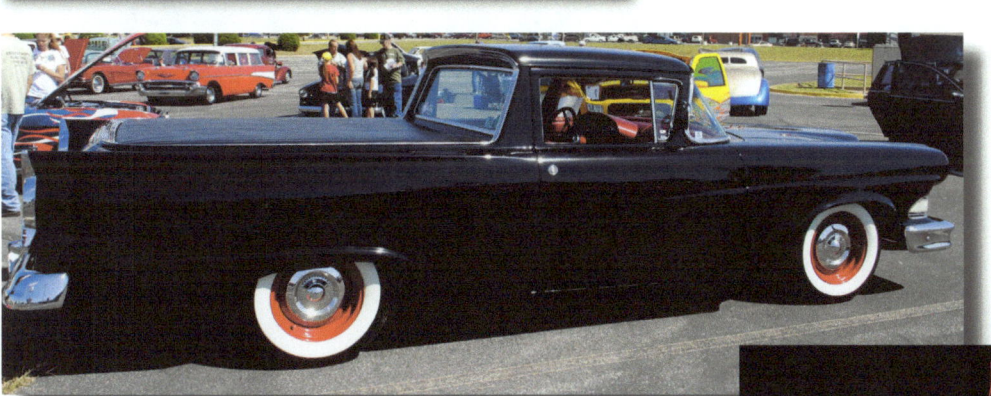

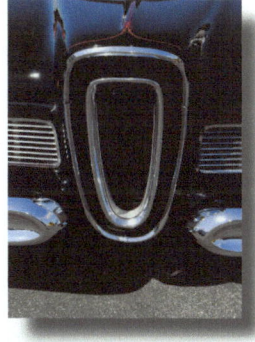

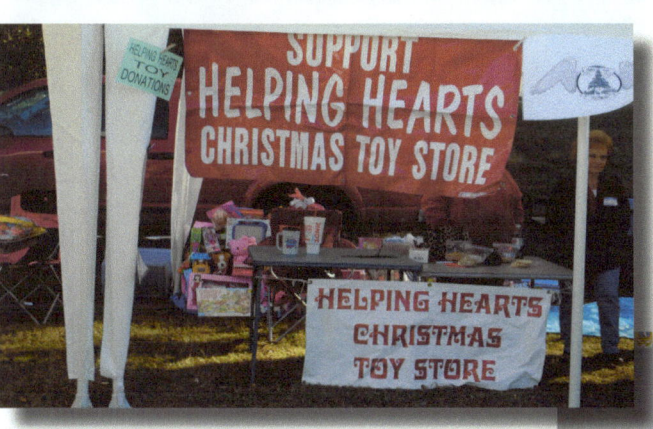

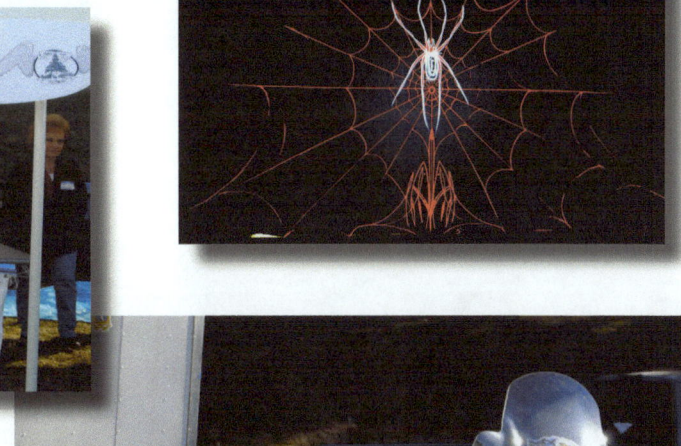

Many hosts possess some radically hot rides, and they are no different. Thanks for taking your infatuation of classic cars and motorcycles to the next level for hobbyists like myself, as well as the blessed souls you assist each December. You all make it look effortless.

MICHAEL SHIVERS

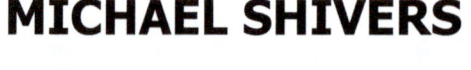

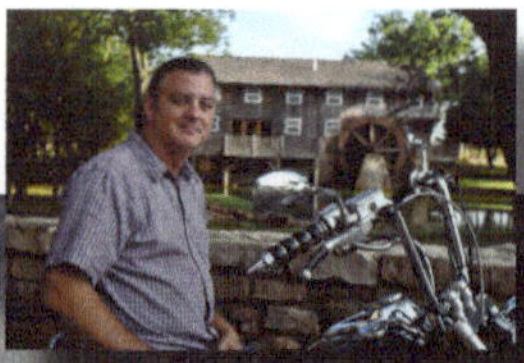

Host of an inaugural car show to sponsor a women's collegiate soccer team, Michael Shivers shows off one of his other multitude of interests, including this innovative creation. He morphed this 2000 Yamaha V-Star motorcycle as a tribute to one of the Classics, The Bel Air.

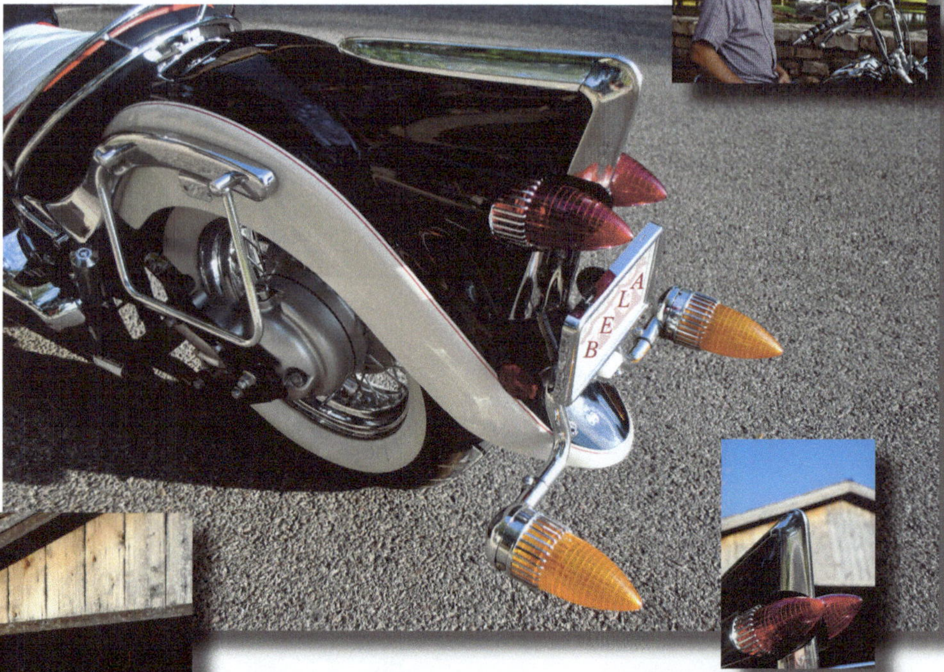

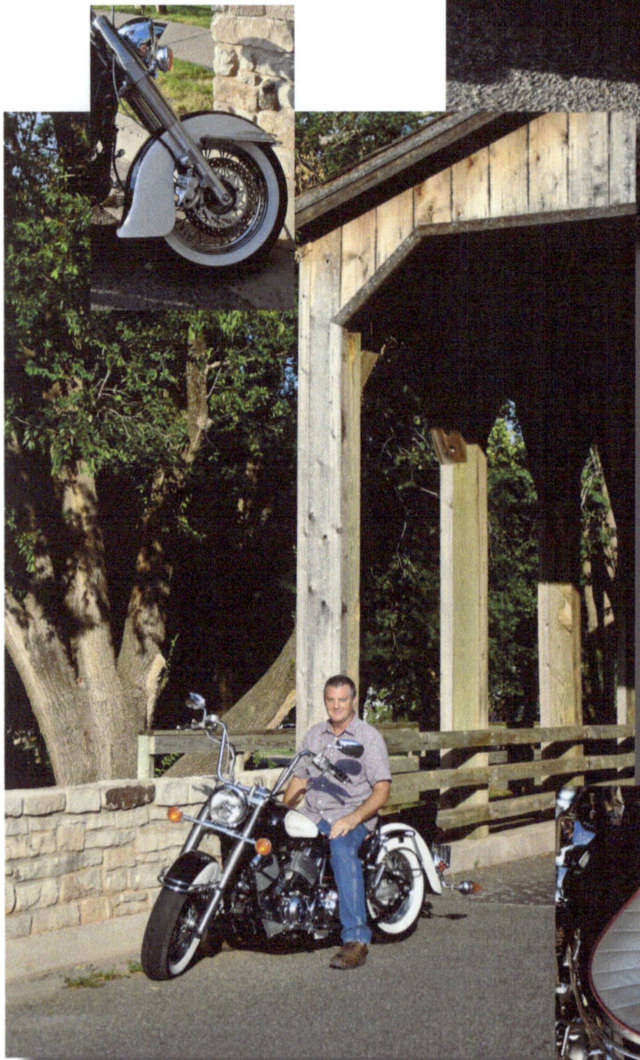

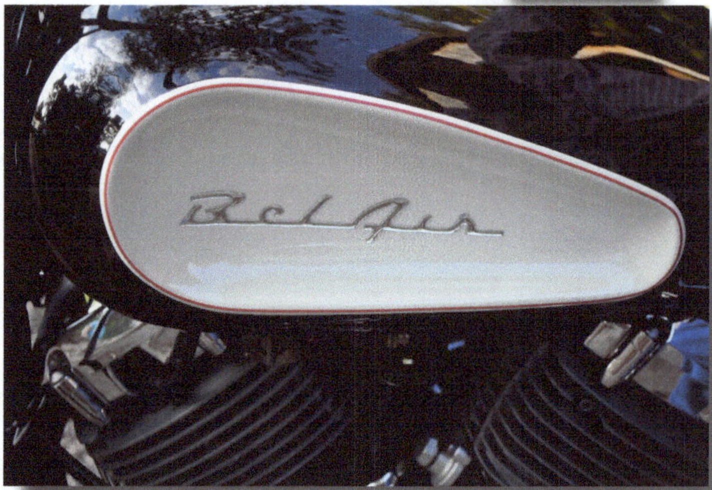

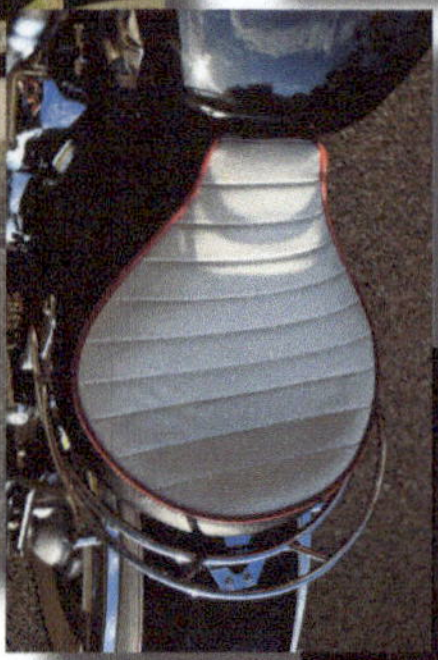

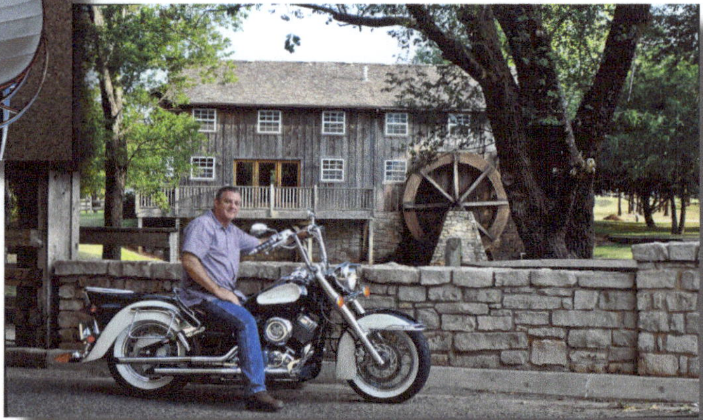

As apparent by these shots with his period piece of art harkening back to a pride in workmanship from a bygone era, Michael loves his job. All who know Michael appreciate his friendliness at shows, and here duly as well, while he takes a breather near an equally breathtaking scene.

69

CENTRAL TECH AUTO SHOP CLASS

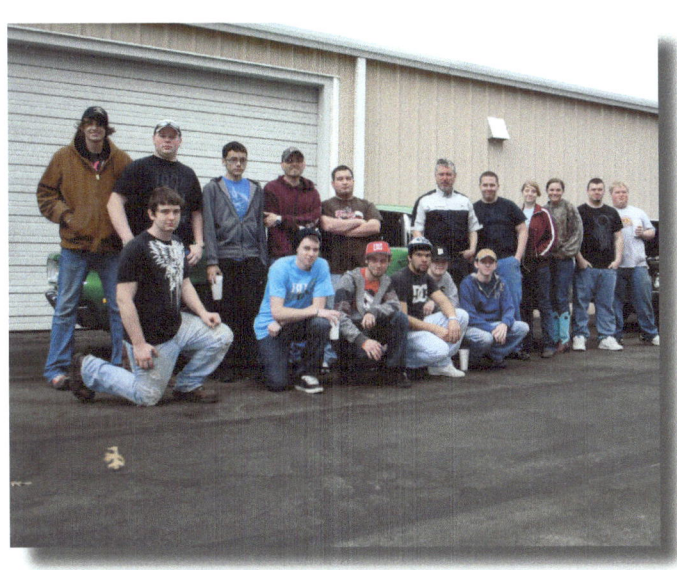

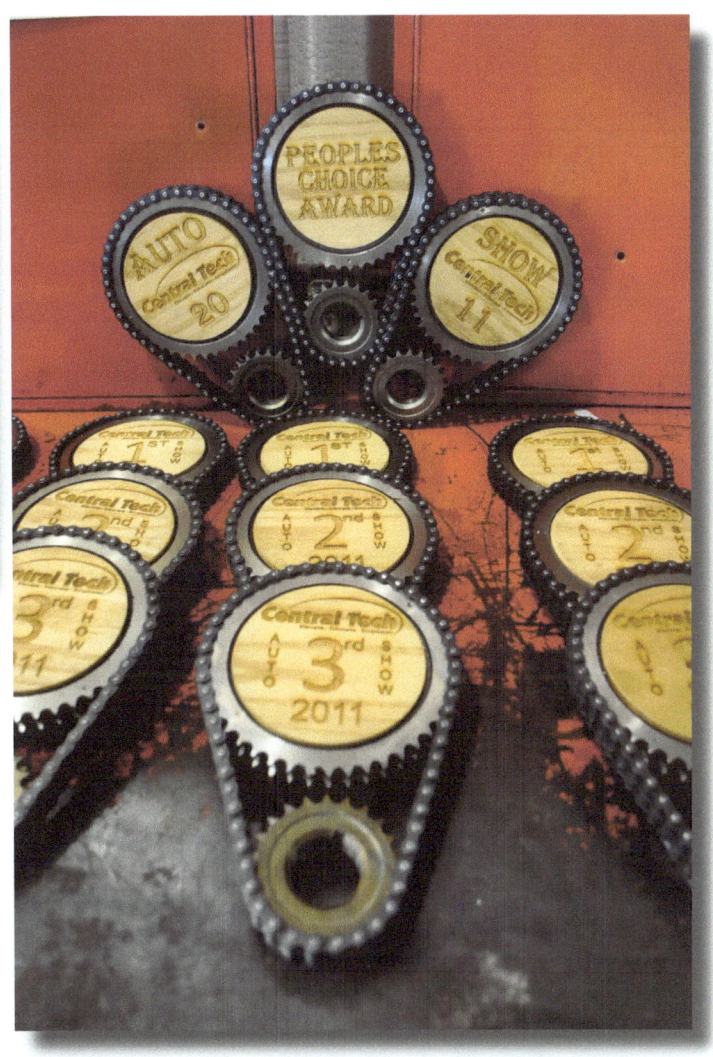

This polished group of auto shop students who hosted their Votech's open house and car show weekend, "Take 5" with me. The leader of the pack is instructor Jim Rogers, known far and wide for his trophy making dexterity. In fact, his awards constructed from a fly wheel, and showcasing the wood-fired engraving of the school's wood shop class were so popular, they were commissioned for at least two other regional car shows I am aware of. On this late, February cloud-filled day, however, Mr. Rogers' upper echalon made their own event famously memorable for us all. Thanks for your hard work, while helping your community.

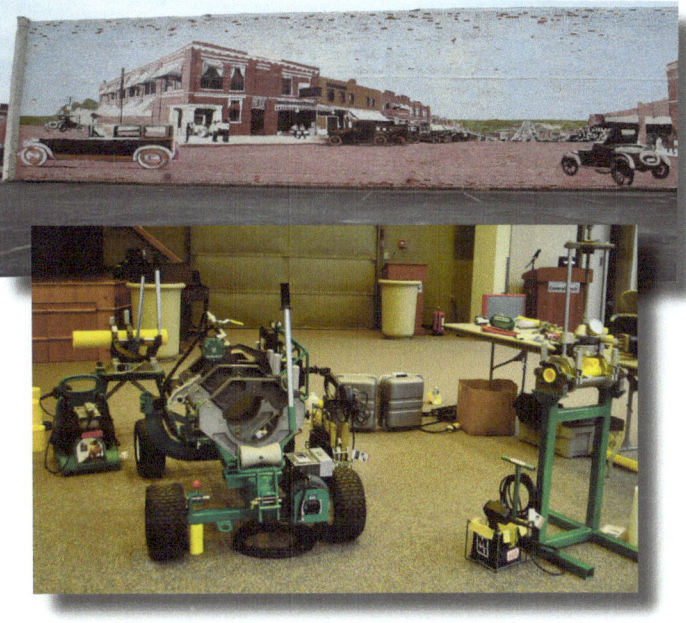

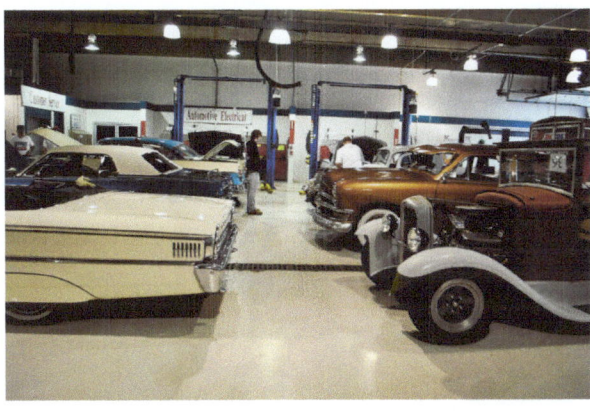

THE ARTISTS

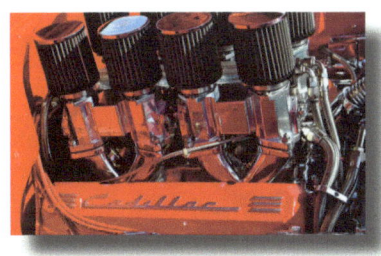

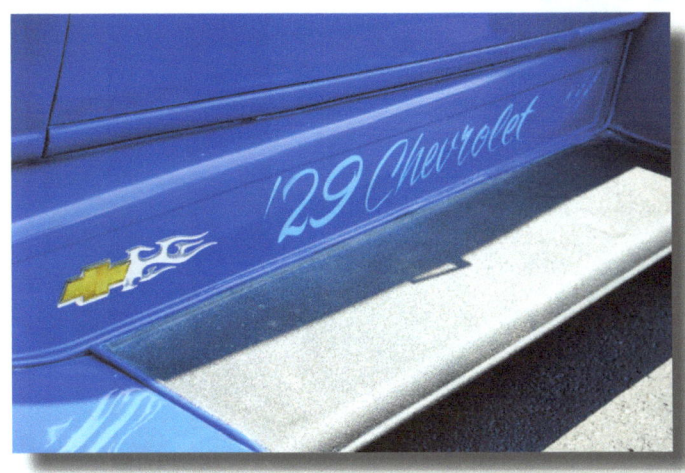

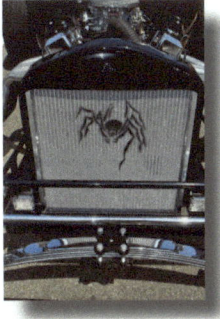

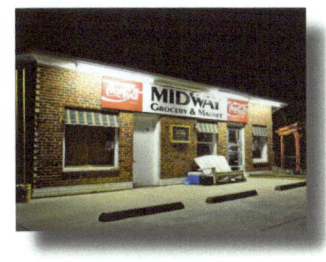

Just as many of the hosts exhibit prolific artistic ability with their own cars and motorcycles, so too do the talented people in this chapter. From keeping our rides in tip-top shape under the hood, to helping present the most detailed appearance, to a just down right righteous savvy in the air brush and auto body departments, an abundance of gorgeous endowment abounds to be put on display in the pages to follow. I even count the cuisineers catering the car-oriented events as pivotal. They definitely play an alluring part in keeping one going down the road, not to mention providing the fuel energizing one such as myself to shoot hundreds of photos.

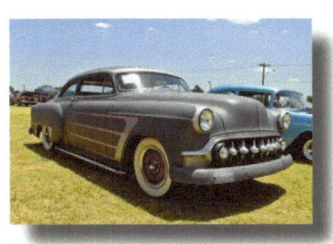

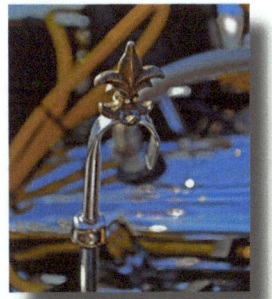

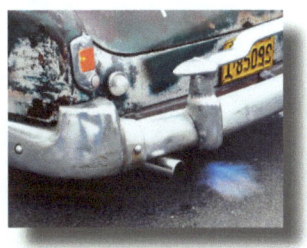

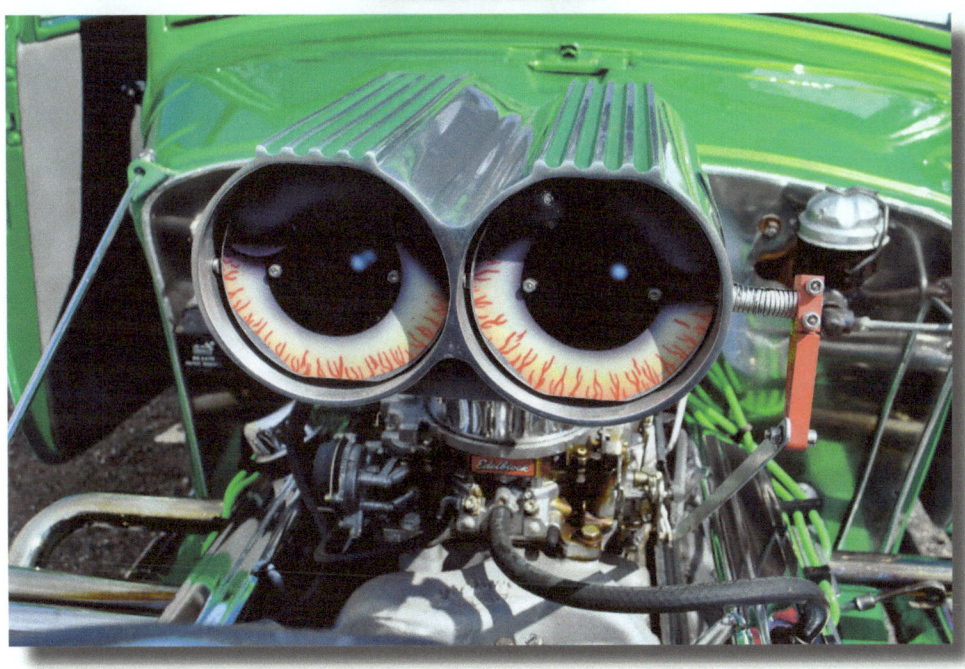

THE Z3 IS IN THIS DETAIL

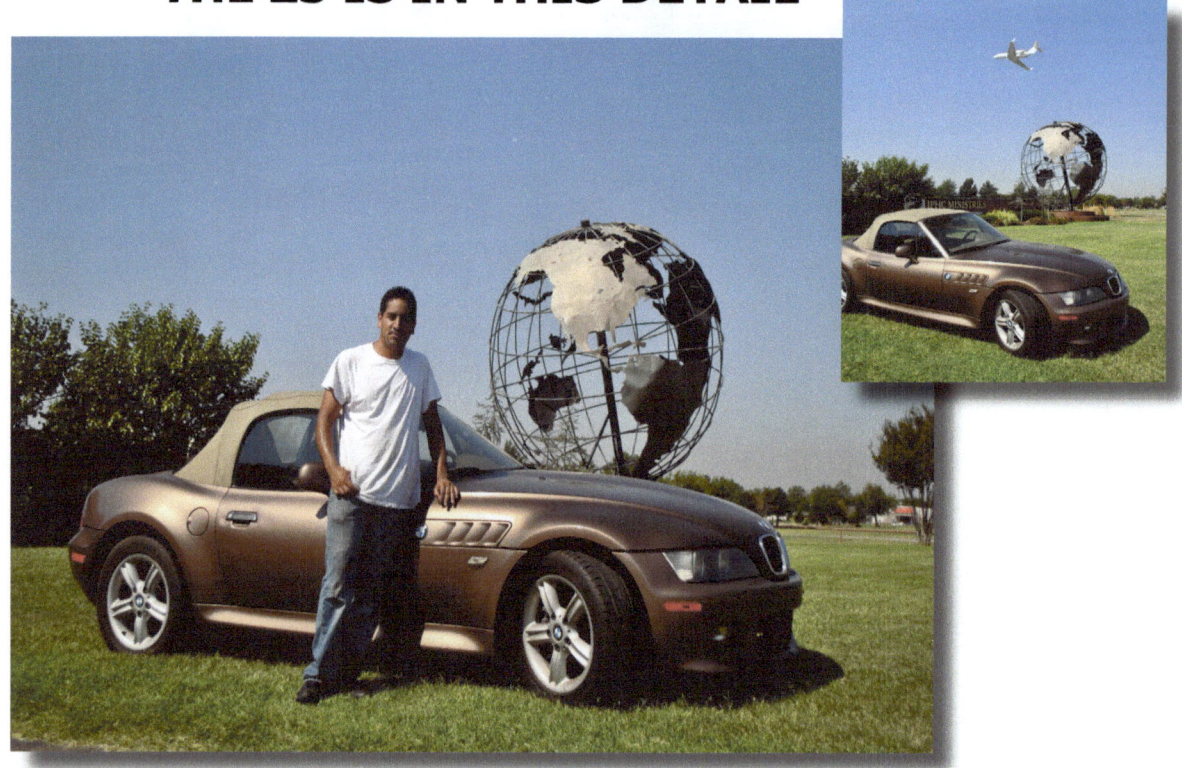

Mr. Omar Ortega has just finished polishing up the interior of this
Golden Millenium edition BMW Z3 circa 2000.

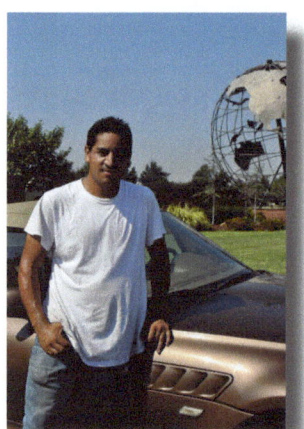

His employers may be the ones about to transfer ownership
of this clean-in-every-way unit, but we were in possession of
the key at that moment, and had a field day giving these 189
horses one more joy ride.

Those at his place of business will understand if he has to shine up the chrome all over
again after the abundance of drool that occurred during our "Out of this World" photo
shoot. We chose the main entrance to the Pentecostal H.Q., marked significantly by an
oversized, also gold, globe.

FAIR WELL J&L

It is with immense sentimentality that I find cause to mention an institution on the southside of OKC., J&L Automotive. Mr. Jimmy McConnell, the name sake for half of these familiar initials, recently retired from the Auto Repair Biz.

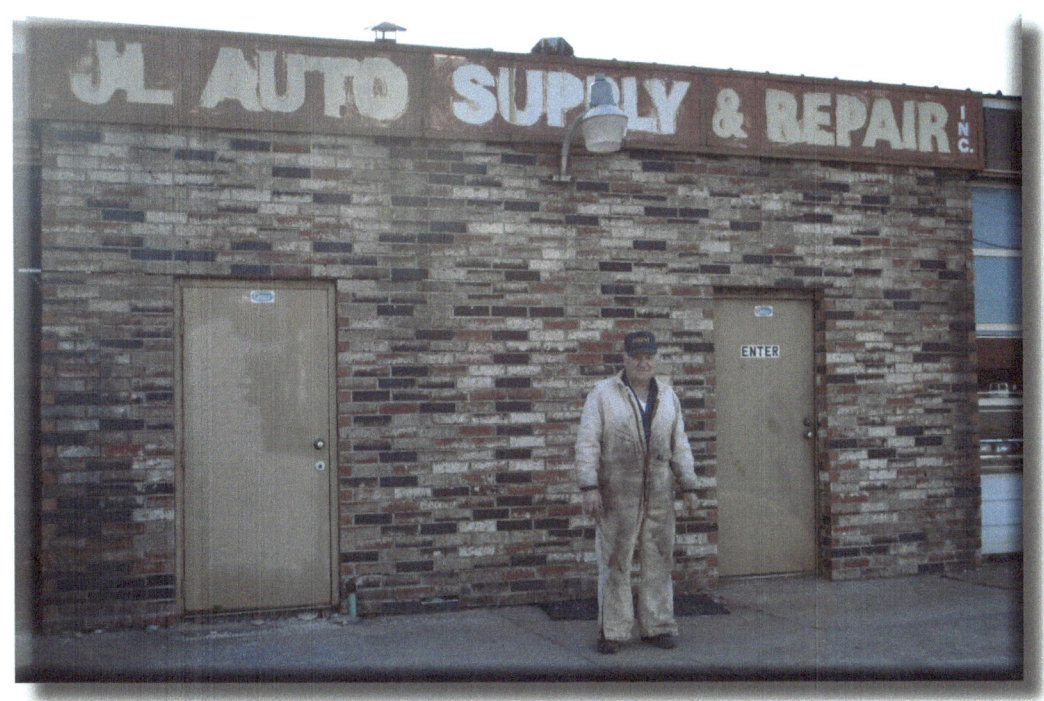

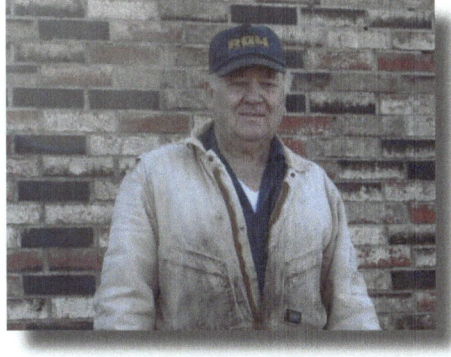

I caught up with Jim while he cleared out his once-booming shop. Many a family car have passed through these garage doors to be handled personally by Jim himself, as well as his best bud Billy. All with that no nonsense, albeit soft spoken, T.L.C. they dished out so well.

Partner Billy, who had already fled the scene before this paparazzi crew could catch a shot, was actually the knight in shining armor one fateful day as I was motoring out of town to go acquire my Ghia. He precisely connected the mystifying trailer we rented to transport it home. Trying to do this on the house, my cohort Margo and I would have none of that, managing to tip the rascal mercilessly.

Thanks, you guys, for all the years of dedicated service to autos and their oft befuddled owners everywhere. Happy retirement and life wherever you go.

A V.W.'S BEST FRIEND

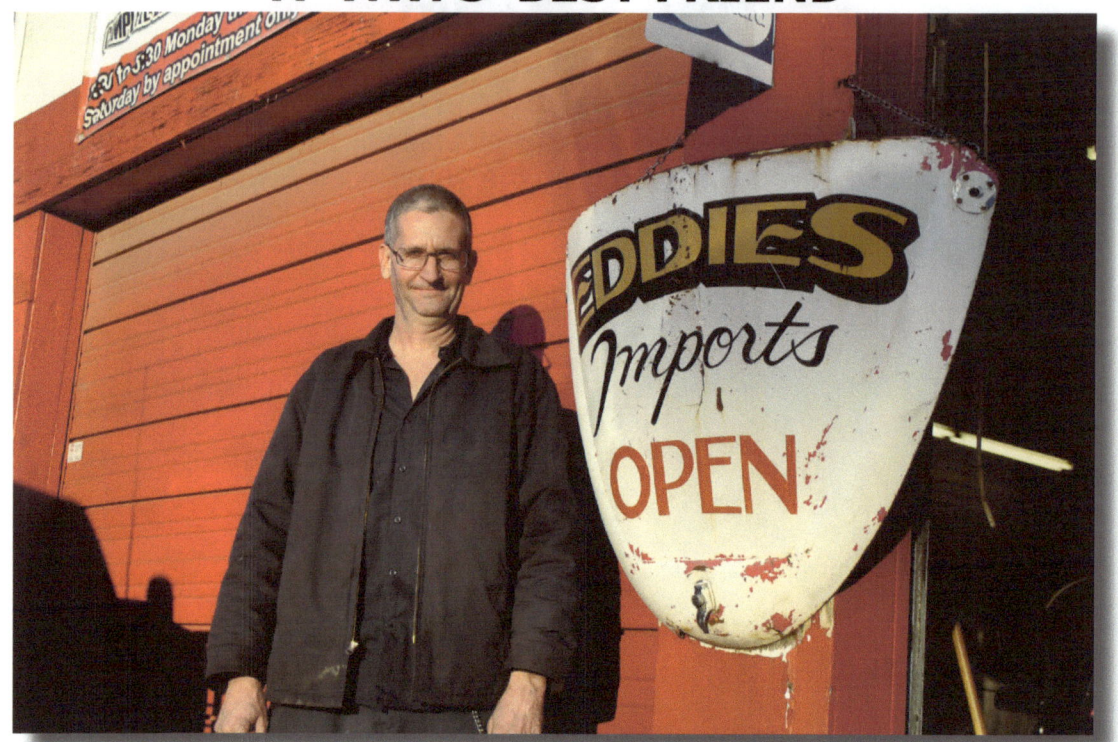

Standing sentry at the threshold, is the famous proprietor of the Best Lil' V.W. and foreign repair shop in OKC., the one and only Eddie of Eddie's Imports.

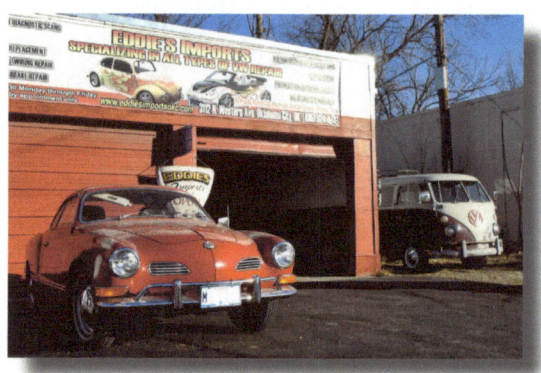

In business and in love with Volkswagens for eons, Ed's the man to get under your hood when your beloved "Herbie" is under the weather. Thanks Eddie for all of your help and advice through the years.

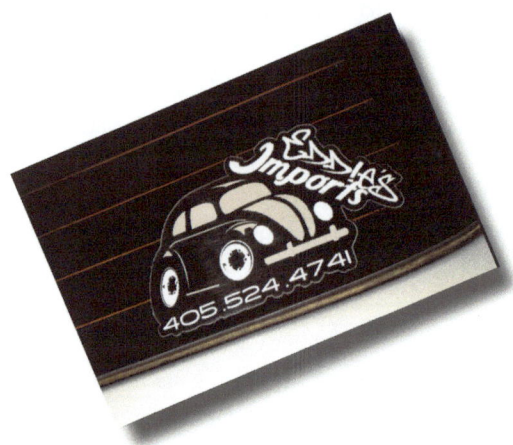

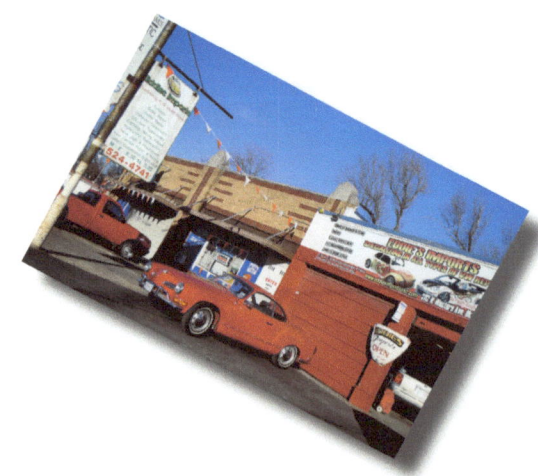

THEIR DISHES ARE ALWAYS..."GONE IN 60 SECONDS"

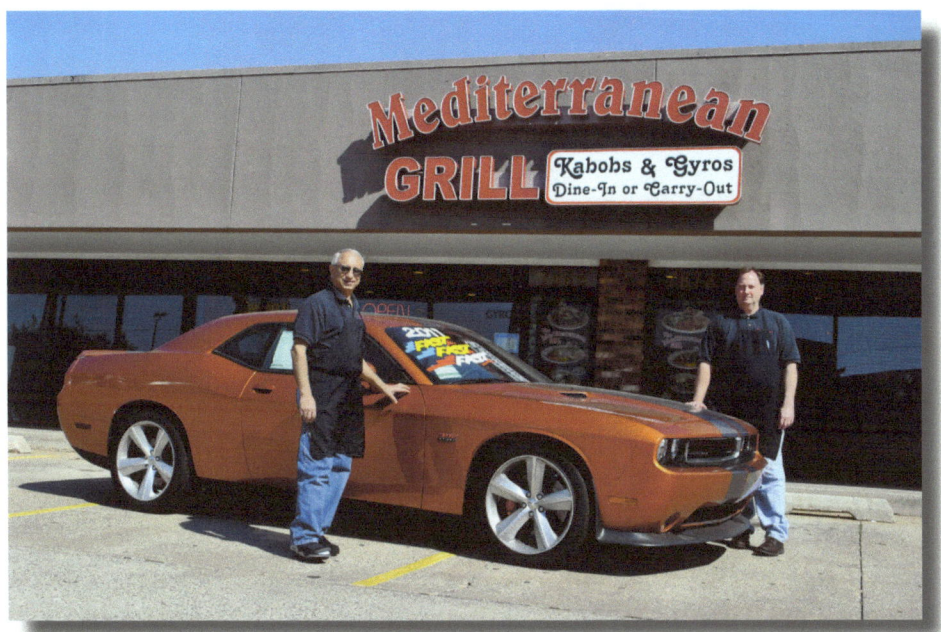

Fred Faroozan and Andy Slagle, brother-in-laws and co-owners of the delectible award winning Mediterranean Grill, take ten with this incandescent 2011 Dodge. We had the indulgence of framing this shot courtesy of Jim Pit, the go-to guy for handling transporting show cars to demos at the dealership he is under the employ of. We tried to talk the boys into obtaining this dreamcycle on steroids as their catering vehicle. Maybe that will manifest for the trio.

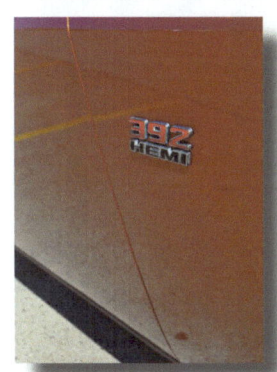

It bears the same warmth in color as the interior shades gracing this yummy eatery. I have spent many a time on the way to car shows, as well as afterwards, indulging in that appetizing atmosphere and gourmet Mediterranean cuisine.

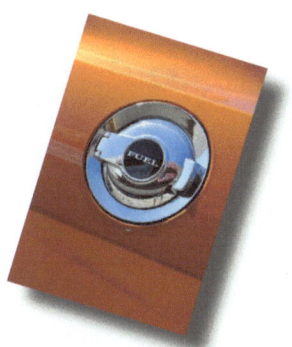

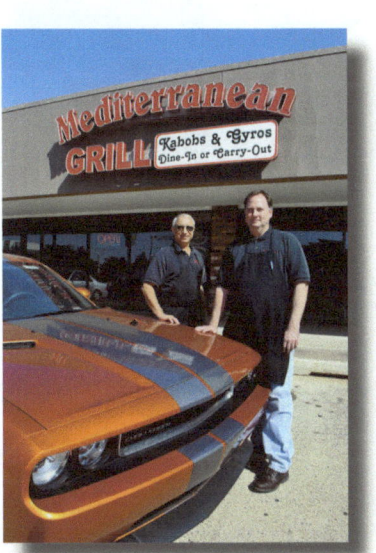

Thanks for cooking up such tasty meals and lasting memories. In my opinion, you have no "Challenger" save the show car you are posing with.

EATING UP THE ATTENTION

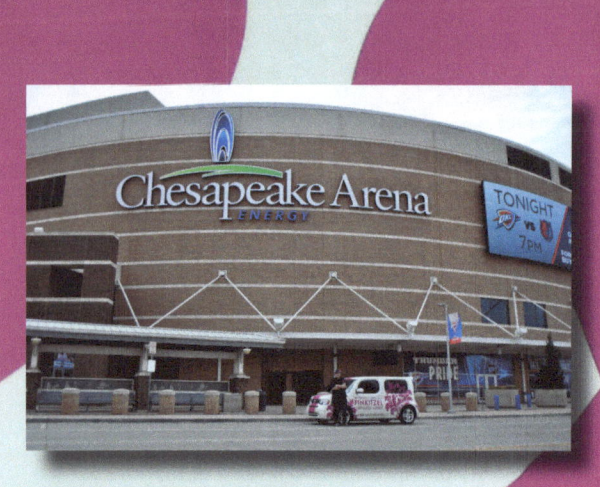

Jacob Menchaca takes a detour with the delivery s.u.v. for the downtown Oklahoma City cup cake shop "Pink Kitzel," translated in Yiddish to tickled pink. Which coincidentaly I was when granted this shot.

The color not only applies to this pink ride, but also fits the entire interior of the sacharinely-welcoming establishment's hues. This may be a Cube, but its famous for representing round bits of sweet pastry heaven. I know I am not the only one who would love to see the "Cupcake-Mobile" roll into one of our car show's parking lots. I will have to pitch the idea. In the meantime, it remains a fraternal after game (and car show) hot spot, being just down the street from where our city's N.B.A. Thunder plays.

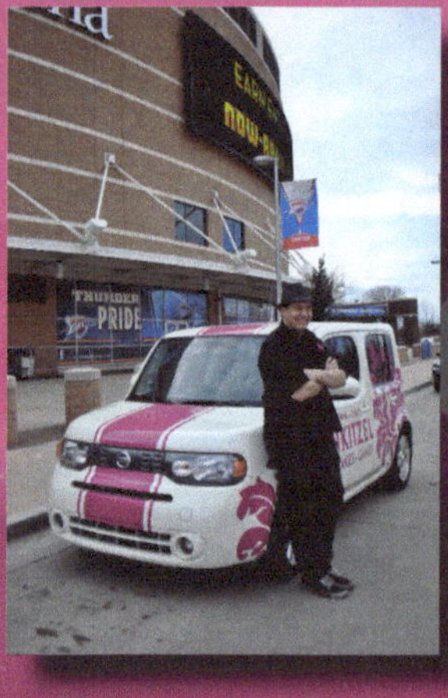

We just had to grab a few shots in front of the 2012 Division Champ's stadium.

MIK'S ARTWERKS

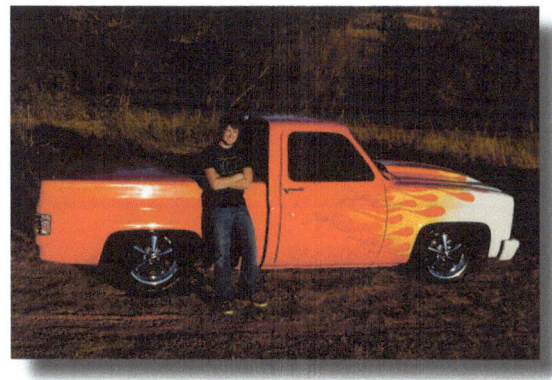
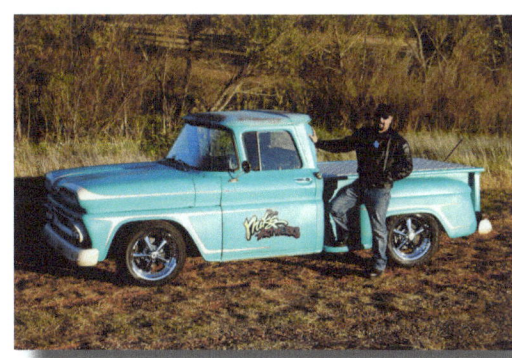

Herein, among the eclectic good company of the Artist chapter, are featured two mellow members of the "Miks Artwerks" team, accompanying their study in Chevrolets. Mik, and son Michael Ofsak, are celebrated far and wide in Oklahoma State and surrounding areas. These artists are not only well known, but really know their stuff, and generously share that talent for all to see. Here are a some glowing examples of their workmanship, culminating into expansion projects such as this local racer's commissioned head gear jazz up.

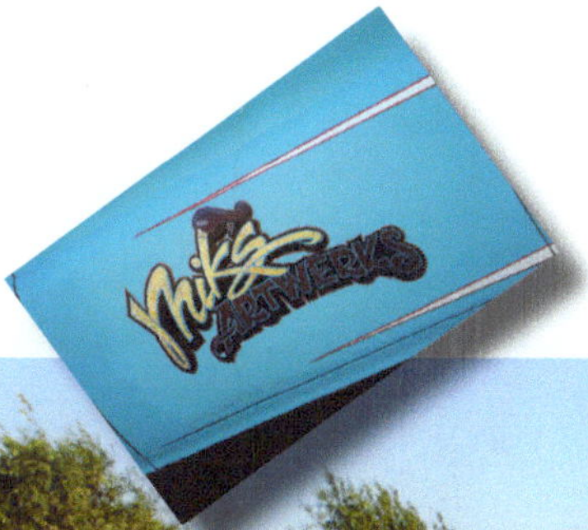

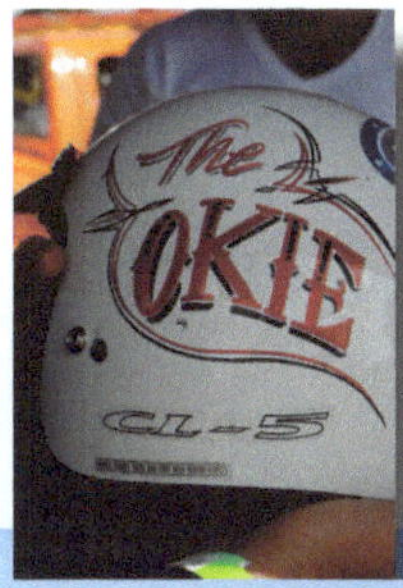

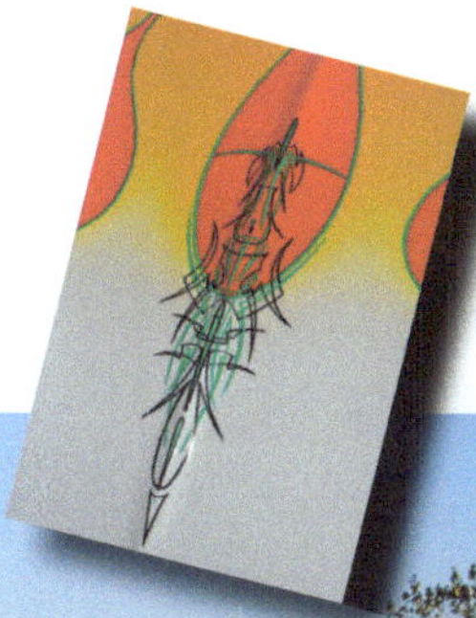

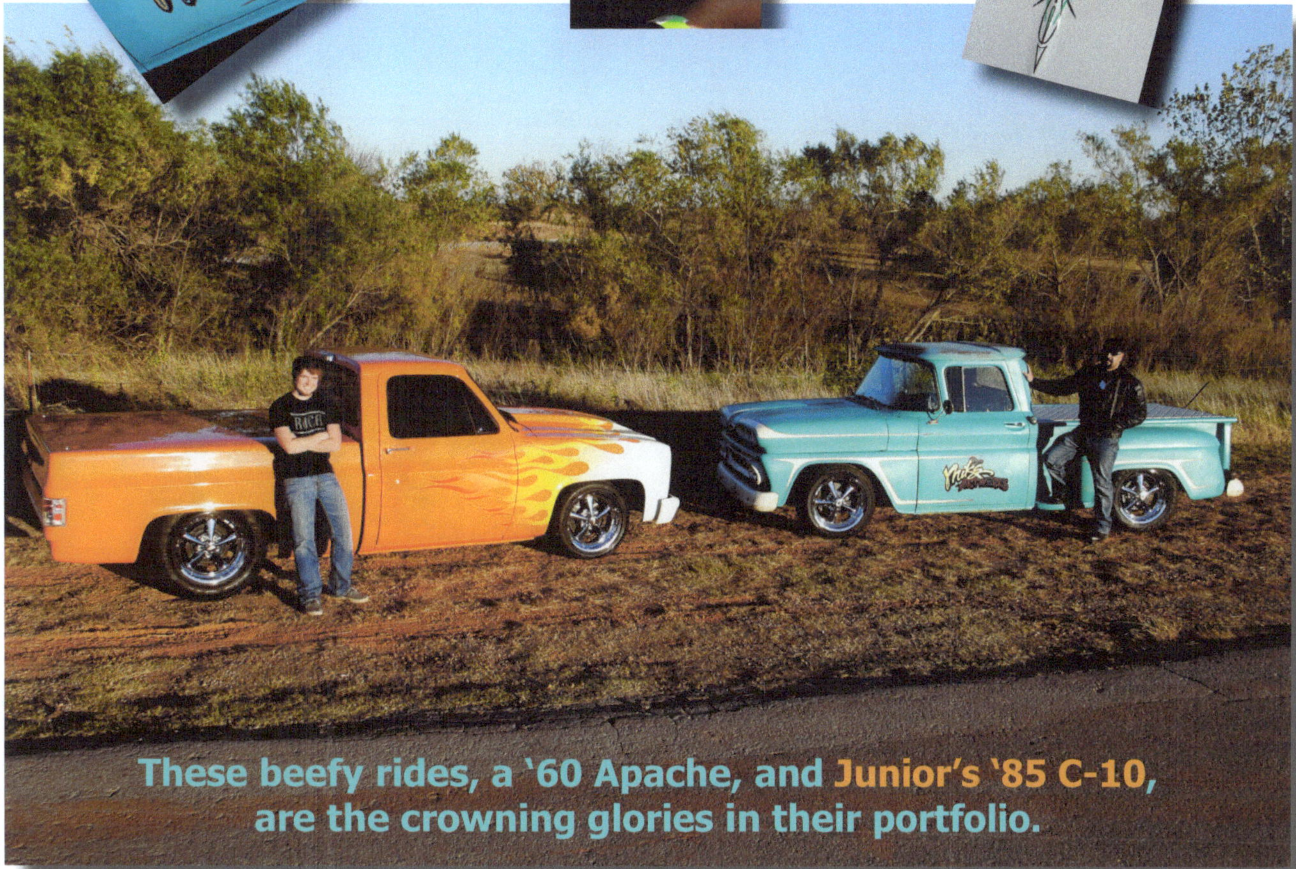

These beefy rides, a '60 Apache, and Junior's '85 C-10, are the crowning glories in their portfolio.

'67 BREW

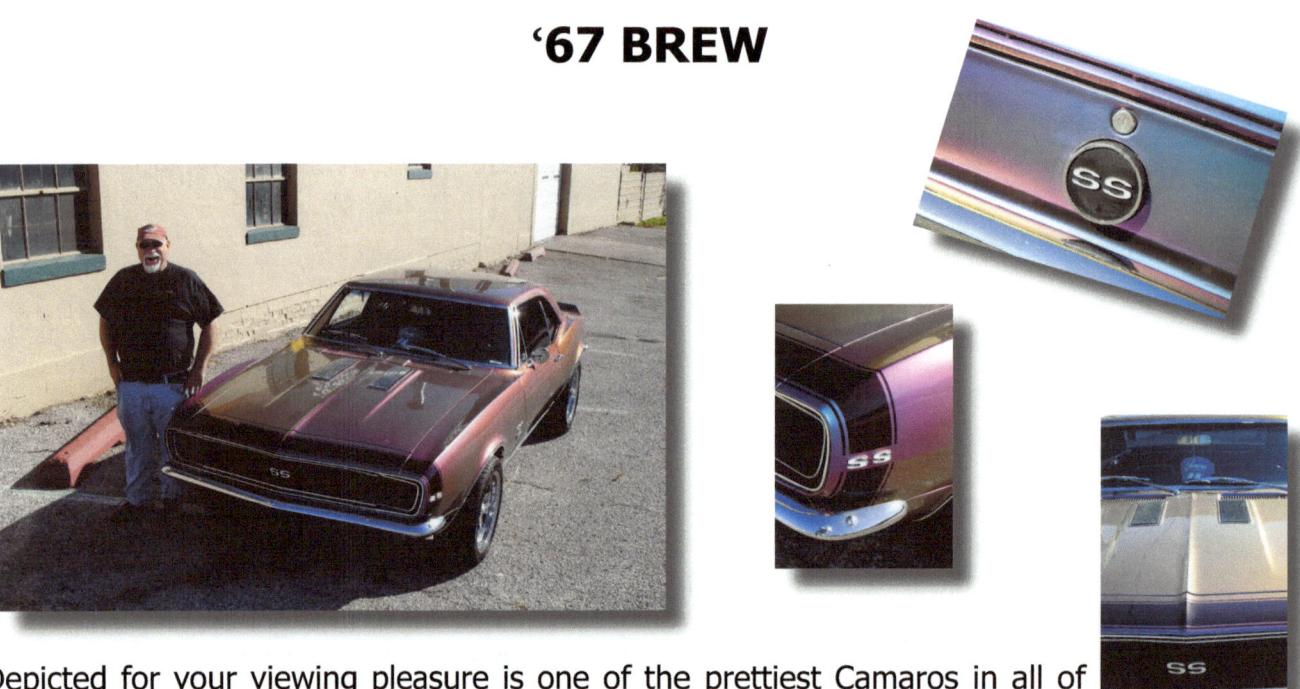

Depicted for your viewing pleasure is one of the prettiest Camaros in all of Oklahoma. With rider Johnny Brewster, of the Rt. 66 body shop Brew and Nick at the helm, and behind the rebirth of this inaugural '67 beast, how could you lose?

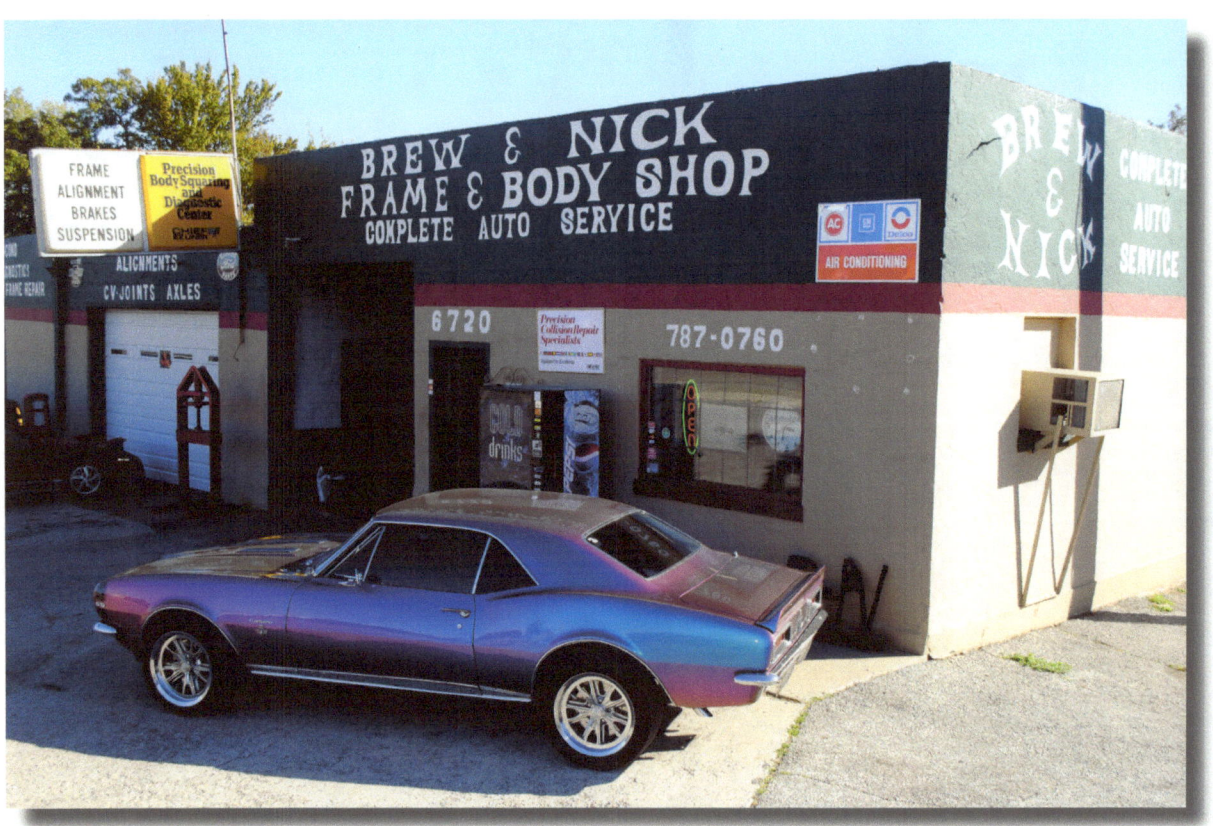

"Brew" as he is known to all, stated that the prismatic pigment gracing this award winning '60s era pioneer set him back about $350 a pint. Thanks for making the sacrifice for our satiated eyes. It is truly a dazzling masterpiece.

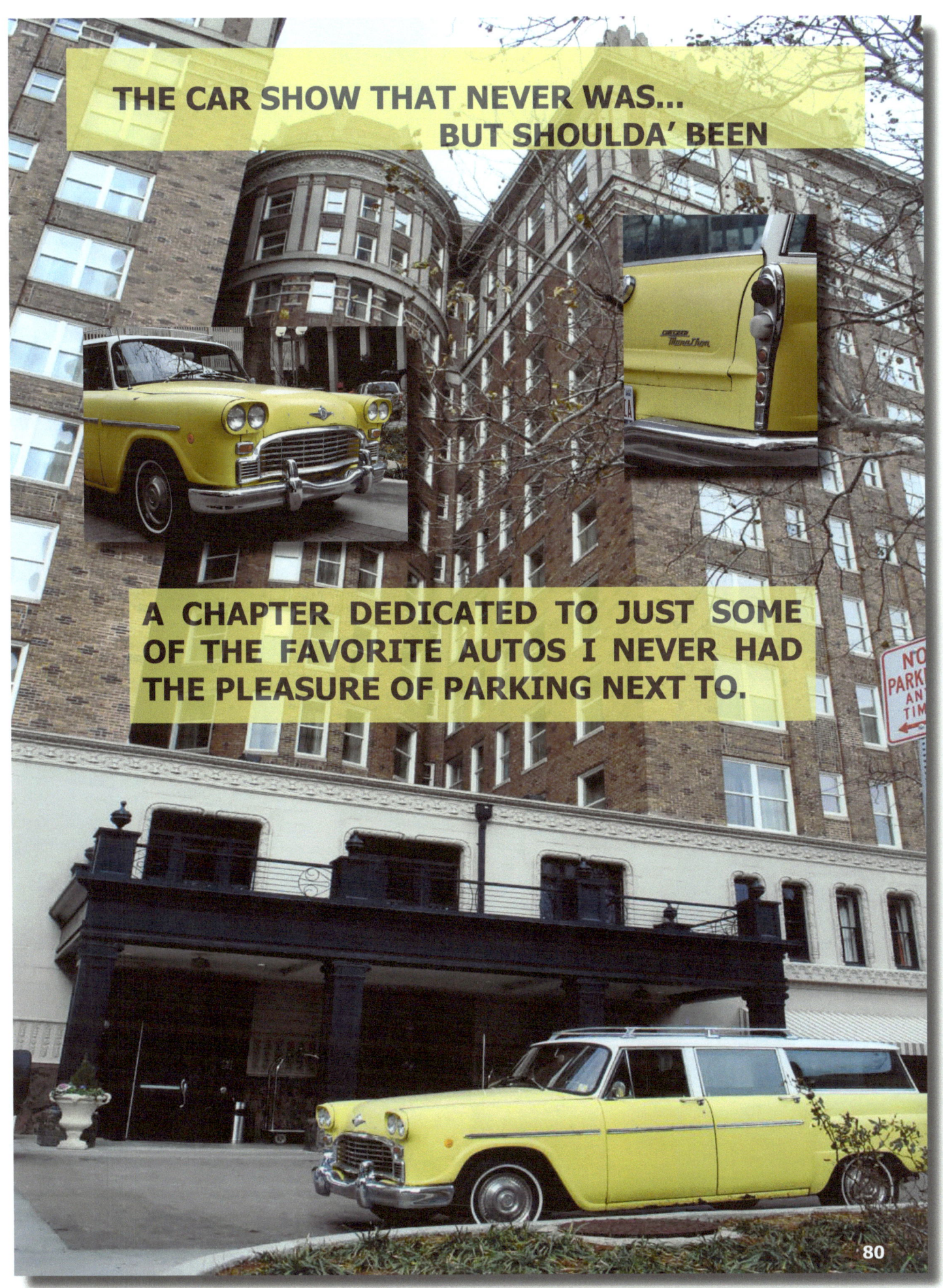

THE CAR SHOW THAT NEVER WAS...
BUT SHOULDA' BEEN

A CHAPTER DEDICATED TO JUST SOME OF THE FAVORITE AUTOS I NEVER HAD THE PLEASURE OF PARKING NEXT TO.

80

MIGHTA' BEEN YOUR GRANDPA'S OLDS...

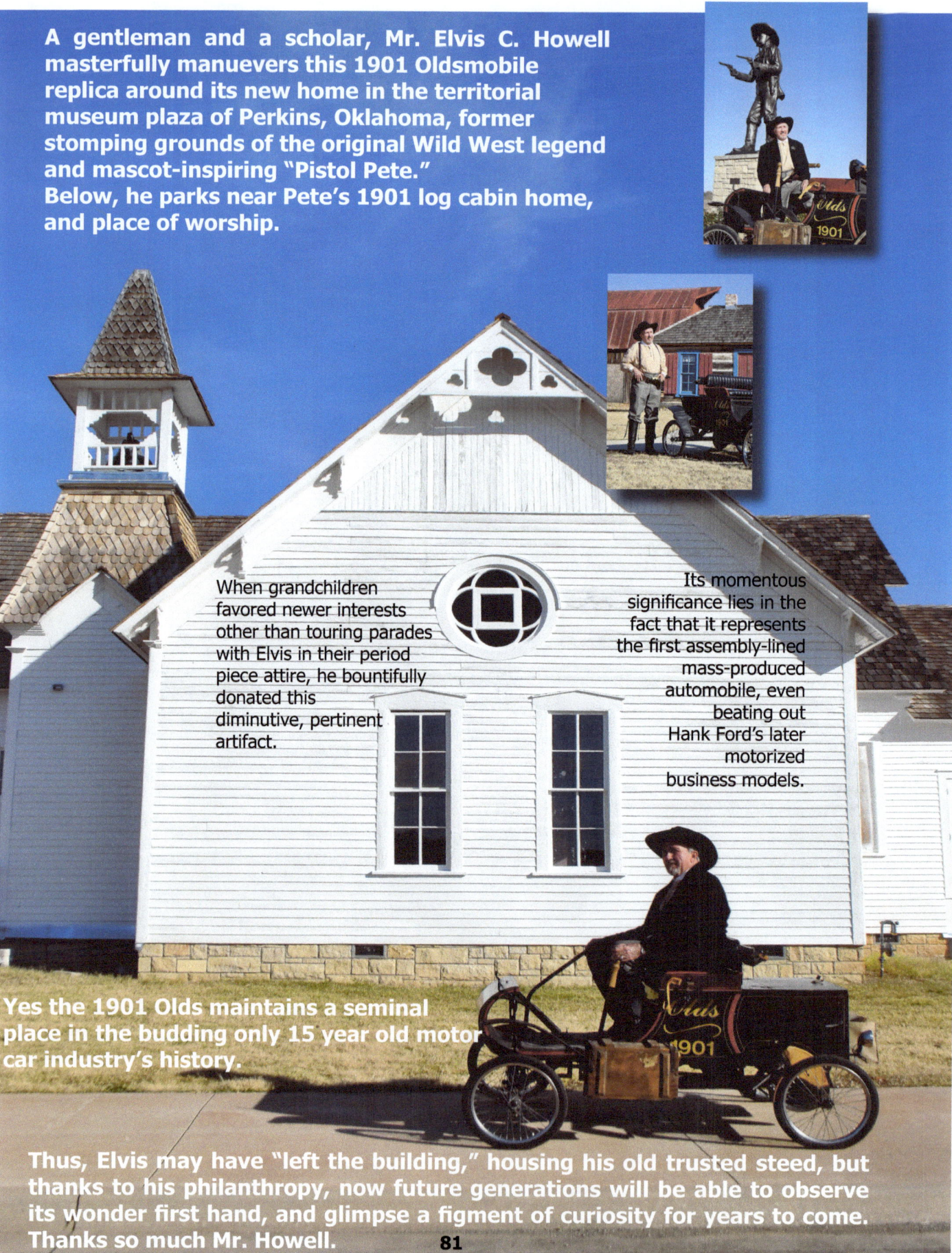

A gentleman and a scholar, Mr. Elvis C. Howell masterfully manuevers this 1901 Oldsmobile replica around its new home in the territorial museum plaza of Perkins, Oklahoma, former stomping grounds of the original Wild West legend and mascot-inspiring "Pistol Pete."
Below, he parks near Pete's 1901 log cabin home, and place of worship.

When grandchildren favored newer interests other than touring parades with Elvis in their period piece attire, he bountifully donated this diminutive, pertinent artifact.

Its momentous significance lies in the fact that it represents the first assembly-lined mass-produced automobile, even beating out Hank Ford's later motorized business models.

Yes the 1901 Olds maintains a seminal place in the budding only 15 year old motor car industry's history.

Thus, Elvis may have "left the building," housing his old trusted steed, but thanks to his philanthropy, now future generations will be able to observe its wonder first hand, and glimpse a figment of curiosity for years to come. Thanks so much Mr. Howell.

81

SMARTER THAN THE AVERAGE BEAR

A truly smart car owner, Megan Elliott, shows off her Smart car near the Automobile Alley section of downtown OKC. In addition to both car and driver hauling an uber-Hollywood look, the piece d' resistance has to be that diva-esque wildly painted hippie werehouse building owned by campy Oklahoma City band the Flaming Lips.

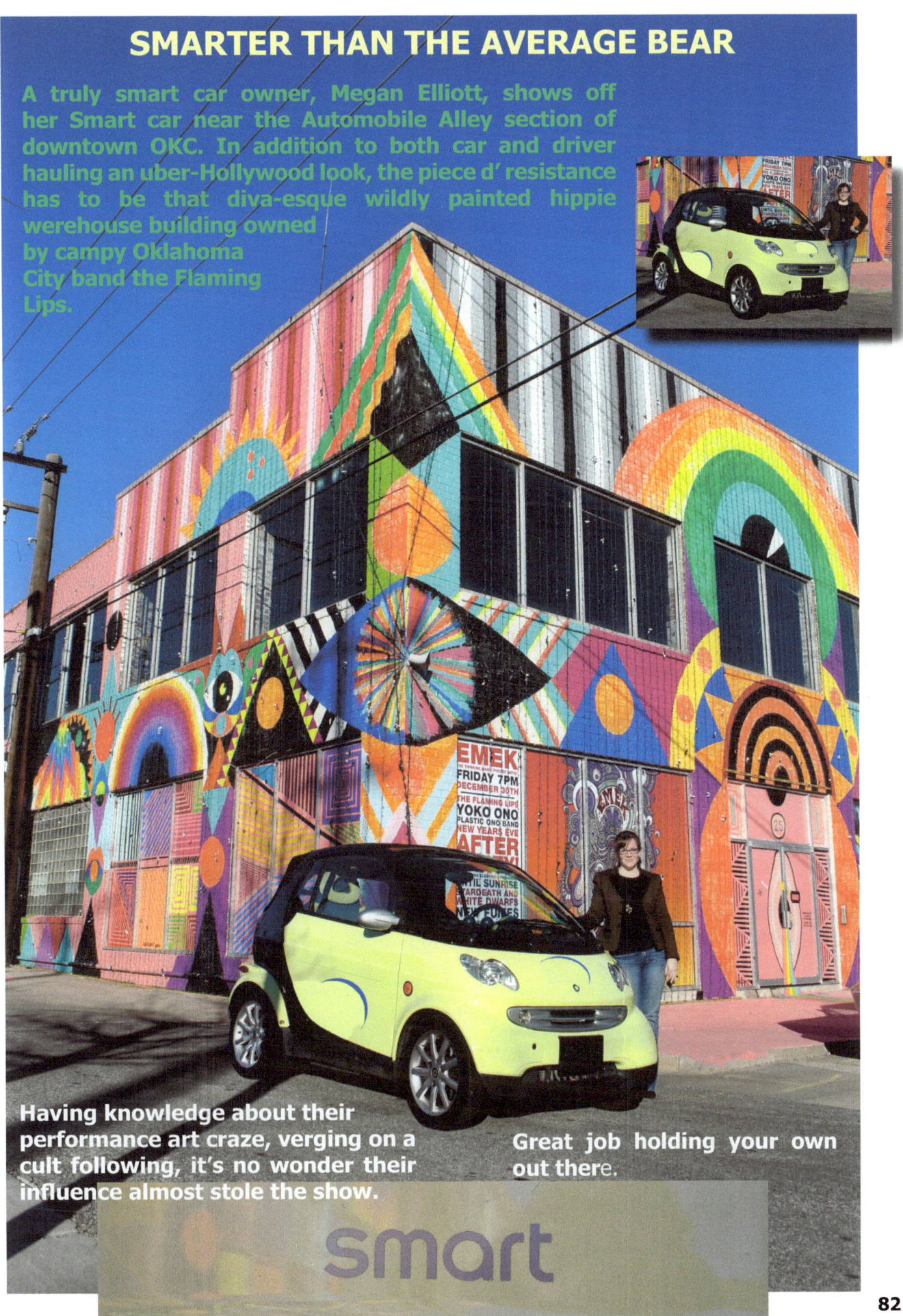

Having knowledge about their performance art craze, verging on a cult following, it's no wonder their influence almost stole the show.

Great job holding your own out there.

smart

SMOOTH SAILING WITH THE AMANTI

On a brisk winter's day dearly venerated neighbors Dale and Sue Waugh generously took some time out of their active Sunday to navigate over to our city's stalwart boat house. The sporting venue is home to rowing championships and even the recent Olympic trials.

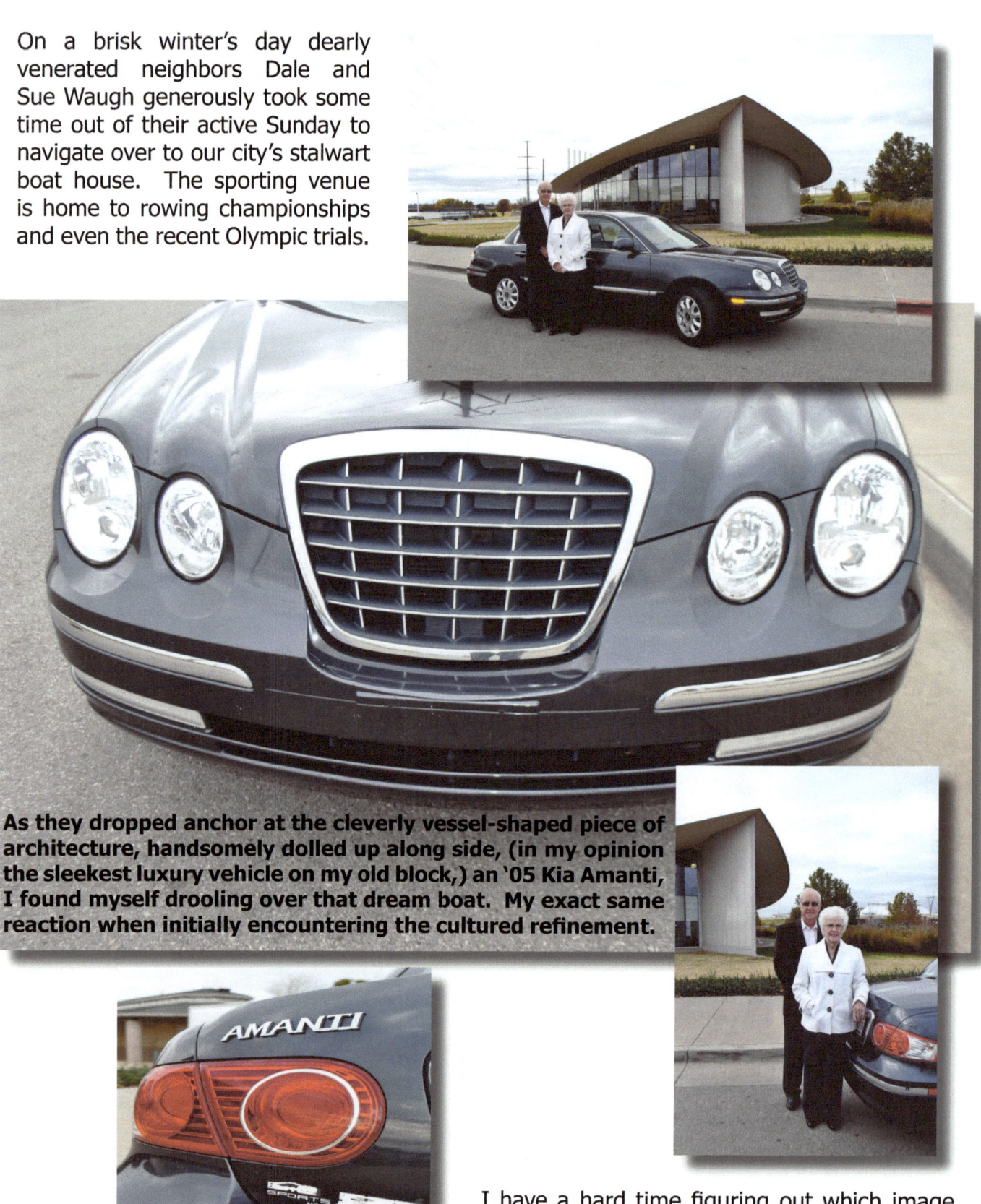

As they dropped anchor at the cleverly vessel-shaped piece of architecture, handsomely dolled up along side, (in my opinion the sleekest luxury vehicle on my old block,) an '05 Kia Amanti, I found myself drooling over that dream boat. My exact same reaction when initially encountering the cultured refinement.

I have a hard time figuring out which image is more visually eloquent. Great models these subject matters. Bravo to all three.

AN ANTIQUE AND A GEM AMONG MEN

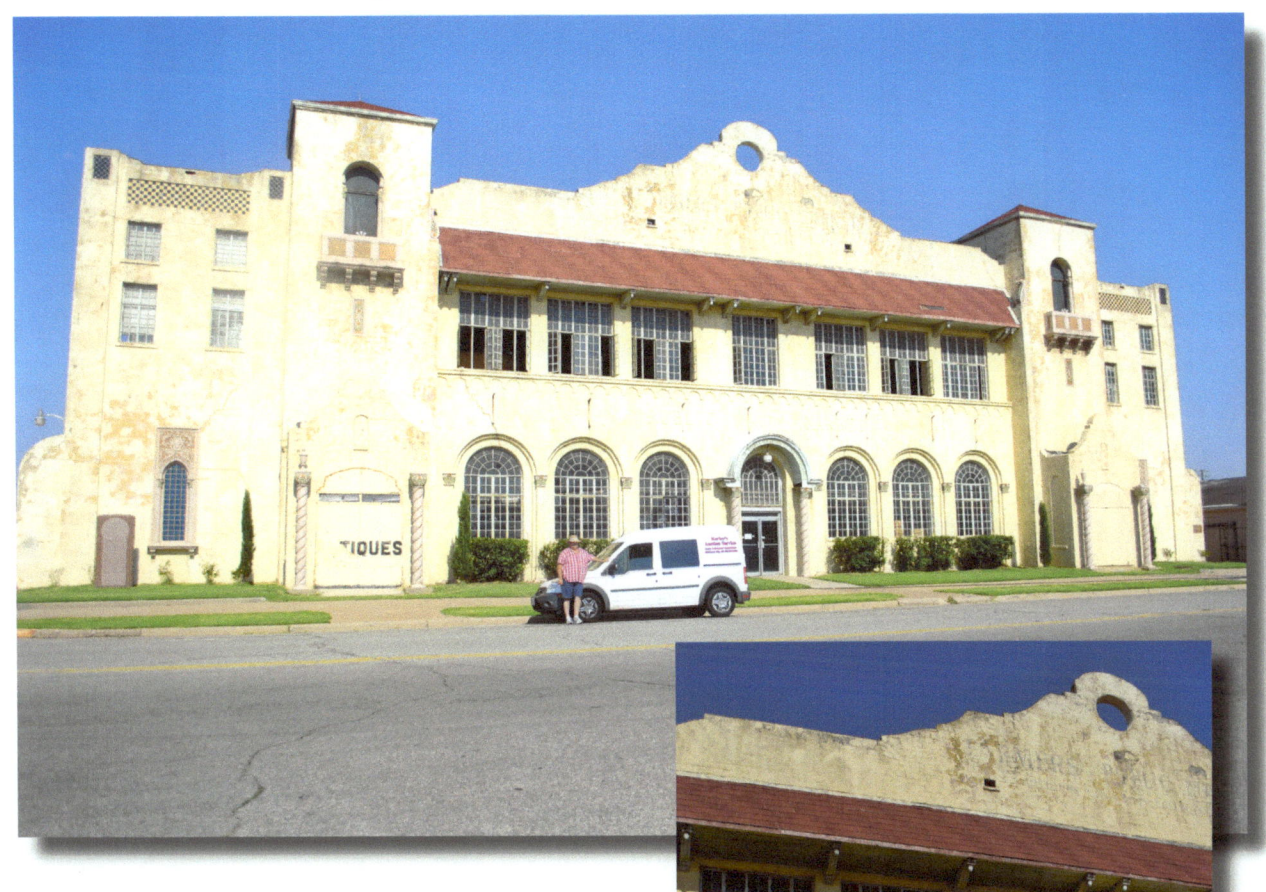

Mr. Pillip Kerley of Kerley's Antiques is just one fortunate vendor lucky enough to head to work at this vintage landmark of agricultural significance near the axis of Oklahoma City. The Farmer's Market building now serves as part time antique mall and special events arena.

Mr. K proudly exhibits his 2010 Ford Transporter utilized in acquiring the enticing finds he purveys in his antique shop. All are bolstered to patronize.

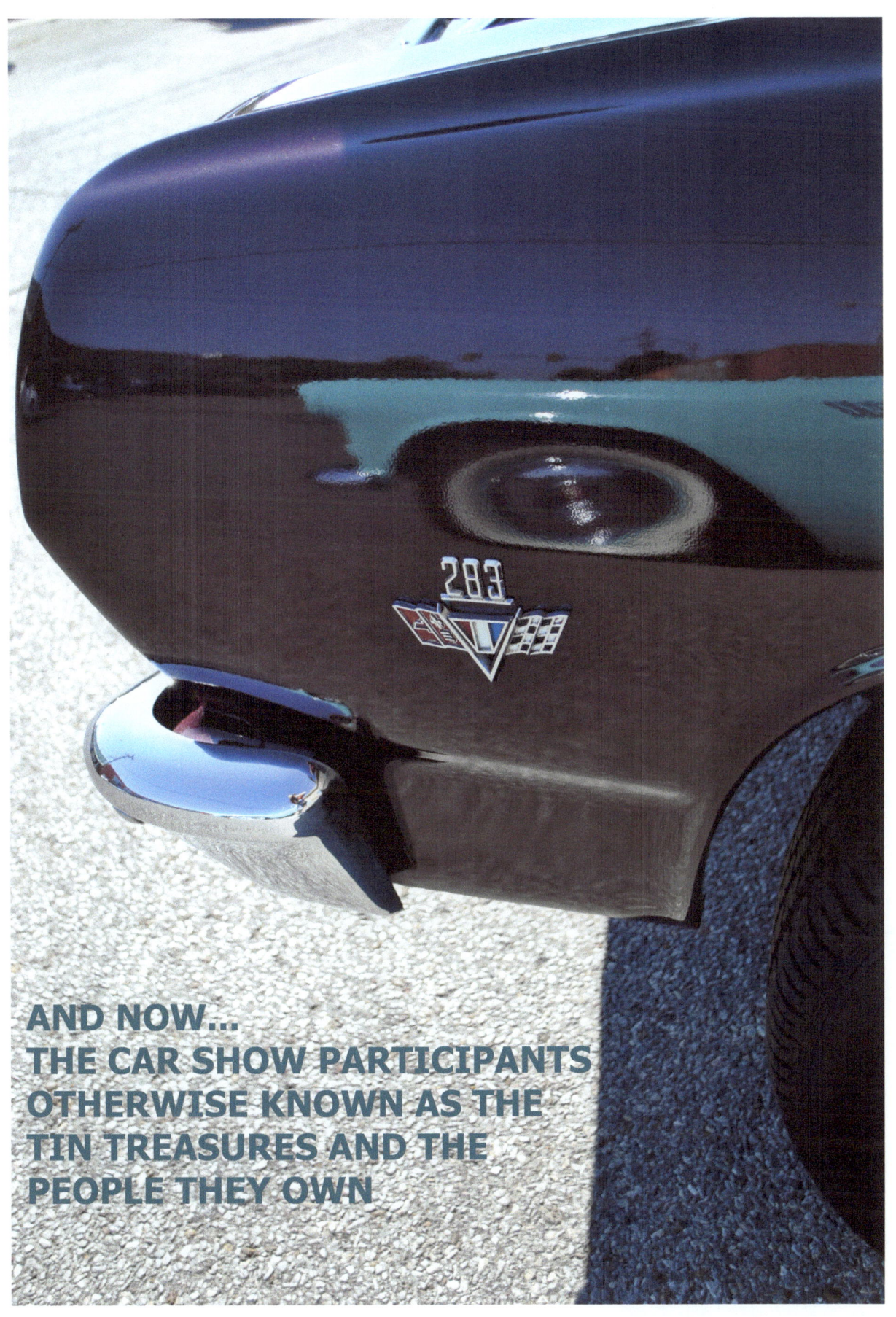

**AND NOW...
THE CAR SHOW PARTICIPANTS
OTHERWISE KNOWN AS THE
TIN TREASURES AND THE
PEOPLE THEY OWN**

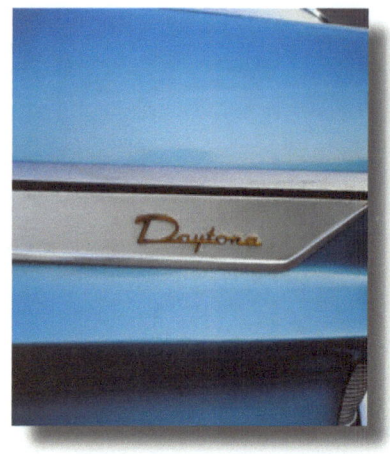

MOPAR

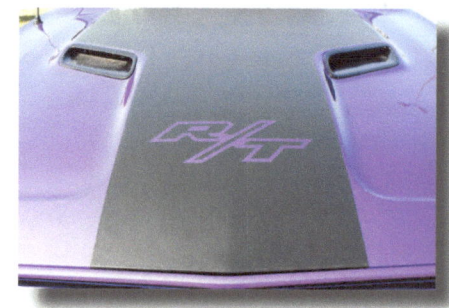

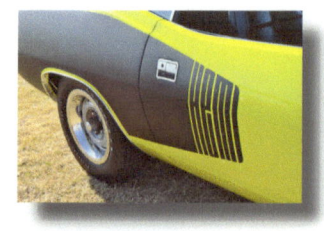

CHRYSLER
DODGE
PLYMOUTH

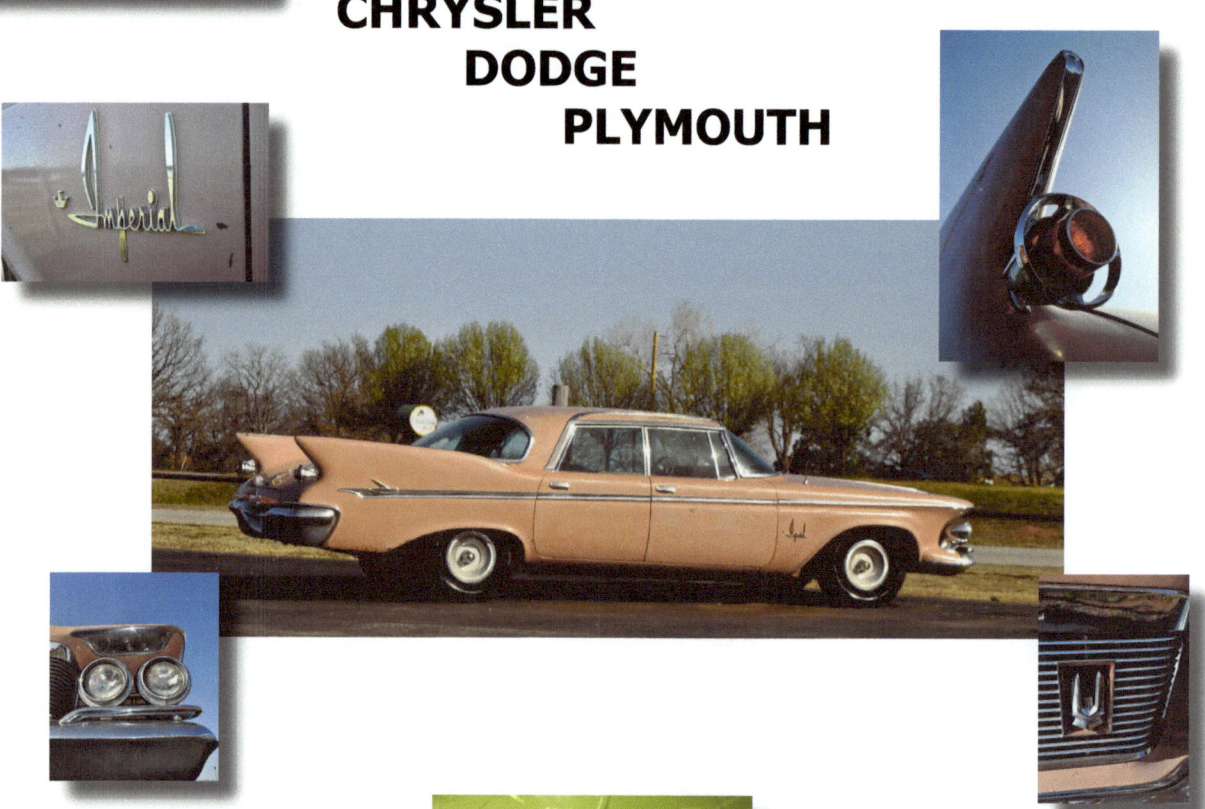

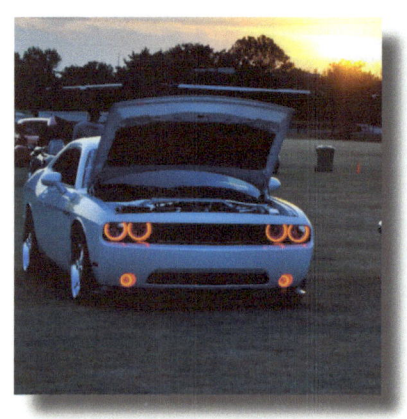

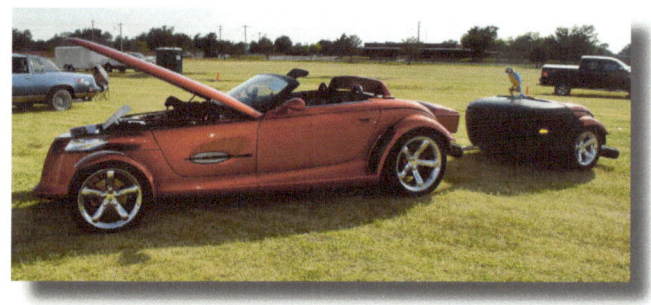

MAGNIF' MAGNUM

Darin Riddles is from a car show family, with everyone from Aunties to his wife and sons showing up either to root for his competitive Dodge Wagon affectionately called "Black Magic," or with a set of their own wheels to present.

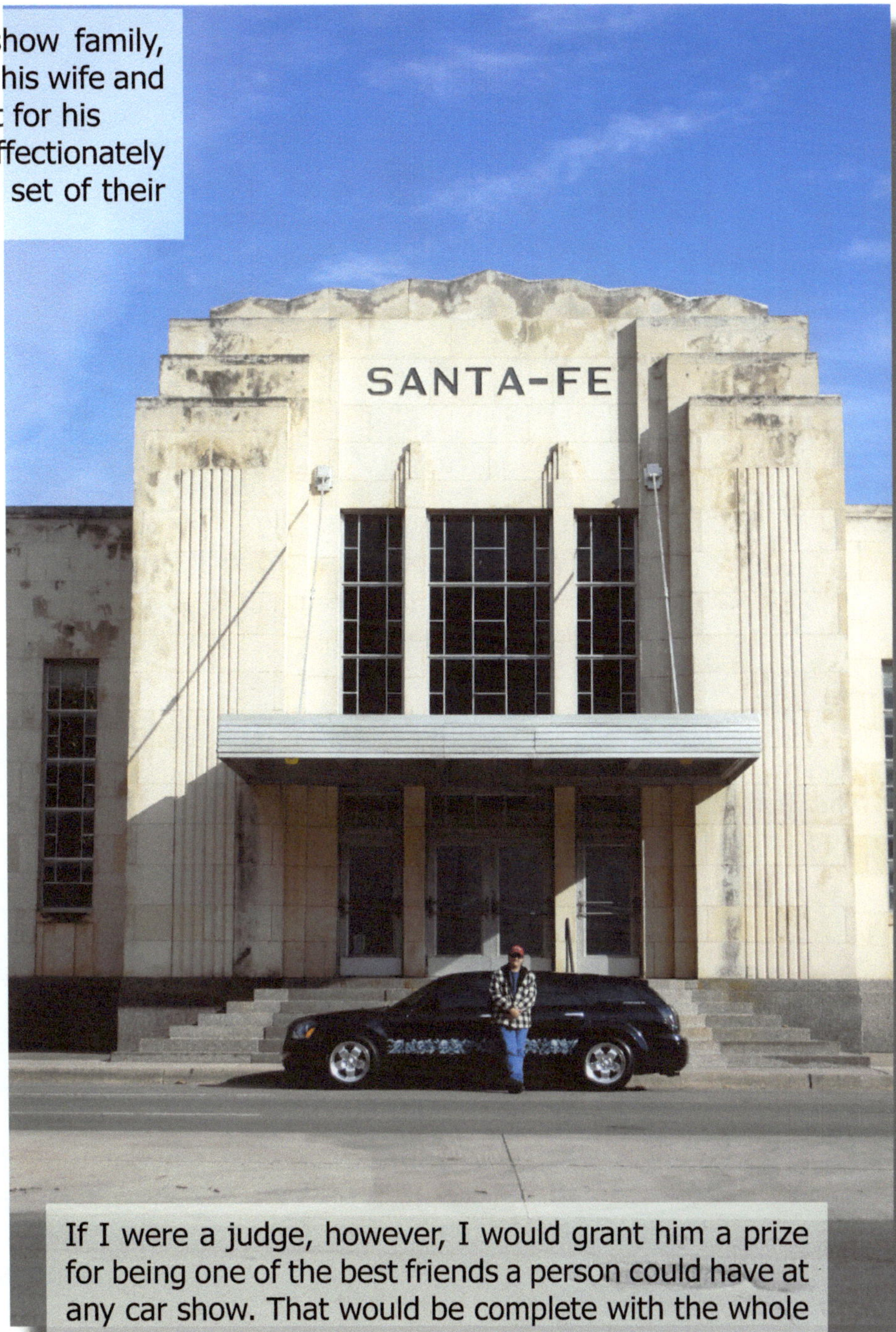

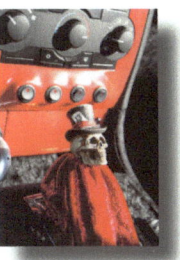

He personally painted all of the colorful extra red elements adding to the macabre effect attained on his hearse, er, I mean station wagon. His ghoulish skull wrap on the exterior definitely fits right in during those Halloween shows, but it's the A/V unit's offerings on the interior that garners the most second glances. He has snagged quite a miscellany of "In Car Entertainment" type trophies to award him for efforts in that department.

SANTA-FE

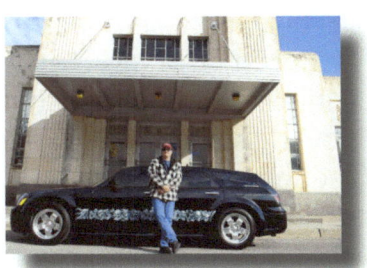

If I were a judge, however, I would grant him a prize for being one of the best friends a person could have at any car show. That would be complete with the whole Hollywood experience...Sworded statuette fellow, and red carpet included. Thanks for always taking the time to share a laugh. Take a bow, Darin, and thank the Academy before the credits start to roll.

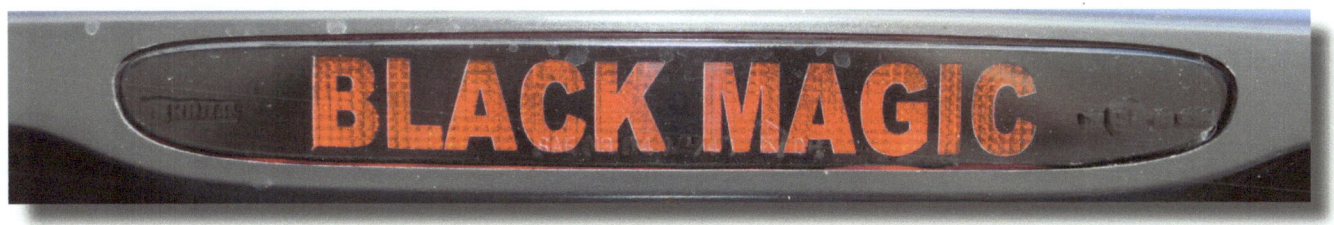

'73 CUDA' DUDE

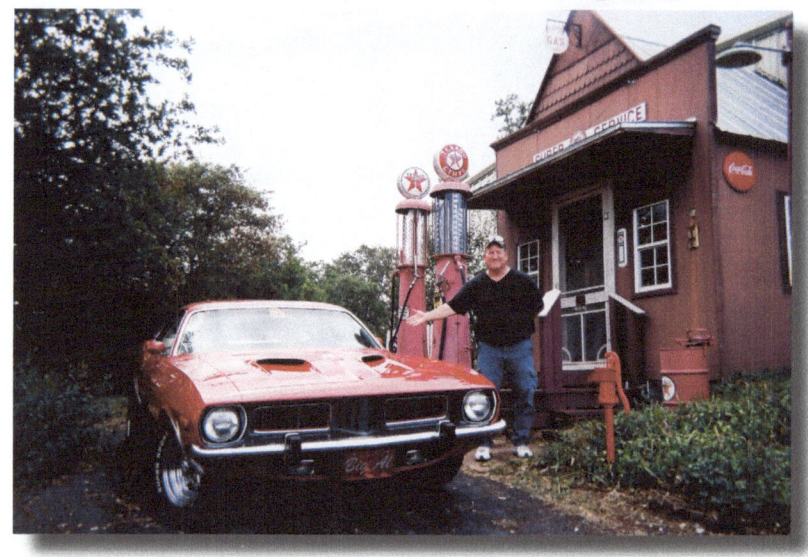

Mr. Alan Ginn, better known as "Big Al" in our local car show band, makes his famous "Vanna" impersonation, while checking out a museum facade complete with faux gas pumps along Rt. 66.

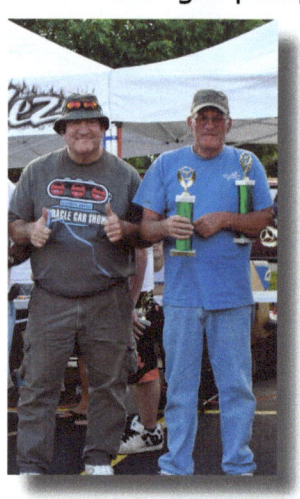

Thumbs up with buddy Ron Langley

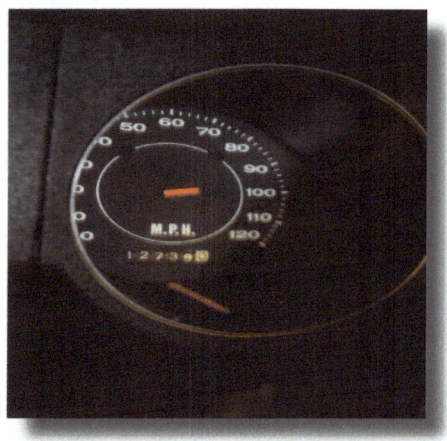

"Big Al" ordered his '73 Plymouth Baracuda while still in the service during the Vietnam conflict. It was waiting for him when he got back from serving our country and they have been inseparable ever since.

Al pointed this fun shot out at a recent car show. It was held at the Grady County Fairgrounds main building. I guess he was racing so fast from the city to get an inside spot (unlike most of us stuck outside in the overflow parking), that he broke his speedometer. I know his Cuda' could beat any of us off the line, so ya never know how fast he was going.

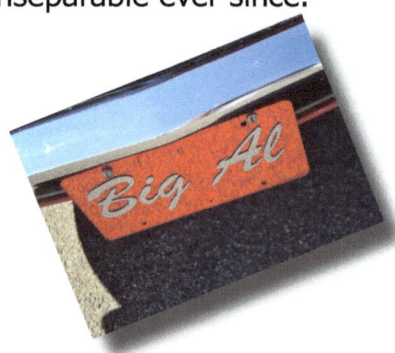

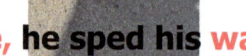

I know one thing for sure, he sped his way into all of our hearts.

RAM HERITAGE

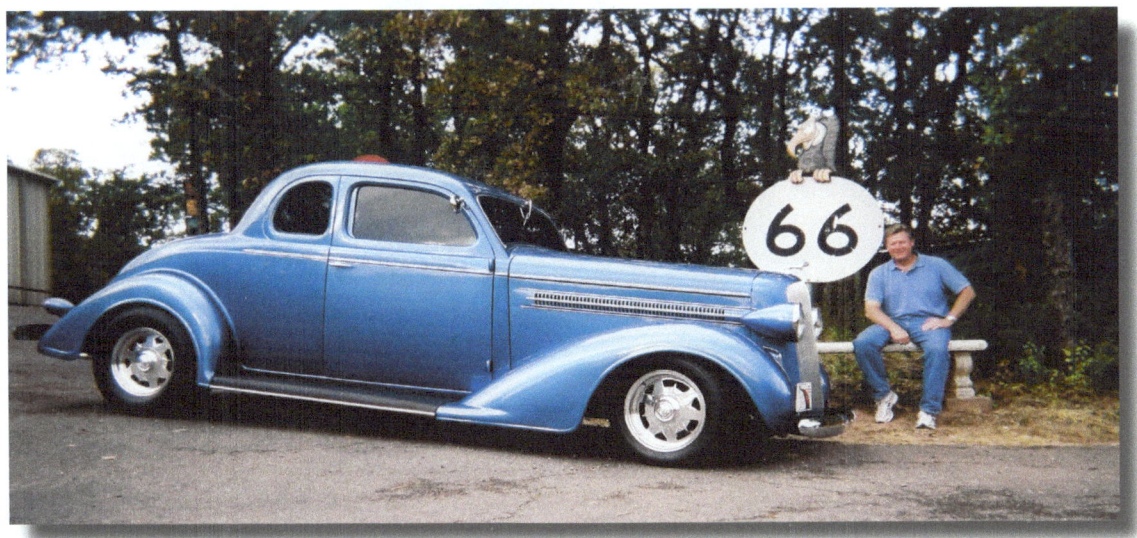

Mr. Jeff Beighle enjoys a rest stop along his journey in quite apropos fashion with his award-winning equally retro blue 1948 Dodge.

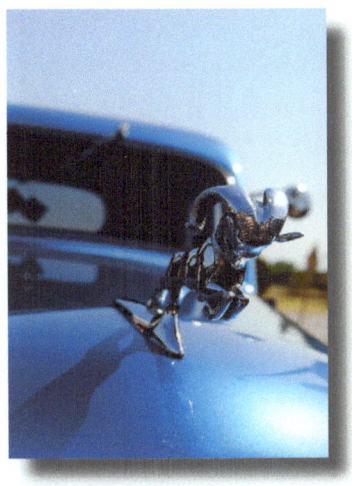

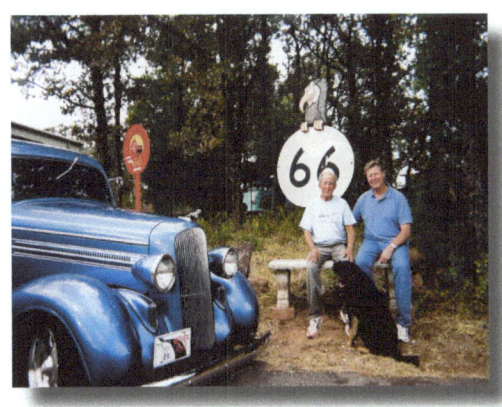

His spot of respite housing this good ole' recognizable street sign is within the gates of a passionately amateur-run Rt. 66 Museum in Arcadia, Oklahoma. The gate keeper, John Hargrove, has quite the assortment of Volkswagens, and other car parts decorating his hallowed installation's walls, not to mention a miniature scale version of another famous tourist waypost on Route 66, the Blue Whale.

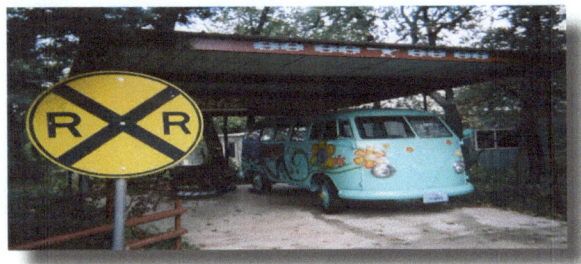

Thanks for the camaraderie over the years at the car shows, Jeff. To John, we ate up the grand tour of the place. Thank you both for sharing your afternoon.

ONE CITY OF OIL RATHER THAN SEVEN OF GOLD,

IS ENOUGH FOR THIS EXPLORER

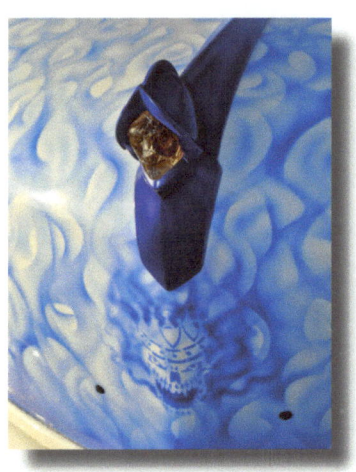

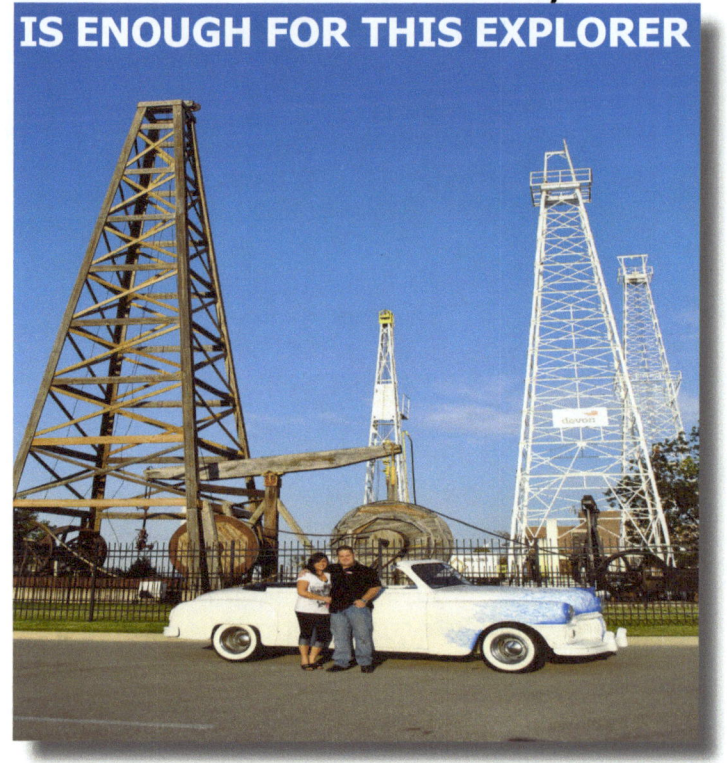

Garrow Herbert embraces the two loves of his life: wife Kaylynne Gilmore, and of course their pampered offspring of the vehicular variety, a luminous 1950 Desoto.

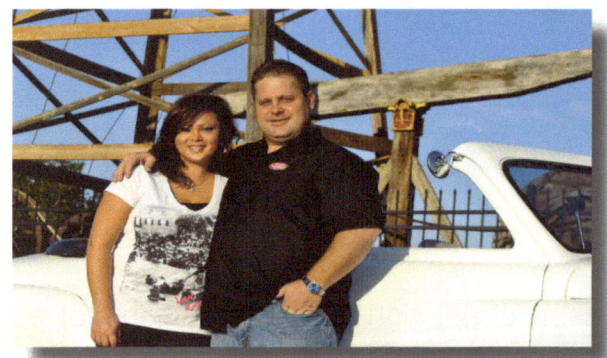

It goes without saying that this impeccably clean flamed stunner is a popular addition at many festive automobile events, including car shows, cruise-ins, etc. We were even behind them in a parade route.

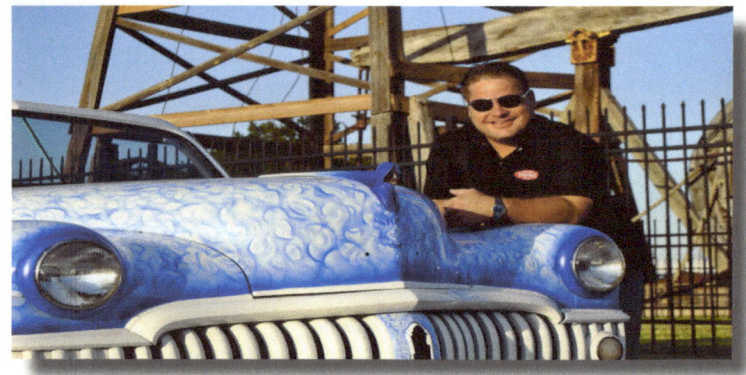

Yes, their car definitely gets all the oohs and ahhhs appropriately due it, but my hurrahs go to their winning personalities & friendliness through the years. My relatives have always said, You must do your best... You can do great things, and be sure to do it all with a smile in your heart. Congrats on pulling that off with your gorgeous car and amenable demeanor.

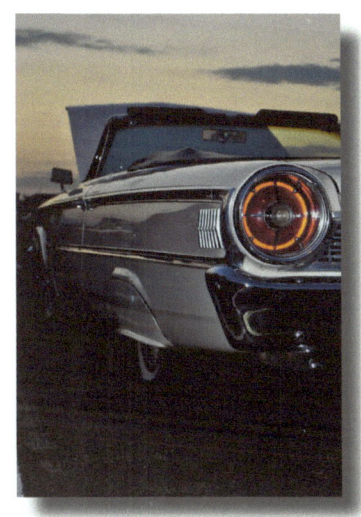

FORD

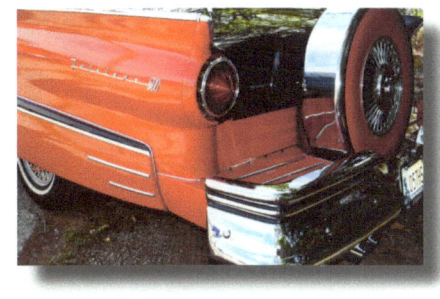

LINCOLN

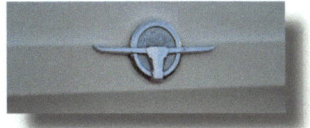

MERCURY

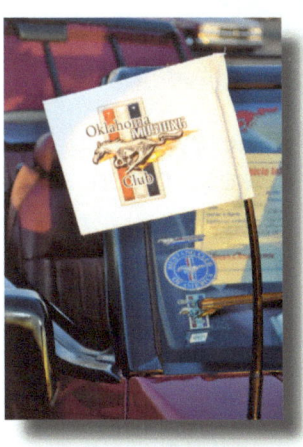

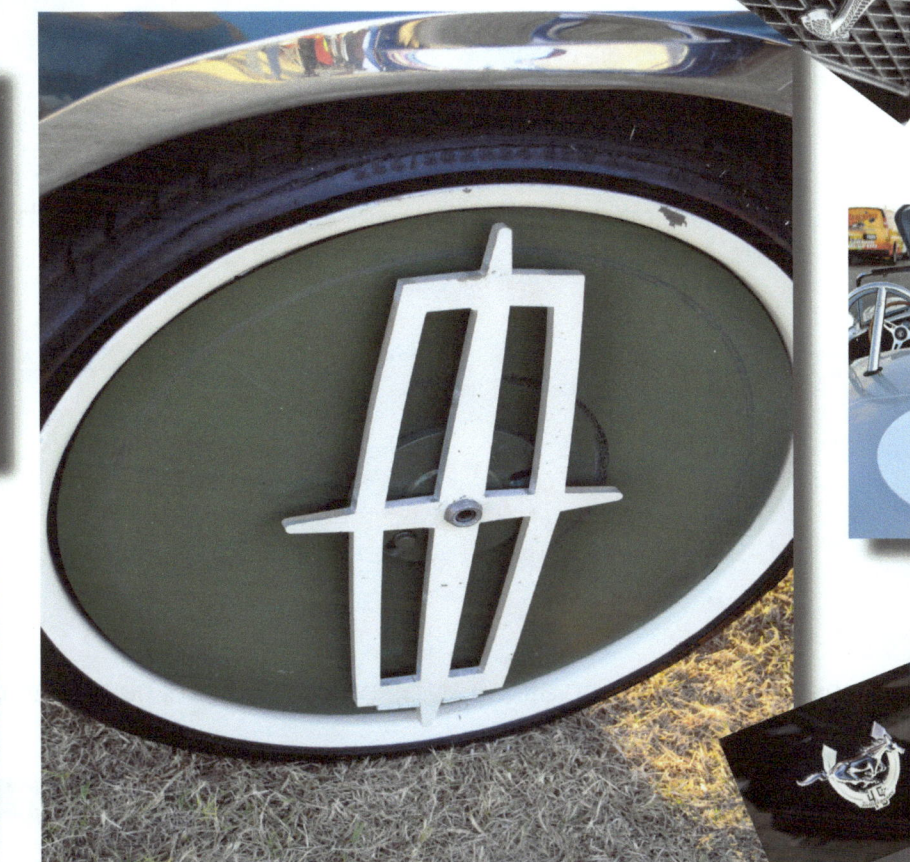

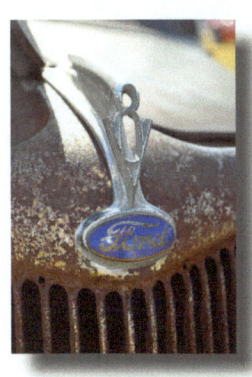

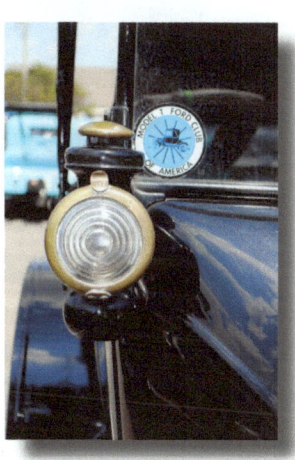

13

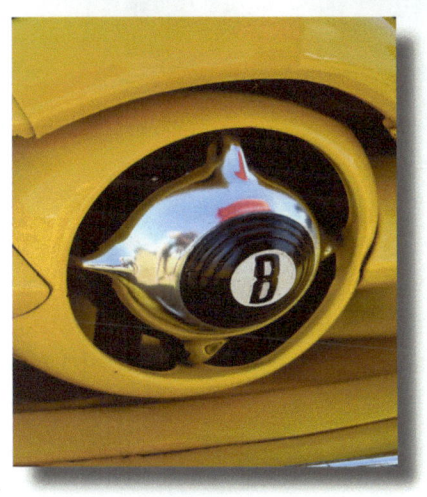

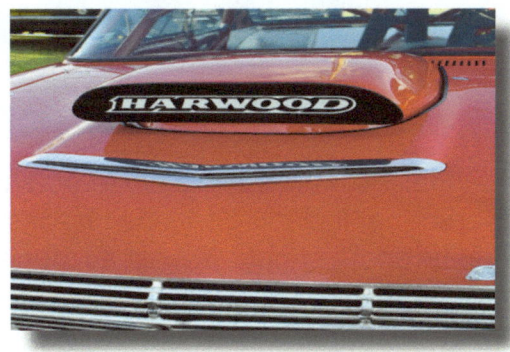

CRAZY 'BOUT THAT MERC'

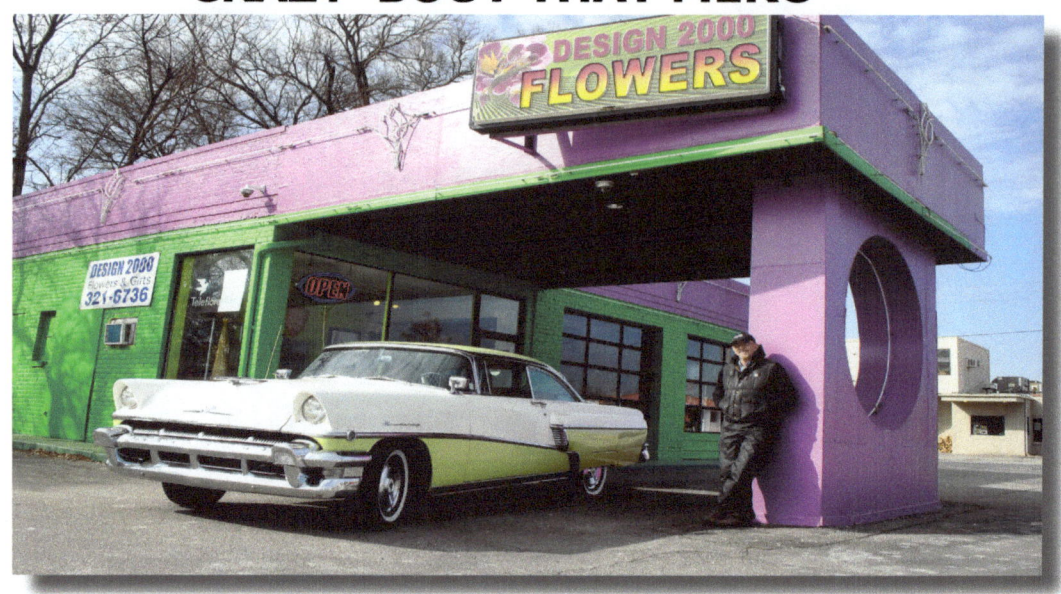

Under the remnants of an authentic repair carport is the '56 Mercury Monterey owned by famed theatrical scene shop professor Michael Fain. In stunning chartruese green and almost original status, he keeps it in pristine well-running shape.

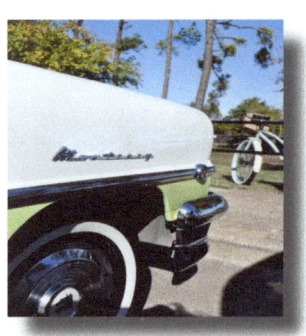
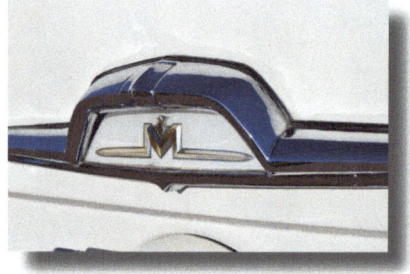
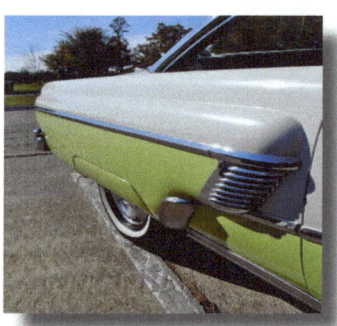

It is as aesthetically pleasing as the stage production sets he helped oversee for years across the nation.

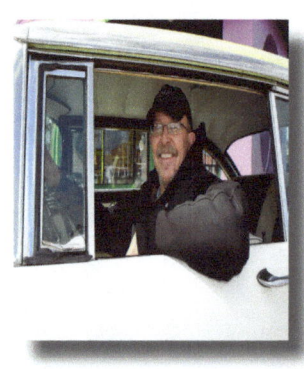
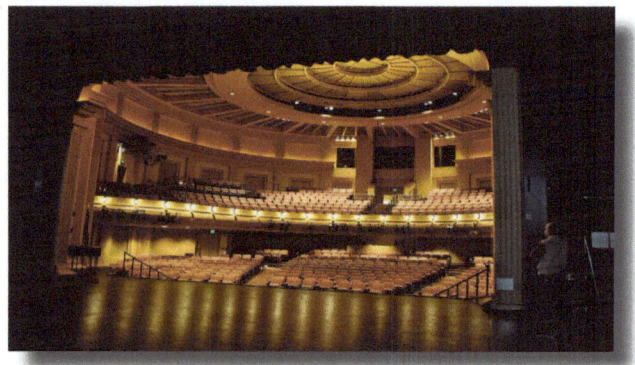

I am honored to say I was under Mr. Fain's wing while at The College of Santa Fe, in New Mexico. Thanks again for everything, including the life lessons way back when, as well as this time outside of class during your photo shoot. You're a trouper to have braved the briskness of the coldest close ups I have ever shot. So glad we got it done, because as we used to say in your backstage... "Done is beautiful."

COLONEL'S COUPE

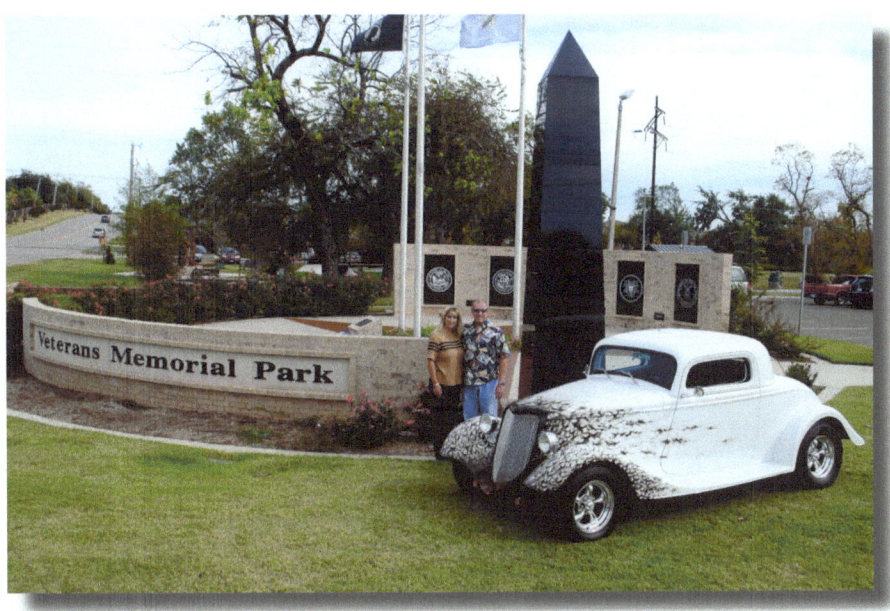

Adorning the Veteran's Memorial in the small Whistle-Stop of Moore, Oklahoma, are Mike and Helen Dill. They are ably chaperoned by their smoke-flamed '34 Ford, which coincidently was creatively embellished by the gent named Mik of this publication's "Artist" chapter. Great job to all on this frame-up restoration.

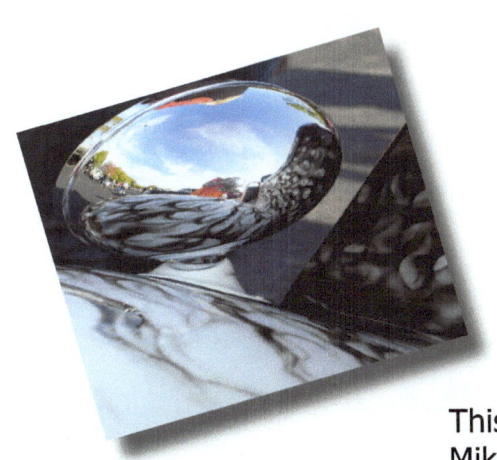

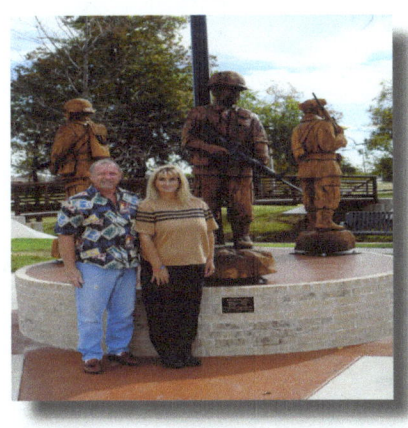

This location is near and dear to the Dill's heart with Mike having made it to the rank of Colonel while in the Army branch of the military for our great country.

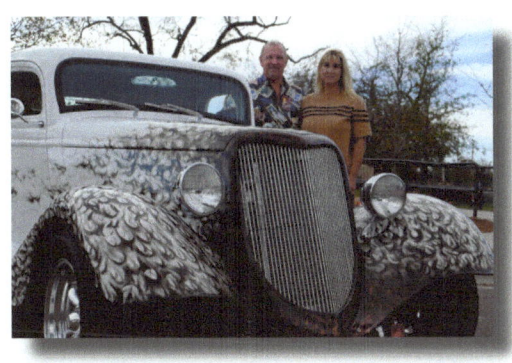

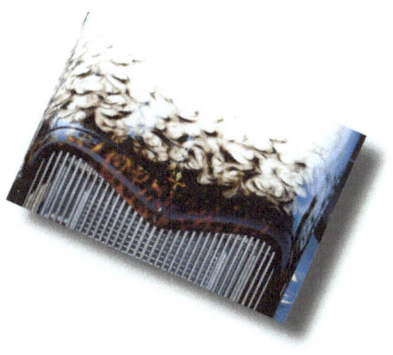

Thanks Colonel, and all of your brood for your loyal service and support.

THUNDERING WAR BIRDS

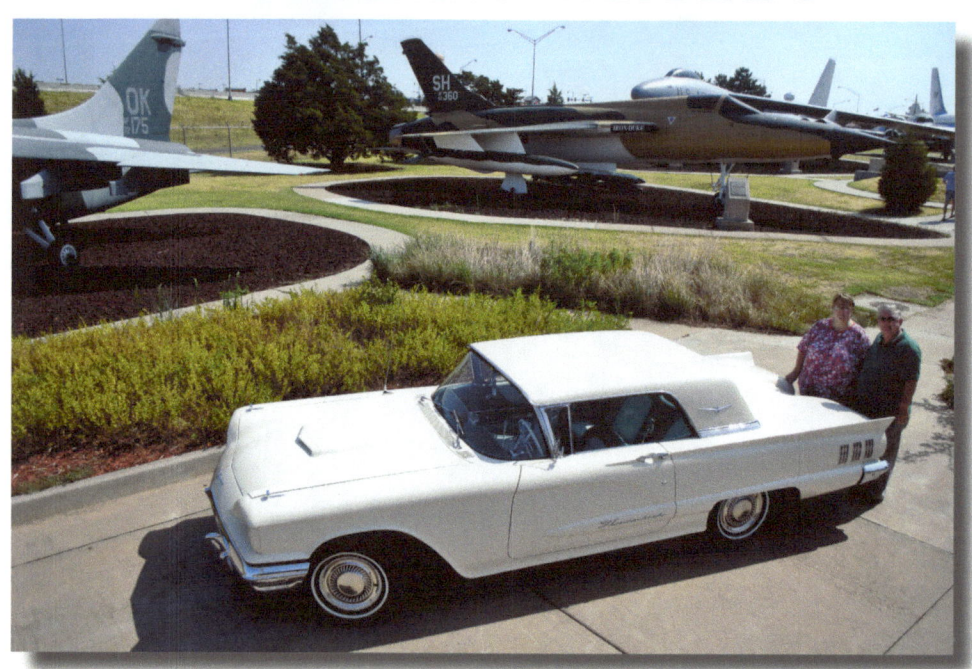

At one with the other birds of a feather on the grounds of Oklahoma's largest Airforce Base, the Adams Family, another venerated Veteran Stephen P. and bride Maggie, stand beside each other in all ways, and in literal terms next to their impeccably clean ally dubbed "Trigger." As seen in the sunlit dash décor, said title is an obvious nod to Steve's best-loved childhood cowboy hero.

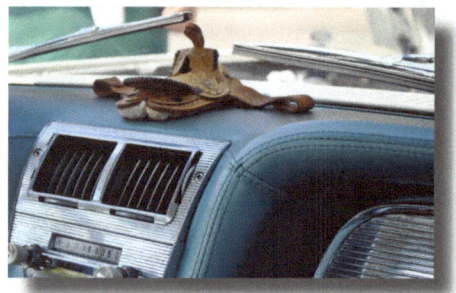
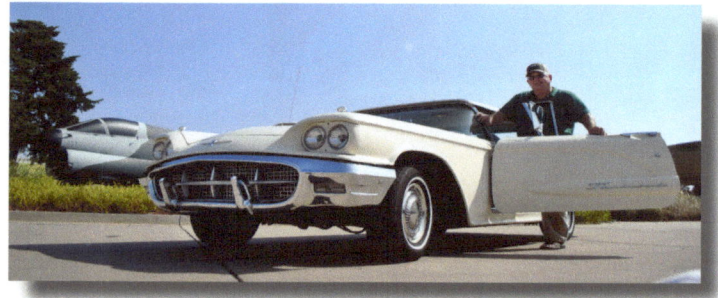

Upon hearing that this 1960 winged creature was on the market, they plunked some savings on "Trigger," who gets gleefully ridden daily without fail. With a 352 Police interceptor engine, I am sure this T-Bird has quite a buck.

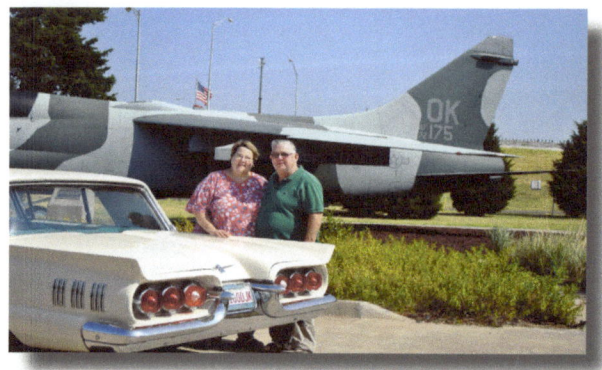

Great way to grab life by the "reins," you two, and thanks for all of the encouraging words while I composed this book.

THE LIGHT OF HIS LIFE...

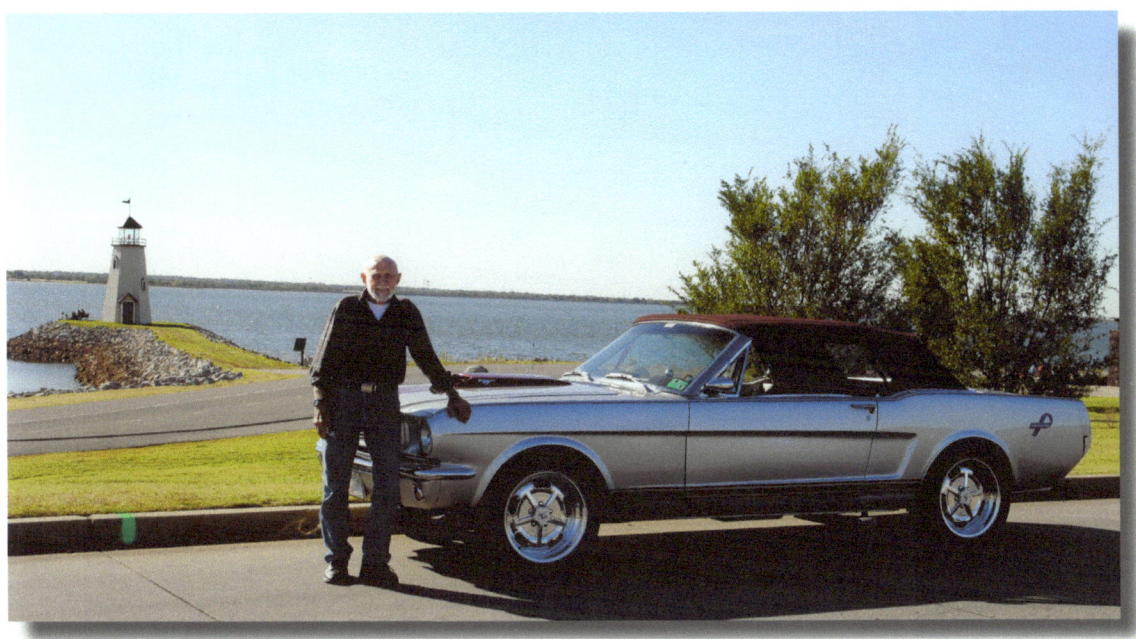

"Luke" Lucas sheds some "light" on his subject in front of the mini lighthouse on Oklahoma City's largest body of water, Lake Hefner.

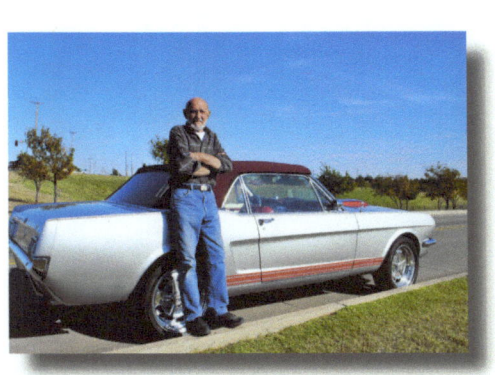

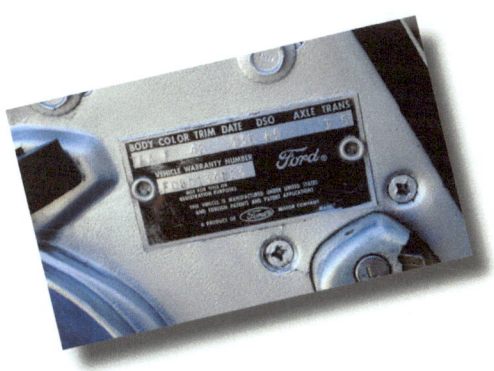

His sweet pony is the first of its breed a 1964 and ½ Ford Mustang. Being a member of the local Stang club he is seen at many a car show, and is a hit every time. He never misses the opportunity to attend the grandiose affair in Kingfisher, Oklahoma dedicated to all things Mustang.

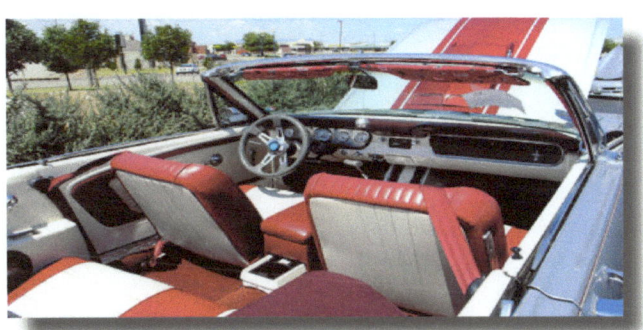

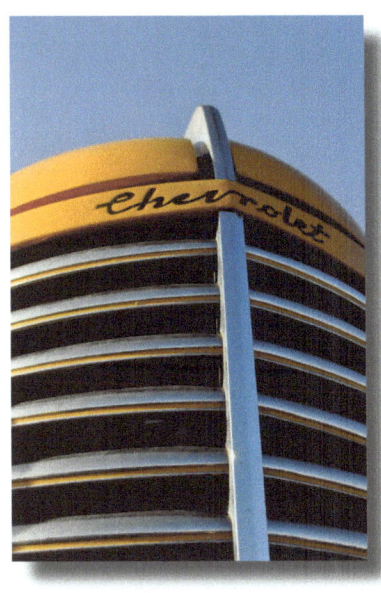
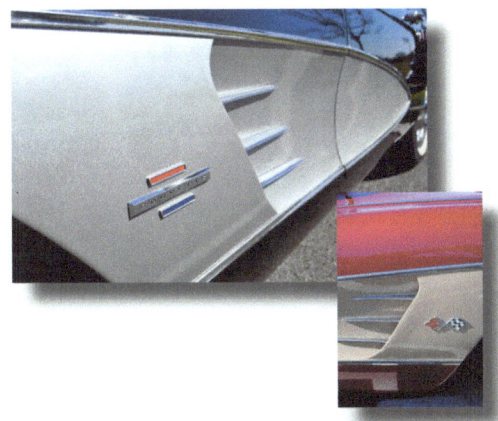
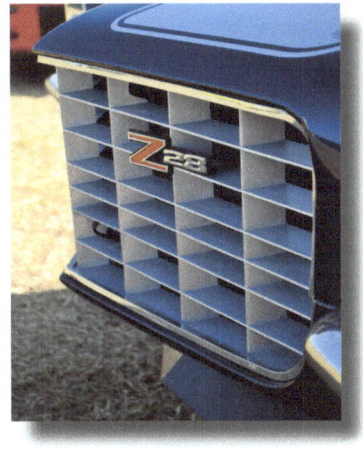
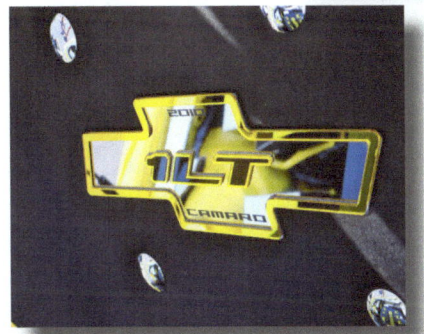
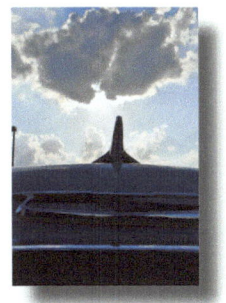

GENERAL MOTORS

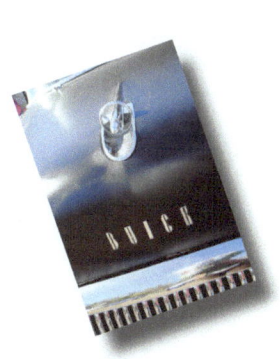
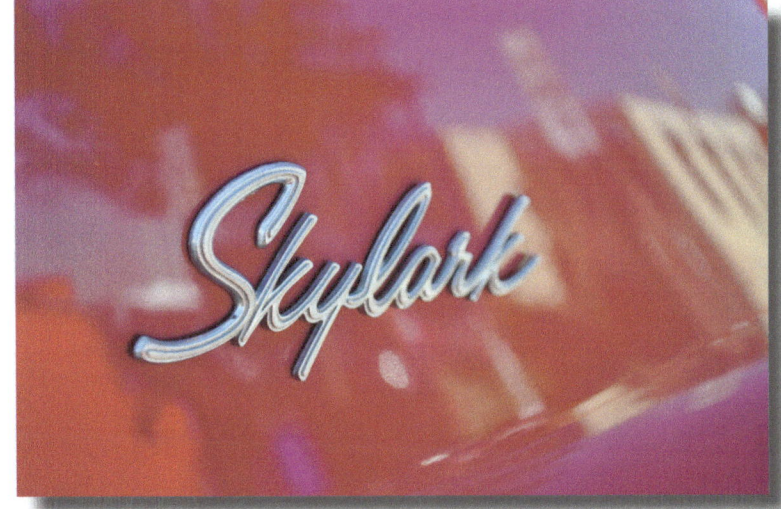
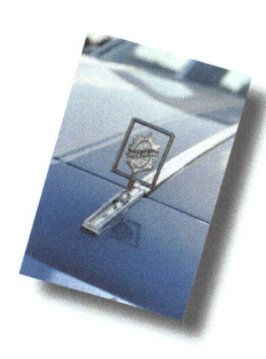
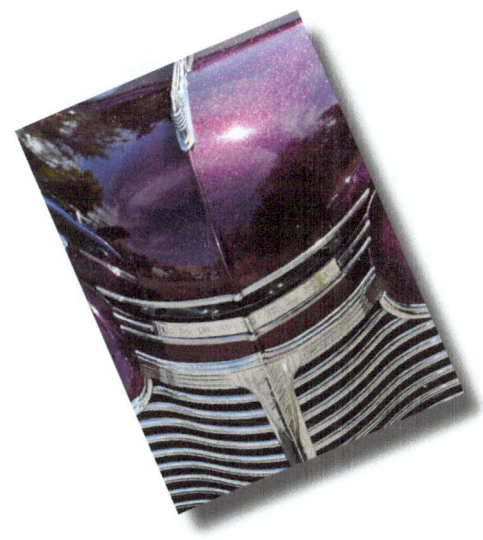
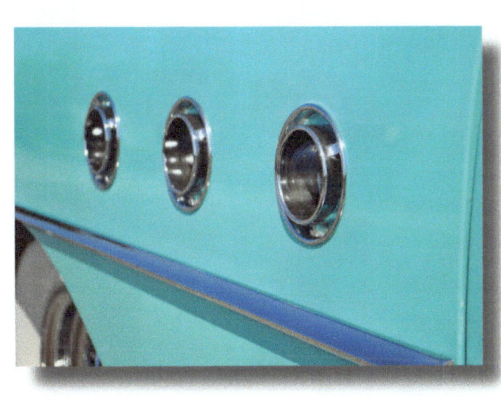
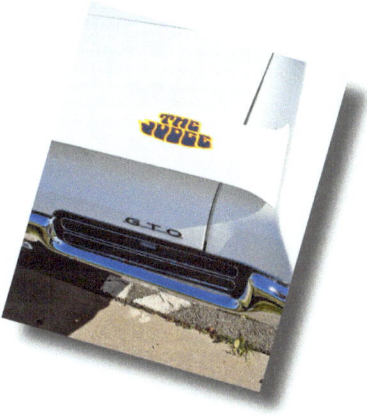

A BEL AIR CONDUCTOR

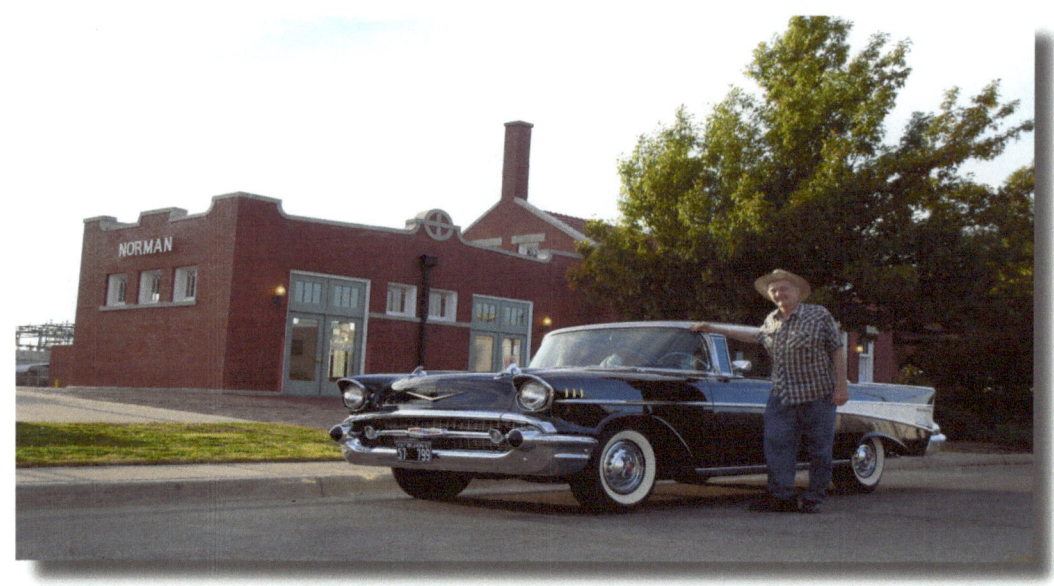

Mr. Vern Clavin may not be this train station's engineer, but he certainly knows his way around iconic American legends like the '57 Chevy.

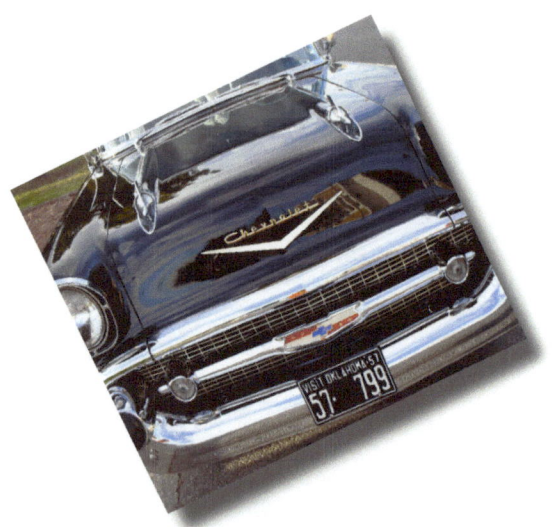

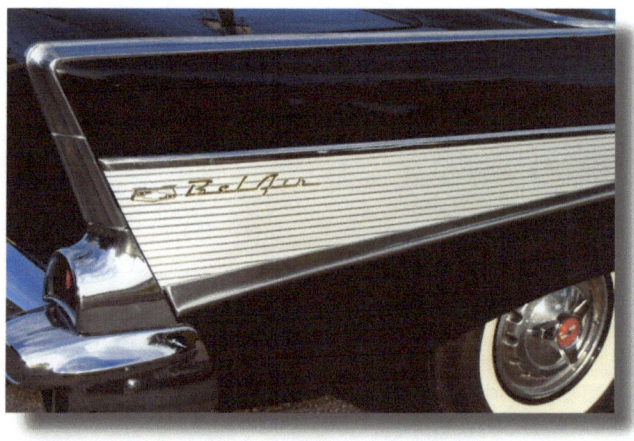

Much like the industrious souls who stoically paved their way West during the advent and explosion of the train revolution, Vern, too, has the unbridled spirit to stay on track. Even during times of infirmity, we would see his gingerly trailered beauty, and that brave smile, belaying any hint of trouble, at car shows near and wide.

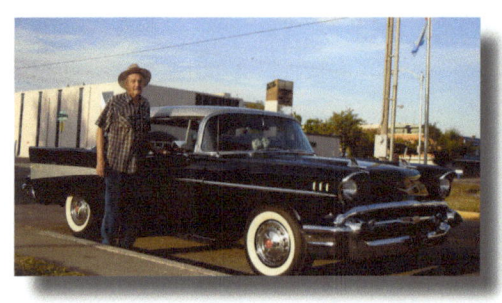

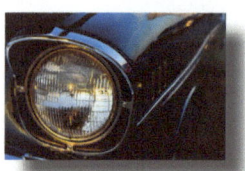

God bless your perseverance in overcoming obstacles. Glad to see you every chance given.

OH HENRYS'

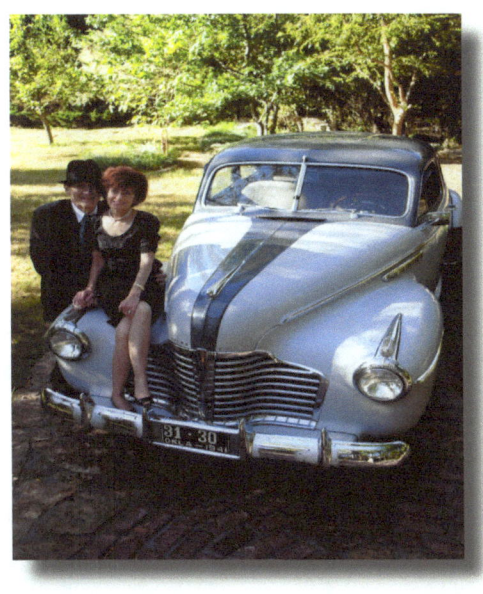

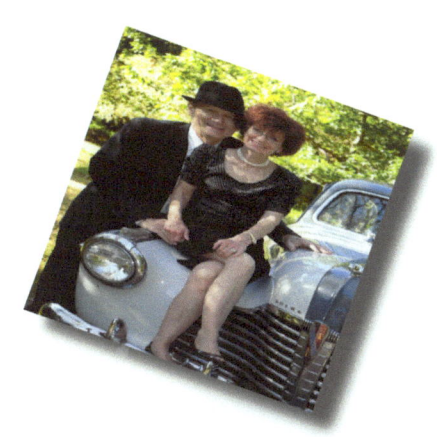

Lyle Henry and wife Eileen Walsh-Henry happily played period dress-up for me with their 1941 Buick. Just a short while ago, things weren't so peachy for Eileen who suffered with debilitating migraines. Hubby Lyle discovered a natural defense solution to help cure his wife, and they continue to help countless others with the fruits of their research and developmental efforts.

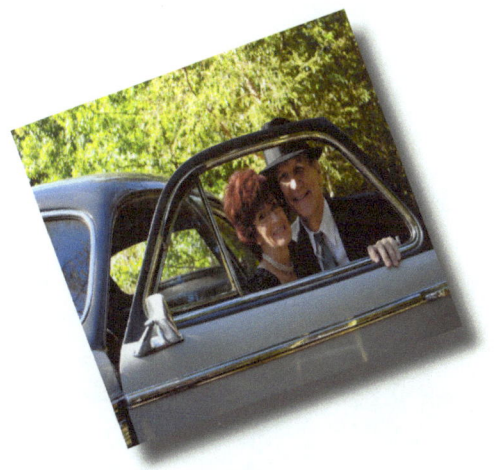

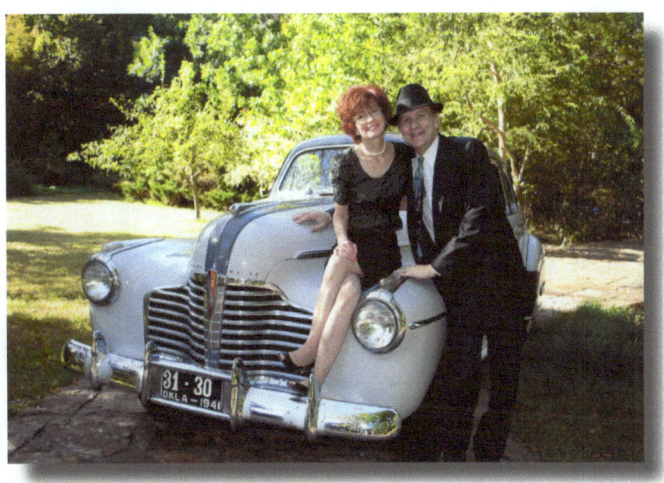

They make a great picture of health and prosperity, portraying that role with real chutzpah as the loving power couple they are, even when the cameras aren't rolling.

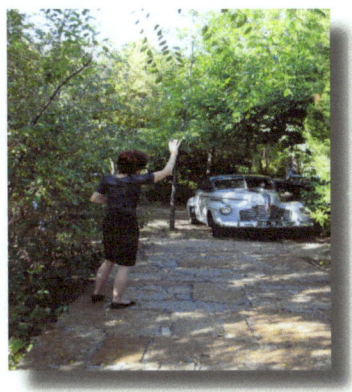

Thanks for sharing your heartfelt story, and posturing so handsomely in my book. Your avante garde looks, and ongoing work, enrich us all.

THE GIFT THAT KEEPS GIVING

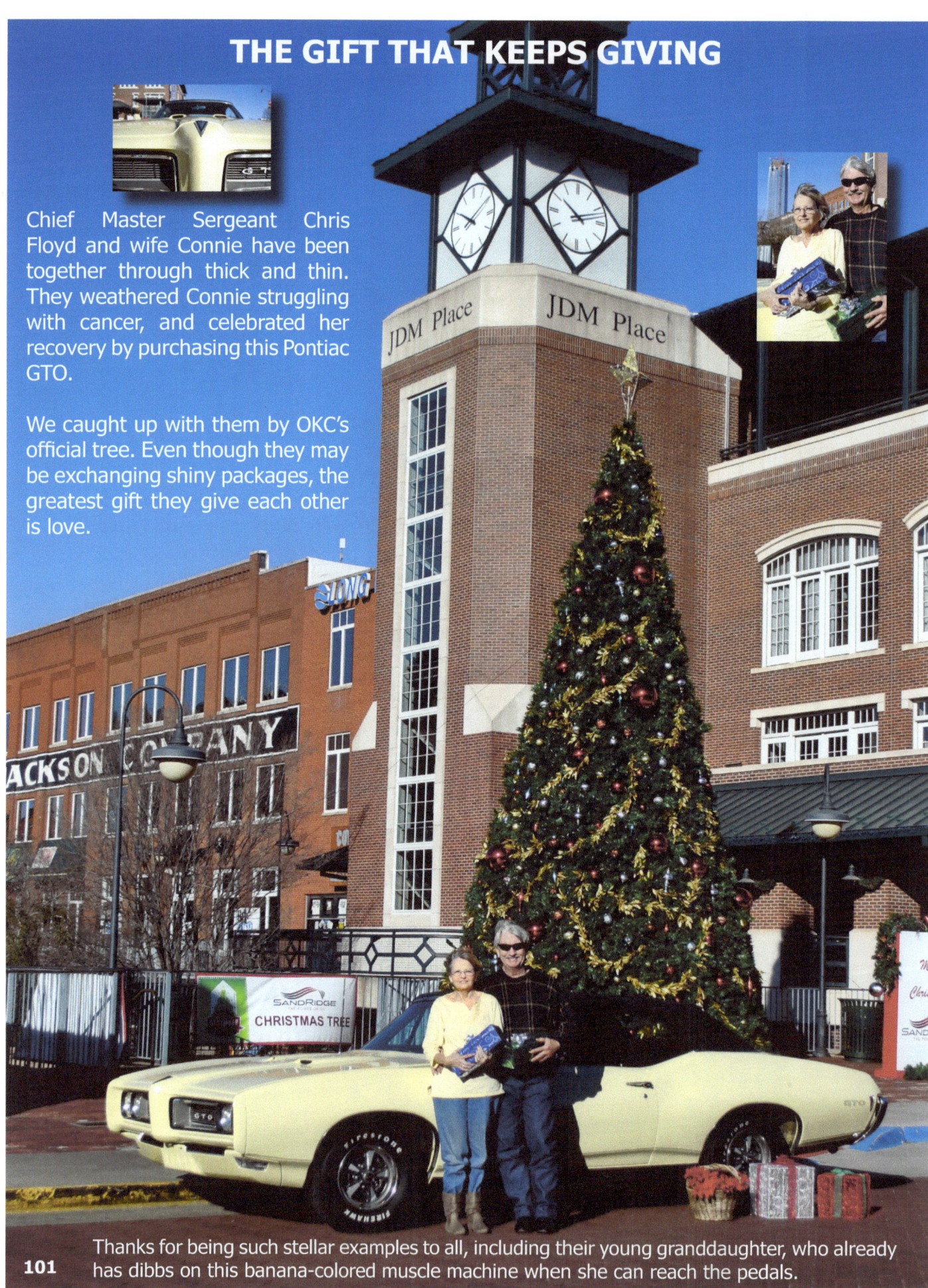

Chief Master Sergeant Chris Floyd and wife Connie have been together through thick and thin. They weathered Connie struggling with cancer, and celebrated her recovery by purchasing this Pontiac GTO.

We caught up with them by OKC's official tree. Even though they may be exchanging shiny packages, the greatest gift they give each other is love.

Thanks for being such stellar examples to all, including their young granddaughter, who already has dibbs on this banana-colored muscle machine when she can reach the pedals.

THE SKY'S THE LIMIT

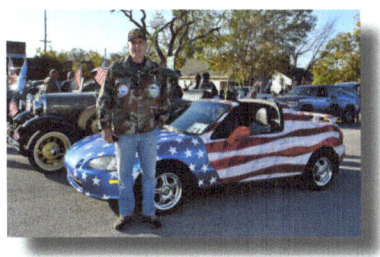

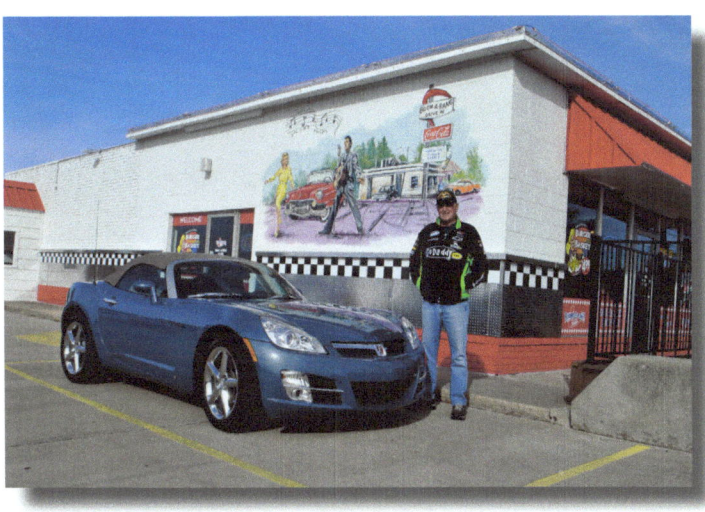

U. S. Vietnam Veteran Donald Garner reveres his country as is inducated by the highly coveted paint job he ordered on his white two door Honda observed here at a Veteran's Day parade.

The convertible he chooses to cruise around in on a day to day basis, though, is this cool blue G.M. Sky from the able designers over in the Delaware Saturn camp. We were invited by Mr. Garner to this '50's breakfast honky-tonk during his car organization's weekly coffee rendezvous.

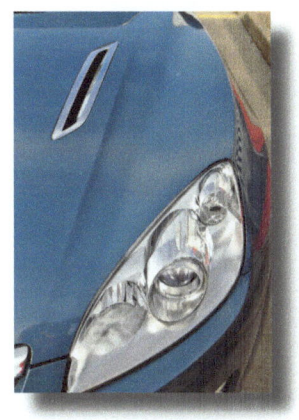

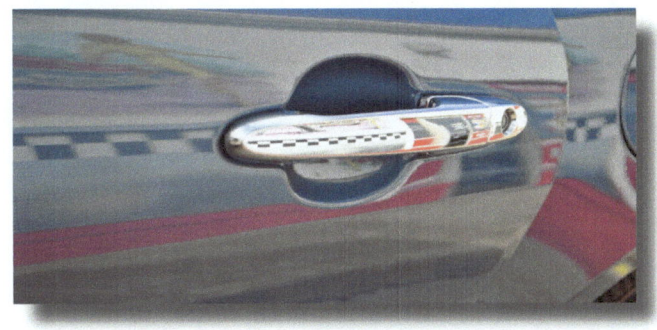

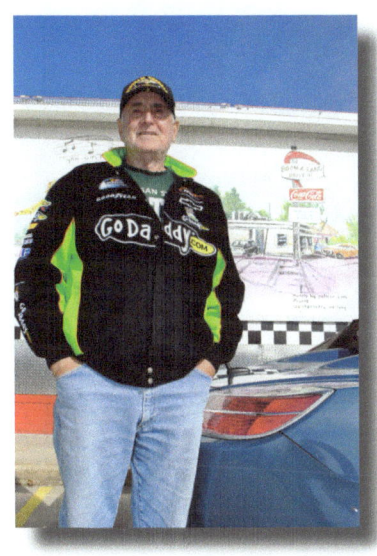

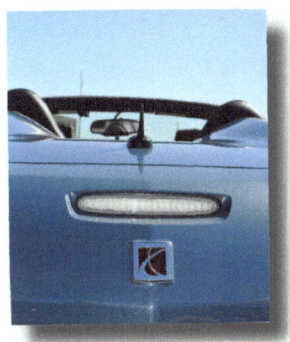

Thanks to all, including Don, for serving our country and still supporting American companies whenever possible.

GALACTIC ADMIRERS

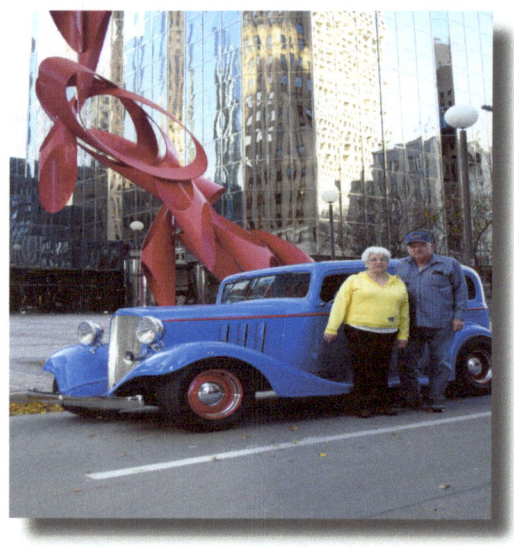

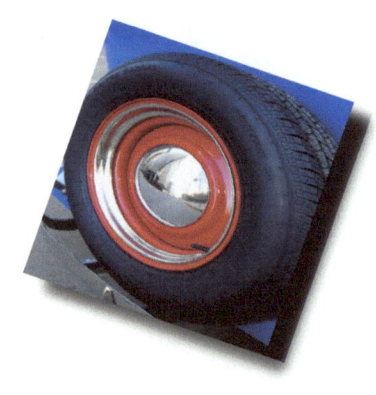

"Leading" the way at Leadership Square, in their matching '34 Chevy, are my long time neighbors Fay and Charlie Creech. The Oklahoma City intersection's sculpture these luminaries gaze upon is titled "Galaxy."

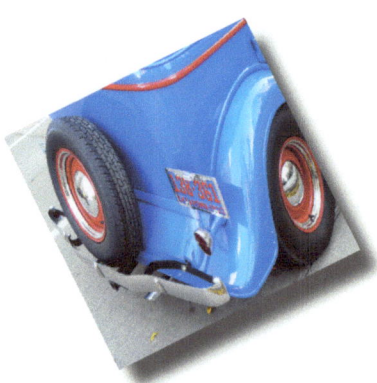

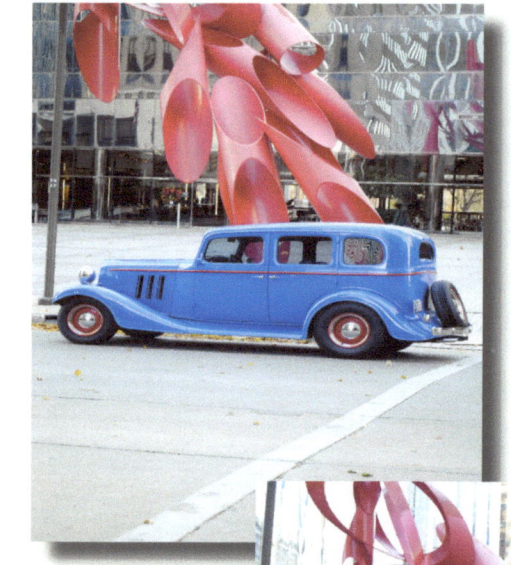

They have primarily Ford-fostered even older restorations through the years. Glad they chose to baby a blue Chevy this go around. It worked out perfectly for the shot.

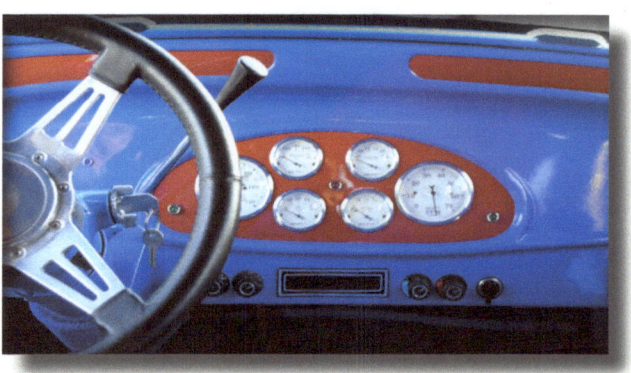

I dug our ride around downtown during this photo session. Thanks also for helping mow when we are gone. You all would be a credit to any neighborhood.

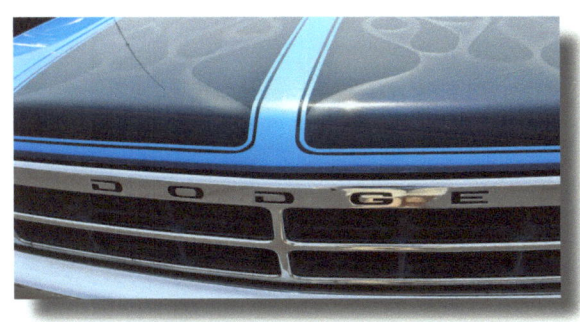

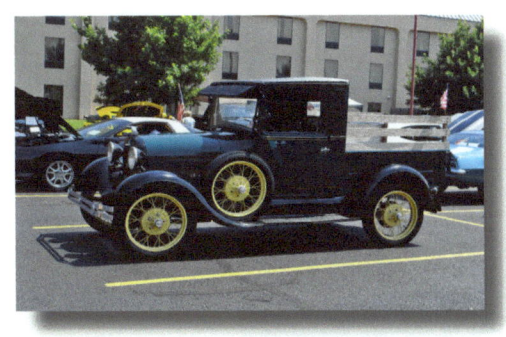

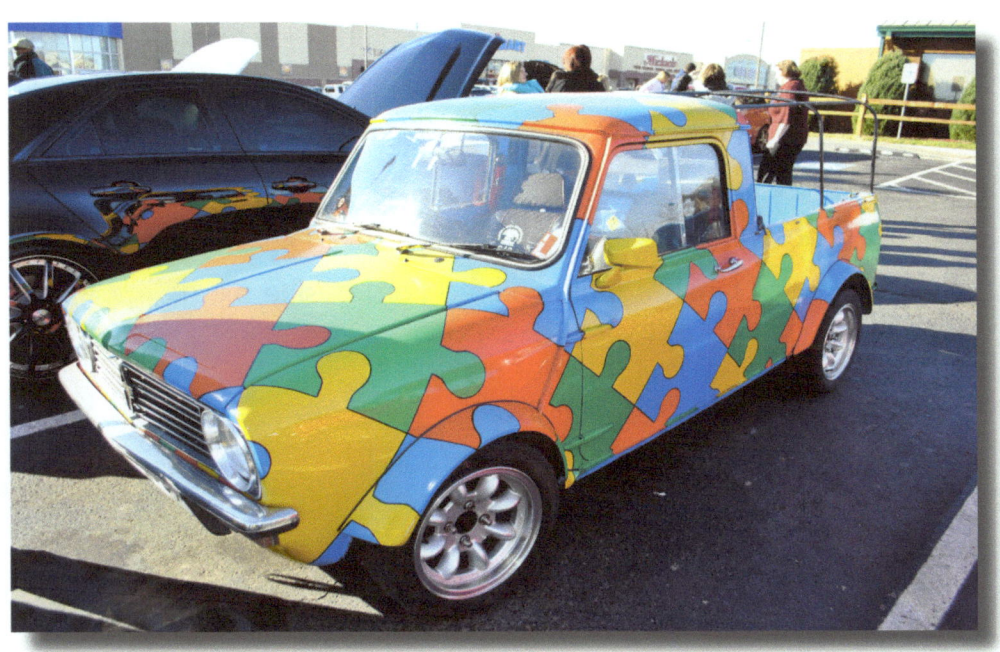

TRUCKS

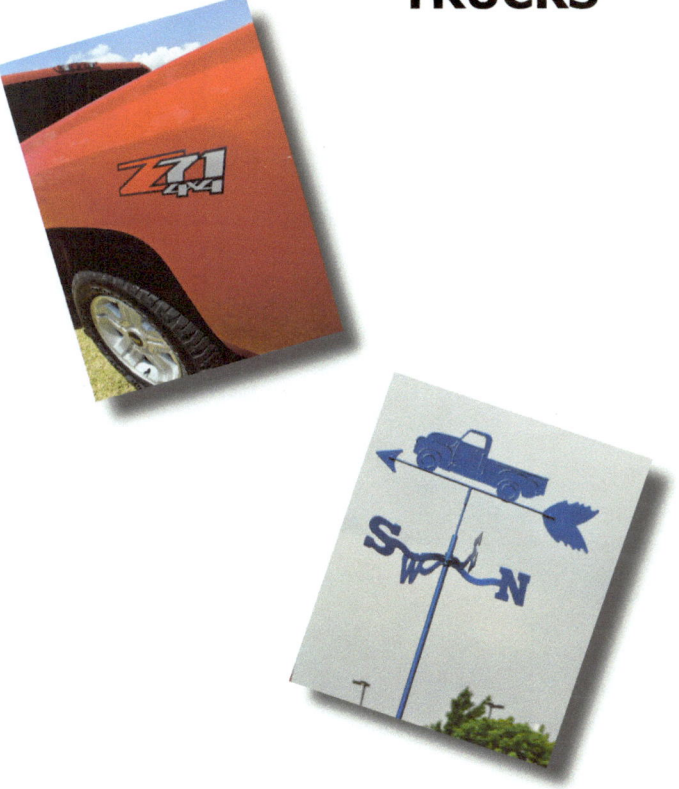

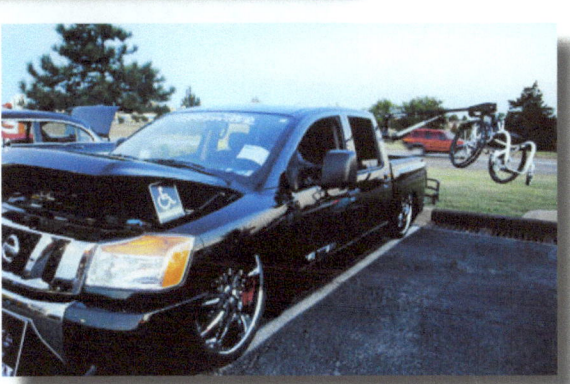

Retrofitted Nissan owned by artist Travis Tollett, the 1st Quadriplegic racer in the Pike's Peak Hill Climb

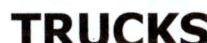

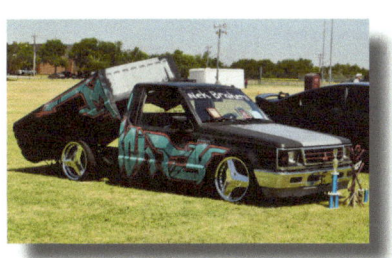

FULL SIZE CHAMELEON

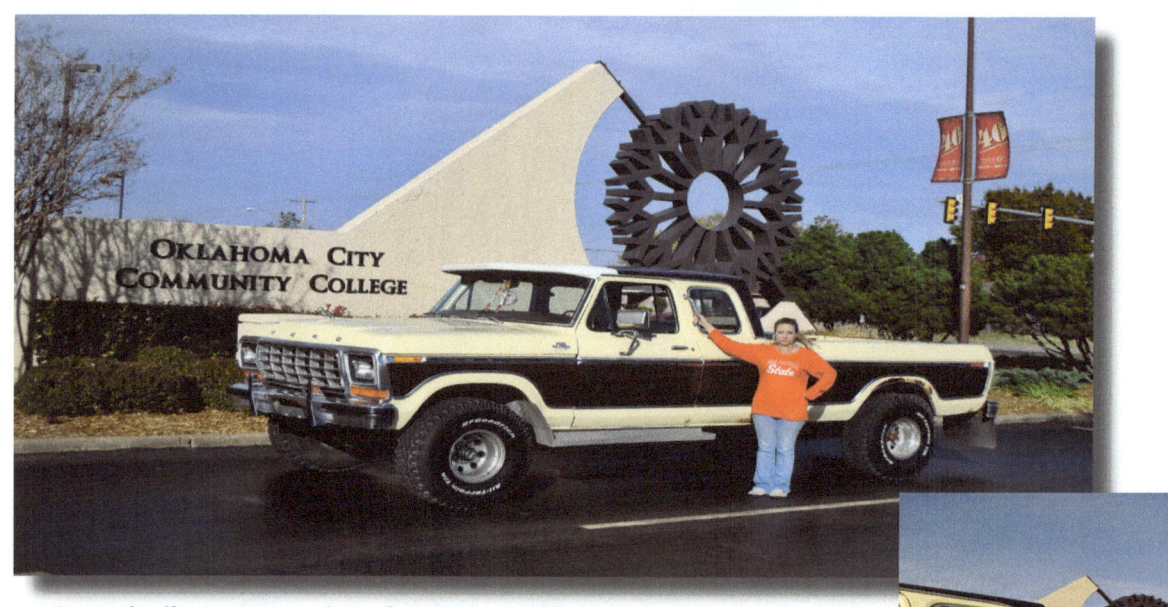

Ms. Lesa Campbell positions her family's multi-colored Ford beside a perfectly coordinating entrance to the city's ever-expanding community college. And in an additional show of support for Oklahoma's higher education system, she comfortably sports an Oklahoma State University fleece.

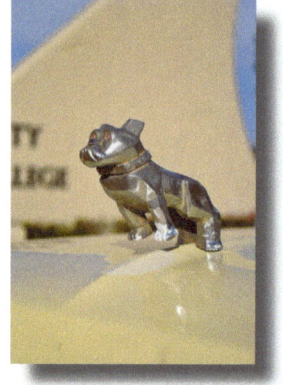

In a ode to all things colorful, this suburbanite's home, situated quite near the ivy walls of O.C.C.C., boasts a cornucopia of eye-catching objet de'art, much of which is dedicated to the automobile transit world.

That "bully" hood ornament is proof positive that they support the trucking industry which has taken care of them through the years.

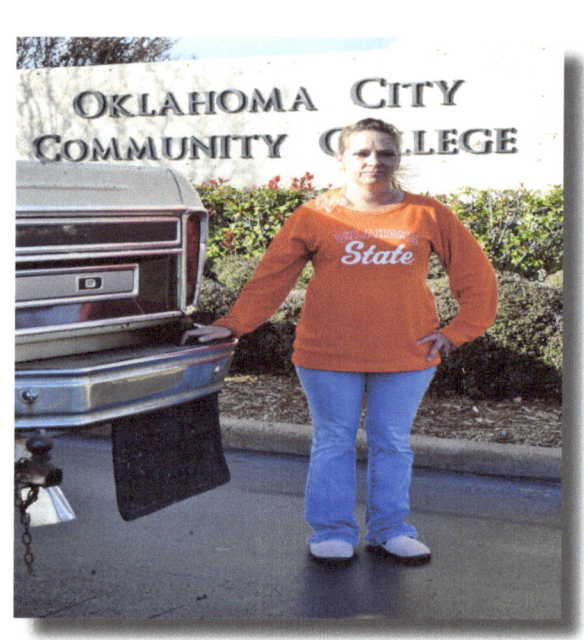

Thanks for taking the jaunt virtually across the thoroughfare from your home sweet, (and sweetly decorated) home, to the campus for these fraternally sanguine shots. Keep on trucking good buddies, and that's a 10-4 over and out.

ONE OWNER BRAGGING RIGHTS

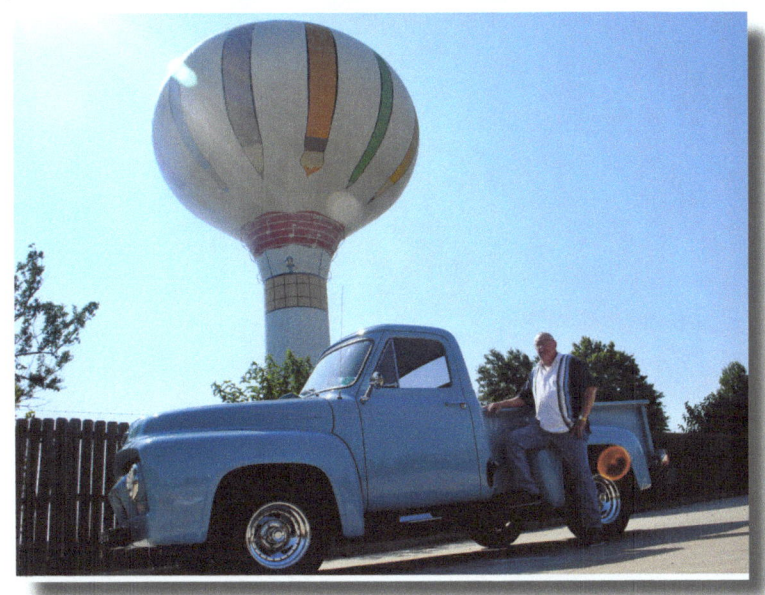

Paralleling the concept behind this South Oklahoma City's balloon-like water tower landmark, Mr. Carl Anderson's '54 blue Ford truck is all-original. The fact that his was passed down to Carl from the initial owner, his father, makes the loyal provenance all the more enduring.

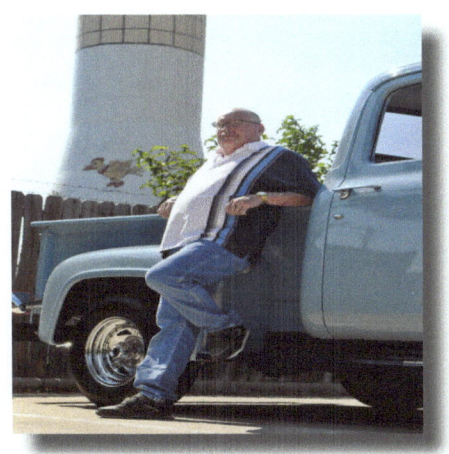

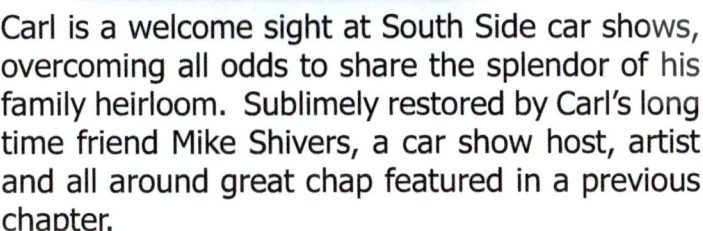

Carl is a welcome sight at South Side car shows, overcoming all odds to share the splendor of his family heirloom. Sublimely restored by Carl's long time friend Mike Shivers, a car show host, artist and all around great chap featured in a previous chapter.

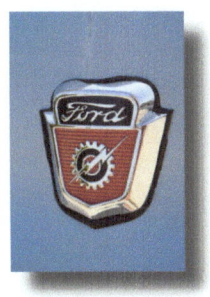

What a treat to behold firsthand the artifacts found at one's local car show. I cannot show enough gratitude to the sponsors and organizations who create such wonderlands of man-made timeless beauty & preservation. Thanks must also be sent to the participants, individuals like Carl, who brave blistering heat, freak snow storms, and, in our Oklahoma, turbulent winds to bring a smile to the faces of kids from 1-100 when we get to see and hear history found, or in the making.

ANCHORS AWEIGH

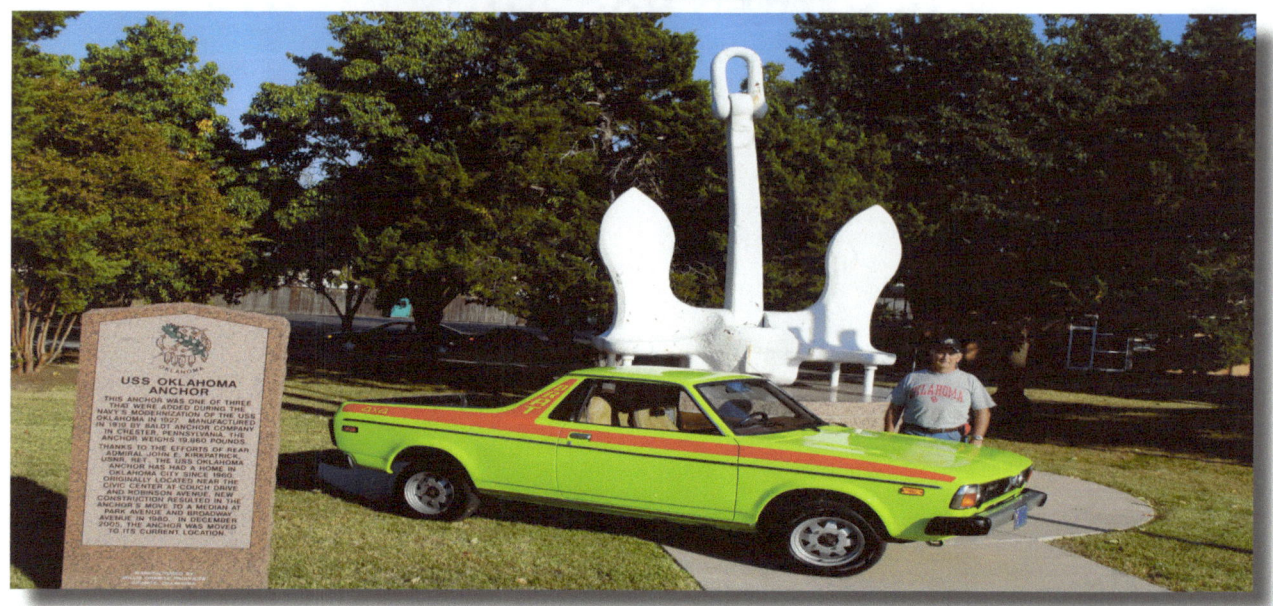

Ideal for a distinguised seaman who served our country in the Navy Seabees from '67-'68, Ray Robison and his 1980 Subaru take the star board side of a vessel's vestiges. It is the actual anchor from the U.S.S. Oklahoma, now forever top side in downtown Oklahoma City.

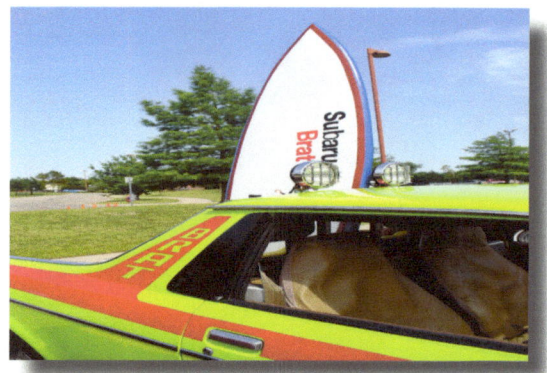

I guess, pardon the pun, that makes this actually a Naval rather than Army "Brat," boasting a 1.6 liter four speed four wheel drive. Although barn-found embedded in the terra firma under an apple tree of his wife's family's homestead, he fabricated a faux fiberglass surfboard prop used at car shows, to remind him of his other lady, the sea.

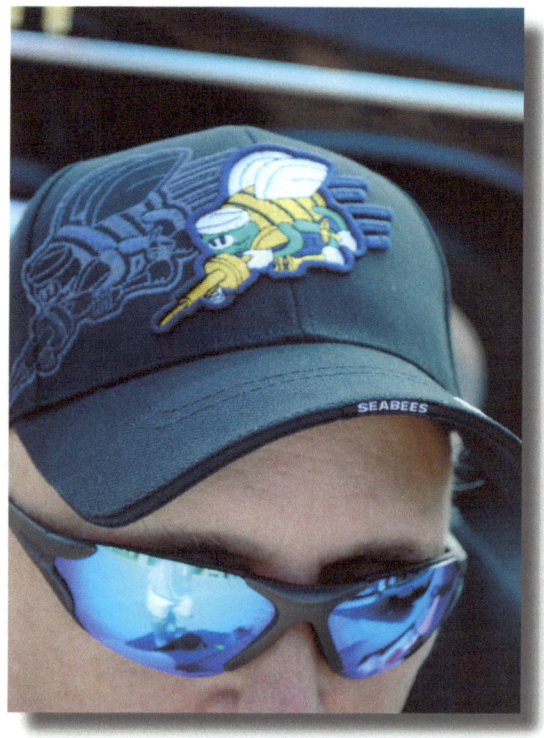

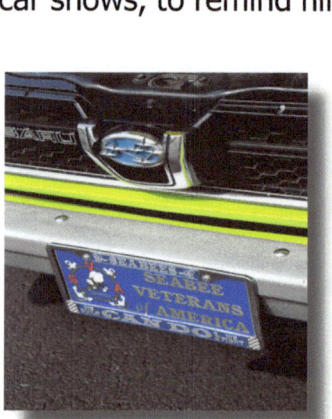

Thanks for "Bee-ing" an important and industrious part of the armed forces, and for your continued kindness back here in the contiguous 48. You were one of my first photo shoot volunteers, and I couldn't be more gratified with these early snaps of your photogenic efforts...

SCOUT'S HONOR

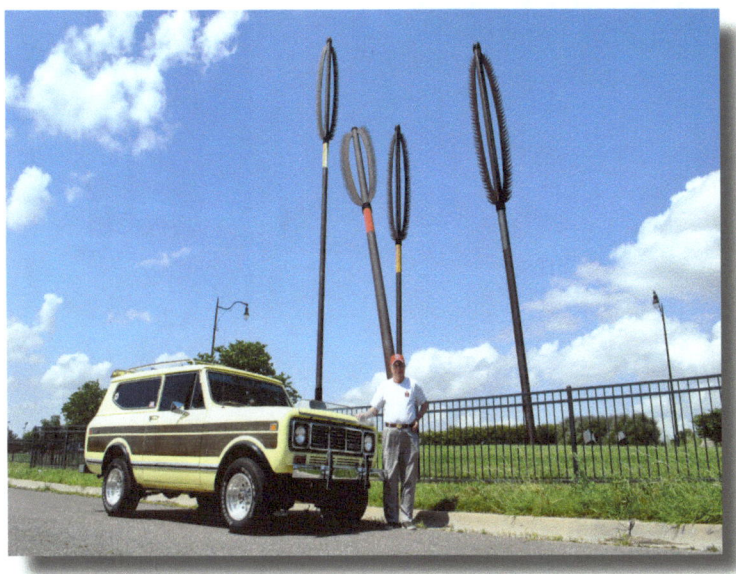

Nestled among the arrow sculptures spearing the Oklahoma International Airport ground's landscape is a 1970 International Scout owned by longtime fan Mr. Jerry Page.

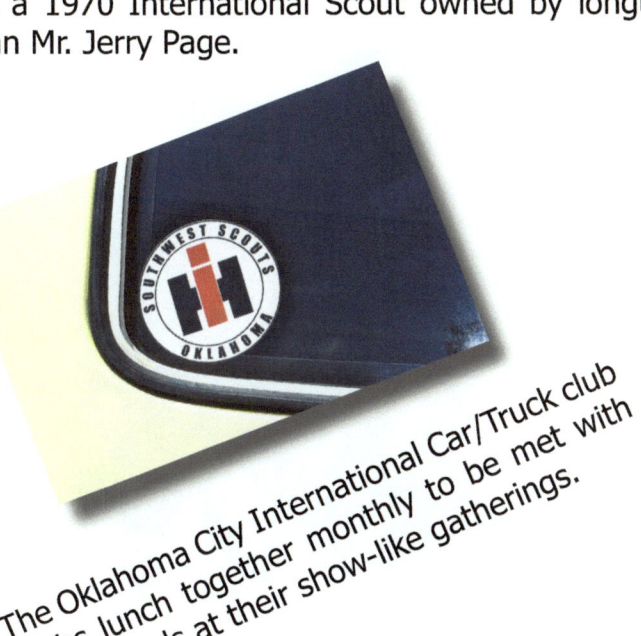

The Oklahoma City International Car/Truck club grabs lunch together monthly to be met with avid crowds at their show-like gatherings.

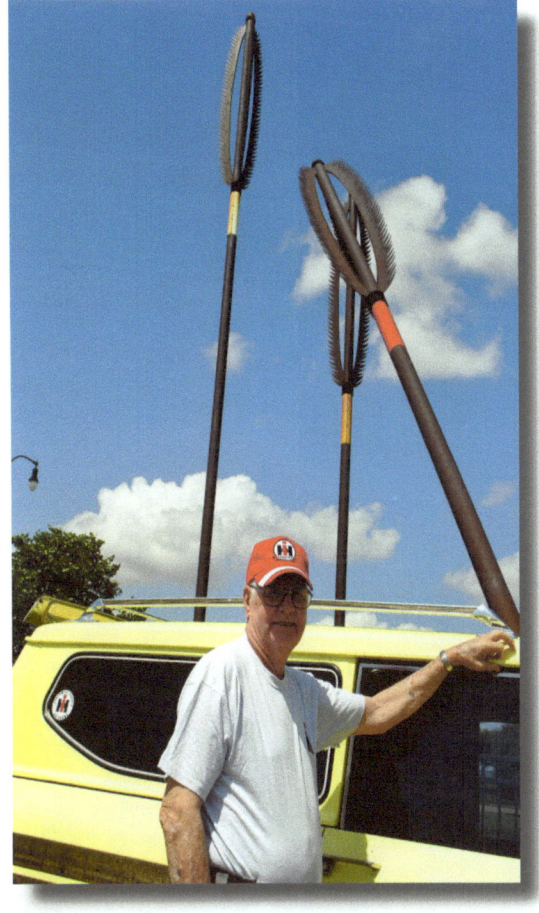

Both Jerry and his father were employed by the International-Harvester Company. His Dad worked for them when tractors were the original mainstay of the sales department, and Jerry himself during the expansion period of this century-plus year old American corporation.

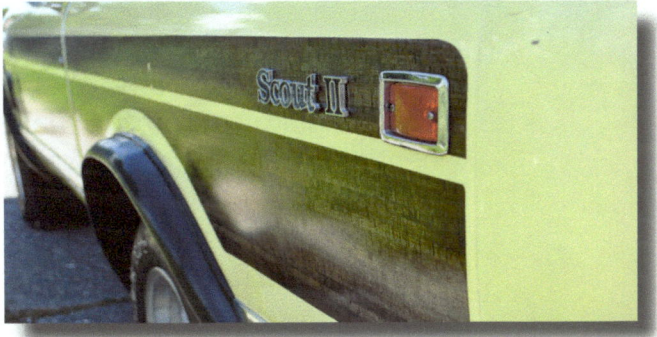

Thanks for cheering me on to finish this book, and for the painstaking conservation of this rust-free rarety for all to appreciate.

FOUND A LEGUME...

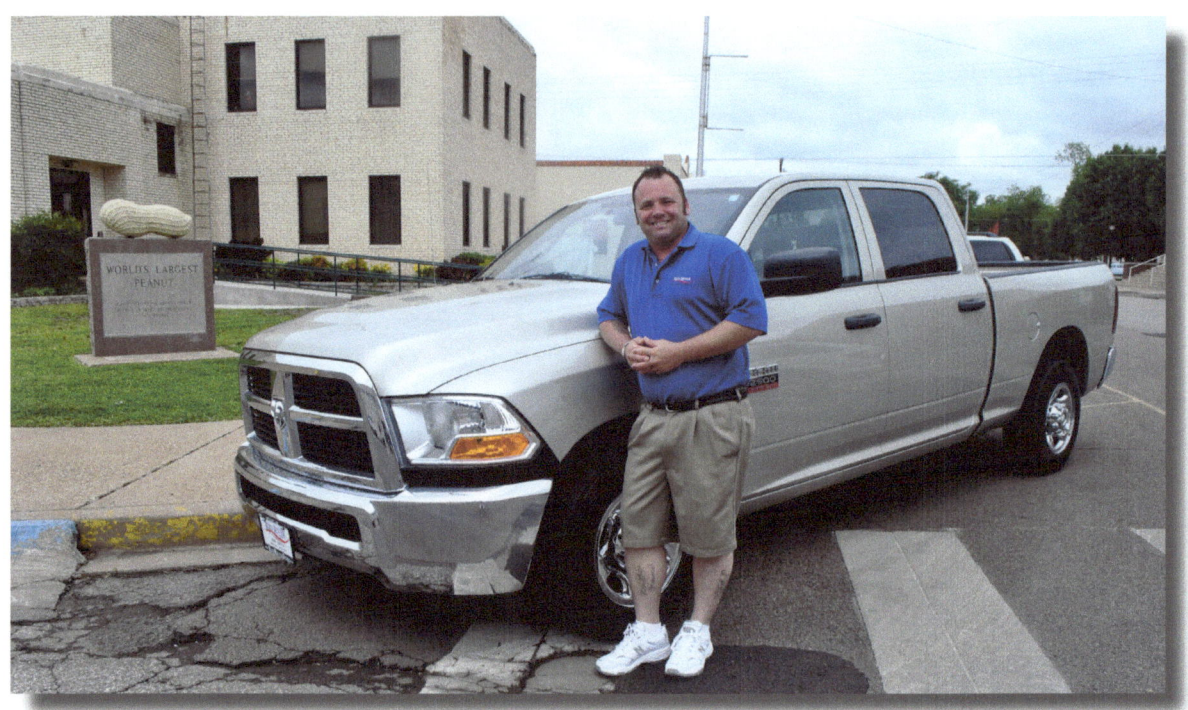

Mr. Shannon Spaulding presents a 2010 Dodge Dakota in front of the world's largest concrete peanut.

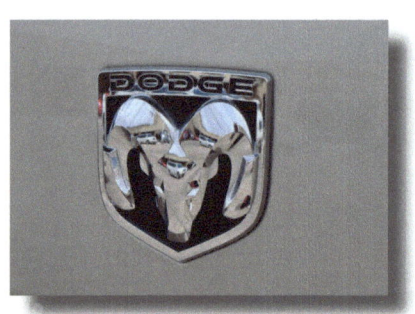

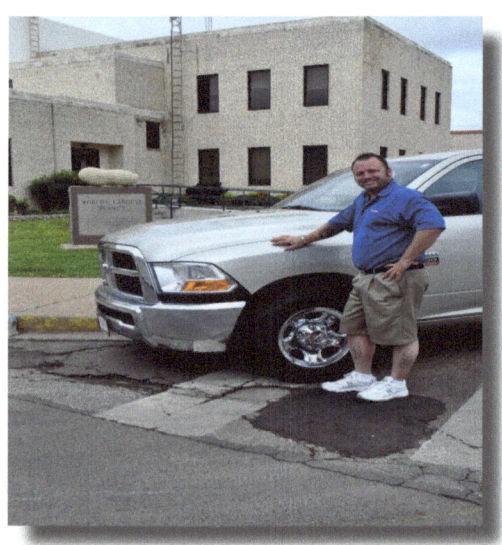

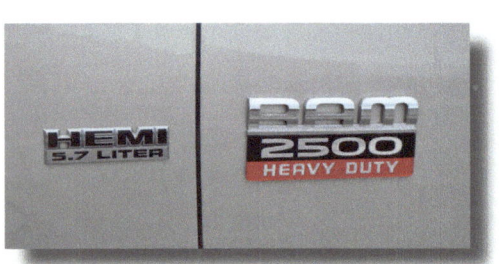

The Magnolia-lined streets of Durant, Oklahoma once yielded quite a crop for that salty snack's industry, hence the city's largess for the tourist department, giving props to their veritable nest egg. I just like how we were lucky enough to find a similarly painted truck to match the perched goober.

Thanks for being "nutty" with us today Shannon. We are all the butter,

-er make that "better" for it.

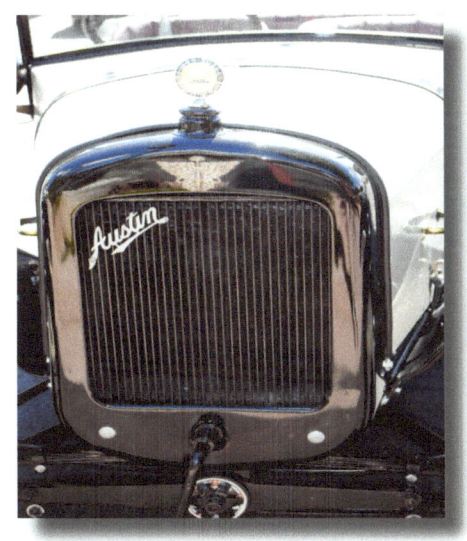

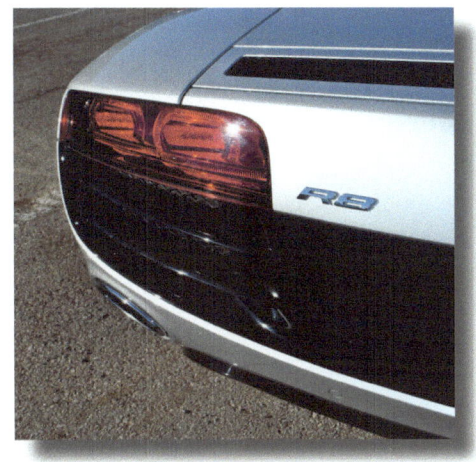

IMPORTS

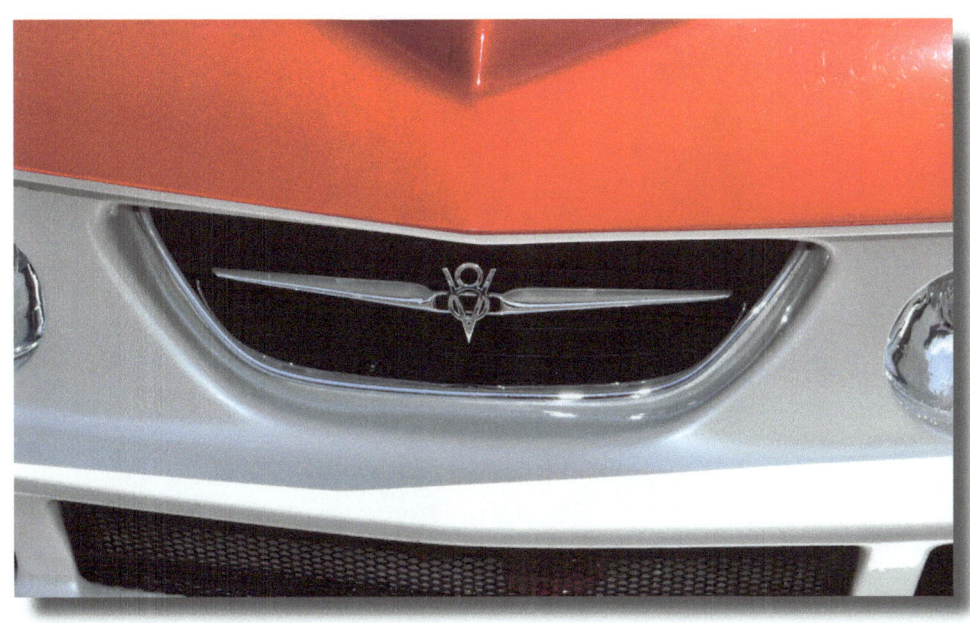

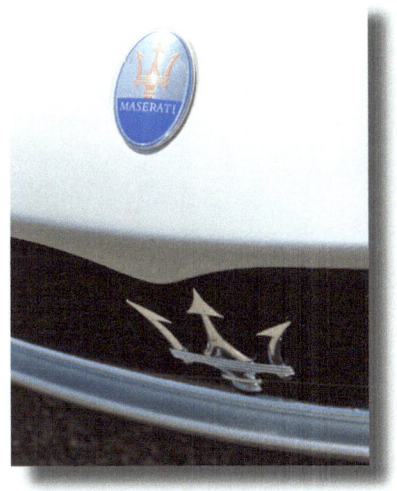

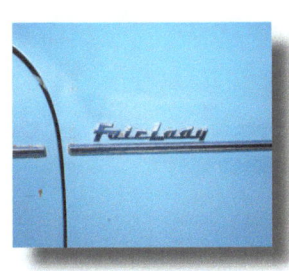

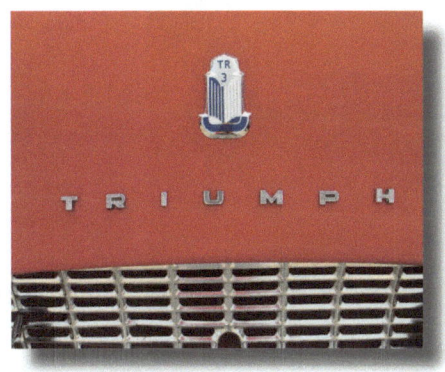

"LAMBO" FIELD OF DREAMS

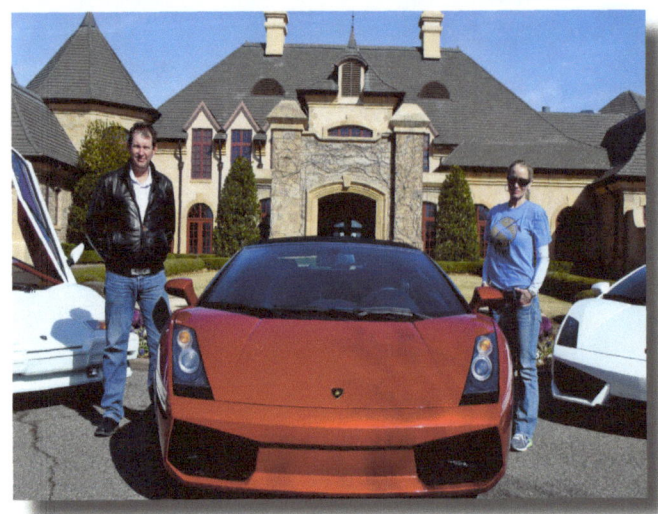

Mr. Jerry and Mrs. Cindy Hunter own the thriving nationally renowned company, U.S. Fleet Tracking. Their signature positioning service is used for, as the name logically implies, fleet control. Locally, one such application has their devices utilized on Oklahoma police cruisers. With contracted clients as far reaching as the N.F.L. Superbowl organizers, it goes without saying that they are a busy team.

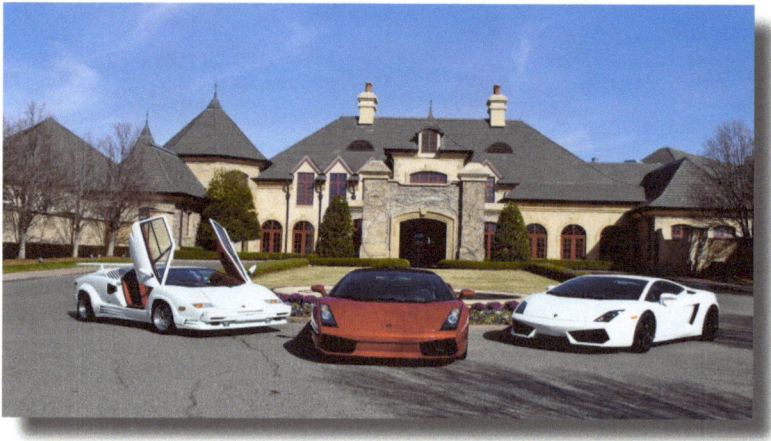

Lucky for me, the Hunters took a much deserved "time out," as they say on the football field, from their oft-times hectic schedule to sun their "livestock" at a favorite Edmond clubhouse. Lucky for you perusers, they posess an extensive plethora of exotic cars, including this rare collection from one of the most prestigious car makers on this green earth, Lamborghini. The white machine to their left was even used in a big budget action film recently, driven by none other than "McDreamy" himself.

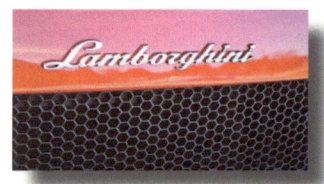
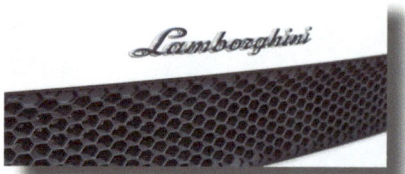
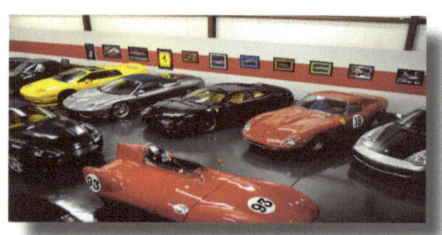

Thank you my young entrepreneurial friends for your willingness to help an up-and-coming author with budding photographic tendencies. Thanks even more for keeping tabs on commerce's goods, as well as keeping those convoying the commodities safely and securely on the streets every day. May prosperity continue to 'follow' you.

MILKMAN'S NEW WHEELS

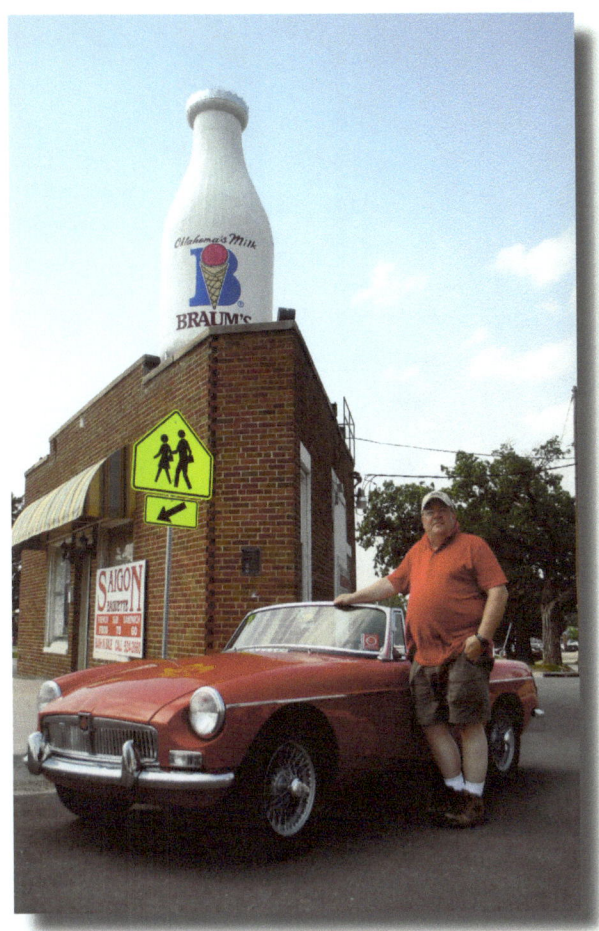

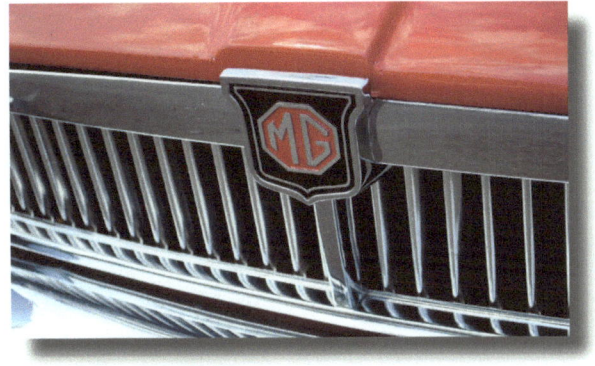

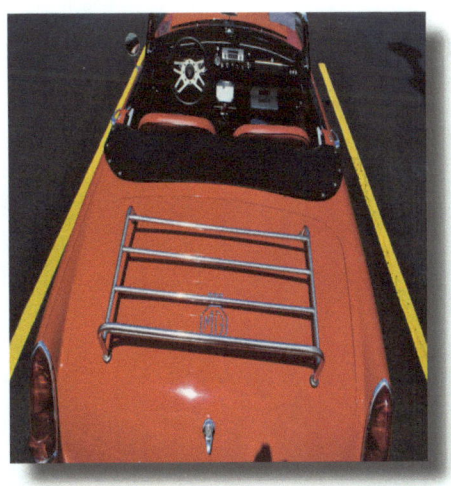

Mr. Tony Brewer deftly flaunts his pristine little red M.G. He "gets his kicks" in front of yet another landmark not far off the beaten Rt. 66 path in the preeminent Asian dining District of Oklahoma City.

This old diminutive satelite office now houses a delectible Vietnamese sandwich shop. As is obvious by the ostentatious milk bottle atop, however, one can see it has had a different purpose altogether in its heyday, rife with neighborhood milk delivery.

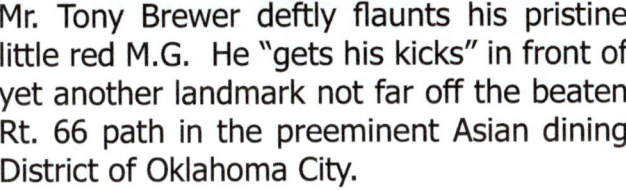

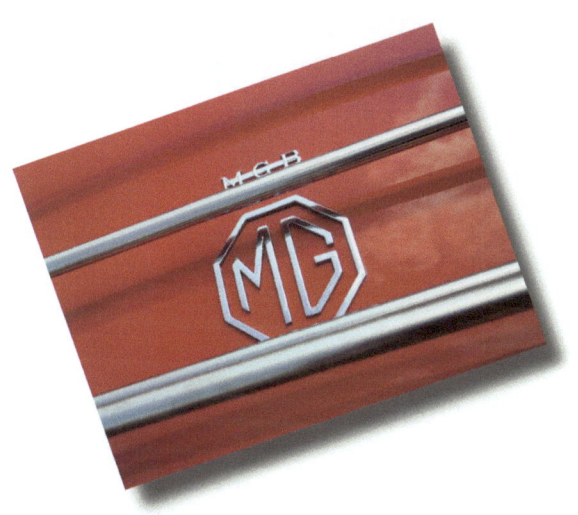

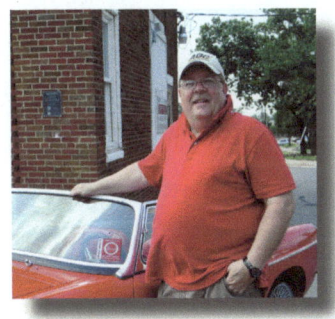

I bet your average Joe would love to have gone door-to-door totin' his bottles in these scarlet letters.

MANANA, MANANA, TEQUERO MANANA...

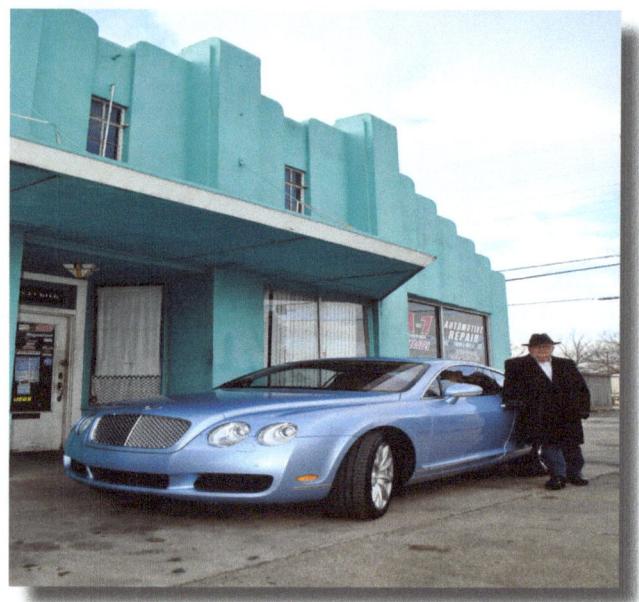

Mr. Jim Rutherford graciously allows me to set a vintage scene in front of one of the more visually appealing structures in university town Norman, Oklahoma.

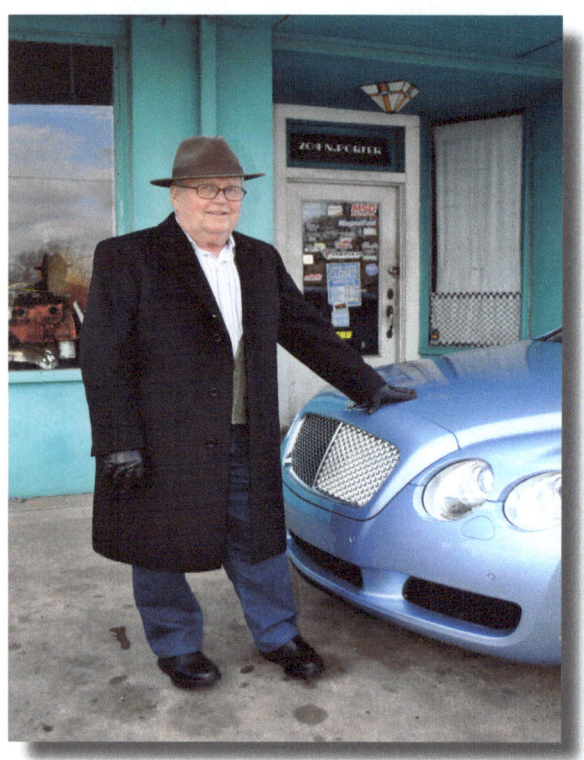

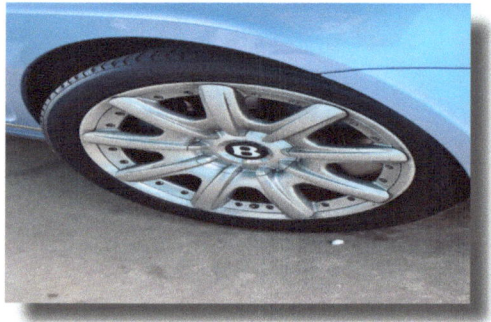

The combo of Jim's powder blue late model Bentley, and the seafoam green presented a study in Art Deco color schemes. I was similarly appreciative of Mr. Rutherford's decision to deck out in his Sunday best.

He was looking every bit the part of the quintessential upper crust gent. So much so it led him to relay a charming vignette. Owning several autos and being fans of theatre, particularly in this case the "Annie" story, his wife dotingly teases him as described: Obsequiously imitating one of the show's butler characters, she occasionally inquires something along the lines of "Mr. Warbucks, will you be driving the Bentley, or the Rolls today?" Also relating in my passion for all things automotive and theatrical, I couldn't help but chuckle. I hope you do the same as you contemplate this tre-riche motor car photo session's back story.

PARKING LOT OF PALS

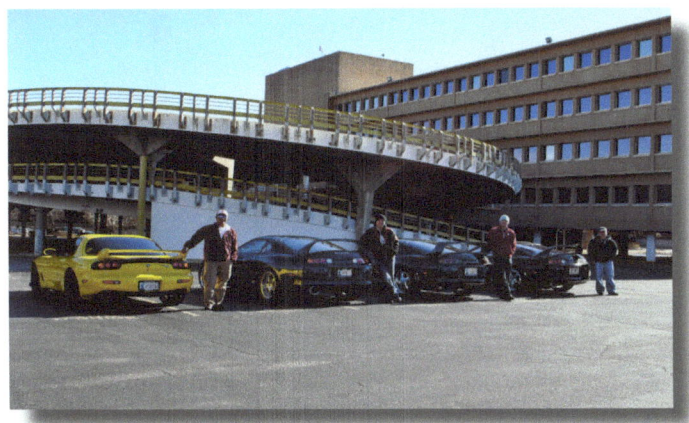

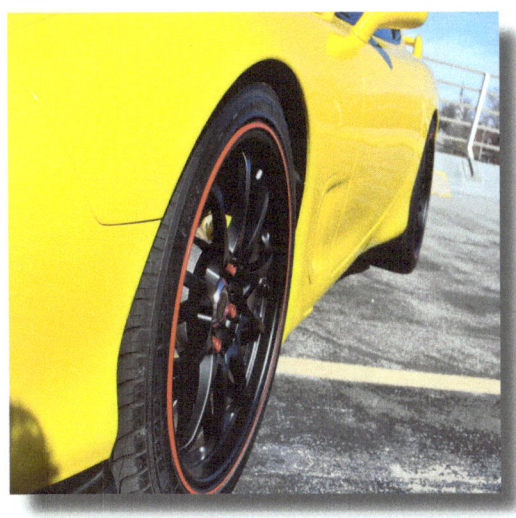

Just like so many other car clubs that gather for the week end tradition of coffee and breakfast, so too does this enterprising group of friends linked mainly by their love of cars.

We met up just north of Oklahoma City, one effervescent winter, day after a nationally known coffee house's monthly car cruise-in show to capture these pin-up boys with their super-speedy slickly-tuned imports.

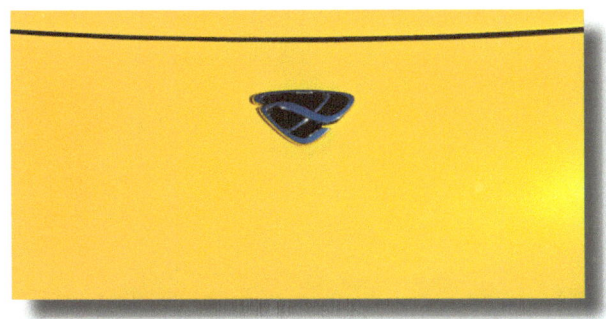

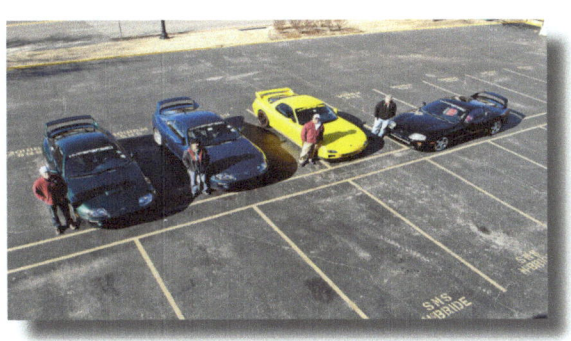

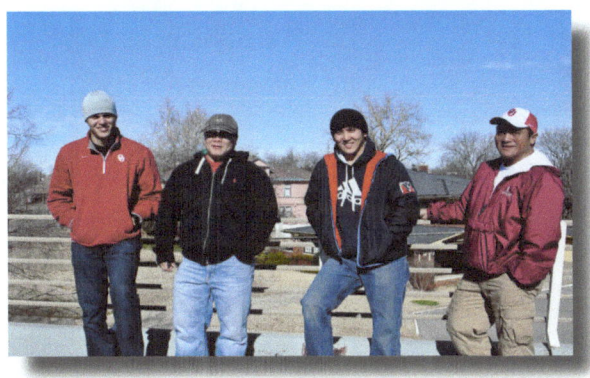

Alphabetically are Song Choe, Long Nguyen, Son Nguyen, and Angel Rivera. Thanks fellas for being so acccomodating and willing to head back out after the crisp morning show, to one of the city's coolest visually captivating parking garages for these images. Hope you have many happy Saturdays to come.

JAZZY BLUES...

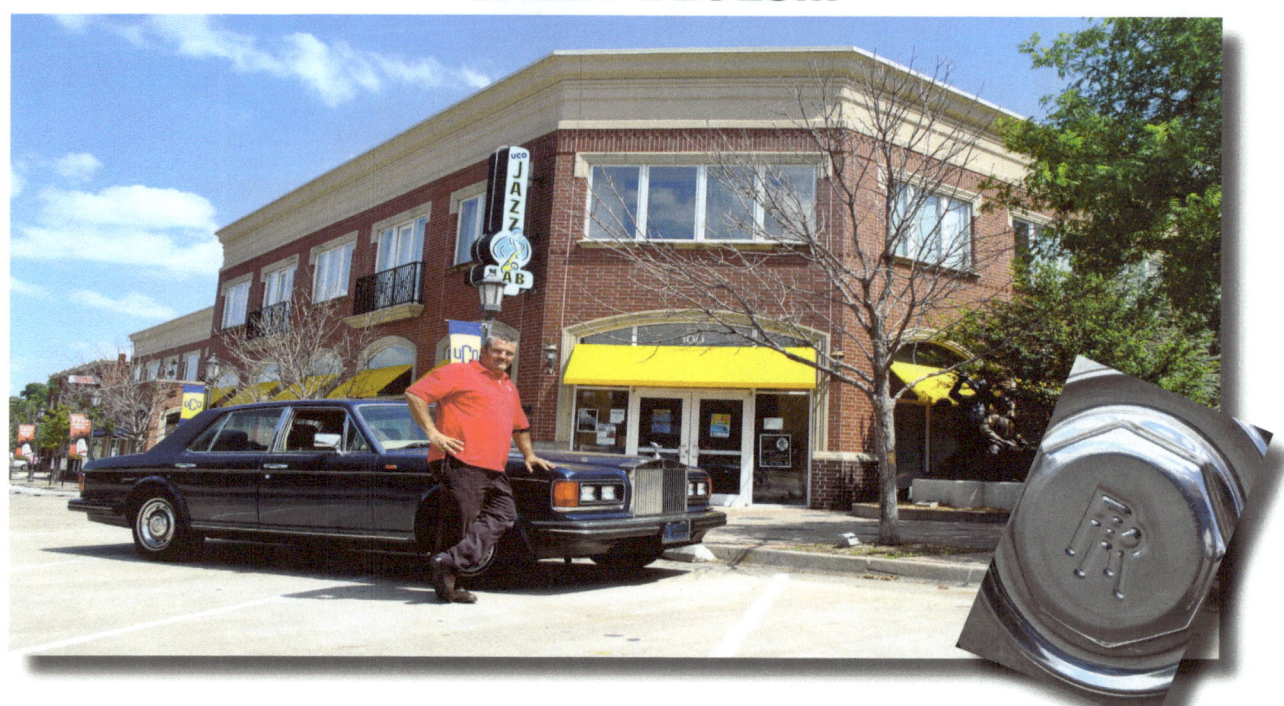

D.J. Morrow parks near one of the metro's first-string musical forums, The University of Central Oklahoma's Jazz Lab, home to every stage of performance art in the genre, from instruction to top-name marquee billing.

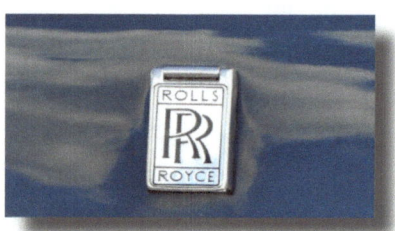

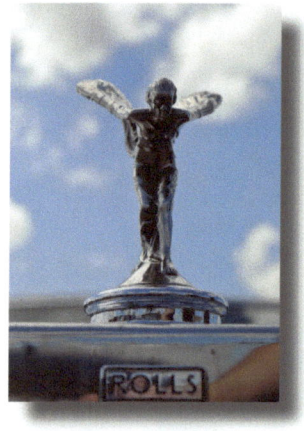

Today the headliner of the show is this classy Rolls Royce. It almost gives me the "blues" to not "roll" in such a jazzy ride, but we'll just go listen to the music for consolation instead.

Bonnet ornament
"The Spirit of Ecstacy"

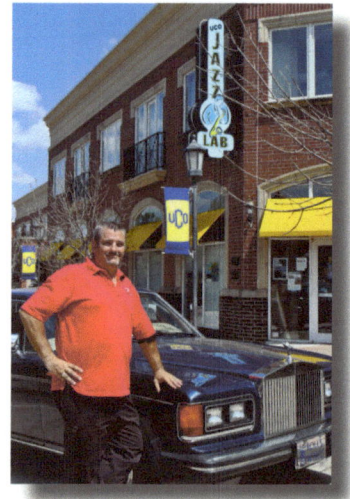

Thanks to D.J., for your spunk, and to your wife for having served our country. If I performed with a musical instrument, its to folks like you I would dedicate a jam session.

BOTTLES N' THROTTLES

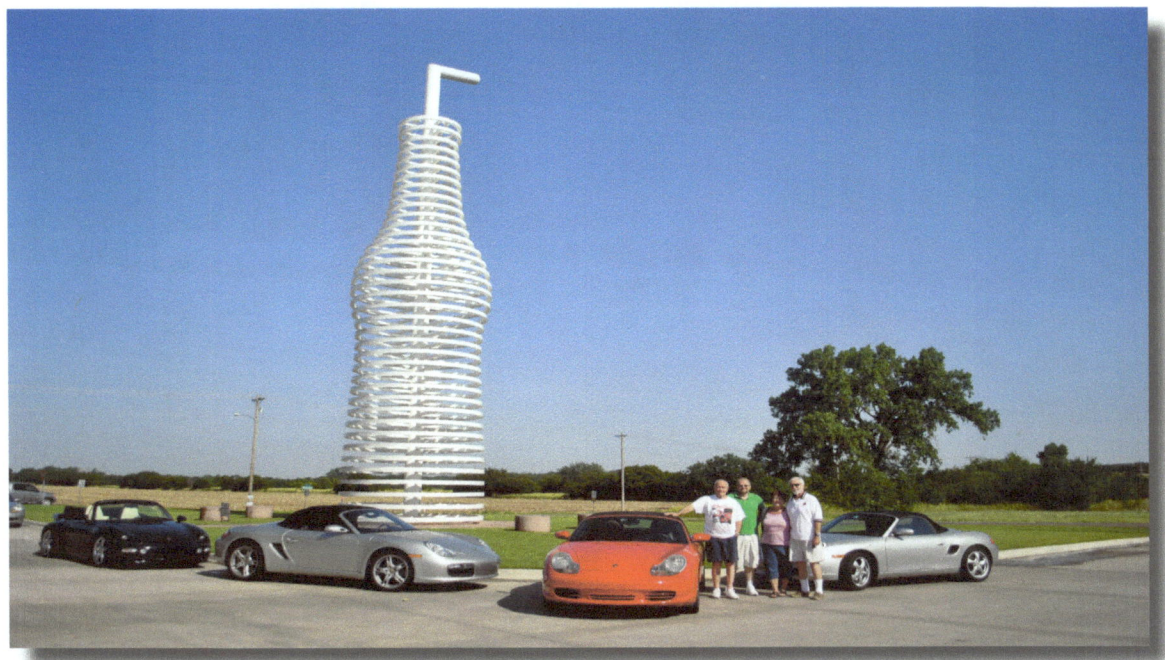

Members of Oklahoma's Warbonnett Porsche Club stood together before embarking on a bucolic group jaunt down Route 66.

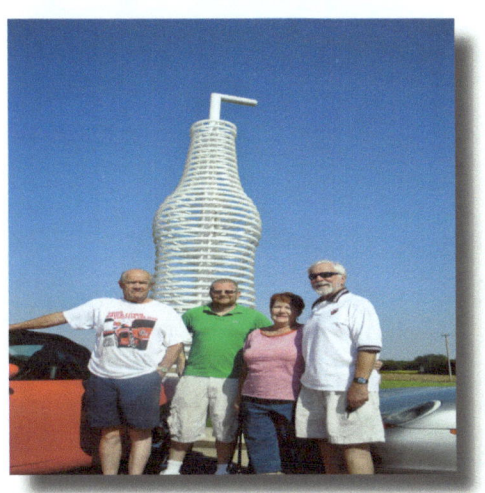

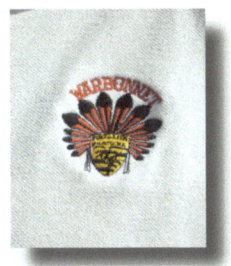

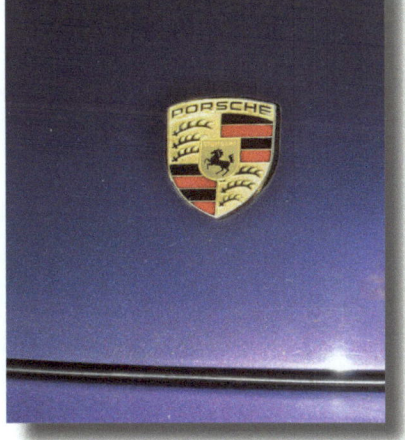

Pictured are Walt and Barb Kendal, Floyd Carter, and transplanted Brit, Dean Wenzel. This pleasant summer's day the club made their starting point at the "Pop's" diner and soda fountain in Arcadia, Oklahoma. Its residents, as one can deduce, are custodians of the world's largest soda bottle.

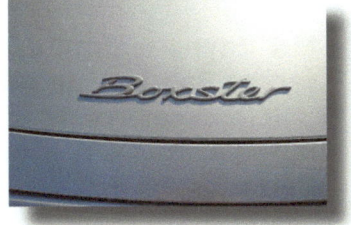

Thanks, Warbonnetts, for sharing your time, and letting us all salivate over that upstanding Italian styling. Bon Voyage, or "when in Rome..." Viagio Sicuro.

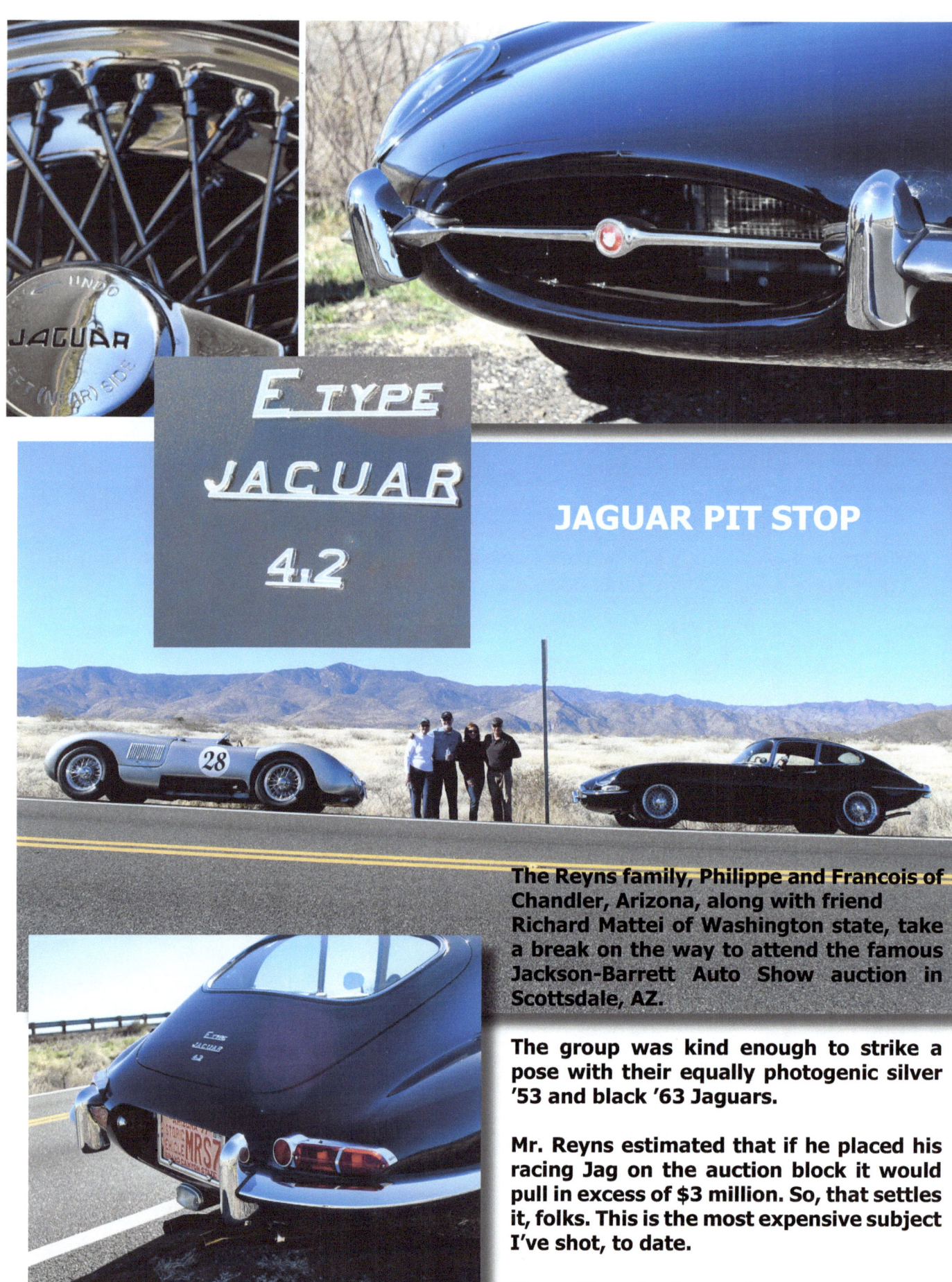

E TYPE JAGUAR 4.2

JAGUAR PIT STOP

The Reyns family, Philippe and Francois of Chandler, Arizona, along with friend Richard Mattei of Washington state, take a break on the way to attend the famous Jackson-Barrett Auto Show auction in Scottsdale, AZ.

The group was kind enough to strike a pose with their equally photogenic silver '53 and black '63 Jaguars.

Mr. Reyns estimated that if he placed his racing Jag on the auction block it would pull in excess of $3 million. So, that settles it, folks. This is the most expensive subject I've shot, to date.

Happy Travels, Compadres.

117

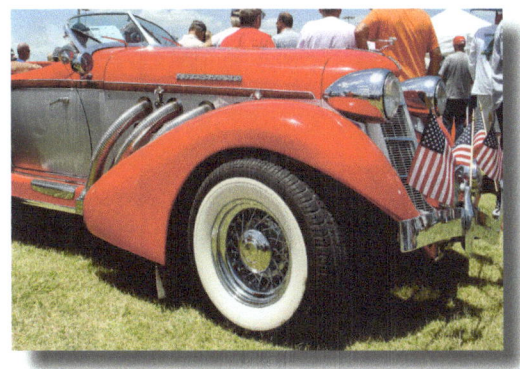

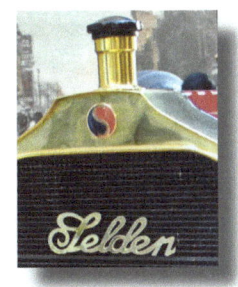

Rare Brass Era 1910

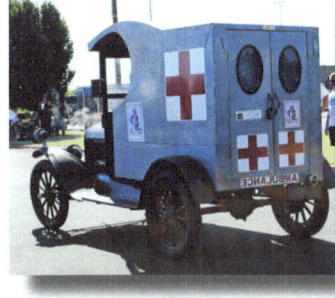

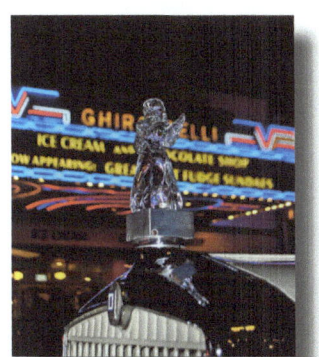

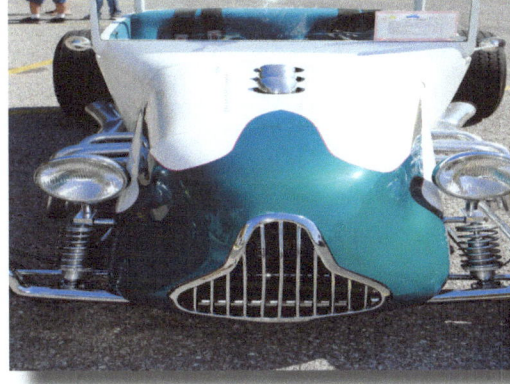

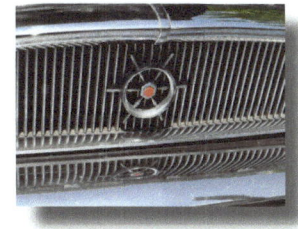

'55 Clipper

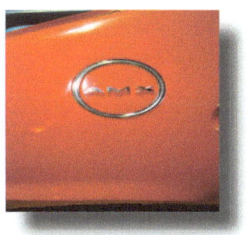

'29 Durant

SPECIAL INTEREST
THAT OBSCURE CAR SHOW CATAGORY WHERE
THE MORE UNUSUAL ENTRANTS ARE PLACED...

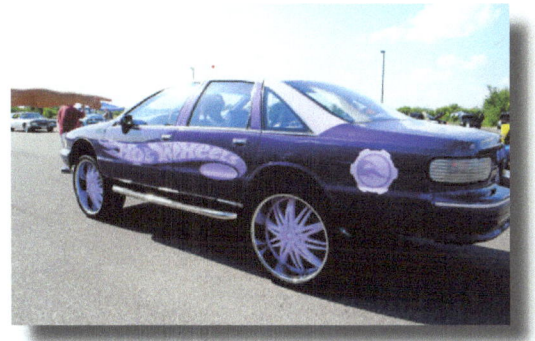

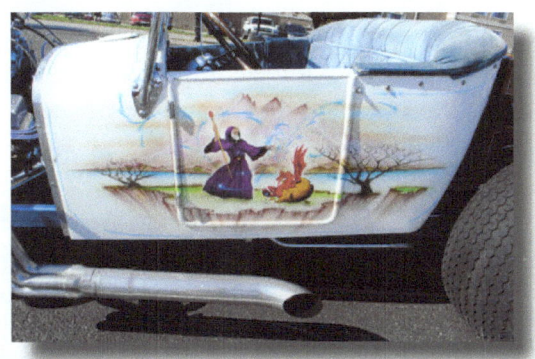

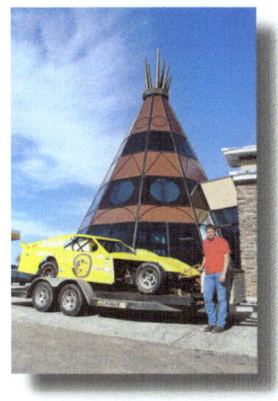

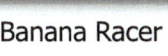

Banana Racer

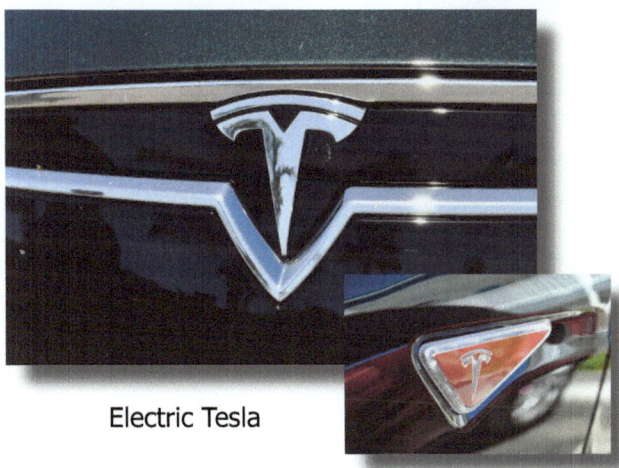

Electric Tesla

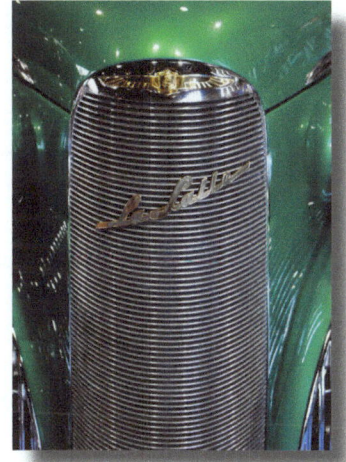

R.I.P. JER...

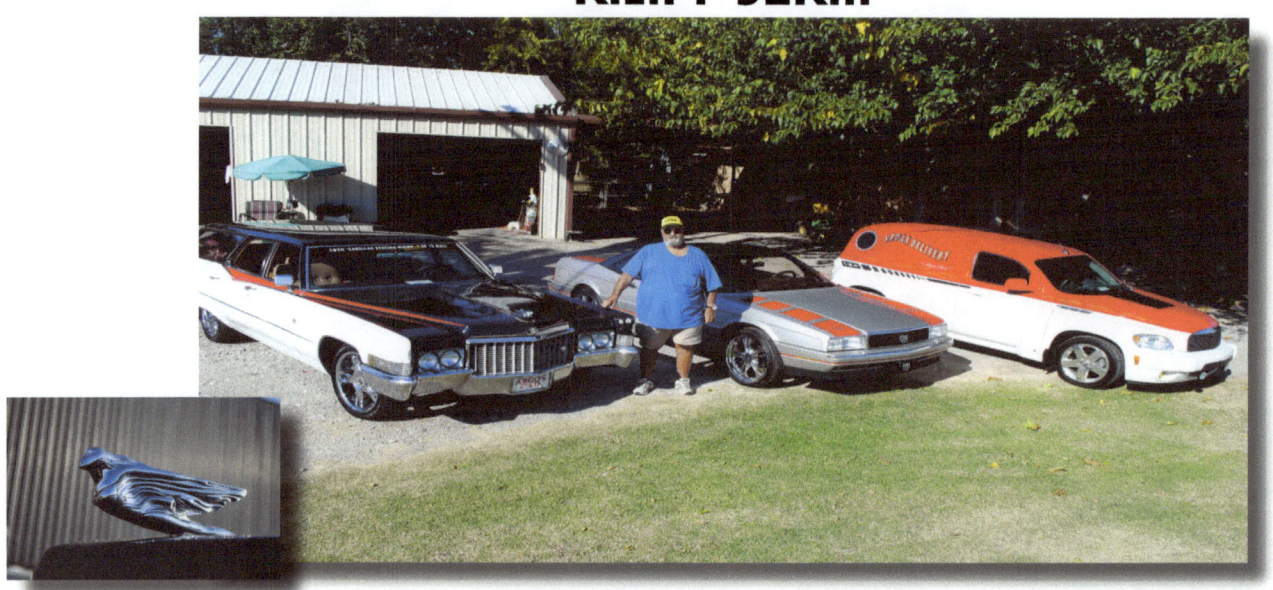

When one would drive past Jerry Argo's waved greeting from his main-thoroughfare facing house in the once small town that is now the burgeoning community of Moore, Oklahoma, you would be reminded of a simpler time.

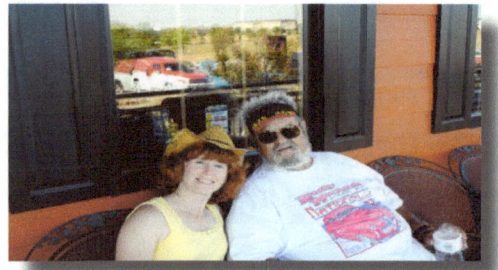

His blithe countenance was like that of other constants of the past... A welcoming grandfather waiting for your arrival from his front porch rocker, or your neighbors chatting amicably on their stoops as you made your way back to the solace of home.

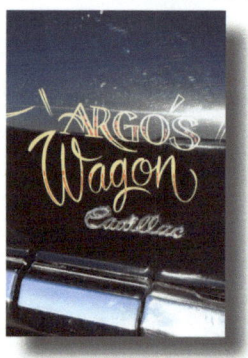

His 1970 Caddie wagon was one of only a dozen.

That praiseworthy, meticulously maintained, Chevy ring was almost as welcome a sight at the many car shows he attended, that is except to his rivalry in the "Special Interest" category. The competitors were really only content with Jerry, not his scene-stealing prize winners.

When time and illness began to ravage my colleague's vibrance the last summer of his days on our planet, Jerry tried to get as much living done as possible. I know I speak on behalf of all who knew him, either on the car show lot, or day to day, when I say, we are so grateful to have gotten to know Mr. Argo.

Hope you are burnin' rubber on those streets of gold paving Heaven's city limits.
I'm wavin' back...

A "STUDEE" STUDY...

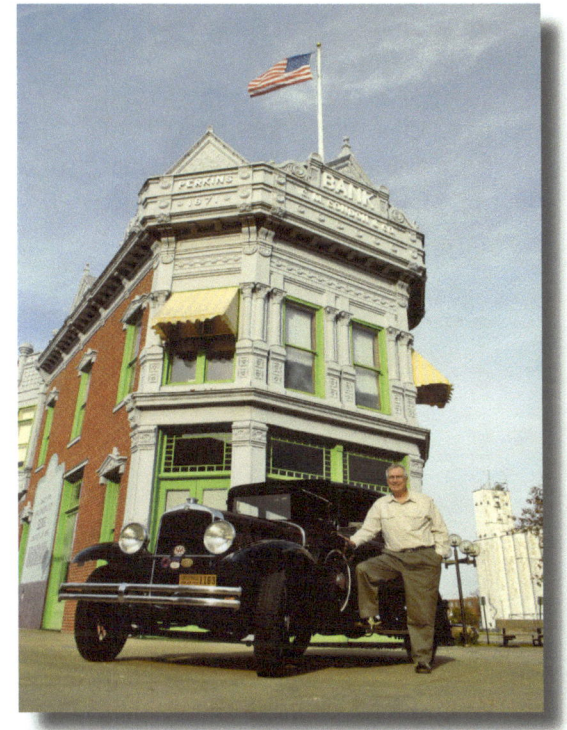

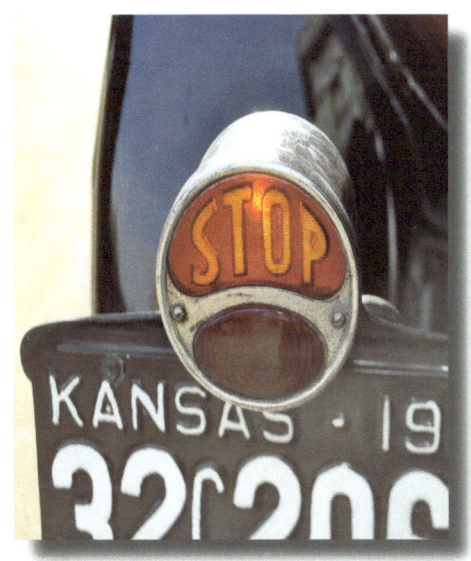

Along with the luxurious Brewster carriage and automobile company of days gone by, the Studebaker was once known for its sturdy wagon that traced the trail across our country's wild frontier.

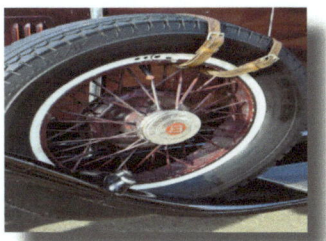

Just as the inhabitants of all cultures, races, and creeds in this land we call America adjusted to the changing landscape, so too did many companies adapt into different iterations with the onset of the auto industry. Personifying the Studebaker company's success during their foray into the art of vehicle creation is the extravagant spirit found in Coffeeville, Kansas resident John Alvey's '29 Dictator.

To properly complement the subjects I chose the fitting backdrop of a late 19th century work of architecture that no doubt must have seen the Studebaker's original timber and canvas form hitched out front, in the stead of John's new-fangled trend-setter. It is just one of the two banks the infamous Dalton Gang simultaneously tried to hold up. Consequently the town-folk in this case fought back and are staunchly known to this day as the "Defenders."

Flawless restoration Mr. A. Congrats on "defending" your Studee against the attacking sands of time.

WIND UP TOYS

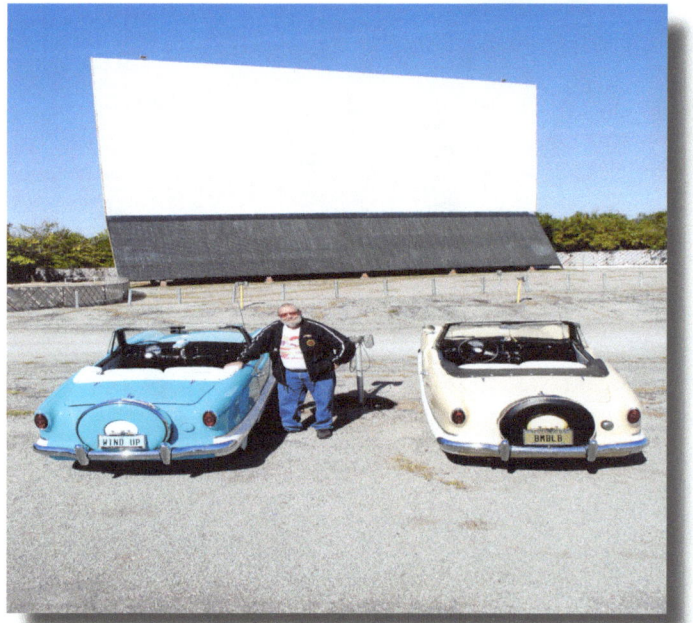

Bill Russell favors Nash Metropolitans. He has owned 12 through the course of his life. It was his first car, and remains his favorite.

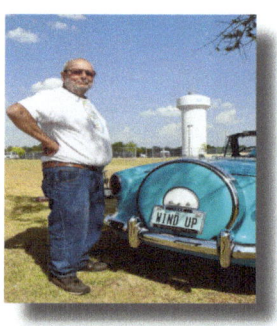

With his '59 & '60 Metros in tow, and all decked out in Nash attire, Bill chooses a couple of prime spaces at Oklahoma City's last remaining drive in theatre, The Winchester. Thanks to the projectionist, Mr. Lindy Shanbour, for granting us the pleasure of meeting at his establishment for this photo shoot. The whole city thanks him for keeping the edifice running so nimbly. Complete with a neon animated cowboy sign one will see in my sojourn's V.W. Chapter, the legendary inspiration point was the picture-perfect locale for a coupla' retro Metros.

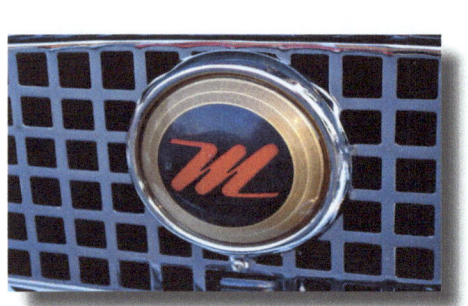

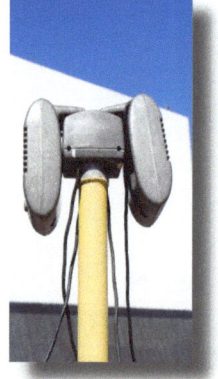

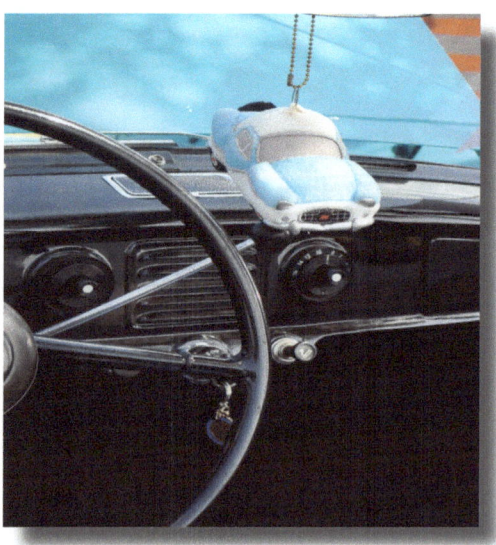

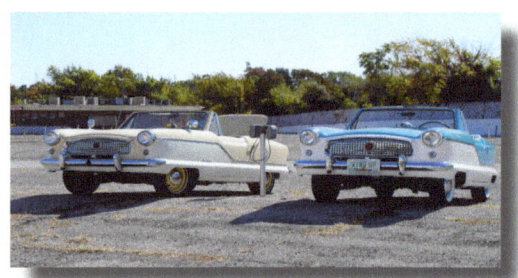

Thanks to Mr. Russell for coordinating the appearance of our two starlets today, and for all the esprit de corps at the car shows.

STARSKY N' HUTCH CAR

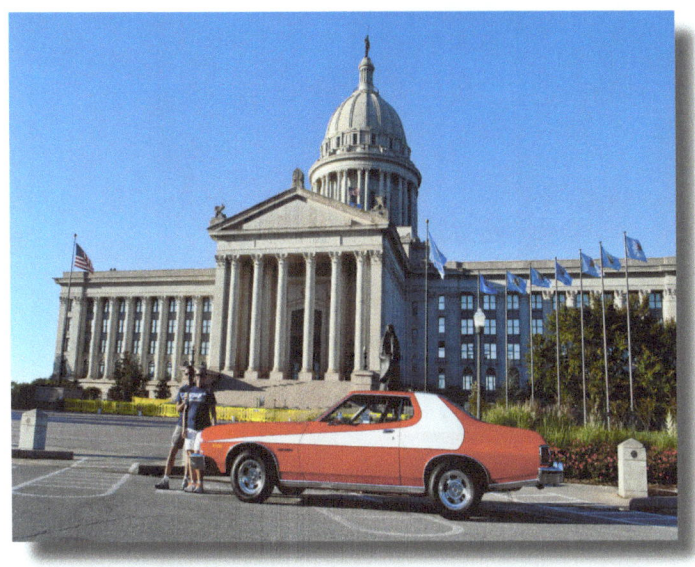

Greg and Lisa Geisler position themselves prominently in front of their Oklahoma City Capital building. Even though Greg works around famous sports figures in his occupation, and Lisa participates in many charitable activities, their Torino is the V.I.P. hero/celebrity in this instance, having been one of the original autos used in the '70s show "Starsky and Hutch."

This is definitely a Ford family with Greg having long been a fan of the Torinos, even owning one in high school and cruising past this sight almost every day during that period of his life.

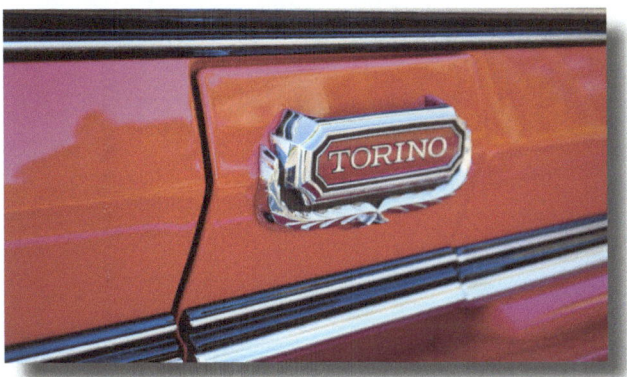

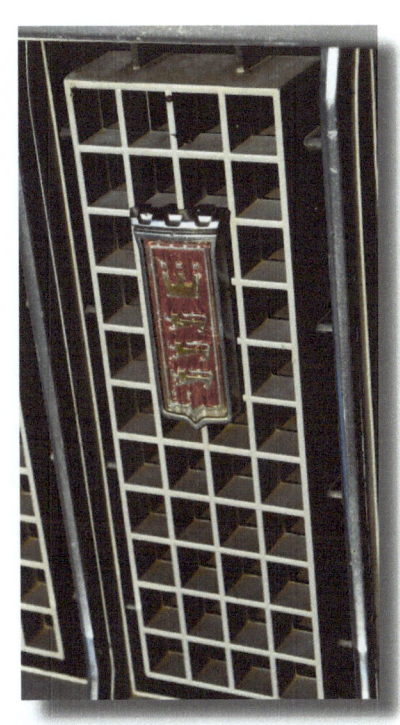

They however have to be in not the Celebrity/Hero chapter, nor Ford section of this publication, as all of their four wheeled family members (including several signed by automobile designers, and even a Presidential Limo,) constantly tie or beat out the contendors in the Special Interest car show category time after time.

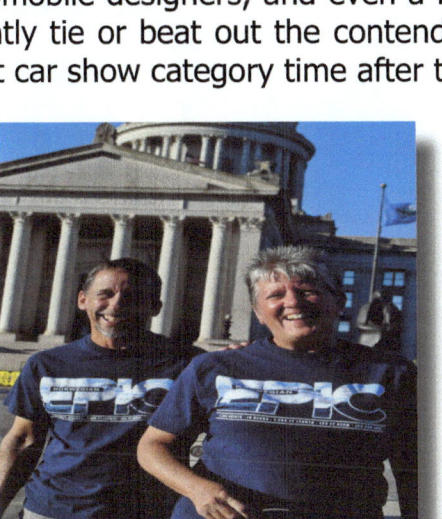

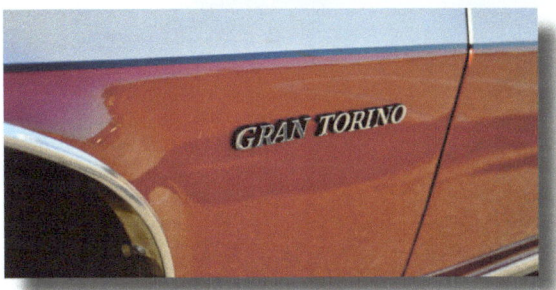

EXPRESS PONY RIDE

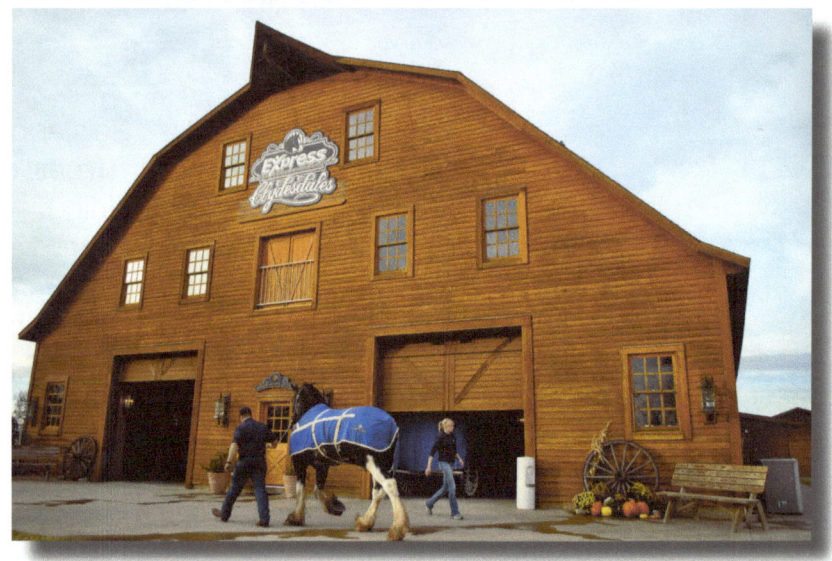

Trotting out their show trailer, with the legendary work horses that comfortably ride within, are Tabitha Minshull, and Kurtis Wheeler. Contentedly under the employ of the Express Personell company Clydesdale Barn, they get their, as well as their co-worker's, of sorts, exercise in daily.

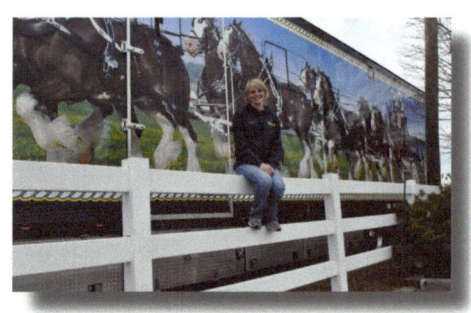

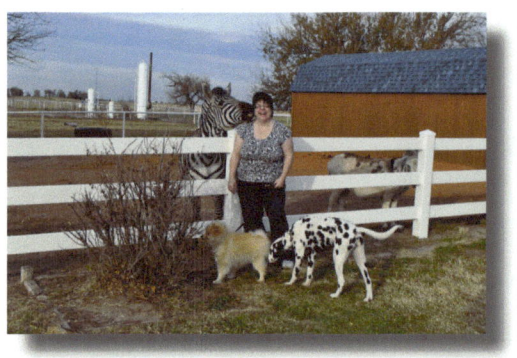

This barn serves the community as a free attraction full of the company's ceremonious signature black parade Clydesdale horses, as well as other farm animals admirers can visit, not to mention a zebra.

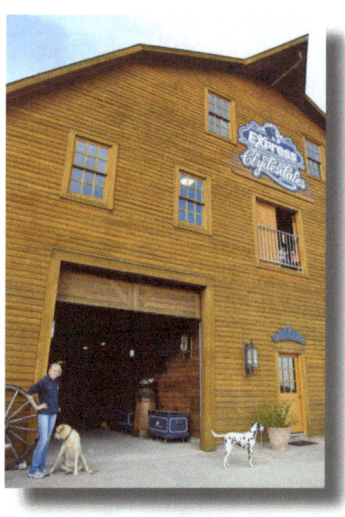

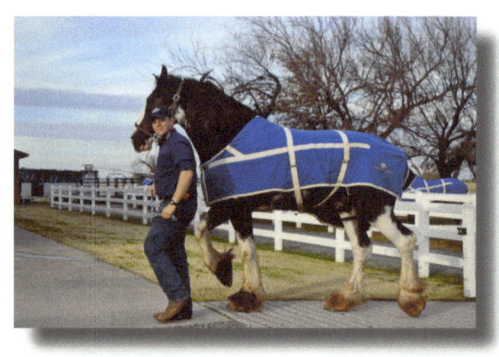

Glad you all are here to share in the glory of nature.

CELEBRATORY "LAWS"

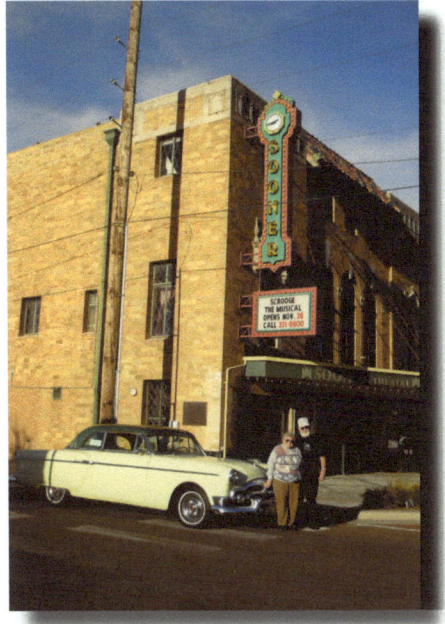

Leland and Lucille Laws of Spencer, Oklahoma bolster car shows all over by admitting their 1954 Packard into the merriment.

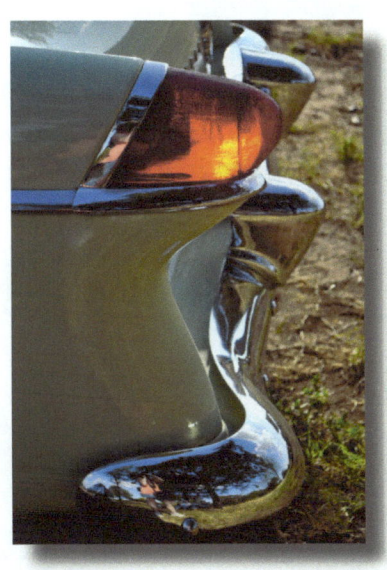

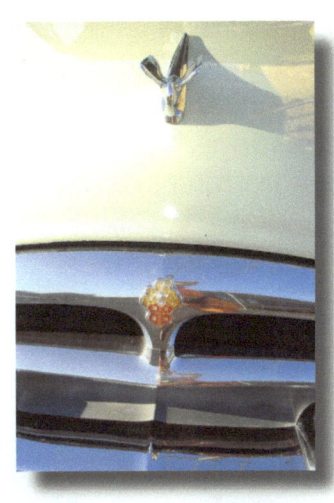

This temperate dusk they took a quick detour by Norman, Oklahoma's oldest theatre for a quick photo after yet another car show. They were hurrying home in preparation for their 53rd wedding anniversary soiree in less than T-minus 24.

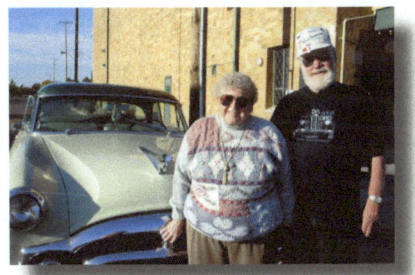

Sure wish we could honor you all by throwing a commemorative car show on the day of your actual special milepost.

F.M. & CAR SHOW ROADY

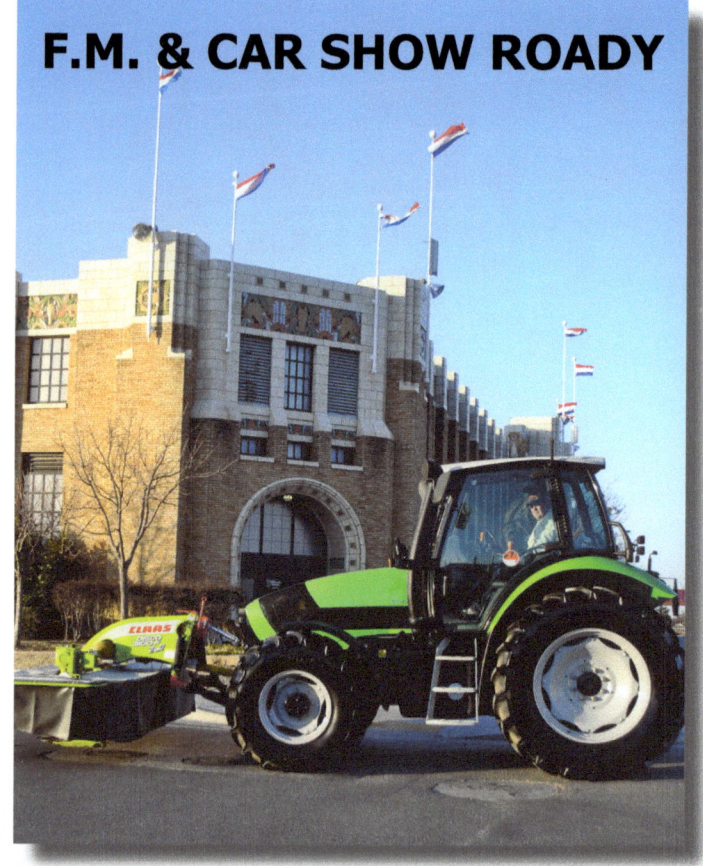

Mr. Chris Sloan of Stigler, Oklahoma was spotted at a farm and car show by the familiar Pavilion on the Tulsa Fairgrounds. His Deutz Fahr tractor, an excellent example of refined power, boasts the strength of the farmer's prize bull, with all the comforts of home in its air conditioned cab. And to think this Agrotron M610 could be yours for a cool $85,000.

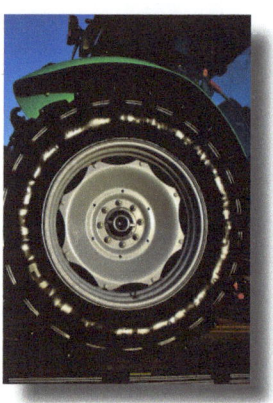 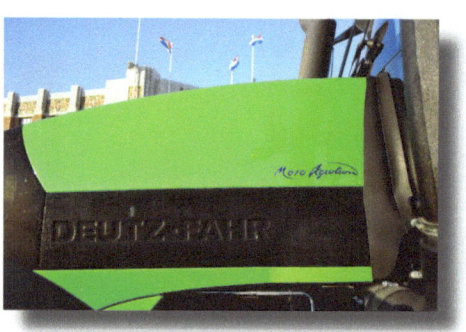

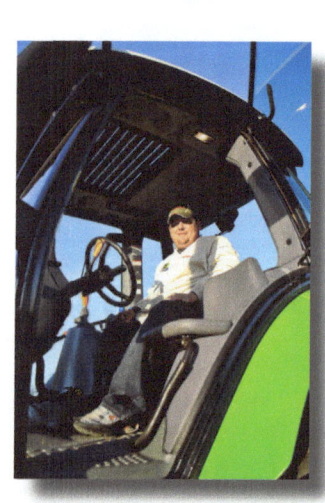

I unfortunately wasn't in the market. However, whenever a tractor is present in the special interest category of a Southern state's car show, the operator is never at a loss for clammering fans. Thankfully Chris had enough time, while fighting them off with a stick, to take a cruise around the parking lot, which doubled as our catwalk for this shot. Taking full advantage of a coveted WPA-era setting, and that spectacular sunset, I tried to capture their best sides.

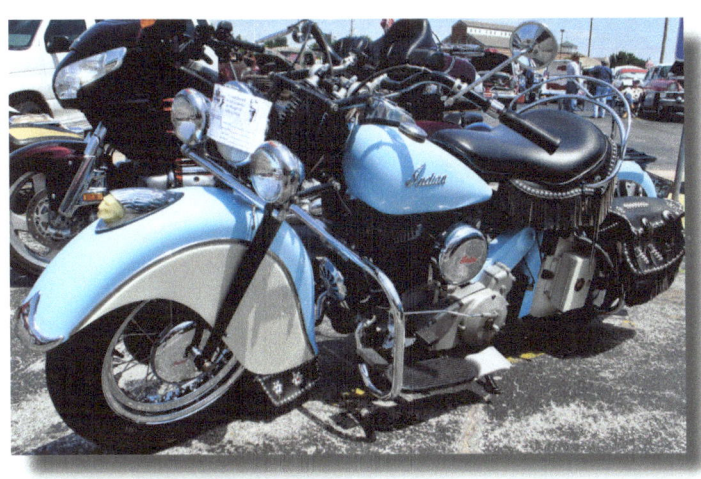

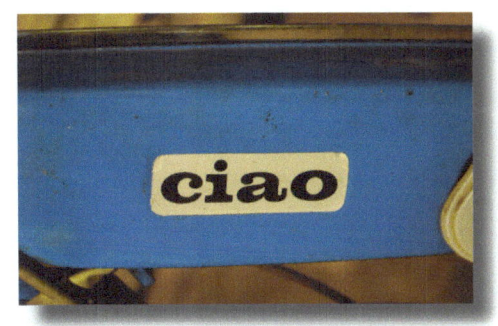

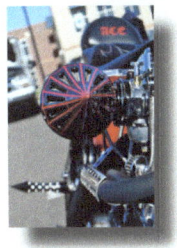

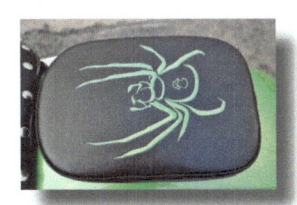

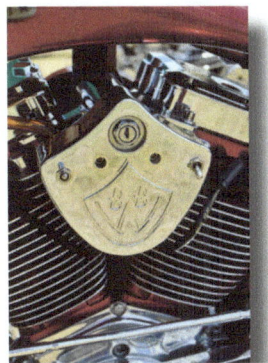

MOTORCYCLES

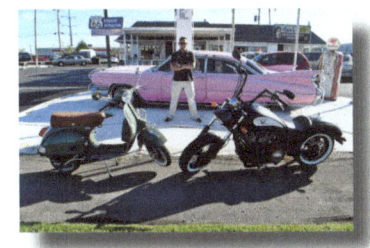

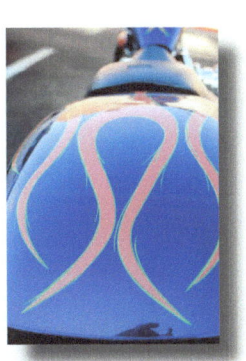

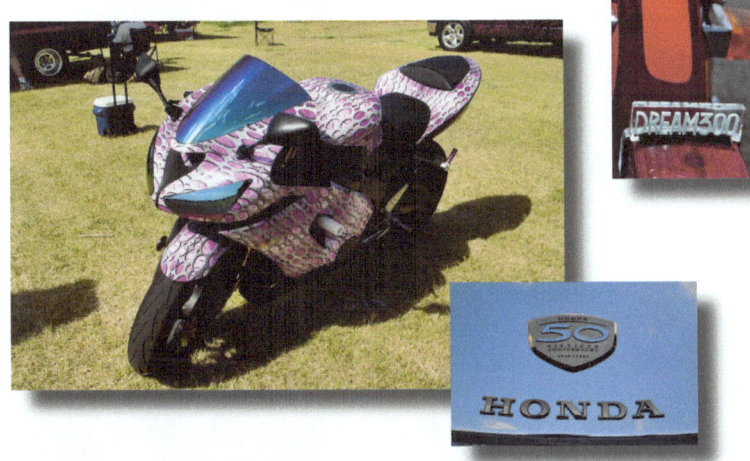

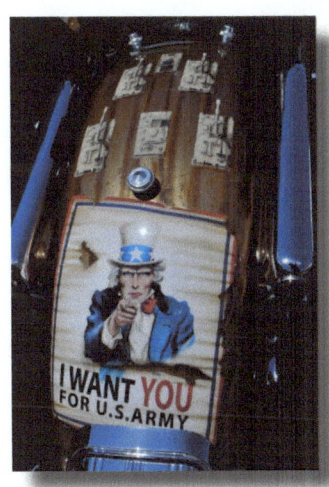

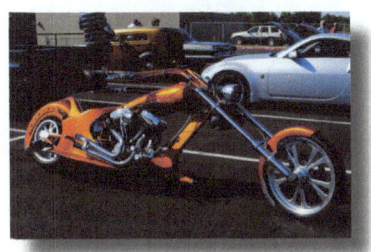

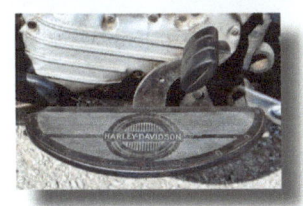

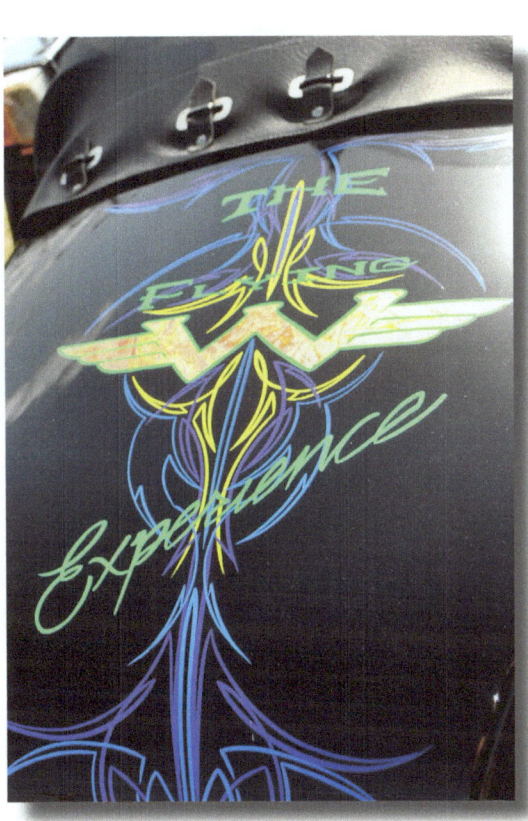

ROAMIN' WITH THE WOODEN NICKELS

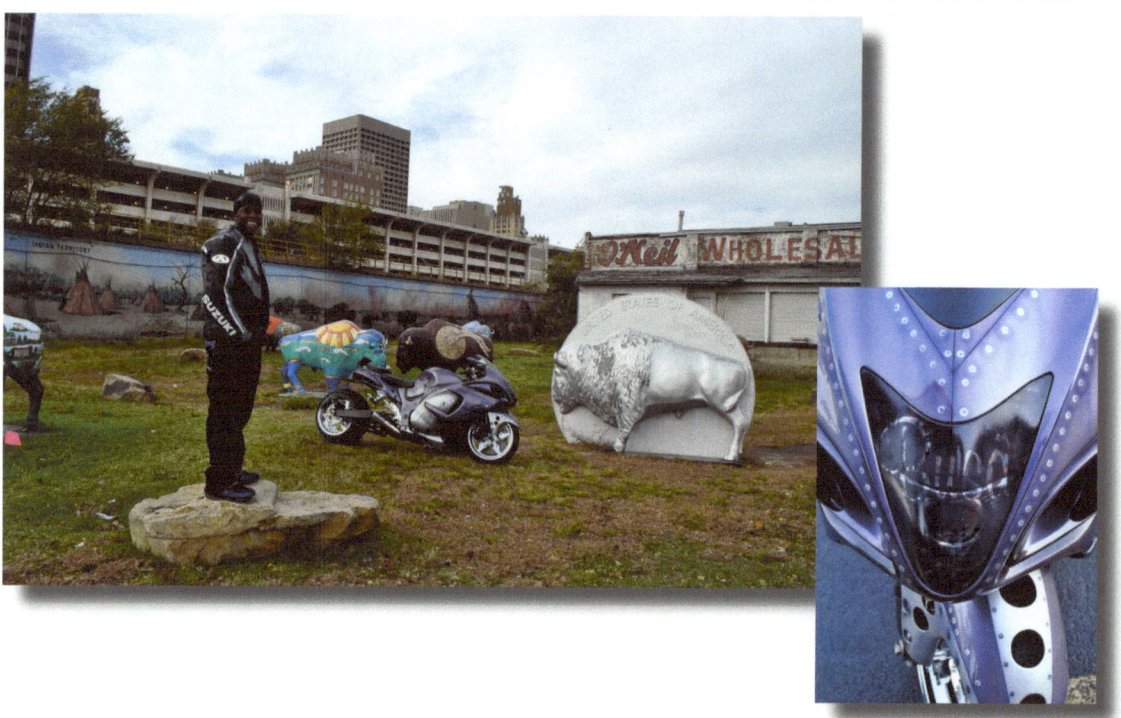

Outfitted in matching digs, is our model for the day De Troy Jarrett. Sporting a coordinating purple Suzuki Hyabusa, we toured around the old Oklahoma City warehouse district called Bricktown.

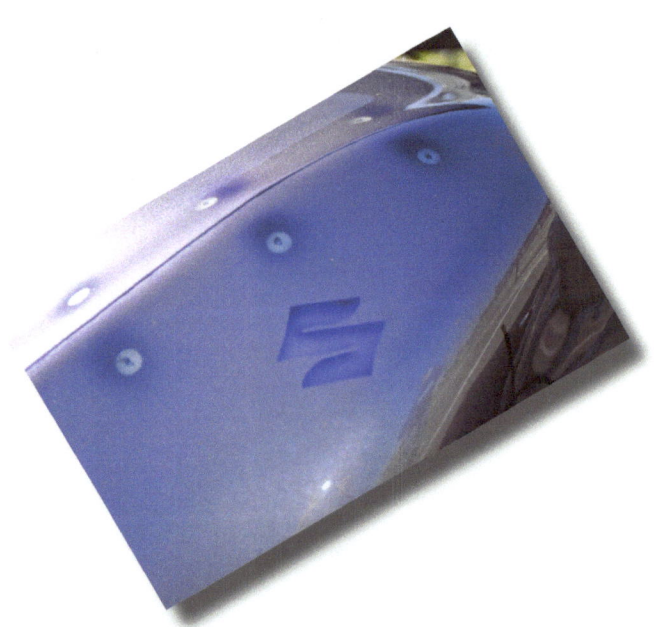

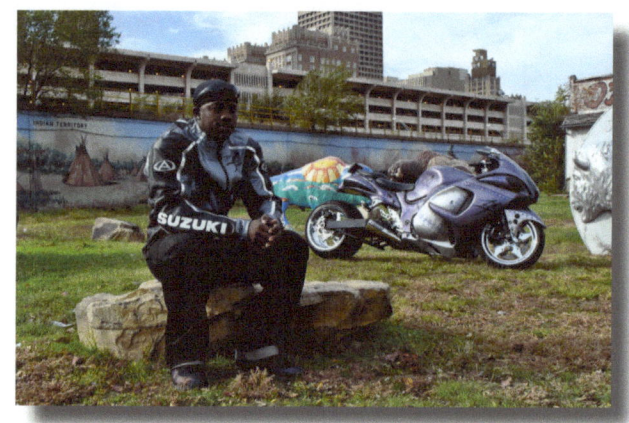

We ended up at the innovative "Buffalo Corral." This is an art project which commemorated the state's Centennial in 2007, and honored the state animal, the Majestic Buffalo.

Thanks to our equally camera-ready rider DeTroy for being so open to ideas and suggestions. You really as they say, "Oughta' be in pictures," as your pensive stares share an intensity beyond your tender years, and that smile is utterly wide-reaching. Hope you really go far.

"WHIZ" BANG OF A GOOD RIDE

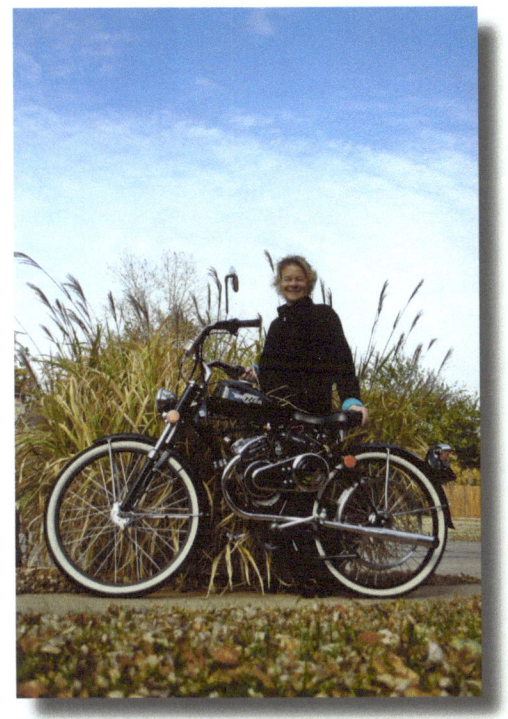
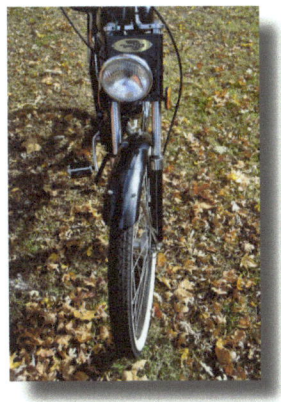
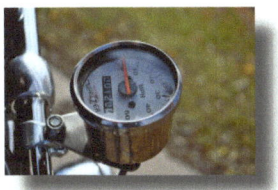

Although this electric bicycle appears vintage, its peddler, Mrs. Lani Malysa, actually has the best of both worlds. The 2008 Whizzer comes equipped with all the modern accoutrements a newer scooter can afford, but harkens back to an arguably more idealistic genre of cycle.

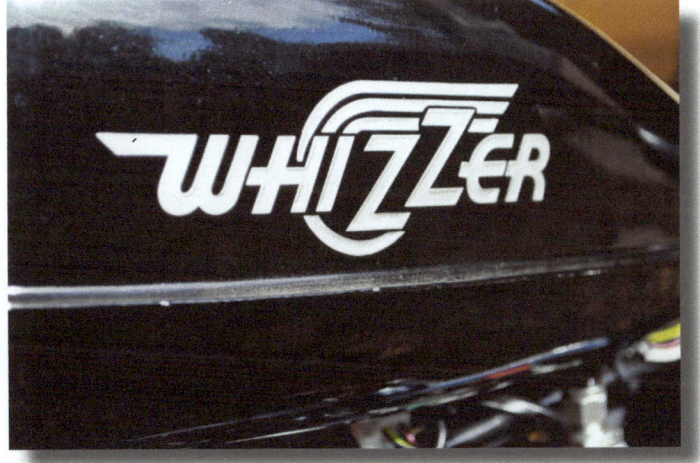

Lani, if you might remember, was shown once before in our Celebrity and Hero chapter escorting the mayor of her home town Norman, Oklahoma, in a Veteran's Day Parade. She is associated with Veterans in training as well as an accomplished Naval instructor. Thank you for sharing your time and rosy visage within these images of your specialy motorcycle. We all also appreciate how you Honor those who serve our country.

SPEEDY CAFE

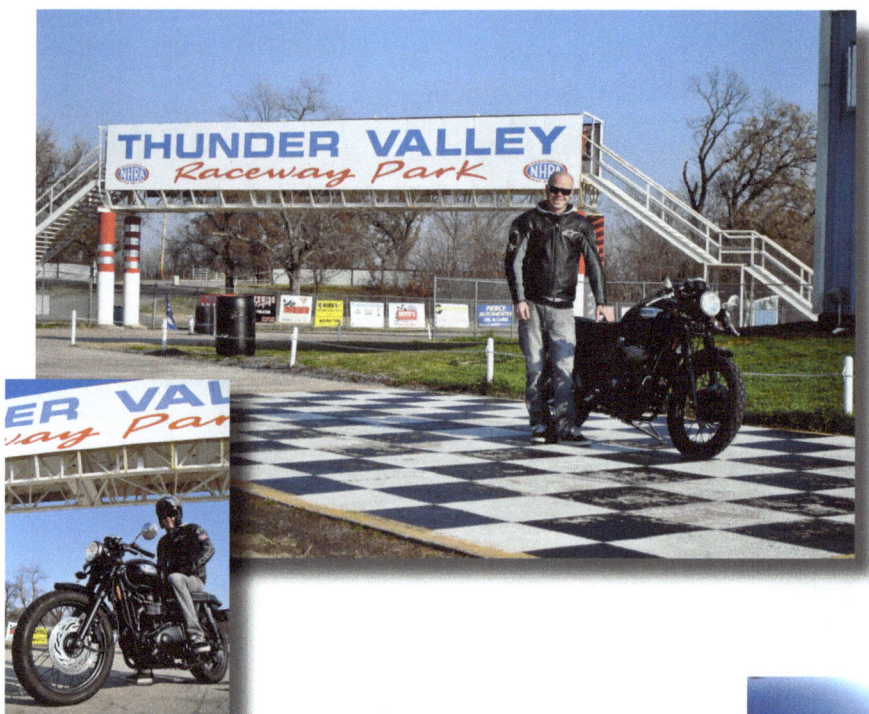

Thanks to Michelle at the N.H.R.A. Sanctioned Thunder Valley Race Track in Noble, Oklahoma, we were blessed with the opportunity to spend a comely afternoon playing on their world class sprint track with Cody Curran.

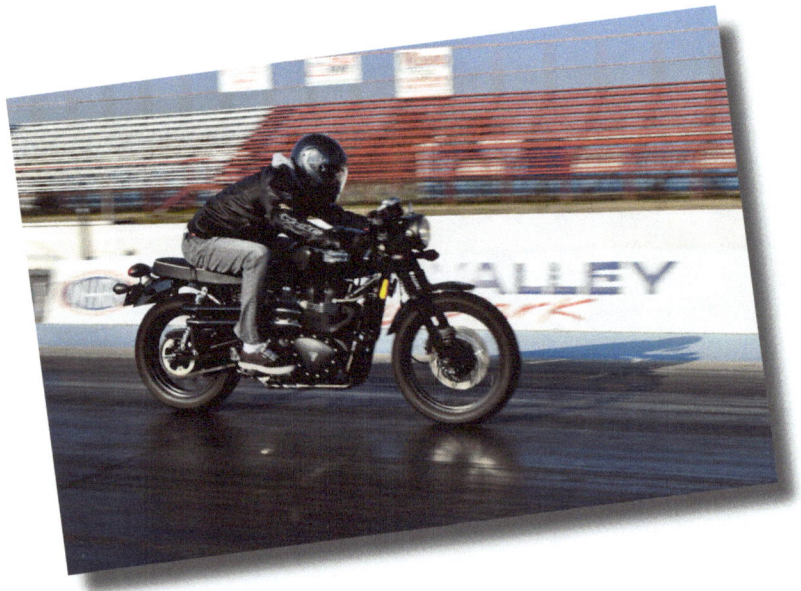

Cody, whose wife is actually a Veteran, found this charitable automobile photography book close to his heart, and was only too happy to donate his time to the project. Plus, who could pass up an opportunity like this to test out the limits of his hot rod bike? This already sleek Triumph was converted into something resembling a "Cafe Racer," and man, it lived up to its description: it was faster than lightning.

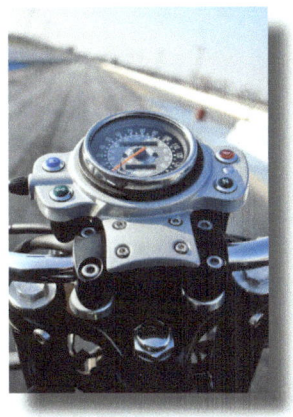

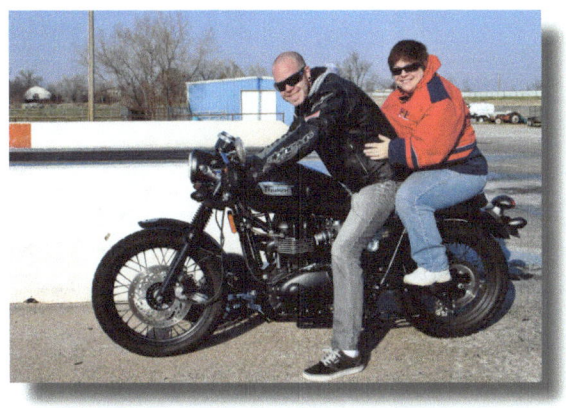

He even offered Margo and I rides, to which there was no ounce of hesitation in our hearty affirmative answers.

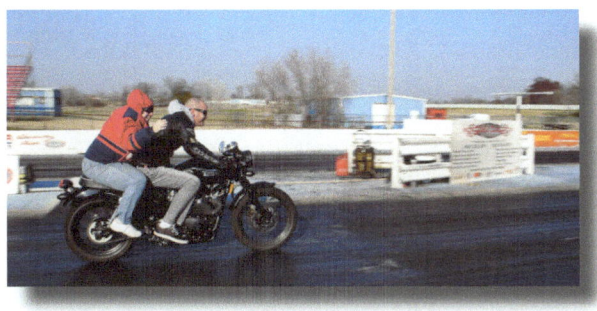

She was full of fortitude, whereas I held on for dear life, with not much regard for anything but surviving the quickest speeds I have ever reached driving, or riding on a cycle. What a gas! Thanks to you Cody for your generosity of spirit, and to the Missus for serving our country.

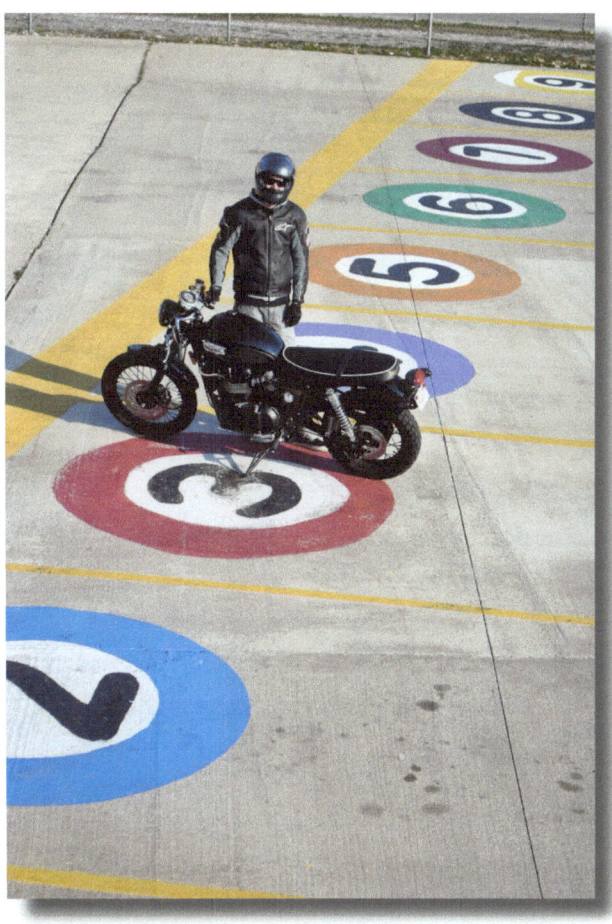

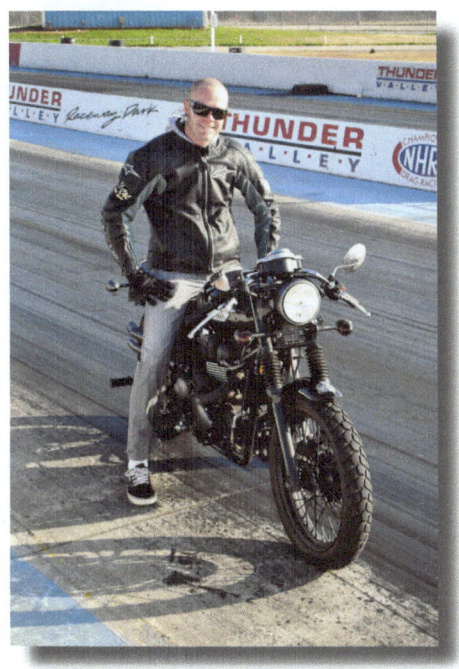

ITALIANS AND STALLIONS

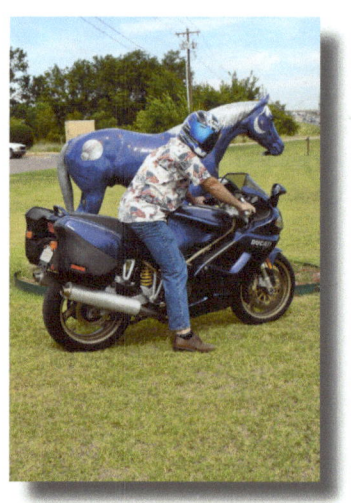

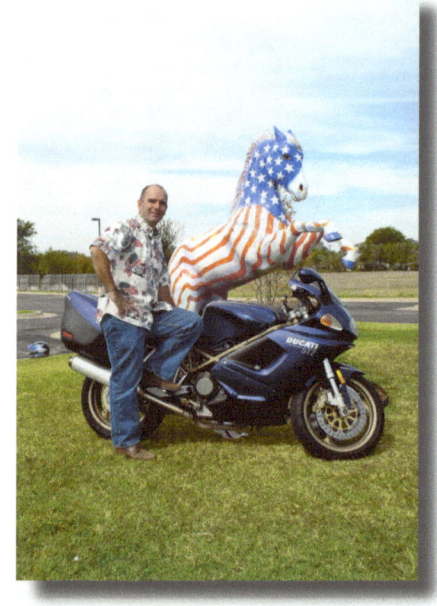

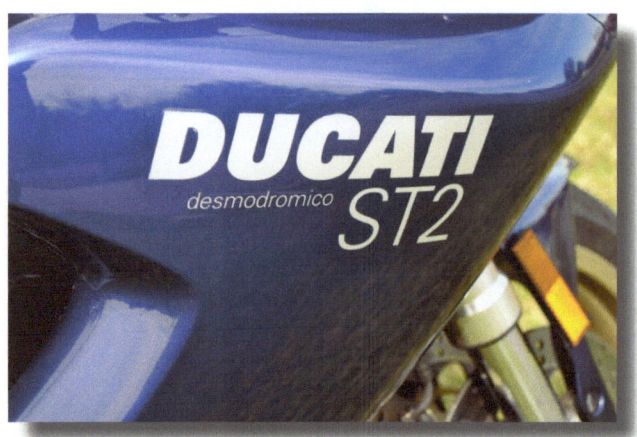

Mr. Curtis Smith of Shawnee, Oklahoma, home to several elegant galleries, takes our art appreciation to the street. He was the consummate professor, showcasing his belissimo Italian-born Ducati with several examples of the city's recent outdoor display

Impassioned artists, in conjunction with each business reflected, competed to have their talents emblazoned upon the many mustang canvases throughout town. My mom rode along for this photo shoot. Having grown up around race horses as a child, she thoroughly jubilated in this guided tour.

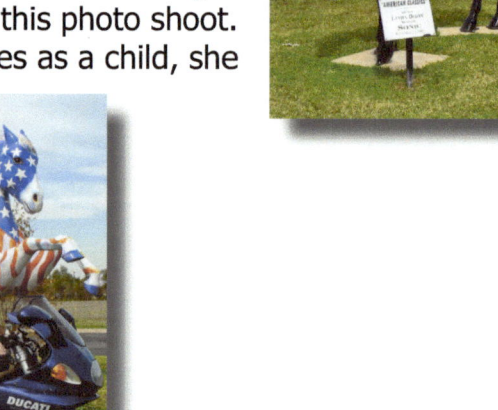

Thanks, Curtis, for the lesson, and for keeping your own swift piece of mobile magnetism in such museum-quality shape.

ARCHWAY TO A CYCLING FAMILY

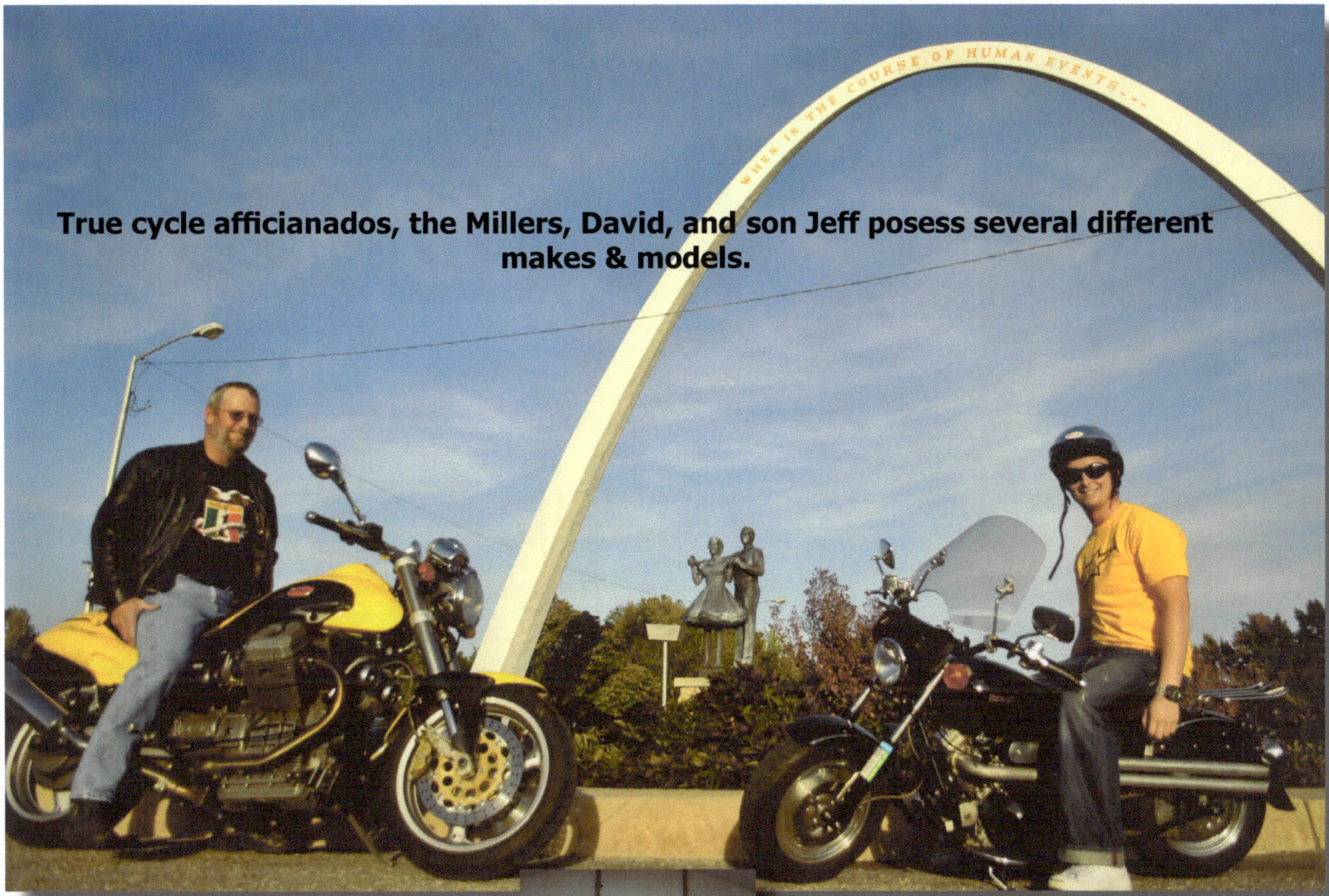

True cycle afficianados, the Millers, David, and son Jeff posess several different makes & models.

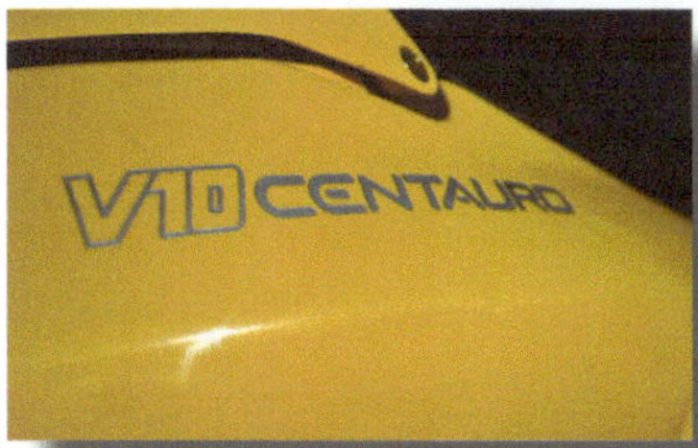

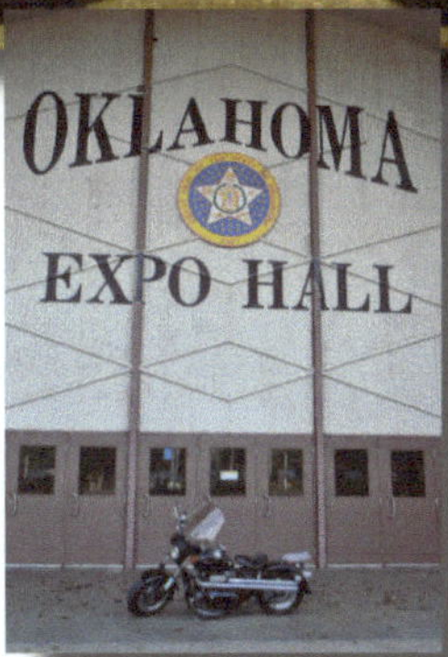

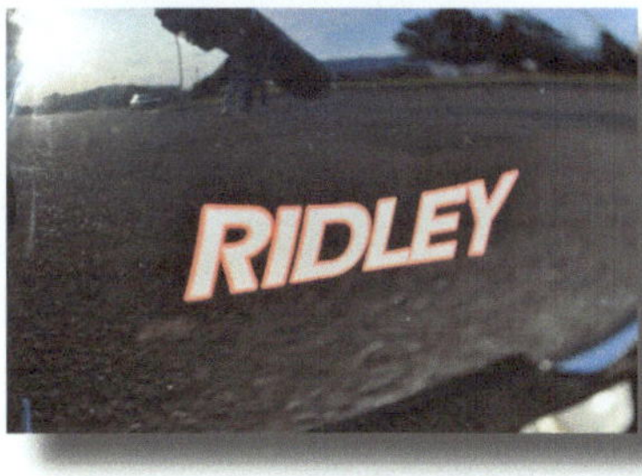

The choices brought to the Oklahoma State Fairgrounds today consist of their procurement's creme de la creme. Davie is sporting his strikingly yellow Moto Guzzi with matching apparel to complete the ensemble. Jeff's mini is nothing to scoff at, being a tad more uncommon. His stone pony is the Oklahoma made and manufactured export from the short-lived "Ridley" company.

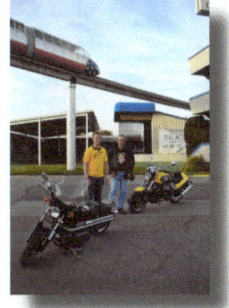

Thanks for being willing to share in your vast knowledge of motorcycles and cruising such a long distance to tarry under our state's answer to Missouri's Arch. May safe rides be always in your future.

THE WINDMILLS ON OUR MINDS

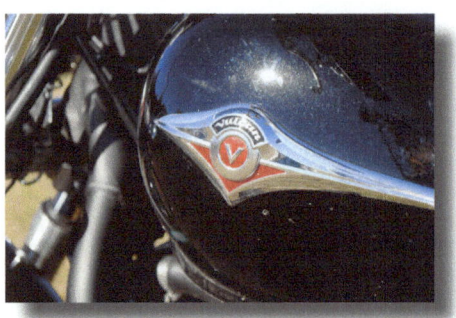

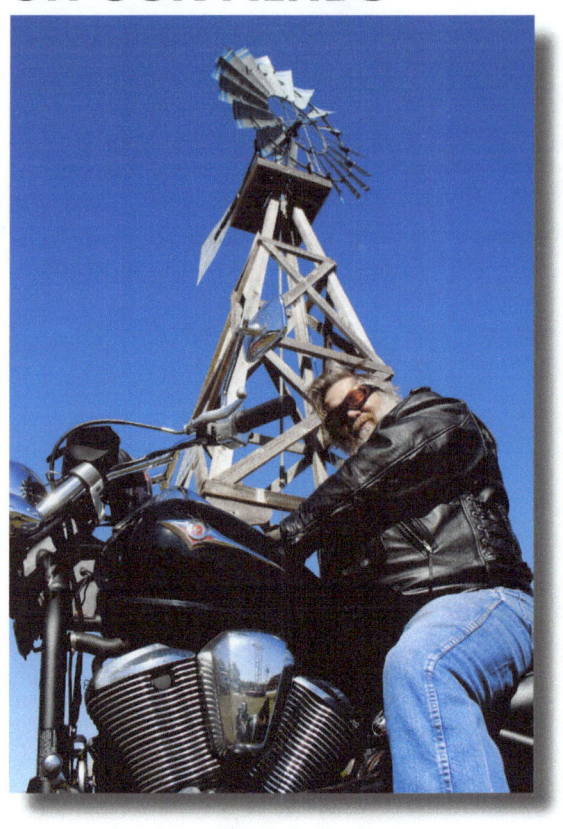

Harrah, Oklahoma Cycler, Curtis Ryan, and his '08 Kawasaki Vulkan, breeze by a sight not too unusual in his perpetually wind-filled state.

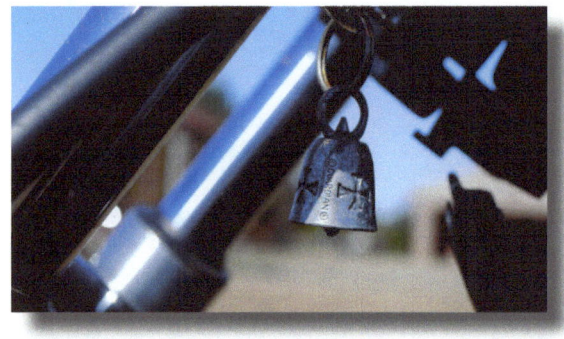

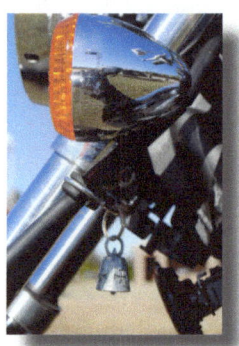

That bell, if you didn't know, is a good luck charm for bikers. It must not be purchased for oneself, but should be bestowed.

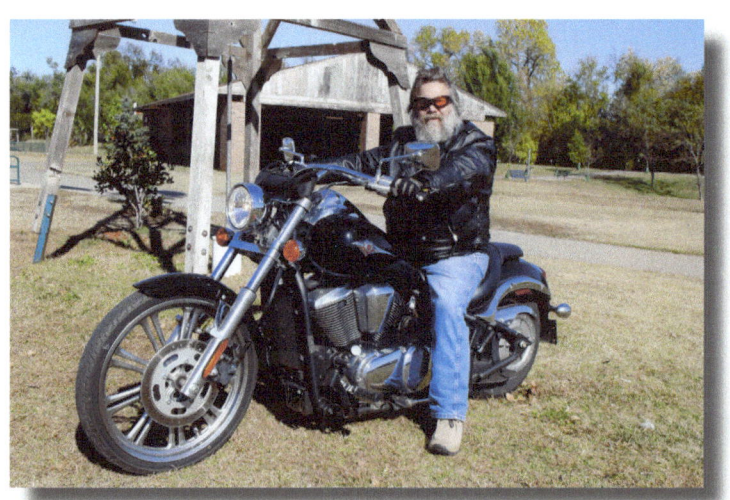

Always the best of luck and safety to you and all bikers.

DAS MOTORAD

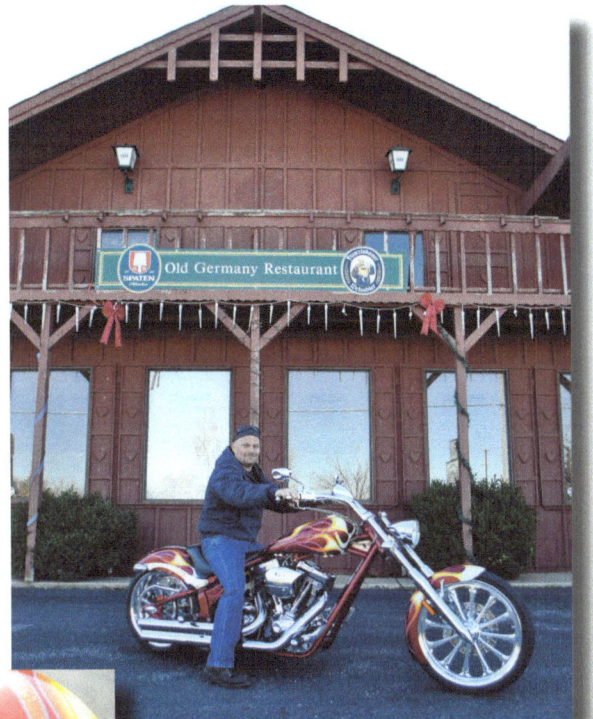

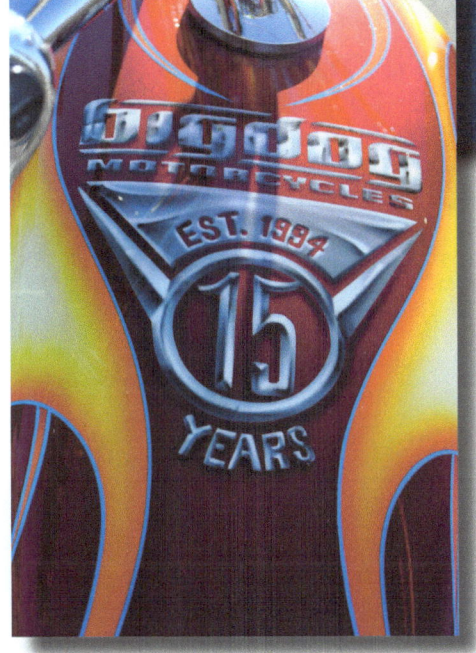

Out for a post-New Year's holiday jaunt are Mr. Daryl Lucas, and his ever-present riding buddy, daughter Kimberly. We crossed paths at this wintery alpine resort-like eatery in Choctaw, Oklahoma.

Their other faithful companion is this colorful Fifteenth Anniversary Edition Wichita, Kansas bred Bull Dog motorcycle.

One can't help but admire the fiercely appointed eye catchers and intense paint job. This is a well taken care of bike that must be the envy of your block. Paint the town the rest of your ride, and year.

BURNIN' OIL WITH THE OILMAN

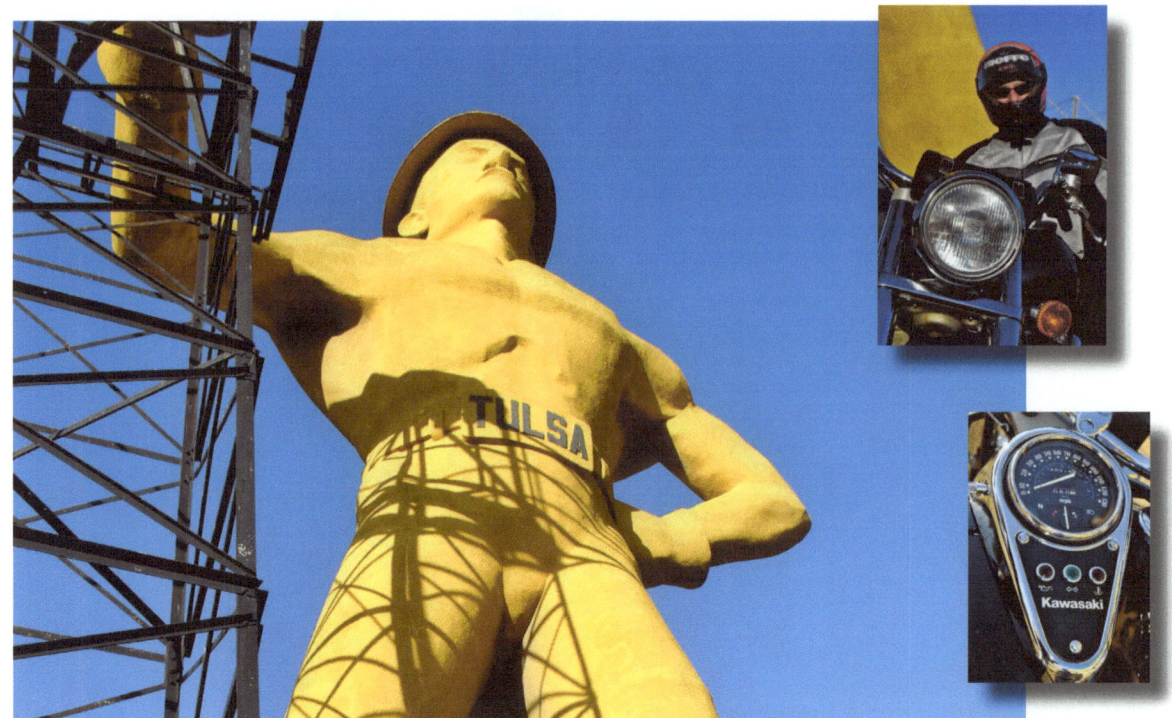

Taming this '03 Kawasaki Vulkan Classic 1500 is Greg Crane of Broken Arrow, Oklahoma. Attending a Toys For Tots show, and charitable poker run on the Tulsa Fairgrounds, we came across this roughneck fella. Counted as one of the largest statues in the U.S., I couldn't count the big fella' out, and knew I had to find a willing participant to frame up.

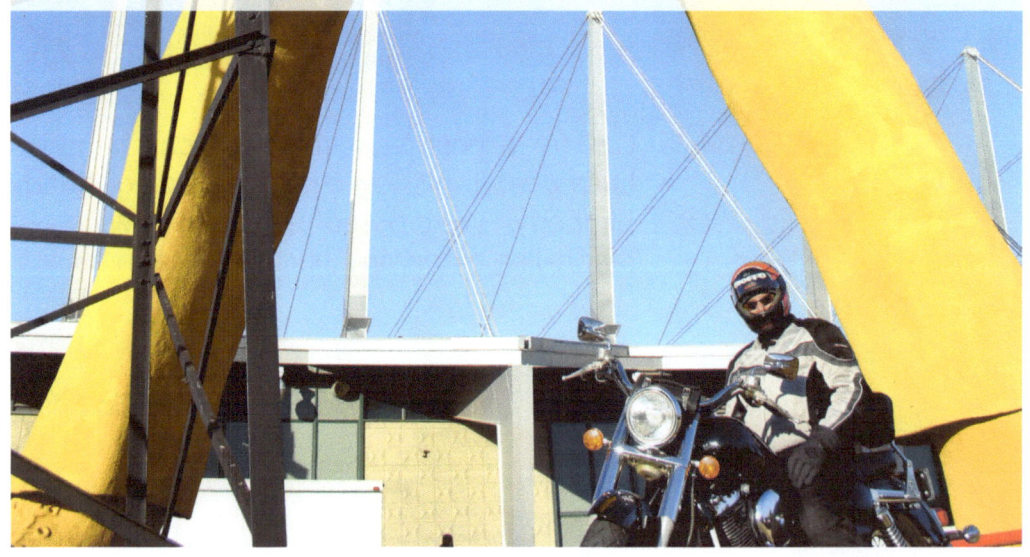

Greg was departing for the toy run portion of the day's activities, heading from the pan to the flames so to speak, as he was slated for a water front starting position. Thanks Greg, and all of the bikers involved for braving those lake-effect winds for the cause. It was estimated to be a successful toy run, so the bitter temps were not all for naught.

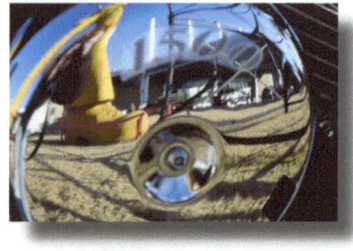

135

VET HOG

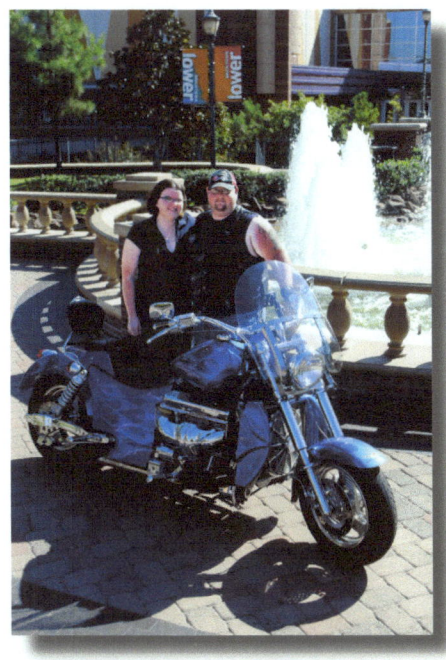

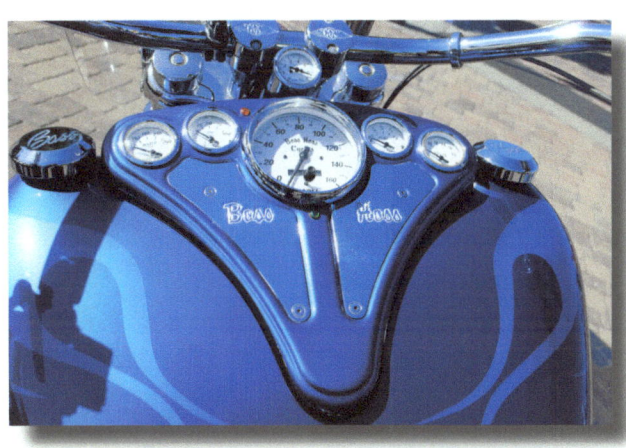

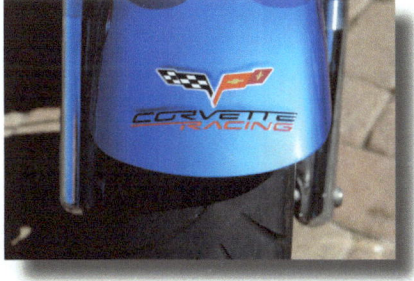

Overflowing with joy since acquiring their hearty 2002 Vet engine motorcycle, Michael and Megan Burns glided over to Lower Bricktown for this fountain side docking.

Complete with a wave of power from the V-12 monster motor they're too cool for school even when the tide rolls into night fall with the azure blue glow their custom illuination package provides.

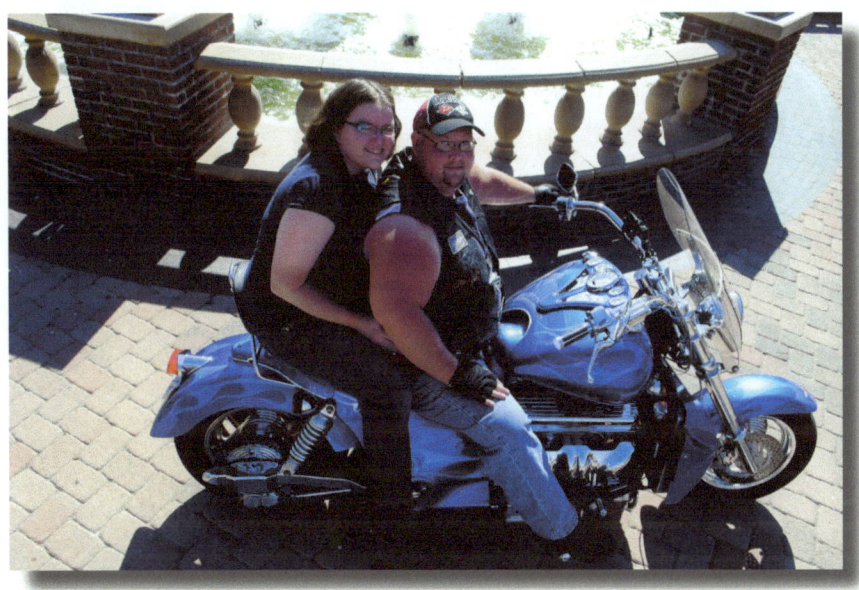

Here's to smooth tarmac ahead.

ROYAL PHOTOS

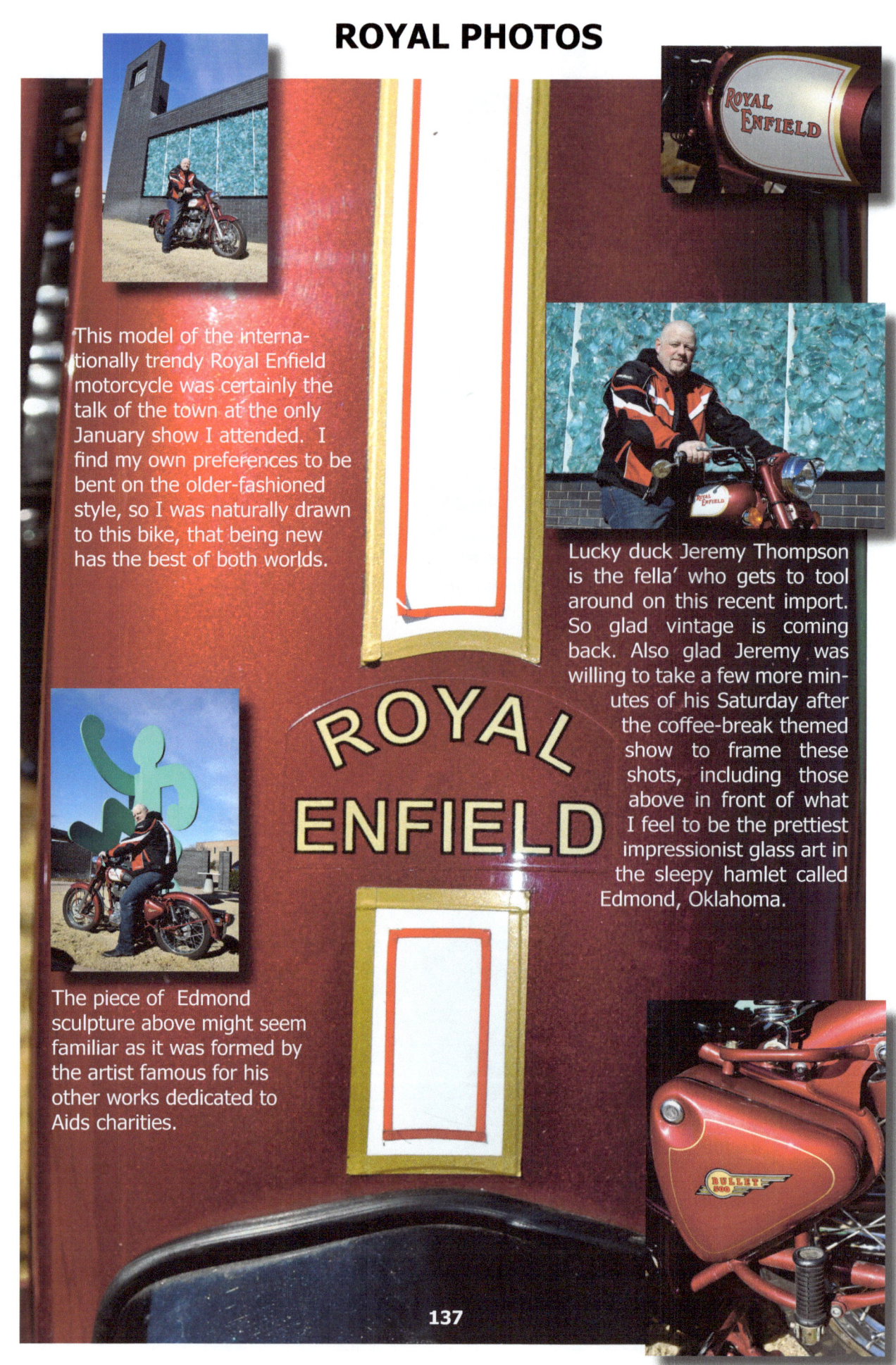

This model of the internationally trendy Royal Enfield motorcycle was certainly the talk of the town at the only January show I attended. I find my own preferences to be bent on the older-fashioned style, so I was naturally drawn to this bike, that being new has the best of both worlds.

The piece of Edmond sculpture above might seem familiar as it was formed by the artist famous for his other works dedicated to Aids charities.

Lucky duck Jeremy Thompson is the fella' who gets to tool around on this recent import. So glad vintage is coming back. Also glad Jeremy was willing to take a few more minutes of his Saturday after the coffee-break themed show to frame these shots, including those above in front of what I feel to be the prettiest impressionist glass art in the sleepy hamlet called Edmond, Oklahoma.

CHOO CHOO CHOSE THIS WINNING BIKE...

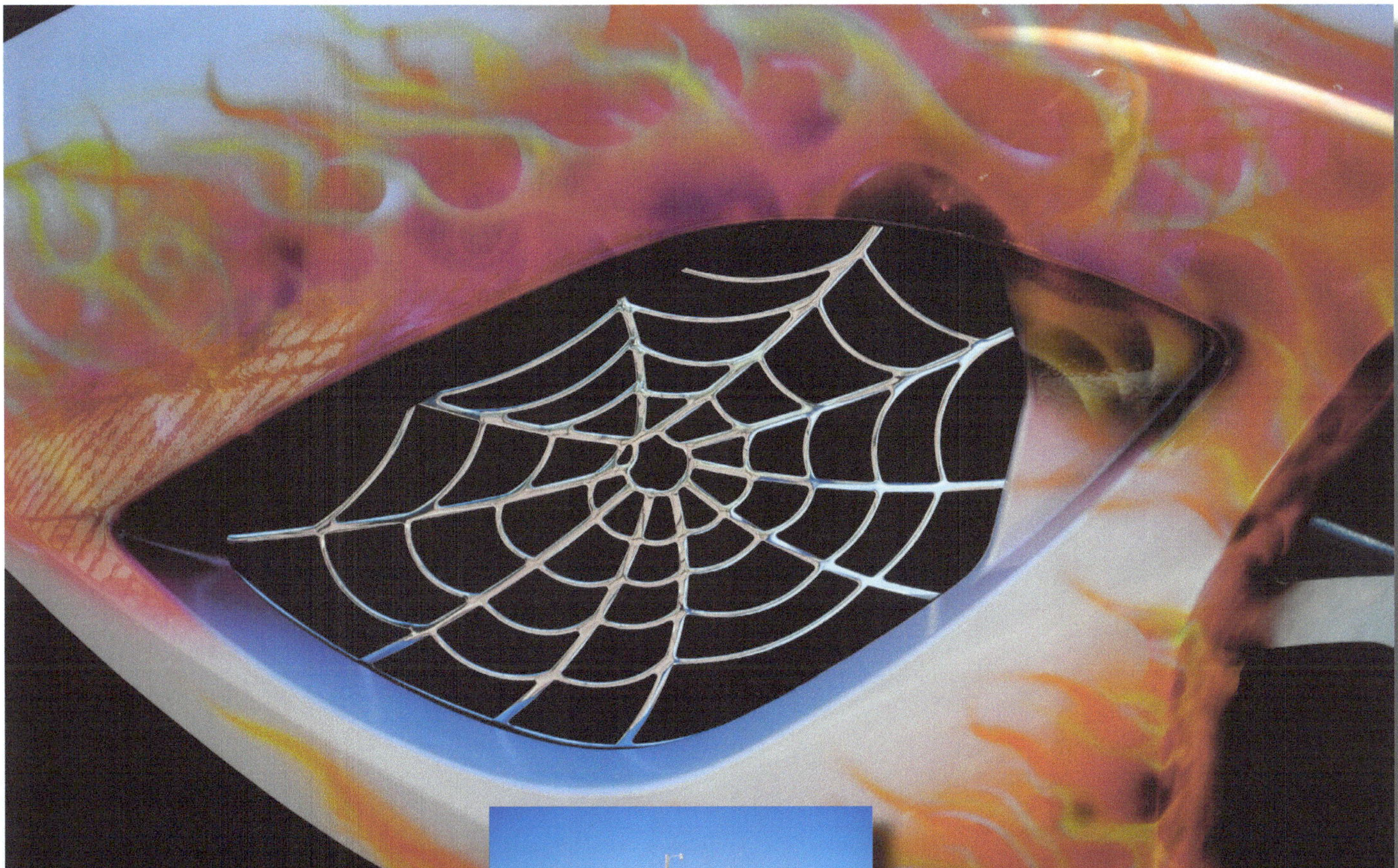

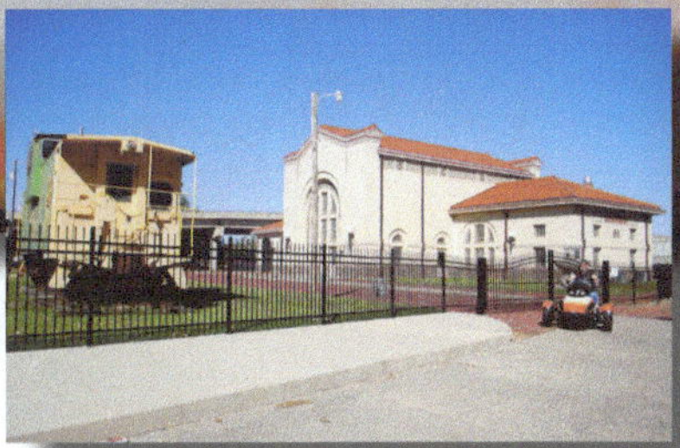

Steering a new 2010 Can Am Spyder, Mr. Larry Whitcomb of Millsap, Texas, was in town for a reunion with his brother in central Oklahoma.

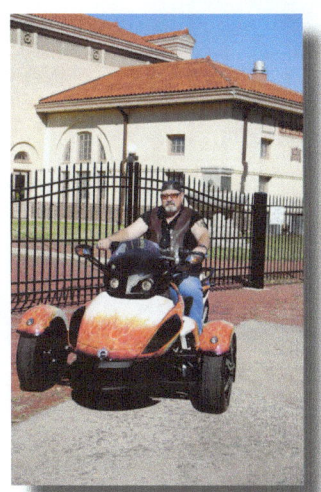

When "bro" casually mentioned there was a car show in his neighborhood, they entered and spent the day showing off Lar's hot ride. Between fielding questions from the colloquial small towners who had scant seen such a boss street legal three wheeler, they caught up on old times.

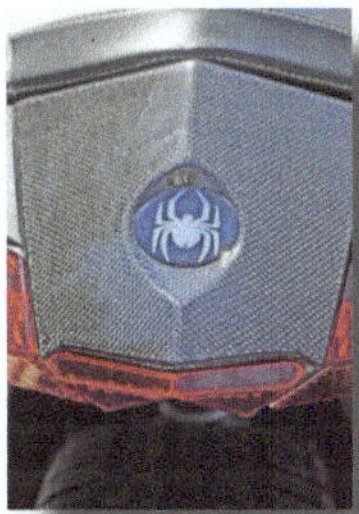

Having a family history of relatives in the employ of the railroad trade, the boys grew up loving trains. We thereby, in line with the ubiquitous theme, prodded Larry along with his spider infested investment, to hang out by this whistle-stop for some photos.

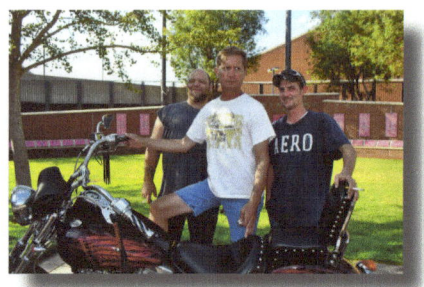

INDIAN SUMMER

I sighted these three football fans, James Bryan, Chris Mathews, & Steve Smallwood while checking out photo locales in Norman, Oklahoma during one of 2011's infamous triple-digit days.

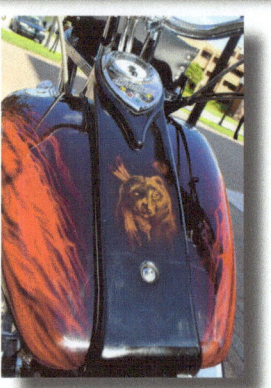

After coaxing our pictured Indian to join us for the fun, we made our way to the University home of these fella's favorite team. They're posing appropriately enough in front of the beloved stadium with, in the foreground, the All American Plaza wall listing every one of the school's "All American" players.

James, a stroke survivor, was forced to sell his trusted steed this late model '02 Custom painted Indian Motorcycle. Luckily, with a little help from his friends, James was able to enjoy at least one more afternoon ride.

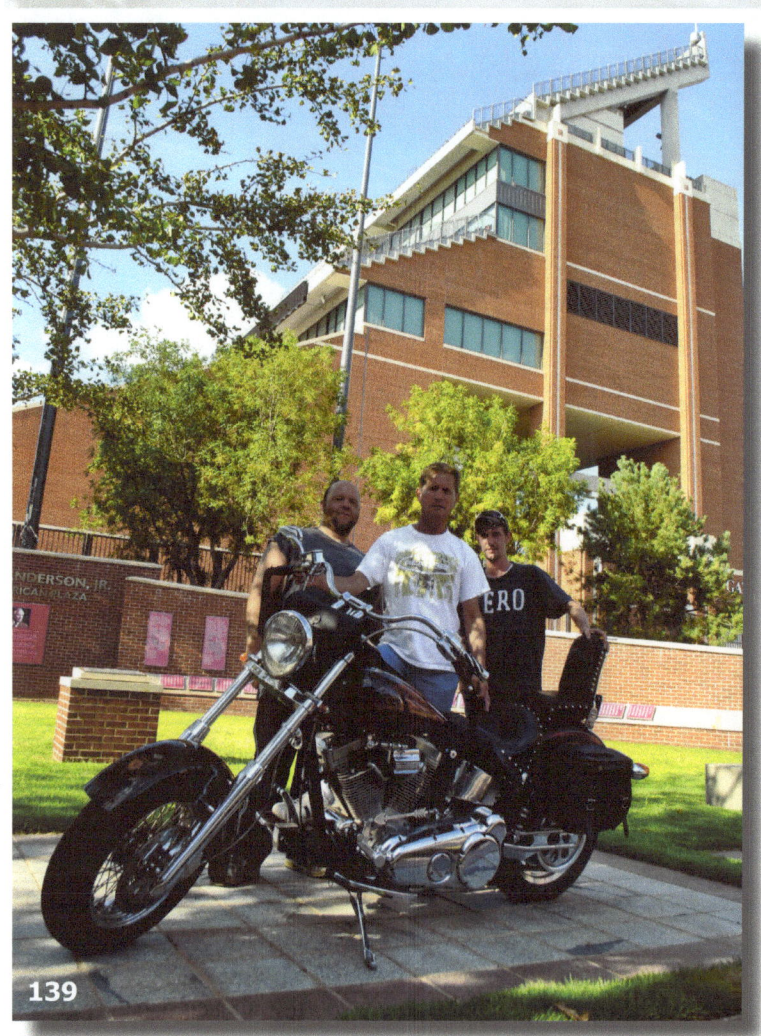

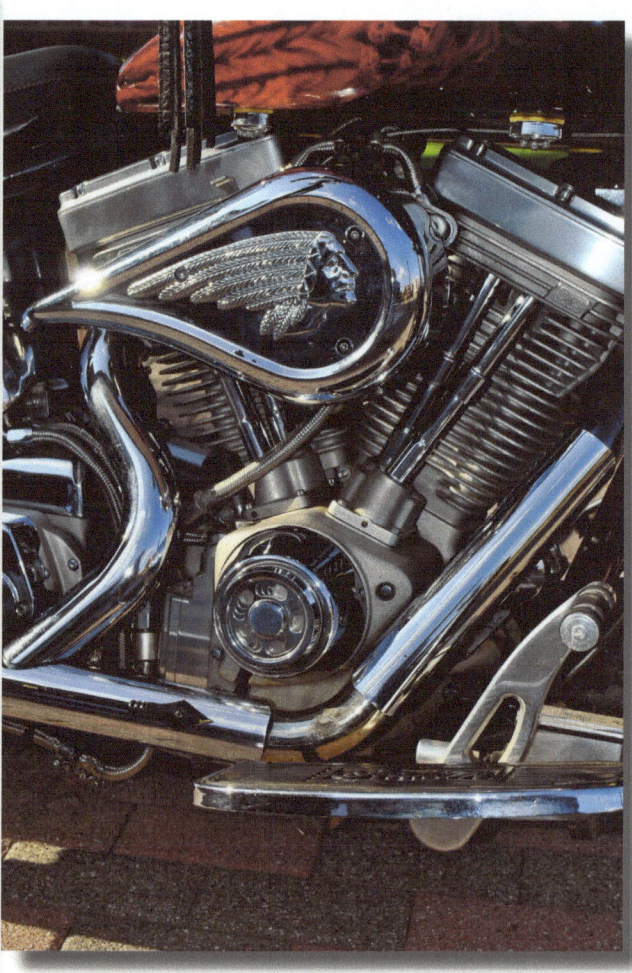

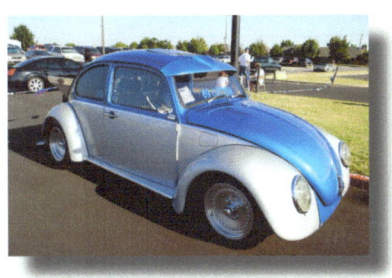

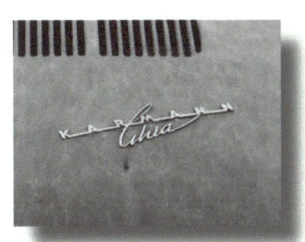

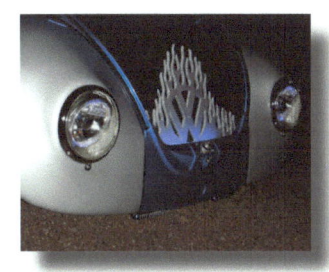

VOLKSWAGENS

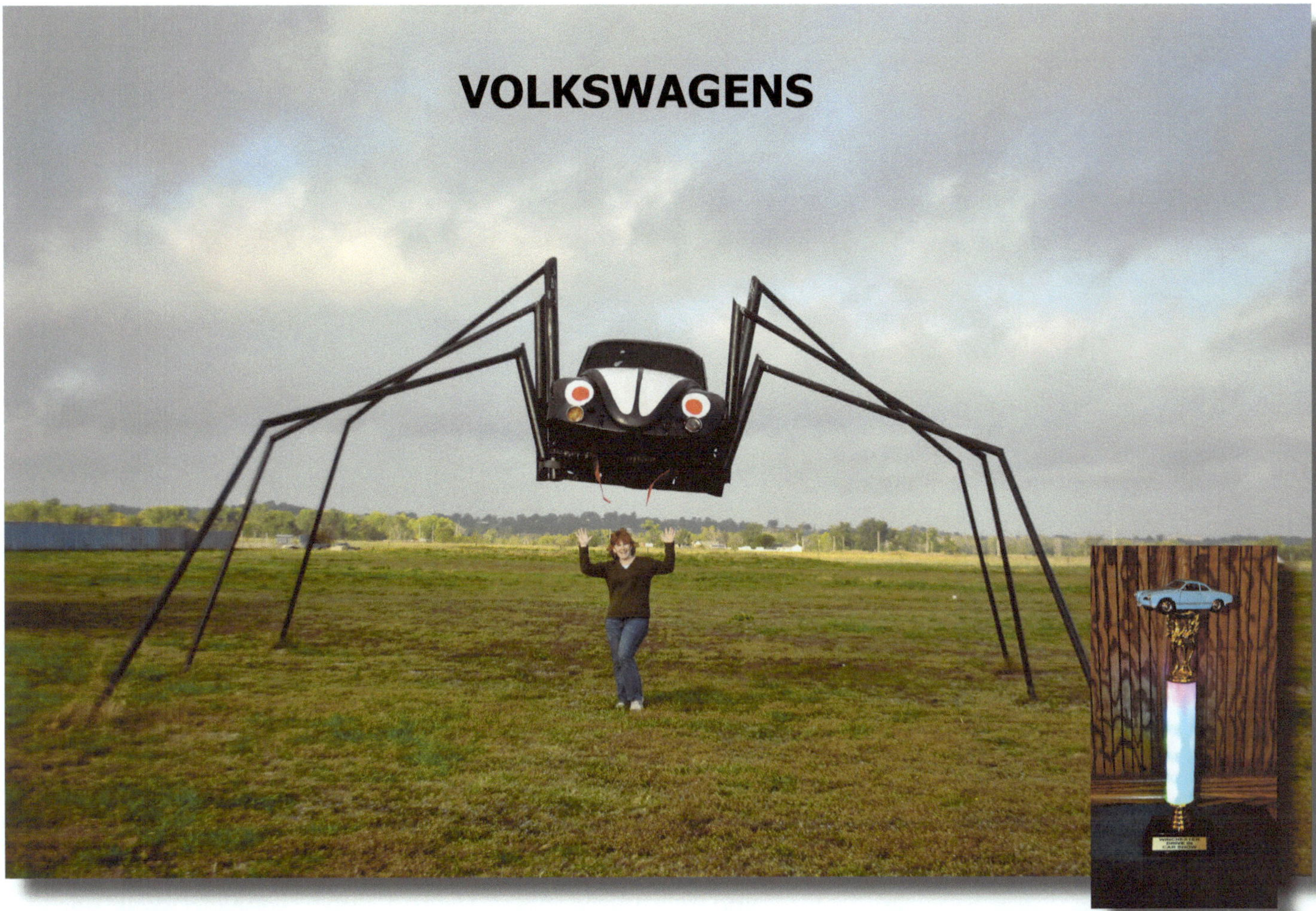

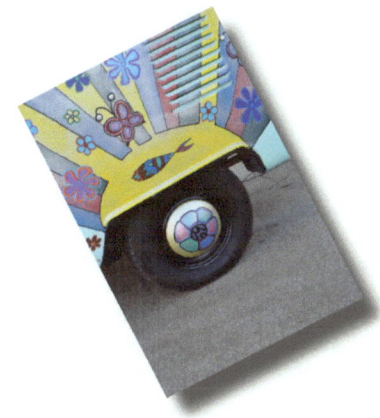

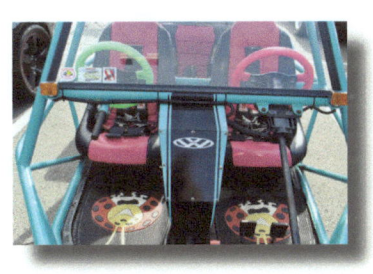

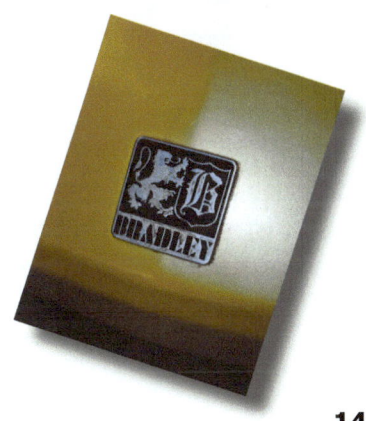

CLUBBIN'

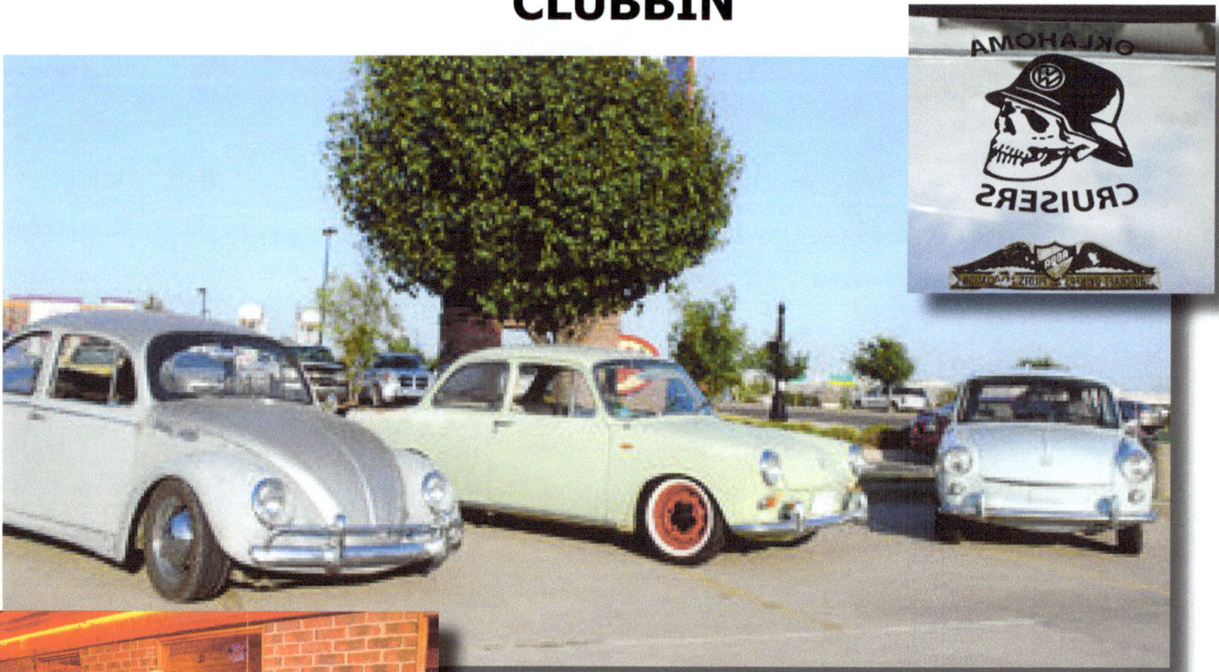

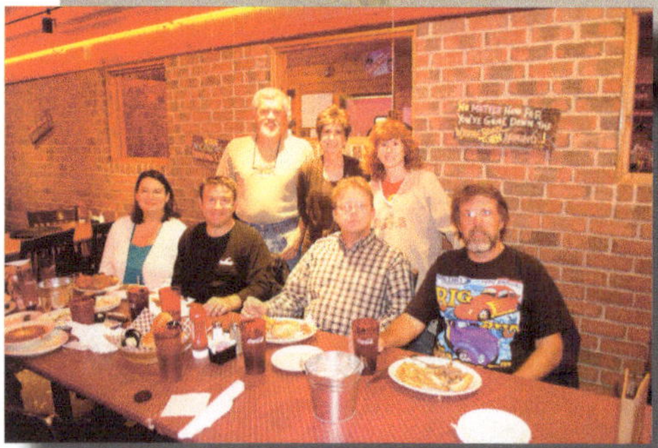

Members of the Volkswagen enthusiasts club I proudly belong to, the Oklahoma V.W. Cruisers, gather for a picture during our monthly meeting.

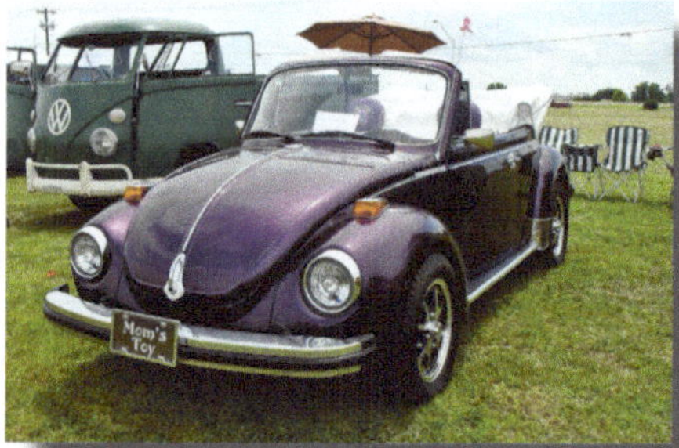

Brenda and Mike Card own his and her Volkswagens. Mike's = an olive green camper bus that looks like it rolled off the show room floor. Bren's = a '78 Super Beetle affectionately dubbed "Purple Passion." She brags that she must be the only woman in America who got hysterically excited over receiving seat belts for Christmas one year. Of course they were purple and matched regally.

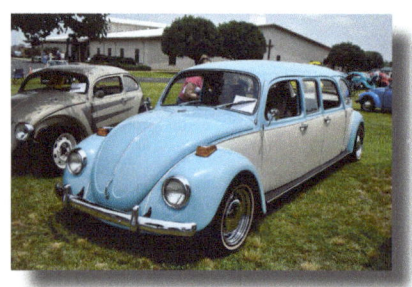

Michael Hathaway and Anet Price cruise around in a '66 Beetle. They hadn't brought it that day as there was inclement weather, but just like this crowd pleasing limo, all the "Herbies" in the club are a welcome sight at the big V.W. Show listed in the Car Show Chapter of this book.

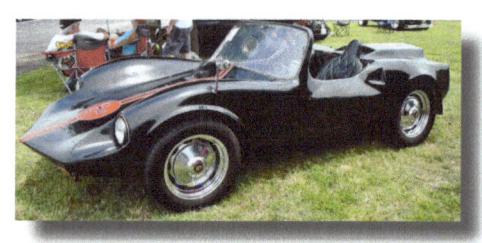

CLUBBIN' STILL...

Stephen Smith, seated, is a true aficianado, in possession of not only a '65 Bus, a '68 Beetle, but also one of the initial '58 Karmann Ghias, known as the Low Light model. Last but not least in our snap shot is Mr. David Westenberger, who can be seen at the local drag strip track racing his V.W.'s. The modified rides include two non-street legal Dune Buggies, as well as another Ghia, his '74, the last year of the breed. Not in attendance was our illustrious President, who owns the pictured sea foam green 1500 below.

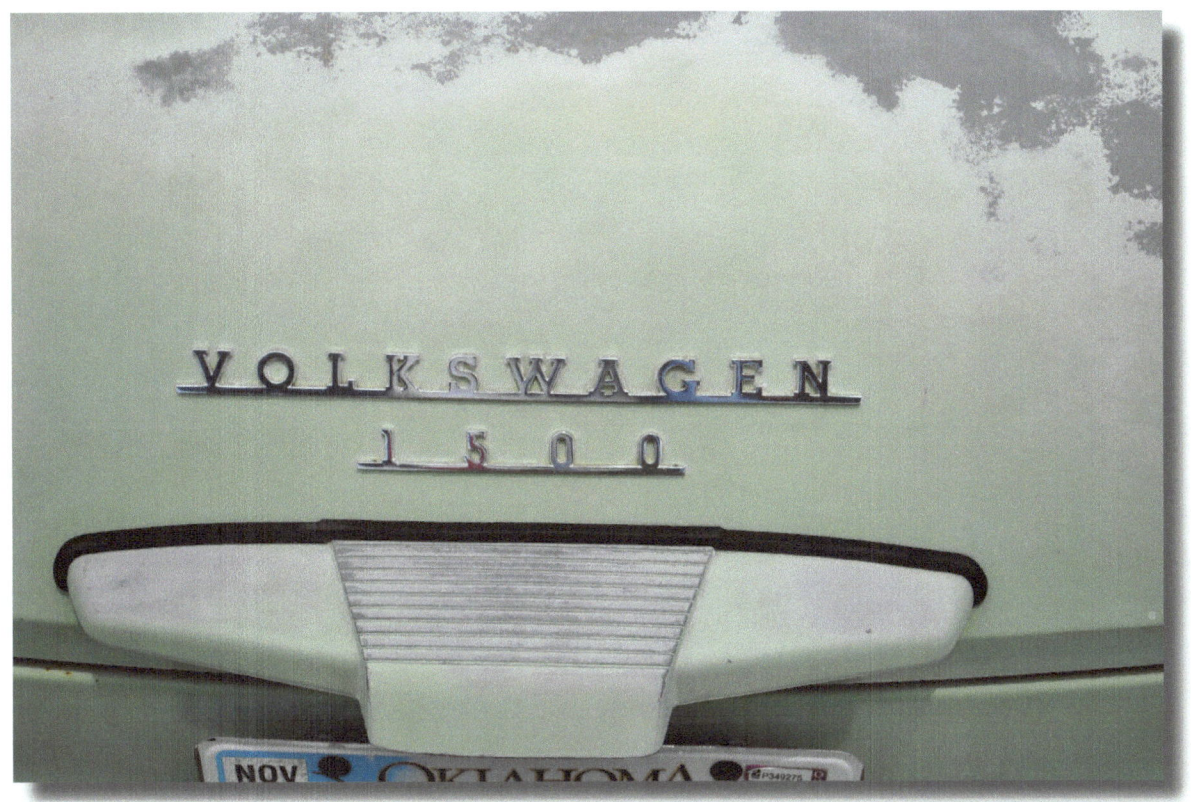

Also missing that night, among others, is one of my best pals from the organization, Mr. Kyle. He is the fella' who introduced me to this motley crue, and he owns a slew of a caboodle himself. The list includes Dune Buggies, Beetles, a Notch Back, a Fast Back, and an almost as rare V.W. Drop-Side Pick Up Truck or two as seen in part of the family portrait below.

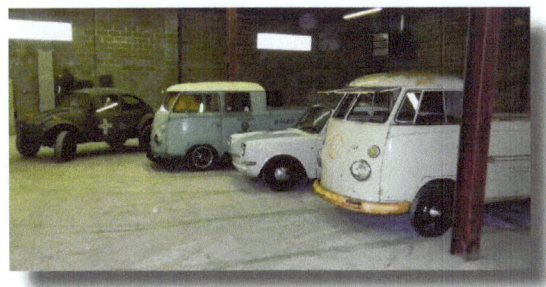

Check out our forum if you're interested in joining, or just want to see these magnificent specimens and more at any of the upcoming events.

BUGGING OUT AT THE IN

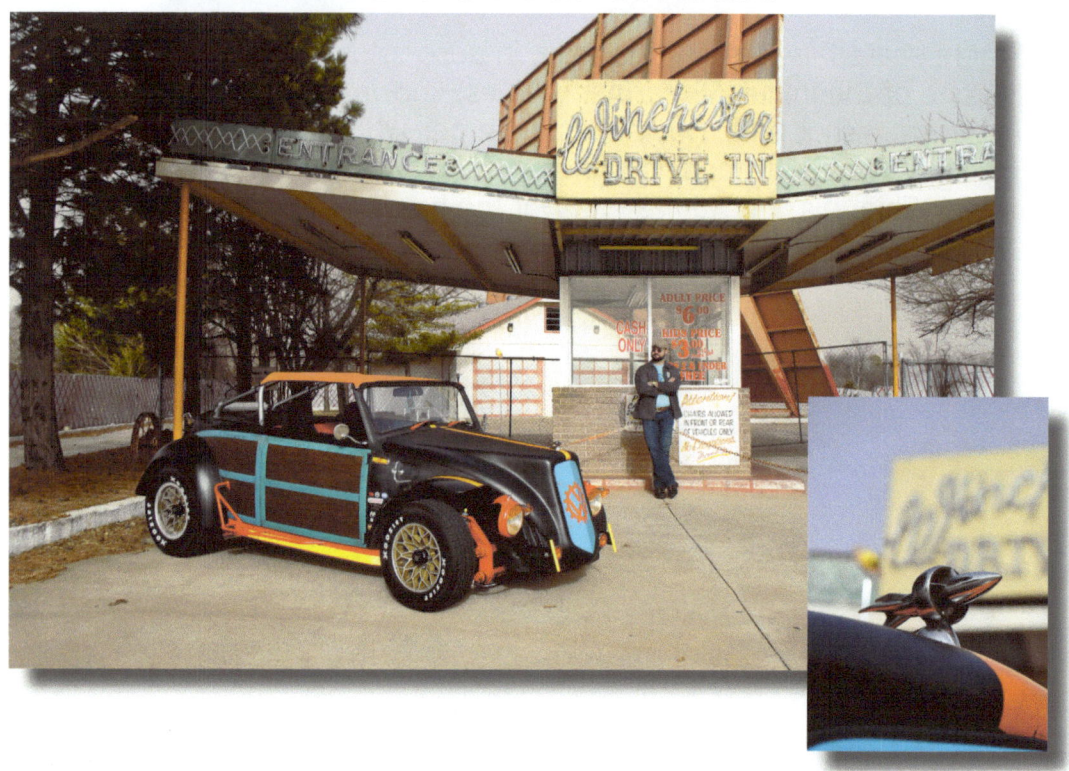

Arriving early to snag a front row at Oklahoma City's remaining drive-in movie theatre, The Winchester, is Mr. Eric Rich. Eric's interpration of this vintage Volkswagen Beetle, bearing the name "Dub Tub" is choc full of imaginative modifications, including a handmade cover, reflective paint job, and a souped-up engine any hot-rodder would be ecstatic to test.

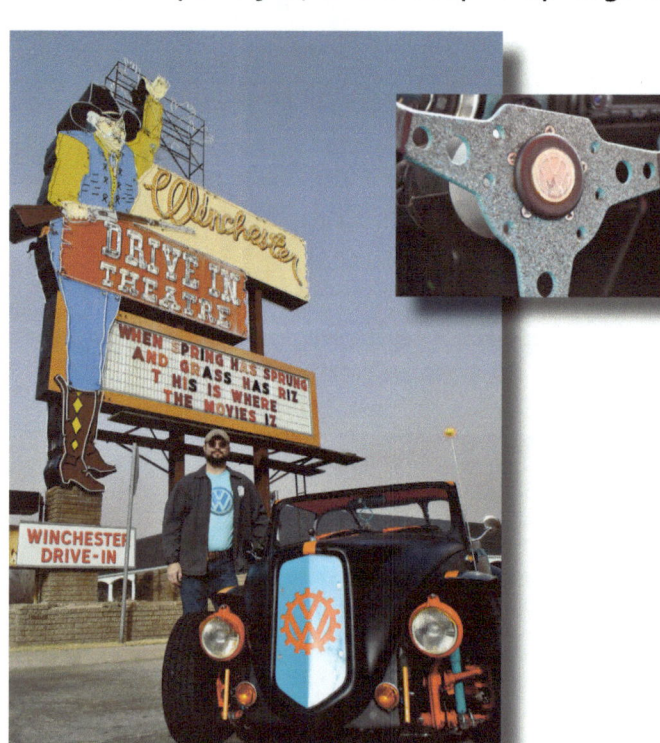

Eric, also a member of the V.W. Club just seen, has been a good friend to all, and an integral part of the Oklahoma City V.W. scene for years.

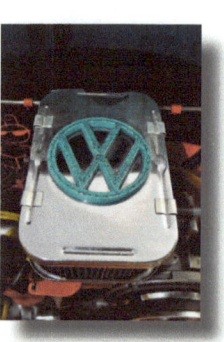

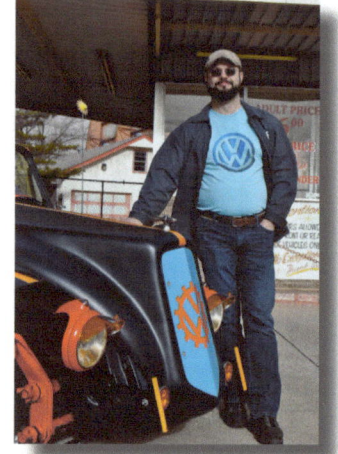

MECHANICS TO THE MILE OF CARS STARS

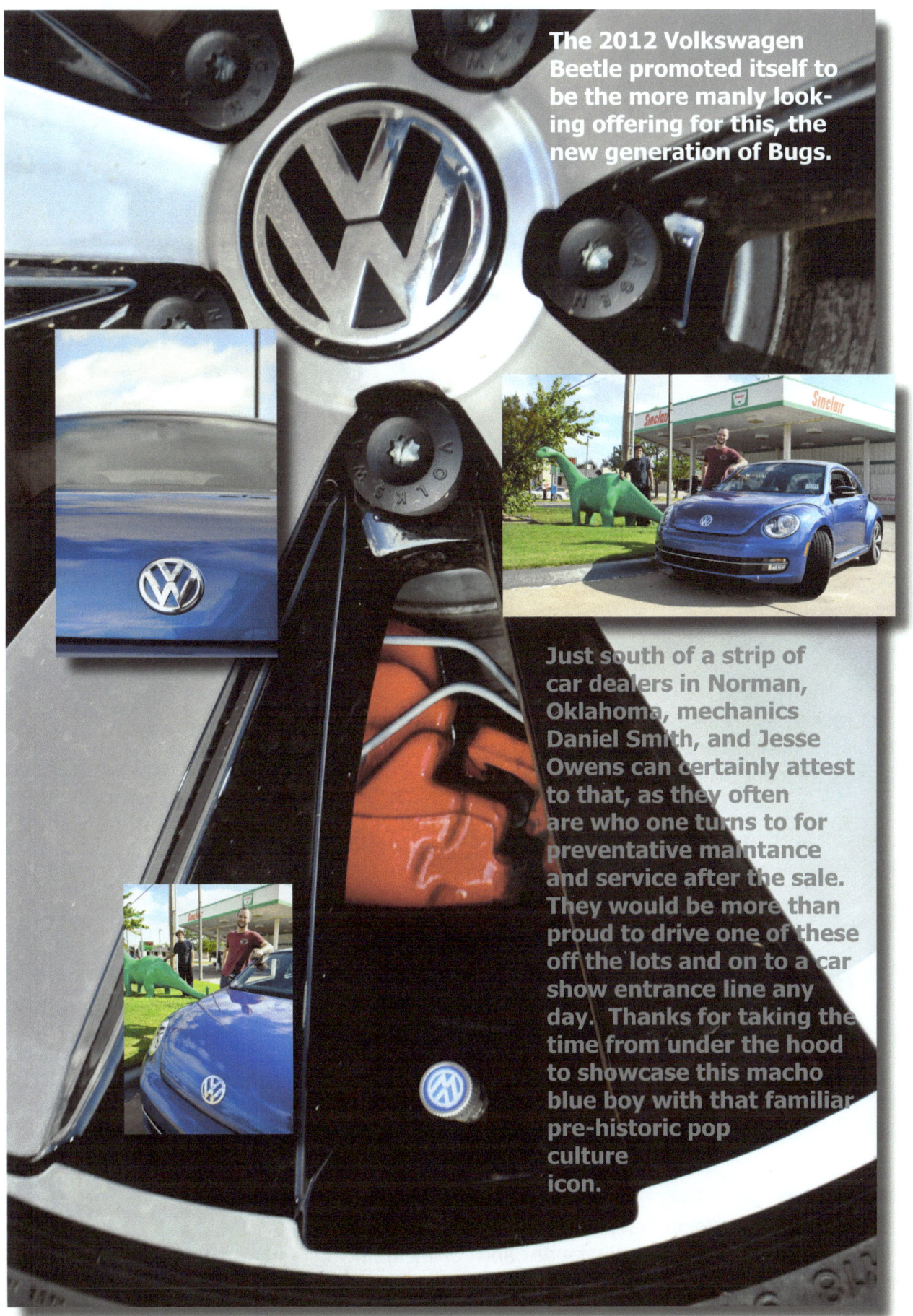

The 2012 Volkswagen Beetle promoted itself to be the more manly looking offering for this, the new generation of Bugs.

Just south of a strip of car dealers in Norman, Oklahoma, mechanics Daniel Smith, and Jesse Owens can certainly attest to that, as they often are who one turns to for preventative maintance and service after the sale. They would be more than proud to drive one of these off the lots and on to a car show entrance line any day. Thanks for taking the time from under the hood to showcase this macho blue boy with that familiar pre-historic pop culture icon.

A FAMILY AFFAIR

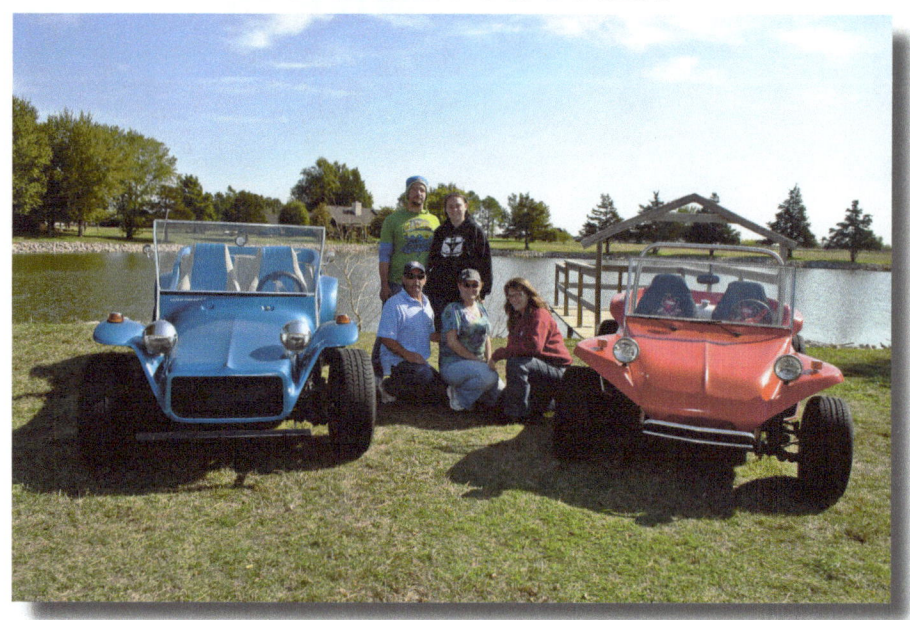

The Elliotts spend a day at the park along with the four wheeled fraternal twins in their dynasty.

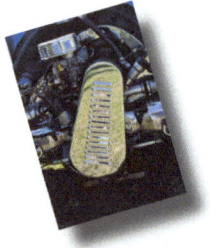 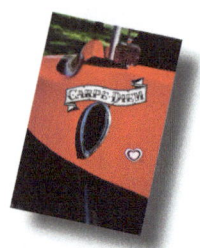

Mom Sherri Elliott, & daughter Lindsey McCracken, caretake these bouncing babies, cruising together to car shows across their metro area.

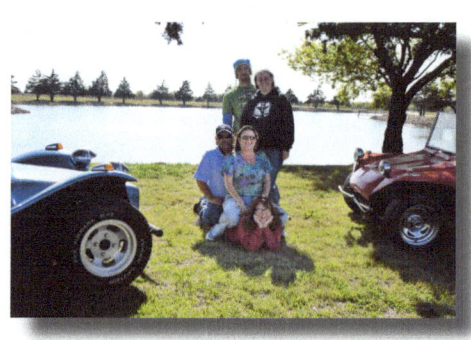

Everybody got in on the act in this wrestling match, including Dad, Dennis Elliott, Sissy, Heather McCracken, and family friend, Joshua Garner.

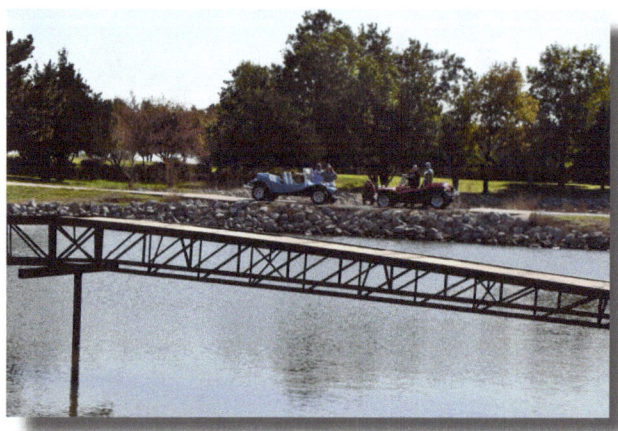

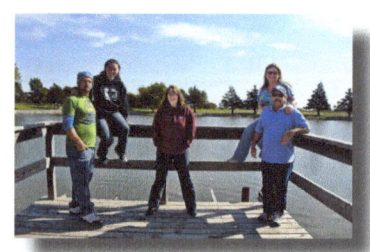

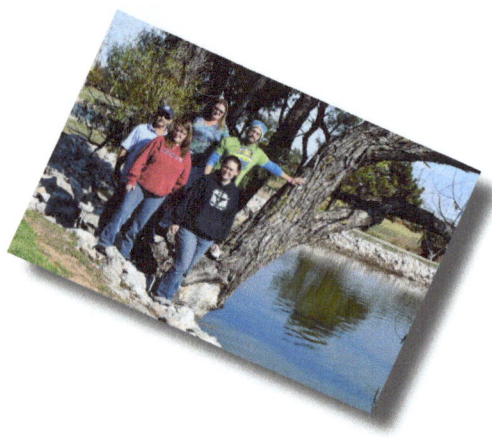

It's always preferable to have such senses of humor in our midst. Thanks for my daily laugh, and for including your Dune Buggies in this family reunion.

HAPPY CAMPERS

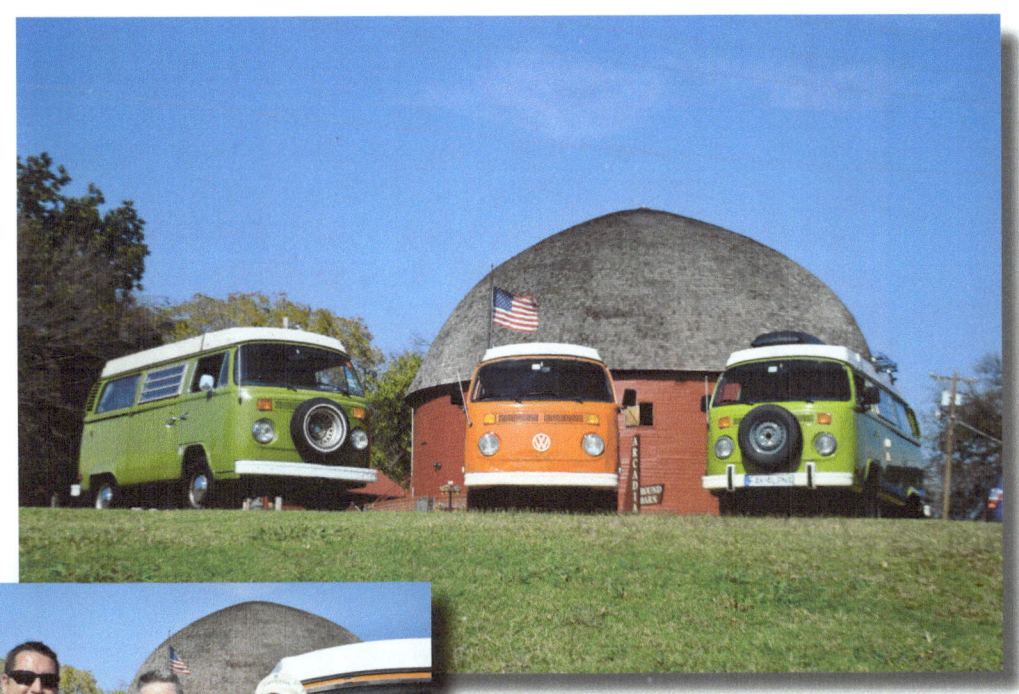

Johnathan Joyce, Donald Waggoner, and James Stuart, are veritable modern day Three Musketeers when it comes to Volkswagen fanticism. This trio of Volkswagen Vans are not just show cars, they have actually maintained camping functionality, and are used for that purpose on a regular basis.

Inseparable in their kindred inclination to a V.W. Bus, and unbeknownst until meeting this bright sunny day, Don and John even wore the same fan tee.

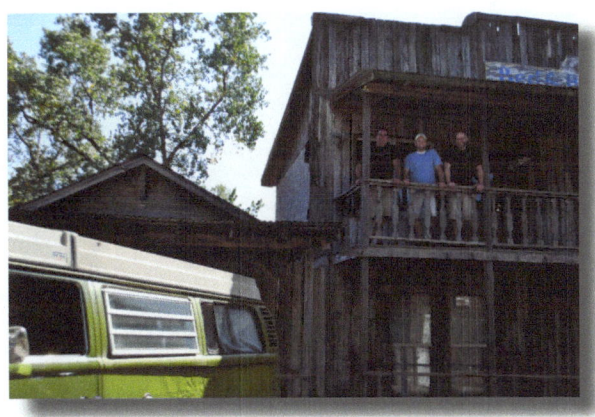

The perfect picture of uniformity, we find them stationed in front of Arcadia, Oklahoma's claim to fame, the indelible souvenir, the Red Round Barn on Rt. 66, & this "campy" renovated hotel relic from past road trips of heydays gone by.

Many thanks for sharing a bit of your time away from your family, otherwise known as the fellow tin can tenters.

REST IN...A VOLKSWAGEN

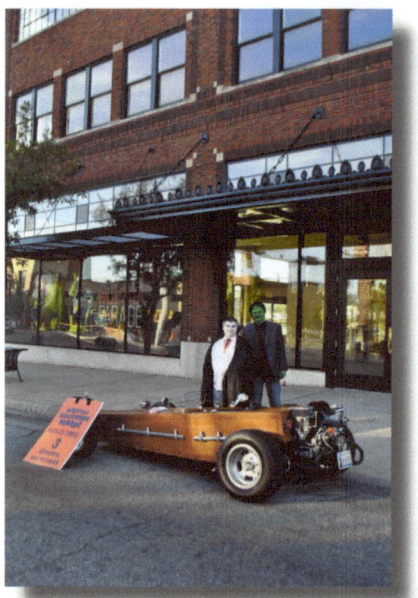

Oklahoma auto-modification king "Diamond-Dan" Carter and Franken -er, I mean "Herman," er - I mean J.R. -- get prepped to lead the Capital's annual Halloween Parade. Luckily Daniel, a.k.a. "Grandpa," has this fitting coffin cleverly disguised as an automobile to retire to in case they drain the night away and sun-up catches them unaware.

Nothing like a converted Karmann Ghia to calm a vampire's nerves. I personally find my own Ghia sufficiently thrilling already, but my night life is a tad duller than that of this vamp and his sidekick.

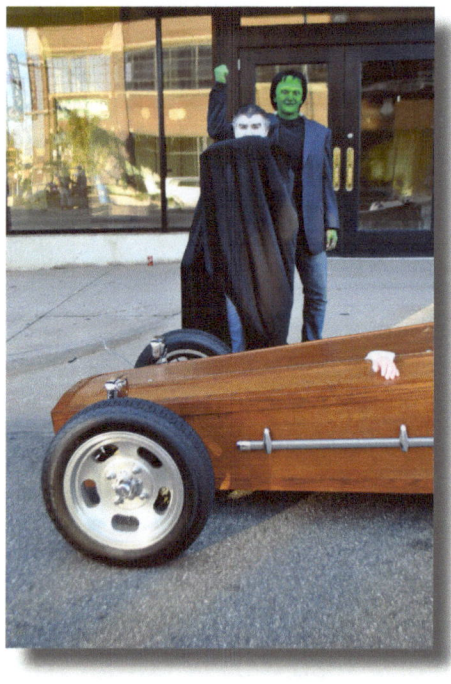

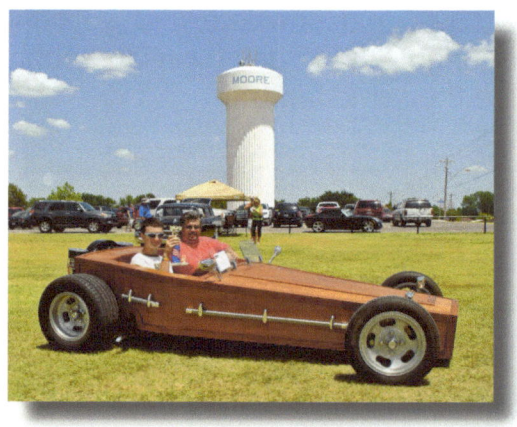

The Day Walking alter-egos.

In all seriousness, spooktacular spirit by the character actors and make up job by their friend Clint Tyson. Furthermore, splendiferously gnarly job on this V.W.'s transformation. The hand-paned woodwork and finish is flawless. What a skilled craftsman.

HOOD ORNAMENTS &
LEFT OVERS

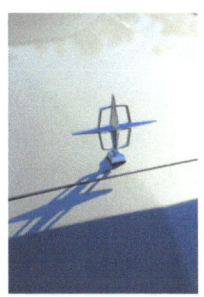
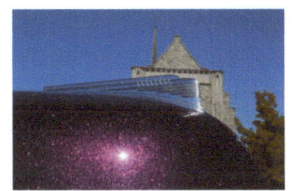
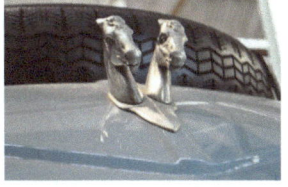
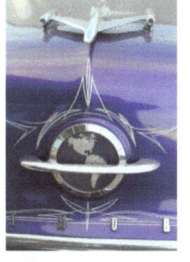
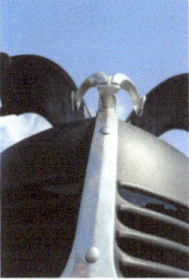
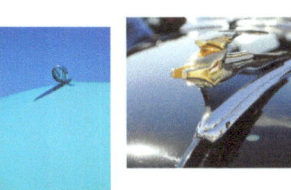
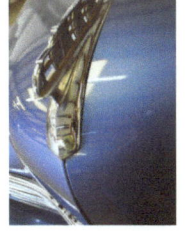
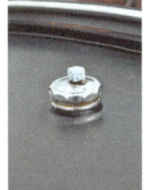
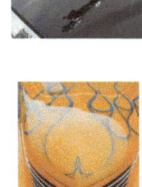
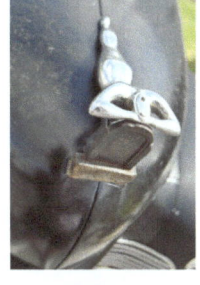
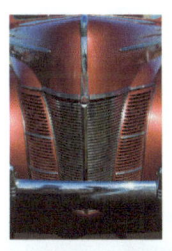
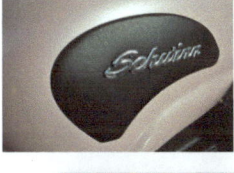
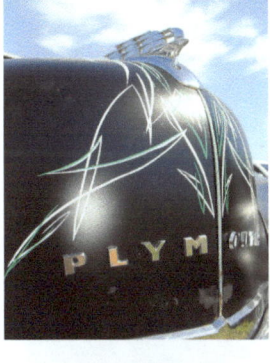
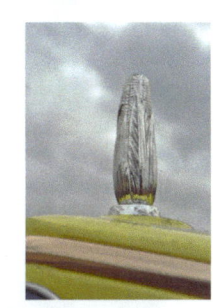
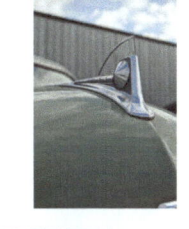
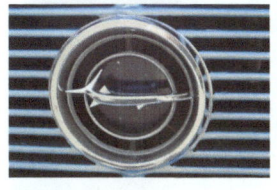
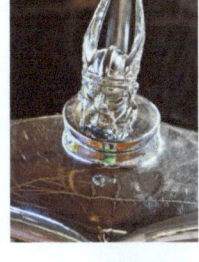
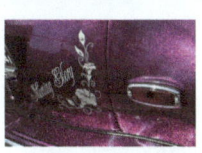
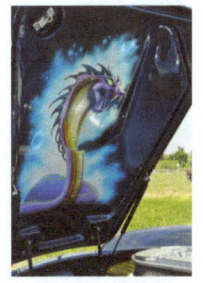
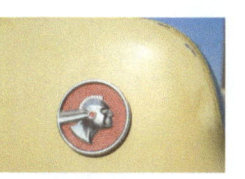
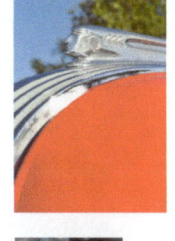
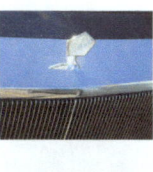
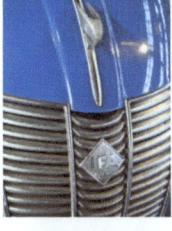
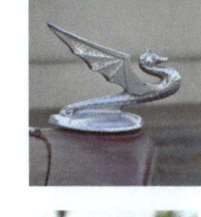
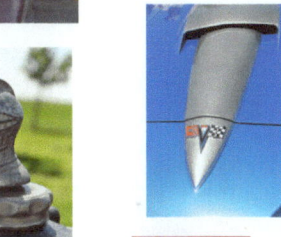
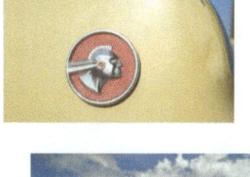
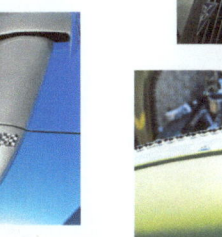
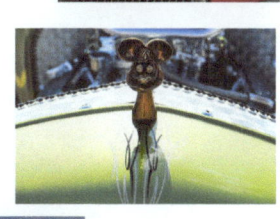
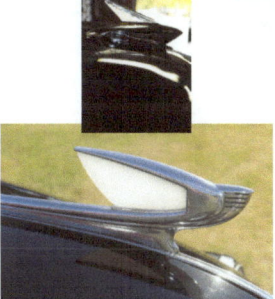
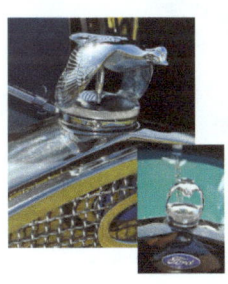
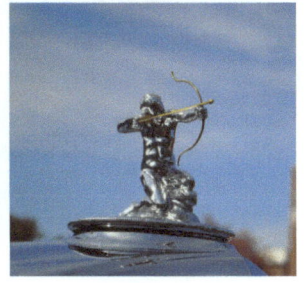
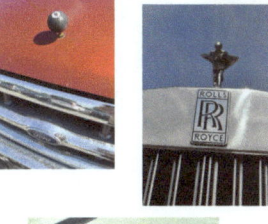
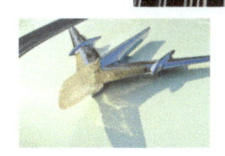
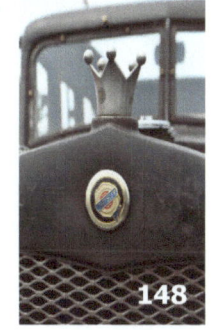

BACK TO THE '007

Armed with an authentic Walther (thanks to Dad's gunsmithing knowledge ,) Mr. Gary Dean of Catoosa, Oklahoma, serves as our "Bond" look-alike in the following page's Hollywood-esque ending sketch to close out this project. Shortly after this photo shoot Deano took it upon himself to seek talent representation, and now actively pursues the dream so many of us have. The old standby, well-wish of "Break a Leg" is of course bestowed upon you. But in the meantime, along with Cliff Wallace, the owner of Digital CDR, and his loaned time machine, we have to spare a moment for one more bit of play before anyone becomes a thespian player. In a total homage to film, and those non chick-flick offerings, the pic below begs the question… "Dude, where *are you going* with my car?"

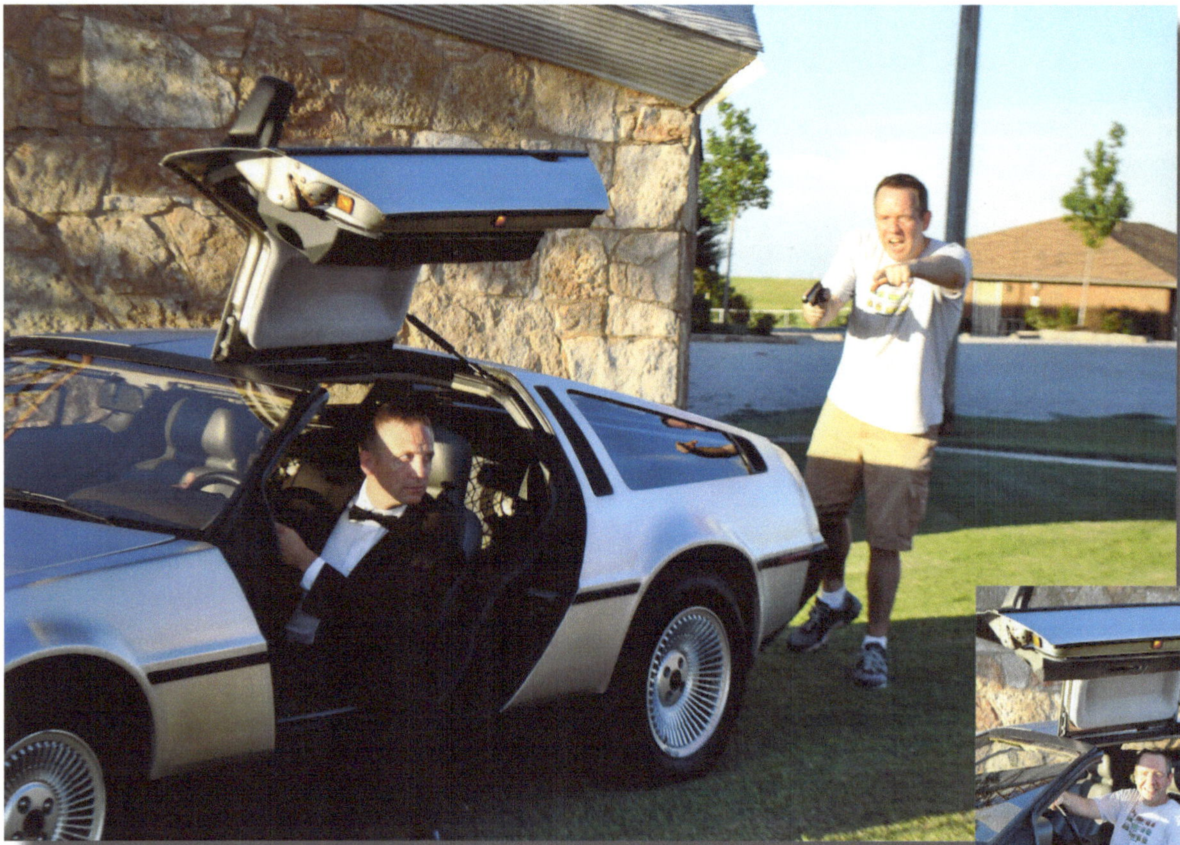

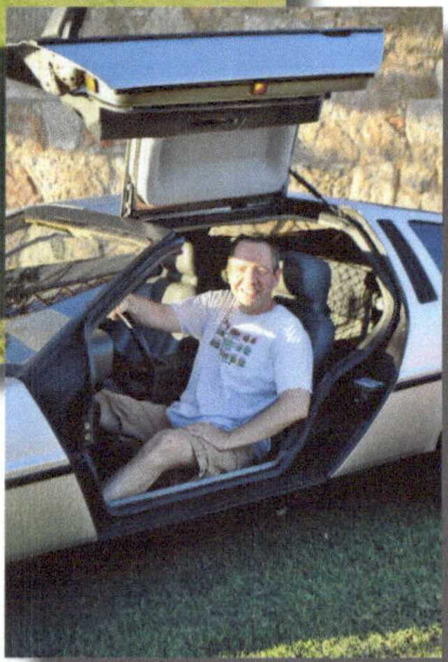

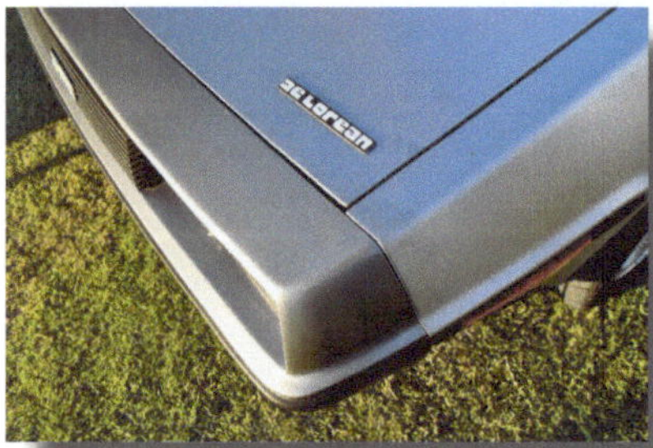

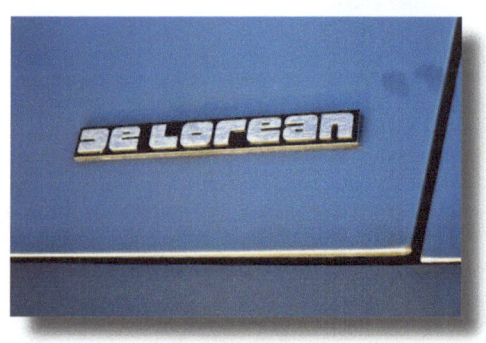

THE END

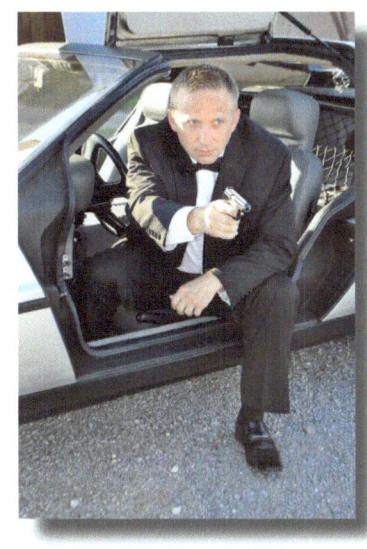

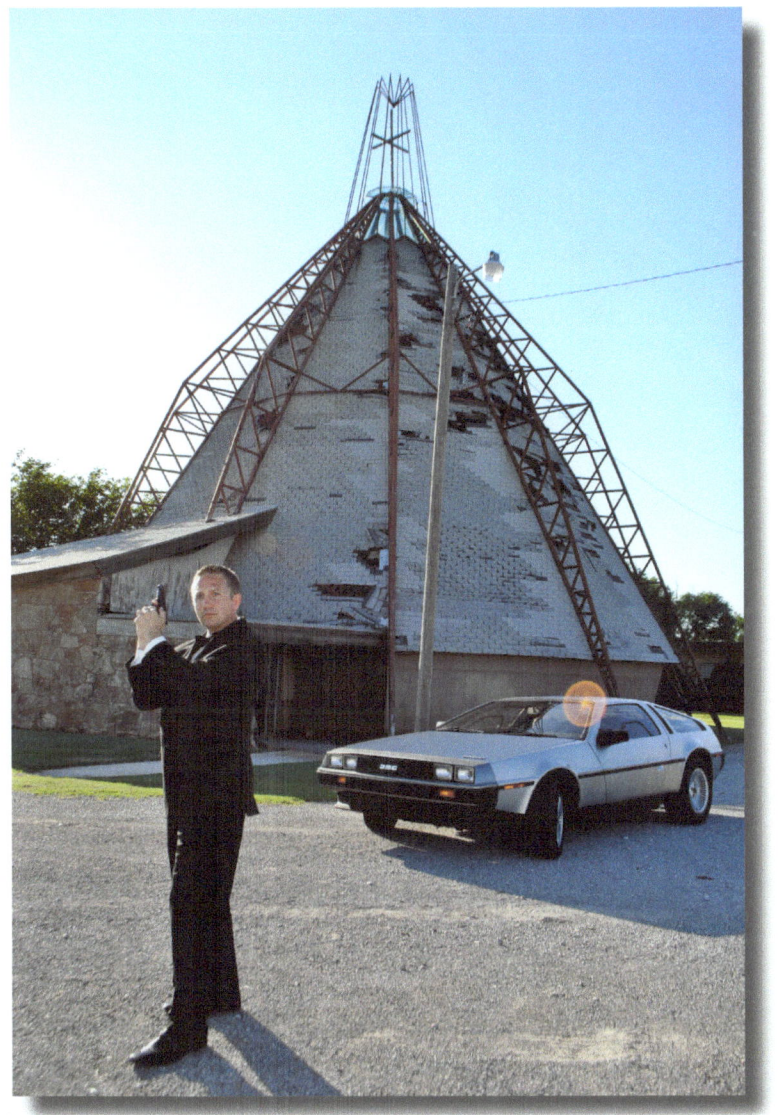

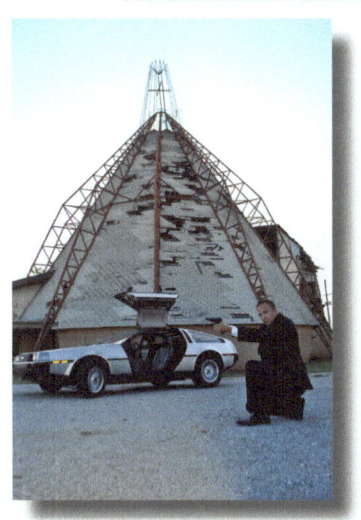

On location at
"The Wig Wam,"
created by Bruce Goff,
a student of
Frank Lloyd Wright.

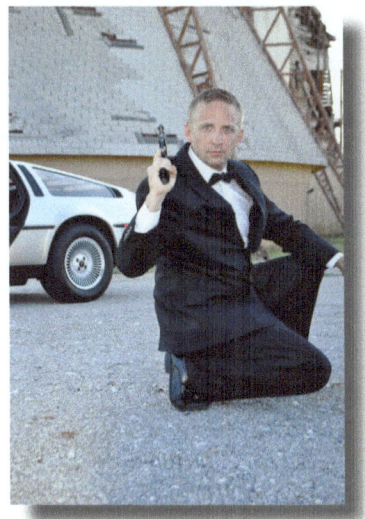

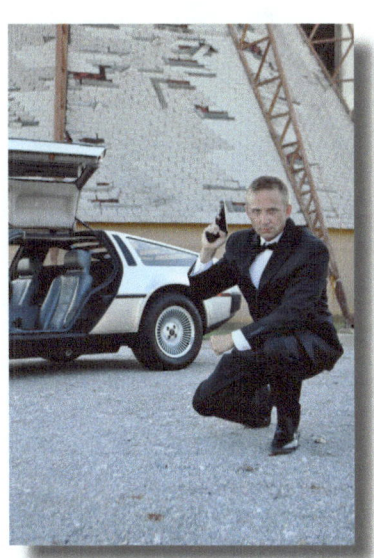

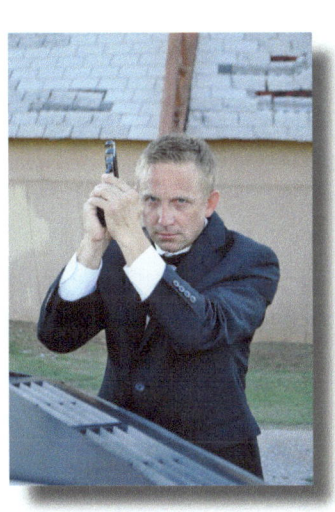

EPILOGUE

Wow! What an odyssey this has been. From concept to fruition seemed interminable, but just like the Centennial year Oklahoma marathon I completed in last place, the point is, at least I finished. And just as in the competitive instance, whereby the reporter interviewing me on my last few steps, revealed I had broken local records for languidity, time-wise, my authored accomplishment too will live on. Bully for me, I can actually be a pinch more boastful of this finish-line crossing. In the happiest of conclusions, words cannot sum up what joy I have had shooting these humble yet well-intended, meticulously submitted, photographs, nor how satisfying it is to relay these summarizations to an audience. Said stories have ranged from the anecdotal to the downright heartwarming.

I will never forget the faces and places, and will summarily be forever grateful to have seen both. I am so pleased to have had the opportunity to be the author of this work; but I am only the messenger -- it's the august interviewees who were the real stars. Whether it be the detail-oriented soul who put their blood, sweat and tears into their ride; the delicate caretaker of the garaged exotic; or the barn-found blossoming diamond-in-the-rough, each car and their owner had a tale to send out into the world. Even those shy candidates herein who looked at me like I had three heads upon my query to shoot their non-show, daily driver, car or bike, recording its biography along the way, (and you know who you all are, wink,) made for compelling additions I am so honored to have included. The one element that links all of these folks of different walks of life, and socioeconomic statures is this one fact: Everybody likes at least one thing about their car, and or has an interesting yarn to share.

As you vicariously experienced, this operation was a headlong venture that found me trekking part of the globe in achieving my life's ambition, finishing this editorial expression of a lasting autophilia bug I have contracted, (that would be the lesser non-narcisstic interpretation of the word accepted in the car show community.) It involved taking in the visions of everything from natural beauty to man-made wonders: Running in the same circles with not just heroes and celebrities, but the essence of the modern-day "every" man and woman. Secret is, we're, none of us, that different really.

What's next for me? I often have pondered that question in recent times as the apex of this composition neared day by day. I went from my fifth appendage being "Dreamer," my well-traveled camera (another similarity among car lovers, we name practically everything,) to my mini memory sticks wherein the seemingly endless sea of photos were chosen and catalogued, to finally carting around, a-la-security blanket style, the bulky file folder containing my many release forms and corresponding article-like captions.

I imagine once the final layouts are decided upon, and this entity that has become my obsession is sent off to whichever printer is the lucky winner, I will pick up the camera equipment again and head back to the work I have grown so fond of. I will probably take some classes, heaven knows I could have benefitted from such training at times, but hey, I hope you agree I didn't do too badly without any formal photographic education.

I know one thing for sure... Chiclet and I will head to more car shows, probably this month in fact, and I hopefully will always have that perky Karmann Ghia parked on the premises.
Thanks for listening to all of the memorable moments, and see ya at the show.

Tiff Mateas

UPDATE

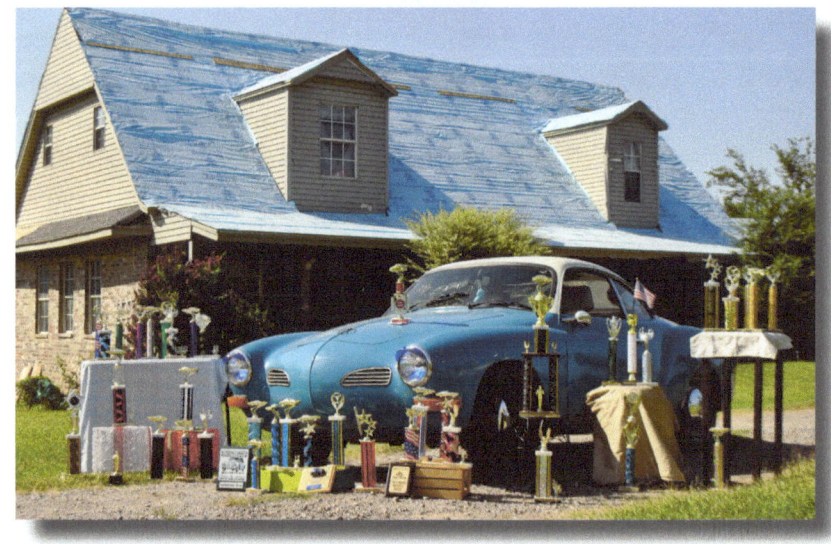

Since penning this book in early May, our lives were literally turned upside down by a massive tornado of the highest rating, an EF-5. Our home sustained such pervasive damage it was rendered structurally unsound, and we had to salvage what we could, including precious belongings such as trophies and photographs. We were the lucky ones though, as 24 unfortunate souls, including innocent children, lost their lives. Sources say a quarter of our little community was decimated. Prior to that fateful day of May 20th, 2013, I was initially going to use this space for sending respectful sympathies to the families of some choice friends, the subject matter of this book, who have passed on of more natural causes. There needs to be mention, however, of at least one ever kind and popular model, Mr. Vern Klavin, who passed on horrifyingly during an additional tornado shortly after the deluge that affected our lives. When the warning signals sounded on what would turn out to be historically the widest recorded twister, he was securing himself, along with his grown children, in a cellar. Before making it to safety, he suffered a cardiac arrest at the top of the stairs. I dedicate these remaining images and thoughts to those left behind suffering similar losses, and I pray, healing.

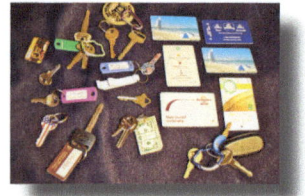

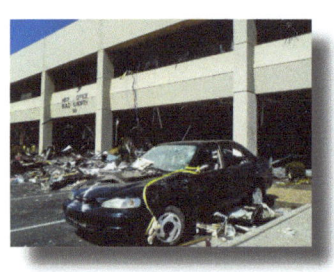

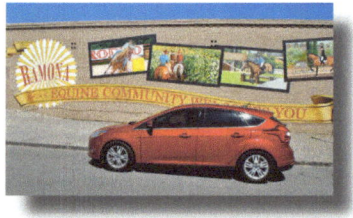

Our keys for various doors/gates, and the transformation to our new keys as so many of us shuffle around hotels awaiting our way home

Before and after realities...We lost both of our daily drivers. I, while running for cover with my Mom at the soon-to-be-devastated Moore Medical Center, closed the door for the last time on the great lil' gas sippin' Corolla Dad lent for transporting Mom to her senior meetings; whereas Margo's wonderful white Suzuki got battered in our driveway as she inside the house, battled with a blowing closet door which all inhabitants, furry or otherwise, huddled behind. We compromised on the new auto with a fuel-friendly Ford Focus in hatchback form for a little more storage.

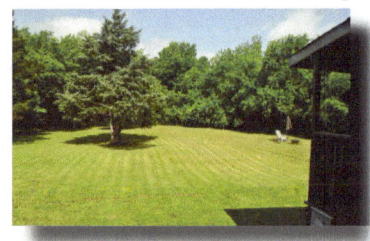

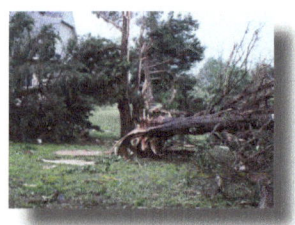

Our freshly-mowed yard the very day before the storm, and just one of the catastrophic sights in our Universe afterward. The Vet Park in my Ford Chapter looks even worse, but The Coca Cola Co. donated $1M for repair, after a national online contest won by an astounding lead established with community votes.

UPDATE CONTINUED

As I pushed my Mom in a borrowed wheelchair to clearer skies upon emerging from the rubble surrounding the hospital where we took shelter, I caught a glimpse of a childhood playground of sorts, The Moore Bowling Alley. It was completely leveled, save for a stand up video game, and several bowling balls.   I for a moment thought of Mr Barbee, whom you met in my travel chapter, and almost grabbed a momento for him, knowing how reverent an object he would feel it is. Fearful of Mom tiring out from having to lug a dozen pounder around as our half mile or so hike to a family pick up point ensued, or worse yet, of some sort of looting missunderstanding, I wisely refrained. Weeks later, while waiting for a tow to cart our debilitated Toyota off grounds to a salvage yard, I approached the fork lift operators cleaning up that once booming area of the now unrecognizable landscape. With my explanation that Mr. Barbee had agreed to creat a respectful memorial to the victims and survivors of our grieving town, the city workers went out of their way to procure for me not only a ball, but a pin used in the lovable alley.

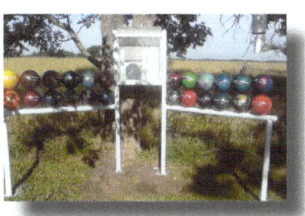

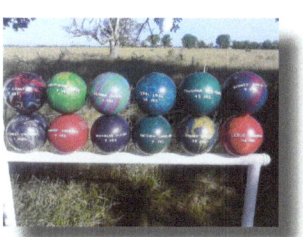

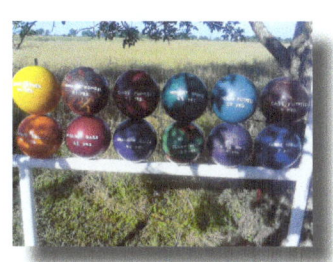

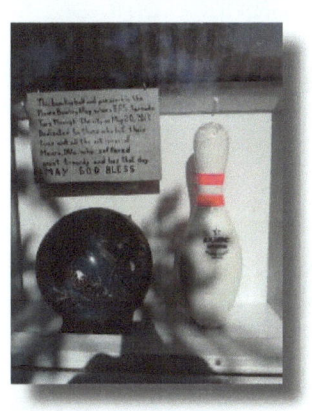

We definitely had to get him some press, and his efforts were appreciated by all who heard the tale, which can be found online at The Moore Monitor magazine dated June 24, 2013. These photos of the tribute are courtesy of Mr. Barbee himself, and the inscription he posted with the middle focal point of his tribute reads as follows:

"This ball and pin were in The Moore Bowling Alley when an EF-5 tore through central Oklahoma on May 20th, 2013. This memorial is dedicated to those who lost their lives, and all the citizens of Moore, Oklahoma who suffered great tragedy and loss that day. May God Bless."

The pictures on either side of the central figure, include bowling balls carrying the names of each individual fatally wounded by the above mentioned tornado, and their age upon leaving this earth.

Mr. Barbee, that is such a solemn creation. Our city thanks you.   I thank you. This is so hard for me to discuss, but I just have to express gratitude to you and all who stepped up to help in whatever whay they could or knew how. I still so dearly miss my world before this tragedy. For me your actions felt like a little closure on a wound we will all feel for years.

WALL OF GRATITUDE

Here's my own well-intentioned memorial section to honor and show thanks to all of the many compassionate people who have helped during my recent times of troubling struggles. My book's data fortunately was spared from the detriment of Mother Nature's wrath, but if not for so many exhibitions of kindness and the countless acts of generosity of spirit, volunteerism, and over all assistance, this creation's completion would definitely not have been as punctual.

Gracious and humble thanks are sent to the benevolent heaven's above for sparing Margo, and my family at large, during the meteorological wrecking balls that plowed through our state that latter part of May 2013. My condolences and prayers extend to the families who were not as fortunate.

The folks at The Moore Family Counseling Center, as well as other agencies and individual therapists, such as Ms. Jamie Leal, who cared for so many traumatized victims left behind to battle all number of stressful emotions, gratis, out of the kindness of their also-saddened hearts.

The staff at The Moore Medical Center who on the day of what we have now quite unconsciously termed "our storm," influenced Mom and I to join them in their work site's cafe safe room after her daily meeting, rather than driving out into the rain. I was unaware of how fast the landborne maelstrom was moving, nor that it was headed right for my home. So in essence, if not for Jana and Bridget at the Inspirations Senior Program, we would have been caught in the middle of the melee as we had tried to pick up Margo and outrun the monster. Thank you, among others, Pam and Jennifer, also with Inspirations, for helping my Mom through her aftermath processing. Secondary mention, from the day of, should be for the angelic nurses stationed near the cafeteria TV sets broadcasting the formation of the monolithic more than a mile wide funnel. They stoically handed out bottles of water and Kleenex to the distraught souls, such as myself, huddled together watching this killer cloud march across our city, right toward our hideout, even as tears streamed down their own tremulous, ashen faces.

On the subject of said broadcast, thank you to since-retired forecasting legend, Mr. Gary England whose concise televised weather coverage prompted me, in our lockdown status, to frantically, amid sketchy cell coverage, dial a warning to Margo appraising her of the wedge's dangerous encroaching proximity and the fact that, after several angles were investigated by Mr. 'E' and staff, the expedient trajectory was indeed still holding our home and her wellbeing directly in its track. She was on an international teleconference at the time and usually answers non-related incoming calls from no one but myself. So luckily after I finally, (literally and figuratively,) snuck a call under the over-loaded wire to her, she sprung into the action of self preservation just in the nick of time.

After the dust settled and the clouds rolled on past both the crosshairs of my home and current location, we safe area survivors, en masse, attempted ascent from the dregs of the still primarily intact structure. I have often said I would also like to shake the hands of the architects who drafted such a well-engineered success. For now, though I will continue to thank whomever I can recollect here within these paragraphs. Praise & gratitude must be showered upon a dauntlessly hale hospital attendant named Handsome, who helped carry Mom over the threshold of the creaky medical center's now non-sliding exit door frame, which had to be torn from the hinges to facilitate our flight. As we all gingerly inched out of harm's way I saw our new-found savior, Mr. Handsome, falter and cringe. I inquired if he was alright, to which he answered that he was just sore from a knee surgery he had under gone less than a week before rescuing us. My heart went out to him, and we thanked him profusely, adding a wish to take care of himself, before he went on his way ministering to the ailing injured.

Thank you to the distressed Superhero families along the side of the main avenue adjacent to the Medical Center in, coincidentally, one of the most severely devastated neighborhoods. Incredulously, amid sifting through the wreckage that once was their beloved homes, many raised thier heads, rushing over in concern for us as we made our way with that, now rickety, wheelchair, in which the physical therapy department had deposited Mom, to reunite with our family members. Offers of help with pushing were flying at our raised consciousness left and right. With well wishes we declined, naturally, as the poor souls had enough on their plates. Those images simultaneously haunt and warm my tired heart.

Thank you to everyone lending their land lines and cell phones to the cause that afternoon. Many folks not only had to fight the jammed telecommunication lines being utilized by worried relatives and emergency personnel, but also, as was in my case, dead batteries worn out from futile attempts to gleen knowledge of my own family members' whereabouts. Thank you to long-time car show pal Nathan Arnett for happening by at one point during the aftermath with a fully charged phone he was sharing. I ascertained the locale of every one of my tribe, save for dear Margo, whose place of refuge according to experts, and my father who tried to reach it through police barricades, had been verified to have taken a confirmed hit. I was frozen in shock and fear untill I finally reached a neighbor, (the best,) Mr. Paul Cardle, reassuring me of her survival via text at approximately 10:30 that evening. At that point, having had virtually nothing to eat besides a candy bar I forced down to avoid "hitting a wall," as they say in endurance sports, I pretty much collapsed in relief and instant hunger. Thank you to Megan and sister-in- law Gina for trying so hard to also get a "20" on Margo. They reported her missing to the checkpoint in charge of locating citizens. Her status was hard to corroborate as she at one point after the initial blow, even visited a neighbor's storm shelter when the skies began to look threatening again. So any of the many emergency crews who inspected both premises, very well may have confused her with someone in the other household. Things were incredibly chaotic with the immense survivor search underway. We are so grateful to all of the heroes dutifully saving lives that day.

Once recomposed from my overwhelm upon hearing about Margo's wellbeing, I set about to speedily devour a great deal of the sandwich meat my baby sis Meg had brought to my folk's house in anticipation of her loved one's arrival, all while determinedly packing several more sandwiches to deliver to Margo, as I was going to get to her side one way or another that night. My Dad and brother Tom Jr., who had just woven a way through the maze of closed roads and downed power lines to retrieve their Medical Center refugees, caught wind of my plan, and were not going to let me go it alone. My aforementioned neighbor Paul advised of the nearest remaining open passage way, and off we went. We made it to Margo's waiting grateful arms less than an hour later on a trip that usually takes a mere 5 minutes across town. The mission was not even aborted when faced with a stranded motorist partially blocking our path, nor when my brother felt a piece of sharp debris pierce the under sole of his steel-toed boots while on foot. Luckily the shard did not penetrate completely through, only leaving a small puncture scrape. Onward we tredged, and for that alone I am so grateful for Dad and Tommy's perseverence. They followed that up with countless hours of tree trunk and junk removal at our homestead, not to mention availing their shoulders, as did all of my family, when I requested hugs, or my tears needed to fall.

Thanks to all of the local food industry and restaurants who comped and donated so many meals in the days and months after the disasters.

I thank all of the animal resources around the state who chipped in to provide any number of supportive services from fostering to supplies. Specifically in our case, we are so happy to have met a couple of Vets in the new area of the city we were forced to scrounged around while finding a vacant hotel room. In parts of an area almost alien to us, we encountered extreme empathy and kindness from Veterinarians Dr. Frank Roberts of the Edmond Emergency Clinic for treating our storm shrapnel-strewn cat, and the Docs at the 23rd Street City Animal Hospital. In both instances we were only charged for medications.

Thank you fellow tornado survivor Susan Benn, and friends for passing along the word about the many other programs in place at the time for our welfare.

Thank you to our main F.E.M.A. representative Kathy Van Note. There was such an outpouring from the overpowering generosity of organizations like The Red Cross, many church groups such as Memorial Road Church, The Baptist Relief Partners, and nationally The Memonite Disaster Service. Major kudo shout outs to the tireless, still ongoing, efforts put forth from non-profits such as Serve Moore, where I had the priviledge of becoming acquainted with a new standard of selflessness in Mr. Michael Grant, of New York. He was wrapping up another volunteer job elsewhere in the country, when our city was ravaged by this big work in project maker. He spent his last vestige of savings to hop a bus our way. A handy man of the truest nature, while in my company, he inspected our HVAC unit, for comfort, and joined with other associates in ridding my home of moldy surfaces for abatement efforts. This enabled me to safely re-enter the property in order to continue retrieving my remaining belongings. Similar humanitarian chronicles were rampant. For instance, free roof tarping and repair efforts went on almost non stop from companies such as Josh Puckett's startup Patriot Roofing.

For all of the packing and moving expertise, not to mention earnest friendship, I want to thank Jeremy, Crystal and David Stephensen, Michael and Robert Shroll Swerer, and Jerry Shroll Hatfield. Then who could leave out Angela Keller. Ang was at the ready so much immediately following the catastrophic event with everything traffic will allow, from her sounding board ear, to bags of burgers or provisions for ourselves and the pets.

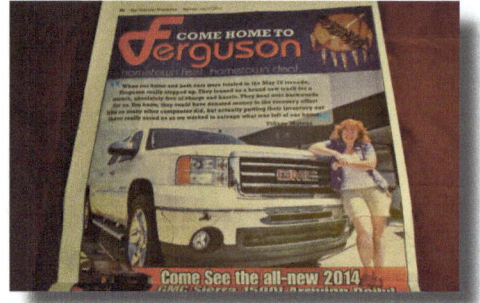

Last but not least, thank you to the congenial management at Ferguson Buick, who donated to the cause not so much in monetary means, but by single-handedly outfitting some 75-odd car-less needy families, including mine, with full-size trucks to meet appointments and even for the purpose of moving belongings to the few-and-far-between remaining storage units. I tried to make my repayment in this testimonial above recorded by the dealer's local news outlet.

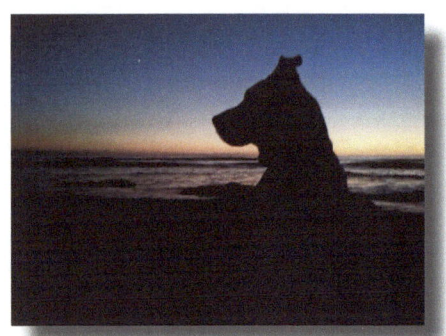

Old...

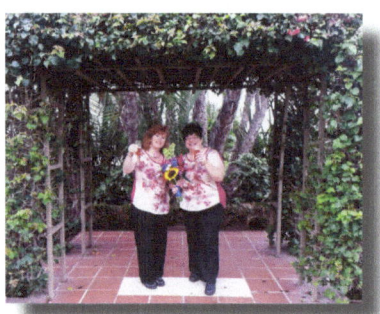

Our legal wedded bliss

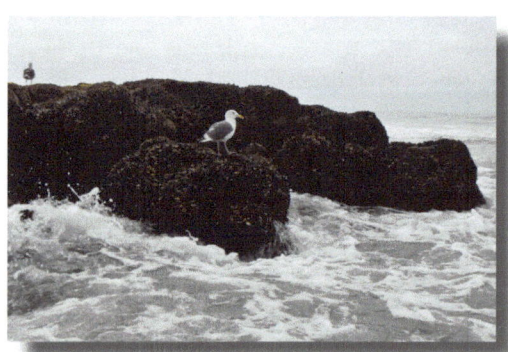

And new feathered friends

The light at the end of the tunnel, you may ask? Well it lies in just what I have conveyed over the last few pages. One must be grateful... even if you have to force yourself to see beyond your uprooted world, in this case peppered with not only sheered tree tops, but also rapid change thrown in the mix. We have since decided on a course of action outside of tornado alley, in SoCal. Despite missing family, it's an opportunity to reap all the benefits offered here in the Golden state, including marital rights, and in separate news, a chance to finally put that acting degree to good use. It may be 20 years since graduation, but it never hurts to try. Wish me kismet, and in the meantime, you can find us at the beach, where the peaceful gurgling of the ocean washes over my bruised psyche.